Samford Whittingham

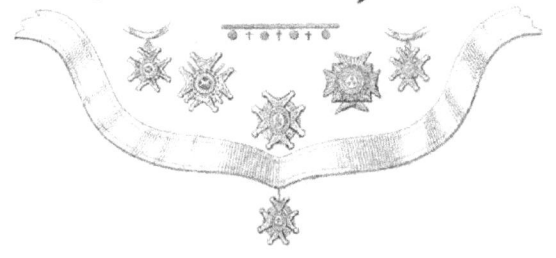

Published by

The Naval & Military Press Ltd
Unit 5 Riverside, Brambleside
Bellbrook Industrial Estate
Uckfield, East Sussex
TN22 1QQ England

Tel: +44 (0)1825 749494

www.naval-military-press.com
www.nmarchive.com

In reprinting in facsimile from the original, any imperfections are inevitably reproduced and the quality may fall short of modern type and cartographic standards.

A MEMOIR OF THE SERVICES

OF

LIEUTENANT-GENERAL

SIR SAMUEL FORD WHITTINGHAM,

K.C.B., K.C.H., G.C.F.

COLONEL OF THE 71ST HIGHLAND LIGHT INFANTRY.

DERIVED CHIEFLY FROM HIS OWN LETTERS AND FROM THOSE
OF DISTINGUISHED CONTEMPORARIES.

EDITED BY

MAJOR-GENERAL FERDINAND WHITTINGHAM, C.B.

NEW EDITION.

The Naval & Militari Press Ltd

TO

HIS ROYAL HIGHNESS

FIELD-MARSHAL

GEORGE DUKE OF CAMBRIDGE, K.G.

COMMANDER-IN-CHIEF,

This Volume is,

BY THE GRACIOUS PERMISSION OF HIS ROYAL HIGHNESS,

Most respectfully Dedicated.

PREFACE

TO

THE NEW EDITION.

———•◊•———

The errors and imperfections contained in the first edition of this work, occasioned its speedy suppression, in order to substitute for it the revised, and, as the Editor trusts, considerably improved volume now offered to the public. His best thanks are assuredly due to those critics who have already noticed the work; because, as may be seen at the end of the Appendix, they have amply justified the opinion which he had long entertained, that the services of Sir Samford Whittingham required only to be better known in order to be fully appreciated by his generous countrymen.

Of those services the Editor hopes that the present volume is more worthy than its predecessor of becoming the permanent record.

It is only necessary to add that the engraving in this edition is a great improvement on the preceding one, and now does full justice to the portrait from which it was taken.

PREFACE.

By graciously consenting to accept of the dedication of this volume, the illustrious Field Marshal who commands the British army has conferred upon the memory of Sir Samford Whittingham an honour, which can hardly fail to convince military readers that his services and conduct are worthy of being recorded. As regards civilians, it is probable that they may be interested in the career of an officer, who, although a *thorough*, was yet not a *mere* soldier: for statesmen, and ambassadors, as well as generals, have testified to his merits, in the most eulogistic terms, and his services were, on several occasions, of a civil as well as military nature. A cursory inspection of the Index of this work would suffice to establish the weight and importance of the testimonies adduced.

In consequence of the services of Sir Samford Whittingham having been principally performed in the Spanish army, and also because nearly the whole of his military career was passed abroad—in America, in the Peninsula, and in the East and West Indies,—it was his misfortune, as regarded his countrymen to be ignored by the many, although most highly appreciated by the illustrious few; whose recognition of merit forms its surest test, as well as its most valuable recompense.

It does not appear that the subject of this Memoir ever contemplated making any record of his services. His brother-in-law, however, Mr. Richard Hart Davis, successively member for Colchester and Bristol, always preserved as much as possible his letters and papers; in the belief that such a publication as the present, would sooner or later occur.

Unfortunately many valuable letters have been lost, including the greater part of General Whittingham's correspondence with two successive military secretaries at the Horse-Guards. The Editor was not, however, greatly surprised, when the letters in question were found missing from their registered places, as he had long believed that their contents had, for the most part, been embodied in Southey's 'History of the Peninsular War.' Indeed a number of details in that work could hardly have been collected from any other source. At the battles of *Baylen* and *Medellin*, for instance, only one Englishman appears to have been present, and yet he is not mentioned by his brother Bristolian, Southey; although from him only could the latter have learned the speeches which *Castanos* and *Alburquerque* addressed to that Englishman. This personal silence confirms the fact in question to those who know how General Whittingham was wont to leave to others the task of recording his merits and services.

In consequence of the loss of the letters addressed to Colonels Gordon and Torrens, the private letters to his brother-in-law, Mr. Hart Davis, form the chief basis of this Memoir; and their frank and unreserved style is particularly suited for such a purpose. But from their voluminous nature, it has been possible only to give brief extracts, as a general rule.

The Editor first projected this work in 1845. Aware that the late heroic Earl of Fife had been the friend and admirer of Sir Samford Whittingham, he wrote to his Lordship to inform him of, and to consult him on, his intentions. The following (omitting only some irrelevant private matters) was the reply of Lord Fife:—

'DUFF HOUSE: *Tuesday*, [post-mark 28 *March*, 1845].

'Dear Whittingham,—I was very happy to have the pleasure of receiving your interesting note regarding the memory of your excellent father, my late intimate and worthy friend. I, of course, am acquainted with much information about Sir Samford, and all that I can possibly do, to forward your views and wishes, shall be with much good will executed; to do justice to the gallant soldier, and talented gentleman, your father.

'Suchet, with whom I was well acquainted, often conversed with me regarding different officers who had opposed him; and particularly mentioned the merits of your father which, he said, might have been followed with bad results to the French, had the war continued much longer. He said, "Whittingham's corps was the best disciplined, and if the example had been followed in many other instances, in different parts of Spain, the French army would have felt the effects in a remarkable manner."

'General Reeves, an intimate friend of mine, who was in Catalonia, often spoke most honourably of your father, although he did not much like those English who were with the *Espagnolles*. . . .

'There are two points to be noticed about your father's conduct, which party and other reasons have rendered obscure: his commanding the troops that marched to Madrid, when the Cortes were assembled; and also at the battle of Barrosa. I shall afterwards make some observations and references about both; and also [give] some details of his services in the early part of the war with [General] Cuesta, and the Duke of Alburquerque, the importance of which were passed over or little known....

'I took your father from Talavera, and, I think, saved his life, in having a very good surgeon of the Guards* every day, and [by having] fed him with tea, coffee and butter, which were [then] of more value than gold; and I obliged him to go from the field in the evening, and made a doctor go with him to my quarters.

'My brother, Sir Alexander Duff, knew your father well, and came home with him from Buenos Ayres. I was nearly being his second in a duel between him and J—— of the Guards. Sir Charles Felix Smith, his second and I made it up; which was fortunate for J——, as your father was a capital shot.†

'Believe me, most truly, [yours]

'FIFE.'

'Major Whittingham, [26th] Cameronians,
    Manchester.'

In consequence of the increasing infirmities of Lord Fife, the Editor did not again trouble his Lordship, nor

---

* The goodness of the surgeon, *in a medical sense*, is disproved in this Memoir.

† No record of this affair will be found in this volume, owing to want of details on the subject. The Editor believes that, either at Cadiz or Seville, the quarrel arose from some expressions on the part of the Guardsman, which were deemed insulting to the Spanish officers.

did the latter ever send his promised information. By his letter, however, he had confirmed to the son, that valuable testimony regarding Marshal Suchet, which in 1814 he had spontaneously sent to the father.* But the effect of his letter was to delay the writing of this Memoir. Regimentally the Editor was then only a captain; and he had not the means or leisure for acquiring that completeness of information, necessary to do justice to a case, which party spirit and ignorance of details, had rendered obscure, in the opinion of a good and friendly judge. Indeed some important facts only came to the knowledge of the Editor, after the death of Sir William Napier and the publication of his life.

The Editor, however, delayed chiefly on account of his roving and unsettled life. He waited therefore till he should have both leisure, and a fixed habitation, to enable him to study the voluminous correspondence of Sir Samford Whittingham and the 'Wellington Dispatches.' At length he has accomplished his task to the best of his ability; amidst the difficulties of selection, rejection, and condensation, and of the loss of many valuable papers; and having also considerably to curtail the MSS. when finished, as too bulky.

The delay brings with it, however, this advantage, that it has facilitated candour and plain speaking; and has also probably given time for the decay of that party spirit, and professional jealousy, by which some facts were formerly greatly misrepresented.

The Editor also trusts that the letters of distinguished persons which are published in this volume, may be in-

* See p. 239.

teresting in themselves, as well as from their being strong testimonies to character and conduct. Next to those of the Duke of Wellington, and of the Marquis Wellesley, the letters of the Honourable Sir Edward Paget, and of Lord William Bentinck, furnish the strongest proofs of the merits of Sir Samford Whittingham. Lord William has an established reputation as a good officer and enlightened statesman; but Sir Edward Paget has not perhaps been sufficiently appreciated. How highly the Duke of Wellington esteemed him, his '*Dispatches*' have proved: but what Sir Charles Napier thought of him is probably less known, and is, therefore, here recorded; on the authority of a living eye—and ear—witness of the circumstances.

In 1848 Lord Frederick Fitz-Clarence, then Lieutenant-Governor of Portsmouth, accidentally met, in the streets of that town, the two soldier-sons of Sir Edward Paget, and asked them to lunch with him that day, as he was expecting Sir Charles Napier, on his way to Osborne to see the Queen. This was at the time, when, at the general call of the country, Sir Charles was about to proceed to India to save that empire from what was then considered as impending ruin. Lord Frederick introduced the young men to his distinguished guest, who, taking them each by the hand, said: 'Ah! if poor Sir Edward had had the health for it, he would have been the man to send to India.'*

Although four portraits of Sir Samford Whittingham exist, the best by far is a small one from which the

---

* As this circumstance occurred some years after the death of Sir Samford Whittingham, it is recorded here instead of in the body of the work.

engraving in this volume is taken. It has, indeed, the disadvantage of presenting him as the undecorated Captain of 1807, instead of the General with his three orders of knighthood and seven medals, or minor decorations. But this defect the skill of the engraver has lessened by making a representation of the decorations under the portrait.

During his last visit to England Sir Samford promised at the request of his eldest niece (Mrs. Harford of Blaise Castle) to commit to writing some of those Peninsular anecdotes with which he had amused his relatives. This promise he fulfilled on his last voyage to Madras in 1840; and the Editor has made use of nearly all these 'Recollections'; placing them in this volume, as far as possible in the order of their proper dates.

Finally, as far as is consistent with the sacred claims of justice to the memory of a beloved and honoured parent, the Editor has endeavoured to justify the confidence placed in him by the highly estimable gentleman, who may be deemed to represent the interests of his celebrated connection—Sir William Napier. This task has been greatly facilitated by the fact that six of the seven grand-children of Sir Samford Whittingham are *related* to that family, one of whose most distinguished members did him a great, even if unintentional wrong.

The confidence in question was expressed in a note concluding with the following words:—

'I greatly respect your sense of honour and justice and am sure that in vindicating your distinguished father you will not forget what is due to others.'

CONTENTS.

CHAPTER I.
1772–1805.

Difficulty in tracing the Family Antecedents—William Whittingham of Bristol—Miss Richardson—Samuel Ford changed to Samford—He would be a Soldier—Old Mr. Whittingham objects to his Son's entering the Army—Samford proceeds to Spain—The ruling Passion—Death of his Father—Returns Home—Gazetted Ensign—Lieutenancy in 1st Life Guards—Disadvantage of tardy Entrance to the Army—High Wycombe College—Sixteen Hours a day Study—Mr. Thomas Murdoch—William Pitt's secret Mission—Note of Hon. W. Eliot—Lisbon—Rogers and Richardson—Mr. Pitt's Thanks—His Death—The 13th Light Dragoons—Early Promotion of the Hon. Edward Paget, the future Friend of Samford Whittingham . . . 1—8

CHAPTER II.
1806–1807.

Secret Expedition under Brigadier-General Robert Craufurd—Captain Whittingham embarks at Portsmouth, 12th November, 1806—Touches at St. Iago—Midnight Freak of some British Officers—Generosity of Portuguese Governor—A well-kept Secret—Arrival at the Cape—How the Secret was discovered—Arrival at Montevideo—General Whitelocke—Order of Battle—Landing near Barragan—General Whitelocke's flattering Offer to Captain Whittingham—Why declined—General Whitelocke's Errors—Question of not loading—Captain Whittingham sent to reconnoitre—Captain Whittingham volunteers to enter the Town—How he reached the Plaza de los Toros—Returns to Head-quarters for Aid—Volunteers again to endeavour to join Craufurd—Joins Nicols and Tolly at Residencia—Proof of Craufurd's Surrender—Successful Charge of Major Nicols—

Captain Whittingham returns to Head-quarters—Suspension of Hostilities—General Gower differs in opinion from Captain Whittingham—Preliminaries of Peace—A disgraceful Treaty—General Liniers—Loss to England by the Surrender—The civic Compliments to General Whitelocke—Captain Cormero's Information regarding the Weakness of the Buenos Ayres Garrison—Durable Friendships contracted at Buenos Ayres—Henry Torrens and the Hon. Henry Cadogan—General Whitelocke's Trial—Brings Captain Whittingham into notice—Duke of Kent becomes his Patron—General Robert Craufurd's Testimony and that of Colonel Gordon . . . . 9—27

CHAPTER III.
1808.

Appointed to the Staff of the Army in Sicily—Takes leave of the Duke of Kent—Arrives at Gibraltar—Acts as Military Secretary to Sir Hew Dalrymple—Obtains leave to join General Castaños as a Volunteer—His Brother-in-law's Letter of Advice—His Appointment to the Staff of Sir Arthur Wellesley—His 'Recollections' of the Battle of Baylen—Castaños' generous Speech to Dupont—The first Englishman who fought in the Peninsular War—Shared in the Victory by joining La Peña's Advanced Guard—Interview with Lord Collingwood—With the Traitor La Morla—Scene at Seville in the Junta Suprema—Castaños' Patriotism—Whittingham made Colonel of Horse—The Englishman's Fall—The Duke of York's Present to Castaños — Colonel Whittingham's Letter to Hon. Henry Cadogan—His prophetic Anticipations of Spanish Failures—Don Santiago Whittingham—Fever at Tudela—A nearly smothered Medico—Disgrace of Castaños after Defeat of Tudela—An *un*distinguished Relative of the Empress Eugénie—Effective Speech to a Spanish Mob—'When the Englishman says it, it must be true'—Things more agreeable as Recollections than when actually occurring—Duke of Infantado sends Colonel Whittingham on a Mission to Seville—Gloomy Aspect of Affairs in the absence of Sir Arthur Wellesley—First Meeting with Lord William Bentinck . . . . . 28—50

CHAPTER IV.
1809.

The Duke of Infantado's Commission—The Duke's Retreat—The chivalrous Duke of Alburquerque—Surprise of Mora—An

Exciting Chase—A Fox-like Ruse—A horrible Incident—A cunning Countess—A complete Humbug—A modest testamentary Request—Letter to Mr. J. Hookham Frere—Bad Conduct of General Urbina—His disgraceful Rout—Alburquerque's Treatment of Traitors—Gallant Charge of Alburquerque and Staff at Medellin—Alava's Heroism—Reforming routed Cavalry—Unfortunately lost Letters—Alburquerque's Laudatory Letters to Duke of York and Lord Castlereagh—Contradictory Orders of Spanish Government—Letters to Mr. Hookham Frere—A Prophecy destined to speedy fulfilment—General Cuesta's earliest British Critic—A constant Source of Annoyance—Sir A. Wellesley's Return to the Peninsula—Brigadier-General Whittingham's Letter to Duke of Kent—Harmony of Frere and Whittingham—Marquis Wellesley's Opinion of Whittingham—Duke of Kent's Letter to Mr. Davis concerning Brigadier-General Whittingham—Lost royal Letters—Interview with Sir Arthur Wellesley—Meeting of General Cuesta and Sir A. Wellesley—Whittingham's Mission to Cuesta—Narrow Escape of Sir Arthur Wellesley—His Remarks to Whittingham—Colonel Roche's Letter on Talavera—Sir A. Wellesley's Dispatch—A glaring Injustice—A truthful Comparison . . . . 51—93

CHAPTER V.

1809-1810.

To Seville for Cure of Wound—Attached to Marquis Wellesley's Embassy—Dr. Kennedy's Treatment—Dr. Knighton—General Cuesta resigns his Command—Sir A. Wellesley's Retreat—Brigadier-General Whittingham's confidential Employment under Marquis Wellesley—Don Pedro de Creus y Ximenes, Intendant of the Spanish Army—Affectionate Letter to Colonel Cadogan—Lord Wellesley's Character—Cadogan's Present to Whittingham—A Judge of Wine—Whittingham Major-General in Spain—Inconvenience of Marquis Wellesley's Ambassadorship—Sir Arthur Wellesley's candid Confession of Error—A Secretary of Legation's Jealousy—Whittingham and Frere deemed too partial to Alburquerque—A justified Preference—Lord Wellington's aristocratic Prejudices—Close of Lord Wellesley's brief Embassy—The Marquis's eulogistic farewell Letter—Genial Shade of Aristocracy—Lord Wellington's Esteem for Alava and Whittingham—Lord Macduff—Lord Wellington's Letter to General Whittingham—Castaños appoints him General of Division—Employed in Isla de Leon—Organizes a select

Body of Horse—Importance of the Balearic Islands—General Whittingham's Promotion to Major in the English Army—Alburquerque relieves Cadiz—His Resignation—Proceeds to London as Ambassador—Dundas translated into Spanish—Mr. Wellesley and General Graham recommend Whittingham's Promotion—Invitation to his Nephew—Colonel Campbell of the Majorca Division—General Graham's voluntary Testimony—Mr. Wellesley's official Praise—Marquis Wellesley's kind Letter to General Whittingham . . . . 94—120

CHAPTER VI.

1811.

The great Difficulty of General Whittingham—Napier and Southey on the Battle of Barrosa—Graham's Assumption of Command—He imputed no Blame to Whittingham—General Whittingham commanded Infantry as well as Cavalry—Disadvantage of trusting to Memory—Whittingham's official Report to La Peña—Ordered to retreat on main Body—Graham's successful Charge—Whittingham's Report indirectly blames La Peña—Accidentally delayed Advance—An egregious Misrepresentation of Facts—General Whittingham's Letter to Mr. Davis on Barrosa—*The Duke's* comprehensive Testimony in favour of Whittingham—The Duke of Kent's spontaneous Tribute to his Merits . . . . . . 121—133

CHAPTER VII.

1811—*continued*.

General Whittingham's arduous Task at Majorca—Financial Duties—A punctilious Governor—Lands at Palma—French and German Prisoners—General Don Gregorio Cuesta again—Letter to Colonel Torrens—Letter to Right Hon. Henry Wellesley—Treatise on Majorca—Letter to Hon. Captain Blackwood, R.N.—Letter to Admiral Pellew—Colonel Torrens's Opinion of Whittingham—Letter to Colonel Torrens—Promotion to Lieut.-Colonel in British Army—Letter to Mr. Davis—Captain Briarly's Mission to Cadiz—Official Delays—General Whittingham desired as Governor—Solicitations from Englishmen—Spanish Jealousies and Intrigues—A nearly exhausted Patience—General Cuesta's Enmity and Insults—General Cuesta's Death . . . . 134—150

CHAPTER VIII.
1812.

Letter to Sir Henry Wellesley—General Whittingham's Visit to Minorca—Colonel Serrano's Report of the Alarm in his Absence—Military College established by General Whittingham—A generous and liberal Spanish Bishop—Voluminous Dispatch to Mr. Wellesley—Importance of the Majorca Division—Its numerical Strength at this time weak—Shocking State of Spanish Officers in Palma—Conditional Resignation of Command—Majorca Division to operate on Eastern Coast under Lord William Bentinck—Letter to Spanish military Intendant—A justified Assurance given to the Admiral—Urgent Request for a Paymaster—General Whittingham embarks with his Division—Resigns his Command prospectively—Is flatteringly requested to relinquish his Design—His grateful Reply to the Ambassador—Successful Affairs of Posts—A military Diversion—The Paymaster Difficulty—A Prospect of Relief 151—168

CHAPTER IX.
1813.

Lord Wellington's Instructions—Lord Wellington refuses the Inspectorship to General Whittingham—The French attempt to surprise Xigona—Treachery of an Italian Regiment—Colonel Walker and Officers of H.M.'s 58th Regiment—Lord Wellington grants the previously refused Inspectorship—His Reluctance to the Measure—Different Style adopted to another Agent—Gallant Conduct of the Spanish Captain Ruti—Generous Conduct of the French Captors—A successful Ruse—A brave Spanish Lieutenant—The French driven by General Whittingham through the Pass of Albayda—General Murray's Two General Orders—Lord Wellington's Dispatch—General Whittingham's Report to the Ambassador—Concentayna Combat—Sir Henry Wellesley's Congratulations—Lord Wellington's Proof of Confidence—Third General Order praising Whittingham's Division—General Whittingham's Report to Sir John Murray—Battle of Castalla—Sir John Murray's Dispatch to Lord Wellington—At Castalla Spaniards rivalled the British—Anecdote from the 'Recollections' .   .   .   .   .   .   169—198

CHAPTER X.

1813—*continued*.

Increase of French and Decrease of English Force—Reputation of the Majorca Division—Death of Honourable Colonel Cadogan—Lord William Bentinck supersedes Sir John Murray—General Whittingham covers the Retreat from Tarragona—Effected without Loss—Whittingham exceptionally favoured by Lord Wellington—An Order more flattering than agreeable—Cavalry unshod for want of Money—A German Aide-de-Camp—Official Jealousies and Persecutions—General Whittingham's Resignation of Command—His Reasons for resigning—Account of passing the Ebro—A drunken Commander—The French murder Colonel O'Reilly—Retaliation by the Spaniards—Great Evils require strong Remedies—Magazines filled in a Week—Lord Wellington feels the utmost Concern at General Whittingham's Resignation—Withholds his Papers till he shall hear again—Gives him a large Command of Cavalry—The Glory and Duty of obeying Wellington—State of Spanish Cavalry—Hazardous Alternative—A fraternal *Epanchement de Cœur*—Training of Spanish Cavalry — Colonel Torrens's Letter to Mr. Davis — Routine carried too far—Lord Wellington resigns the Command of the Spanish Army—Improvement of Spanish Cavalry—A disappointing Peace . . . . . . 199—227

CHAPTER XI.

1814.

Spanish Promotions—A Prayer not heard—Lord Wellington's Fears regarding Spain—Reception of Ferdinand VII. at Saragossa—A triumphant Entry—Constitution unpopular in Spain—The King requests Gen. W. to accompany him to Valencia—The royal Present—Arrests—'The Majesty that doth hedge a King'—The King and Don Carlos's flattering Request—*The Duke's* Testimony to the Merits and Services of General Whittingham—His Conversation with the Duke—Unpopularity of King Ferdinand in England—Appointed Aide-de-Camp to the Prince Regent—Promotion to Lieut.-General in Spain—Sir John Murray's Court-martial—Sir Henry Wellesley recommends General Whittingham to Viscount Castlereagh—The Earl of Fife's Letter— Marshal Suchet's Opinion of Whittingham—Inquisition established in Spain—Spanish Finances—Sir John Murray's Trial—Unlucky 'Buts'—General Mina's Rebellion—

Recollections of King Ferdinand—Triumphal royal Route—The King and the Constitution—Royal Thanks—General Whittingham commanded to continue with His Majesty—General Zayas sounds General Whittingham—His Opinion not approved—Arrests—March on Madrid—Cavalry Field-day—Lieutenant-Generalship conferred by the King—Ministry of War offered—Declined after reference—Takes Leave of the King and Don Antonio . . . . 228—248

CHAPTER XII.
1815-1819.

Sir John Murray's Trial—Sentence of Admonishment not carried out—An absurd Parliamentary Calumny—A Duel prevented by the Speaker—Quarrel adjusted—Colonel Campbell's Letter from Madrid—His Description of the Anglo-Spanish Officers—Gen. Whittingham's Appointment in the Spanish Army—Failed to obtain Employ with British Troops—Want of Rank in the British Army—The secret Dispatch—Aristocratic Nature of Wellington—Commissionership with Austrian Army declined—The Spanish Offer preferred—George IV.'s Aide-de-Campship no Sinecure—Duke of York's Letter to Sir Henry Wellesley—Disappointing Peace—Grand Cross of San Fernando—State of Finances in Spain—General Whittingham's Memoir to the King on the Slave Trade—Why unemployed at Madrid—Royal Favour—Russian Influence—Mr. B. Frere's Engagement—An expensive Honour for Lady Whittingham declined—Legitimately exercised Influence—Explanation of his Conduct to Lord Castlereagh—Declines all Rewards—The only Favour asked of the King—Government declined—Services unrewarded—Starvation in the midst of Honours—Mr. Vaughan's Recommendation of the General—His diplomatic Services to Mr. Vaughan—Diplomatic Services to Sir Henry Wellesley—Introduces his Nephew to the best Society—Marriage of Mr. B. Frere by Proxy—Sir H. Wellesley's Letter to the Duke of York—The royal Reply—Plenty of *Praise*, no *Rewards*—Troubles in Spain—Defence of the King a Point of Honour—Decline of English and Rise of Russian Influence—Secret Negociations by the Russian Minister—Death of Mrs. B. Frere—General Whittingham leaves Madrid—His Success against the Slave Trade—Chamois-hunting in the Pyrenees—Offered the Government of Dominica—Bids Farewell to the King of Spain—An attentive royal Host—Opinion applauded but not followed—The Ambassador's final Testimony

—Nothing ask, Nothing have—General Whittingham's Letter to
Mr. Murdoch—Fruitless Mission of the Count de Corres—Lord
Castlereagh's Testimony of Mr. Davis—Baron Hugel's Descrip-
tion of the West Indies . . . . 249—284

CHAPTER XIII.
1820–1822.

General Whittingham's Arrival in Dominica—Restores Order and
Concord—Anxious to obtain Employment in India—His System
of Government—Favours the Slave Population—Testimonials
both from the Islanders and the Proprietors resident in England
—Boon to the White Soldiers by Sir Samford's Recommendation
—Wilberforce's Letter to the Bishop of Calcutta—His Auto-
graph Letter to Sir Samford—George IV. and the Duke of York's
Letters of Introduction—Sir Henry Torrens's prophetical Letter
—A most delightful Personage — A popular Marquis—Uncle
Toby and Corporal Trim—A Governor-General's Smiles and
Frowns—Visit to Lord Hastings at Barrackpore—His Lordship's
flattering Confidence—How Lord Hastings silenced Ava's King
—Arrival of Sir Edward Paget, the new Commander-in-Chief—
Lord Hastings' great Error . . . . . 285—303

CHAPTER XIV.
1823–1825.

Death of the Marquis of Londonderry—Death of Bishop Middleton
—Sir Edward Paget's flattering Proposal—India should be ruled
by a Viceroy—The King of Oude—A handsome Commander-
in-Chief— Reorganization of Bengal Army indispensable —
Wretched State of military Means—Arduous official Labours—
Encouragement to Smokers—Sir Edward Paget's sole Source
of Comfort—The Mutiny at Barrackpore—Sir Samford's Report
of the Mutiny—His subsequent Defence of Sir Edward Paget—
Death of Sir Alexander Campbell—The *Alter Ego* of the Commander-in-Chief—Sir Herbert Taylor's Letter to Sir Samford—
Illness of Sir Edward Paget— Advice followed Forty Years
later—Lord Combermere's Arrival — First Impressions of his
Lordship—Character of Sir Edward Paget—Parting Exchange
of Presents—The Hookah and the 'Admiral'—Lord Combermere's Advance to besiege Bhurtpore—Efficient Preparations
owing to Sir Edward Paget—Lord Combermere's temporary
Coldness to Sir Samford Whittingham . . . 304—327

CHAPTER XV.
1826.

Sir Samford receives a Contusion at the Siege of Bhurtpore—His narrow Escape—Extraordinary Valour of Lieut. Caine—Defence of Sir Edward Paget—An invaluable Intellect—A satisfactory Letter—A Meerut Scandal—A Meerut Duel—Coolness under Fire considered criminal—Effects of a masterly Letter—Slow Posts caused ludicrous Results—Ill Health of the Duke of York—Sir Herbert Taylor's eulogistic Letter—Defective military Organization in India—Increase of European Force necessary from the Insubordination of Native Soldiers—Sir Edward Paget's generous Letter to Earl Bathurst—How the Means were *created* for taking Bhurtpore. . . . . . 328—340

CHAPTER XVI.
1827–1828.

Two Letters of same Date Ten Thousand Miles apart—Sir Edward Paget's Congratulations—Death of the Duke of York—Captain Seymour's Death—Copy of Sir Edward's Letter to Lord Bathurst reaches India—Aide-de-Camp selected for his Merit—Lord Combermere the Guest of Sir Samford—The Talk of the Garrison—The King of Oude—Lord Combermere's Friendliness—The Reaction of a generous Mind—Lord William Bentinck's Appointment—Sir Edward's Present of genuine Havannahs—Thanks of the House of Commons—Sir Edward's generous Disclaimer of Thanks—Willoughby Cotton's affectionate Letter—A Model of what a Man ought to be—Willoughby Cotton's Opinion of Sir Edward Paget—The principal Promoter of the Passage of the Douro—Lord Combermere's kind Letter—Lord William Bentinck's Arrival—His Request—Sir Herbert Taylor's Opinion of Sir E. Paget—The Confidant of Three successive Kings—Lord Combermere's Proof of Confidence—Sir Edward's Affection—Sir Samford's greatest Ambition . . . . . 341—359

CHAPTER XVII.
1829–1830.

On route to meet Lord Combermere—Takes final Leave of Lord Combermere—Letter of Southey to Mr. Hart Davis—Great Unpopularity of Lord William Bentinck—Captain Caine A.D.C. and the Tigers—Delightful Climate of Meerut—Universal Harmony at Cawnpore Station—Lord Combermere's Letter—Mussourie Hills—India not a good School for young Soldiers—A Home on the Hills—Lord Hastings versus Lord Amherst as a Financier—Accounts mysteriously withheld—Sir Henry Hardinge's Correspondence with Sir Samford—Expected Visits from Lord William Bentinck and Lord Dalhousie—Anxiety for a prolonged Command . . . . . . 360—369

CHAPTER XVIII.
1831.

Visits of the Earl of Dalhousie and of Lord William Bentinck—The Duke of Wellington's repeated Observation to Mr. Hart Davis regarding General Whittingham—Wholly adopted and rejoiced in by Lord William Bentinck—The Duke's Declaration against Reform—The Duke's Loss of Office injurious to Sir Samford—The rival Champagnes—A candid noble Sportsman—Lieutenant (now Sir Henry) Durand—One of the Duke's last official Acts — Lord William Bentinck's opinion of Daniel O'Connell — His Confidence in his Countrymen — A characteristic Letter by 'The Duke'—Lord Hill's Opinion of Sir Samford . . . . 370—379

CHAPTER XIX.
1832.

Mussourie—Chiefs at Simla, with their respective Staffs—Sir Edward Barnes—Bad Handwriting no Proof of Greatness—Lord William on the Royal Discretion—Sir Edward Barnes—The Commander-in-Chief's official Death Warrant — The Duke's Dictum on the Disagreement of Indian Chiefs—Lady William Bentinck—Injustice of Napier's earliest Volumes—The Non-publication of the 'Wellington Dispatches' an insufficient Excuse—The Barrosa Injustice— Colonel Caine's Recollections—Sir Samford writes to Sir Edward Paget for Redress and Satisfaction . . . . 380—384

CHAPTER XX.
1833-1835.

An inauspicious Day—Sir Frederick Adam, Governor of Madras—'Les absents ont toujours tort'—A reckless Rider—A General calls out an Ensign—An unexpected broad Front—Cruel only

to be kind—Lord William Bentinck's Comments on the Duel
— The Governor-General appointed Commander-in-Chief—
Application for the Military Secretaryship—Sir Samford's Value
to Lord William—A very hard Case—Colonel Napier's Statement too favourably judged by its Victim—Sir Samford unjust
to himself—An official Letter on broken Promises—First Meeting since Childhood of Father and Son—The Nilgherry Hills—
Sir Edward Paget and the 'United Service Journal'—Lord
William's Confidence in General Whittingham — Babington
Macaulay, Member of Council—Sir Samford's Admiration for
the Prussian Military System—Requests Sir Edward to be his
Second in a Duel with Colonel Napier—Sails for England in
the 'Curaçoa.' . . . . 385—403

CHAPTER XXI.
1835-1836.

Mr. Davis's Letter to Sir E. Paget—Sir Edward declines to take
Part in a Duel — Sir Rufane Donkin's decisive Conduct approved
by Sir Edward Paget—A double Breach of Faith—A Question
left to the Judgment of the Reader—Interviews with 'The Duke'
and Lord Glenelg—Men of no Party apt to be neglected—The
Compiler of the immortal 'Dispatches' consults Sir Samford—
Lord Auckland's Invitation—His Lordship's Notes to Sir Sam-
ford — The Hon. Admiral Fleeming — Lord Elphinstone —
Lord William Bentinck's Dinner to Lord Auckland — Lord
George Bentinck—Royal Presentation—The King's Questions
—William IV.'s flattering Finale—Sir H. Taylor's Letter on
the Death of Sir William Knighton—The Duke of Wellington
on the same Subject—Sir Samford Whittingham's Reply to his
Grace—Sir Edward Paget's Farewell—Lord William Bentinck's
Farewell—His Lordship's Philosophy—Correspondence between
Sir Samford and Lord Palmerston—Portsmouth Hospitalities—
Embarkation . . . . 404—425

CHAPTER XXII.
1837-1839.

Sir Samford's Second Service in the West Indies—Seeds of Dissension sown in vain at Barbadoes—A profitless Command—Cares
for the Health and Comfort of Soldiers—Mutiny of the Black
Troops in Trinidad—A Roman View of Military Discipline—A
fraternal Difference—'The best Inspecting-General we have'—

Sir Charles Paget's flattering Letter to Sir Samford—Popularity at the Expense of Discipline despised—Appointed Colonel of the 71st Highland Light Infantry—Congratulations of Sir John Macdonald the Adjutant-General—Sir Charles Paget's 'Heart and Soul Remark' to his Brother—An invaluable Inspecting-General —Sir De Lacy Evans—The Hougomont Hero—Dr. Archibald Hair's Congratulations—Lord Glenelg's Letter—Doctor Coleridge, Bishop of Barbadoes—Sir Samford's Joy at the Emancipation of the Negroes — Inspection Visit to Dominica — Sir Samford's Capacity for Labour — A fiery Interview between Wellington and Picton — Yellow Fever in its last Stage — Satisfaction of Home Authorities—Death of Admiral Sir Charles Paget — His Relatives advise Sir Samford to resign—Mr. B. Frere's Letter to Sir Samford — Appointed Commander-in-Chief at Madras — Parting Compliments from the Governor and Assembly—Departure . . . . 426—453

CHAPTER XXIII.
1840-1841.

Returns to England for the last time—Last recorded Meeting of Two old Friends—Moore and Dickens—Duke of Wellington's kind Note—Letter to Sir John Hobhouse on Corporal Punishment—Writes his 'Recollections' at Sea—Arrives at Madras during Lord Elphinstone's Absence—Lord Elphinstone's natural but needless Fears—Reinforcement to China—Letter from Lord Burghersh—Letter to the Hon. W. G. Osborne—Sir Charles Felix Smith's eulogistic Letter—A true Prophet on Indian Affairs —Sir Samford recommends Rapidity of Military Movements—A be-jewelled Rajah—An unworthy Englishman—Evil Effects of the West Indies—Sir Harry Smith's spontaneous Letter to Sir Samford—Evil Results of paternal Prejudices—Letter from the Bishop of Madras—Sir Samford's Loyalty to the Government—Correspondence about the 'Wellington Dispatches' — Sir Samford's Letter to Colonel Gurwood—Sir Samford's last Letters—His sudden Death—Lord Fitzroy Somerset's Letter to the Editor —The Funeral . . . . 454—491

APPENDICES . . . . 493—499

A MEMOIR

OF

SIR S. F. WHITTINGHAM.

CHAPTER I.

1772–1805.

DIFFICULTY IN TRACING THE FAMILY ANTECEDENTS—WILLIAM WHITTINGHAM OF BRISTOL—MISS RICHARDSON—SAMUEL FORD CHANGED TO SAMFORD—HE WOULD BE A SOLDIER—OLD MR. WHITTINGHAM OBJECTS TO HIS SON'S ENTERING THE ARMY—SAMFORD PROCEEDS TO SPAIN—THE RULING PASSION—DEATH OF HIS FATHER—RETURNS HOME—GAZETTED ENSIGN—LIEUTENANCY IN 1ST LIFE GUARDS—DISADVANTAGE OF TARDY ENTRANCE TO THE ARMY—HIGH WYCOMBE COLLEGE—SIXTEEN HOURS A DAY STUDY—MR. THOMAS MURDOCH—WILLIAM PITT'S SECRET MISSION—NOTE OF HON. W. ELIOT—LISBON—ROGERS AND RICHARDSON—MR. PITT'S THANKS—HIS DEATH—THE 13TH LIGHT DRAGOONS—EARLY PROMOTION OF THE HON. EDWARD PAGET, THE FUTURE FRIEND OF SAMFORD WHITTINGHAM.

FOR more than sixty years the subject of this Memoir and his sons have passed the best part of their lives in the public service of their country, in various parts of the world, and without a settled habitation. Owing to this fact, to the local changes in his native town, and to the circumstance that all the early contemporaries of Sir Samford Whittingham have long since departed this life, it is no easy matter to trace in accurate detail the antecedents of the family. Nor is this necessary in a case where the distinction gained by personal merit, unaided by aristocratic connections, is one of the chief justifications for holding up as a useful example to others the career of a military officer.

The father of Sir Samford Whittingham was a respectable citizen of the ancient and honourable city of Bristol. Mr. William Whittingham appears to have retired from business, with an independent, though not large, fortune, and thenceforward to have lived on his means as a gentleman in his native city. He had early married a young lady, who lived in the neighbourhood, who was of Warwickshire extraction, and who was called 'the beautiful Miss Richardson.' They had three children. The eldest, a girl, Sarah, married in 1789 Richard Hart Davis, a prosperous merchant in the Spanish wool trade, who, in 1806, became member for Colchester, and in 1812 was returned for his native city of Bristol (which he represented in six successive Parliaments), and was succeeded at Colchester by his eldest son, Hart Davis, afterwards Deputy Chairman of the Board of Excise.

The third child, James, eventually obtained a small post under Government. The elder of the two sons, Samuel Ford, the subject of this work, was born on the 29th January, 1772. When he grew up, his father desired to train him to the law, in its less brilliant but more probably remunerative branch; but his son revolted at the very idea. From the first he was resolutely determined to be a soldier; and nature had fitted him for the profession of arms.

Tall and broad-shouldered, with a fine figure, and an excellent constitution, he possessed an open fearless disposition, and an enthusiastic impetuosity, with much ambition, all tempered by the most generous and chivalrous feelings. In addition to this, Samford (for into that one word the names Samuel Ford were soon contracted by himself and his friends) possessed much natural ability, very great energy, and a truly wonderful power of application. A bright and winning smile, a large and powerful forehead, neutralized the irregularity of his features, and, coupled with his strong and commanding figure, formed a prepossessing exterior, which manners, always allowed to be singularly charming, rendered very attractive even to strangers, and completely fascinating to relatives and friends.* His respectful and disinterested deference and attentions to the fairer half of the creation was ever one of his most striking characteristics; and he truly was the knight without fear and without reproach. His natural impetuosity was calculated to make great friends or great enemies. If in his career the former greatly preponderated; if the latter were indeed very rare, as is believed to have been the case; this must be attributed to those winning qualities, that never lost a friend, but often won over an enemy. But his father would not hear of his entering the army; and his filial piety was such that he gave up the cherished object of his life till he became his own master.† He even allowed his brother-in-law, Mr. Hart Davis, to persuade him to give a trial to the wool trade, so far as to agree to travel into Spain, and visit the connections at Bilbao of the Bristol House. The desire to travel and see the world attracted him. He proceeded to Spain; there, with his wonted application and energy, he speedily acquired a perfect knowledge of the Spanish lan-

* One of Sir Samford Whittingham's nieces thus describes her uncle's appearance:—'If by the word *handsome* is simply meant beauty of feature and profile, it does not apply to him. But if eyes of matchless brilliancy, and the whole heart and soul animating a countenance beaming with talent and affection, be the test, then his countenance was eminently fascinating and delightful to look upon; as were his manners and powers of conversation, by which he won the hearts of all who approached him.'

To this may be added another peculiarity, which may interest the reader. One of the medical officers called in when Sir Samford Whittingham was dying afterwards declared that he had 'the *largest forehead* he had ever seen.'

† According to the *Bristol Times* (in its review of this work) Samford Whittingham was one of the mounted volunteers composed of the richer citizens, who were enrolled in Bristol in 1797, on a threatened French invasion. No doubt this episode increased his warlike tendencies.

guage and people. But he preferred the society of the military to that of the merchants, and the ruling passion only became stronger and firmer than ever.

Mr. William Whittingham died at Earl's Mead, Bristol, on the 12th September, 1801, aged sixty; a man much respected by his relatives and acquaintances. The part of the town in which he lived has undergone such changes as to be no longer recognizable, thus adding to the difficulties of all researches into the past.

By his father's death, Samford Whittingham became independent. He did not, however, immediately return to England; probably waiting till he should learn if there were any prospect of his being at length able to obtain a commission in the army. Fortunately the rule that prevented anyone above twenty-six years of age from obtaining a commission did not then exist. But it is probable that the further unfortunate delay was occasioned by his respect for his mother, who might have been shocked at the earnest wishes of the father being disregarded too soon after his death. The son appears to have remained abroad till he received the news of his approaching appointment. At all events it was not till the 3rd of January, 1803, that he arrived at the house of his widowed mother, in College Green, Bristol; and on the 20th of the same month he was gazetted to an ensigncy. But he was bent on being a cavalry officer, and immediately proceeded to London to negotiate the exchange.

The following fragment of a letter (which must have been written from London about the middle of February 1803, as it is recorded that he left the Green on the 3rd of that month) was carefully preserved by his mother, and found in her pocket-book, after her death:—

'My dearest Mother,—I have almost concluded the business of the Lieutenancy in the [1st] Life Guards. Lord Harrington, the Colonel, is to give me a positive answer on Monday; and Mr. Greenwood* has no doubt it will be favourable. The price is 2,000 guineas; but out of this will be deducted the price I have already paid for the Ensigncy, &c.'

Samford Whittingham was now thirty-one years of age. At that period, men usually obtained their first commissions at sixteen or earlier. He had thus lost at least fifteen years, and started in the army at a most lamentable disadvantage. If such a thing were possible now, it would be sufficiently disadvantageous. But sixty years ago it was worse. It is true that, thanks to that 'Soldier's Friend,' the Duke of York, the days were past in which English colonels might be seen in long clothes, or Scotch majors be heard 'greeting for their porridge.' But the road to promotion for the noble and wealthy was still wonderfully quick; and many men scarcely out of their teens were often found in actual command of regiments. Mr. William Whittingham's obstinacy had done irreparable injury to his son, rendering it almost impossible for him to expect to live to attain to the higher posts and rewards of the profession of arms, especially as he had nothing but his own merit to rely on in the struggle.

He did not return to Bristol, but proceeded immediately to the military college, then situated at High Wycombe. Although in those days science was not much encouraged in the army yet the zealous soldier was determined thoroughly to fit himself for the duties which he had undertaken to perform. He determined to endeavour to make up for lost time by extra exertions. It is recorded that, whilst at college, he lived on vegetable diet, in order to be able to study *sixteen hours a day*! And his constitution was able to bear for about a year and a half this trying strain upon its powers. He left an impression

---

* The firm now called Messrs. Cox and Co., *the par excellence* Army Agents of England.

at High Wycombe, which, in the memory of more than one professor, was transmitted to Sandhurst College, when the scholastic locality was changed; and of which impression, the editor was an ear-witness nearly thirty years later.

Samford Whittingham appears to have joined the 1st Life Guards in London towards the latter part of 1804. He had made, probably in Portugal, the acquaintance of Mr. Thomas Murdoch, a wealthy and influential wine merchant. This gentleman appears to have been the means of introducing Lieutenant Whittingham to the notice of the Right Honourable William Pitt, the *Premier*, who was then projecting an expedition against the Spanish South American colonies, and was desirous to secure for that purpose the services of a certain Englishman, named Captain Rogers, then in Madrid, in the service of Spain. Rogers was probably the captain of an English merchant ship, though this is a matter of conjecture only. The Life-Guardsman's knowledge of Spain and of the language, and his High Wycombe education no doubt were considered good qualifications for the negotiation in question: and he was of course delighted to be of service to the great Minister of the day.

As Mr. Pitt entered into his last period of office in May 1804, and as Lieutenant Whittingham belonged to the 1st Life Guards only from the 10th March, 1803, to the 14th February, 1805, there is no difficulty in filling up that part of the date of the following note, which is left blank in the original :—

' GREENWICH, 18*th December* [1804].

' Dear Sir,—Mr. Pitt will be glad to see Mr. Whittingham to-morrow morning at any time he will call and send in his name. The sooner he calls after eleven o'clock the less chance there will be of his being kept waiting.

'I have written, by his direction, for leave of absence to Lord Harrington.

'Yours faithfully,
'WM. ELIOT.

'Thomas Murdoch, Esquire,
  'No. 1 Fitzroy Square.'

There is no doubt that the above note was written by the honourable William Eliot, brother to the first Earl, and afterwards himself the second Earl, of St. Germans. The ensuing correspondence has been lost, in consequence of the box in which it was deposited in the care of Mr. Richard Hart Davis having been stolen a few years later. A certain Captain Richards was, it appears, employed by Lieutenant Whittingham to proceed from Lisbon to Madrid in the disguise of a smuggler, and to bring over Captain Rogers to England, and nothing more is at present known of the transaction itself. As regards Lieutenant Whittingham, he obtained the thanks of Mr. Pitt, but declined at the time all remuneration. The premature death of the Minister, on the 23rd January, 1806, was one of Samford Whittingham's earliest misfortunes, preventing his deriving at that time any advantage, either from his services or his disinterestedness. But the Ministry took these services, amongst others, into consideration when, many years later, a small pension was granted to him.

In the *United Service Journal* for April, 1841, this affair with Mr. Pitt is thus noticed in the account of the services of Sir Samford Whittingham :—

'In 1804, Lieutenant Whittingham, at the desire of Mr. Pitt, was selected to proceed to Portugal on a secret mission. This service detained him in that country about twelve months, and during his residence at Lisbon, he was promoted to a company in the 20th Foot.

'Captain Whittingham, on his return to England, was complimented by Mr. Pitt on the very able manner in which he had executed the commission entrusted to him by that Minister; and shortly after a troop in the 13th Light Dragoons becoming vacant, he was removed into that regiment.'

The article from which the above was taken was (there is every reason to believe) written by Mr. Hart Davis, Junior, late Deputy Chairman of the Board of Excise, who was better acquainted than any person then living with all that concerned his uncle, Sir Samford Whittingham. The exchange into the 13th Light Dragoons must have cost a large sum of money; but the amount has not been recorded.

In that same year, 1805, in which Samford Whittingham was promoted to be captain, his future greatest friend and patron—then wholly unknown to him, and two years younger than himself—was gazetted a *Major-General*. This was the honourable Edward Paget (whose brother, Lord Paget, afterwards became Marquis of Anglesey), of whom much mention will be made in the latter half of this volume.

CHAPTER II.

1806-1807.

SECRET EXPEDITION UNDER BRIGADIER-GENERAL ROBERT CRAUFURD—CAPTAIN WHITTINGHAM EMBARKS AT PORTSMOUTH, 12TH NOVEMBER 1806—TOUCHES AT ST. IAGO—MIDNIGHT FREAK OF SOME BRITISH OFFICERS—GENEROSITY OF PORTUGUESE GOVERNOR—A WELL-KEPT SECRET—ARRIVAL AT THE CAPE—HOW THE SECRET WAS DISCOVERED—ARRIVAL AT MONTEVIDEO—GENERAL WHITELOCKE—ORDER OF BATTLE—LANDING NEAR BARRAGAN—GENERAL WHITELOCKE'S FLATTERING OFFER TO CAPTAIN WHITTINGHAM—WHY DECLINED—GENERAL WHITELOCKE'S ERRORS—QUESTION OF NOT LOADING—CAPTAIN WHITTINGHAM SENT TO RECONNOITRE—CAPTAIN WHITTINGHAM VOLUNTEERS TO ENTER THE TOWN—HOW HE REACHED THE PLAZA DE LOS TOROS—RETURNS TO HEAD-QUARTERS FOR AID—VOLUNTEERS AGAIN TO ENDEAVOUR TO JOIN CRAUFURD—JOINS NICOLS AND TOLLY AT RESIDENCIA—PROOF OF CRAUFURD'S SURRENDER—SUCCESSFUL CHARGE OF MAJOR NICOLS—CAPTAIN WHITTINGHAM RETURNS AGAIN TO HEAD-QUARTERS—SUSPENSION OF HOSTILITIES—GENERAL GOWER DIFFERS IN OPINION FROM CAPTAIN WHITTINGHAM—PRELIMINARIES OF PEACE—A DISGRACEFUL TREATY—GENERAL LINIERS—LOSS TO ENGLAND BY THE SURRENDER—THE CIVIC COMPLIMENTS TO GENERAL WHITELOCKE—CAPTAIN CORMERO'S INFORMATION REGARDING THE WEAKNESS OF THE BUENOS AYRES GARRISON—DURABLE FRIENDSHIPS CONTRACTED AT BUENOS AYRES—HENRY TORRENS AND THE HONOURABLE HENRY CADOGAN—GENERAL WHITELOCKE'S TRIAL—BRINGS CAPTAIN WHITTINGHAM INTO NOTICE—DUKE OF KENT BECOMES HIS PATRON—GENERAL ROBERT CRAUFURD'S TESTIMONY AND THAT OF COLONEL GORDON.

TOWARDS the close of 1806, when the secret expedition against Lima, under the command of Brigadier-General Robert Craufurd was organized, Captain Whittingham was appointed Deputy Assistant Quartermaster-General to that force. Early in October, he joined it at Portsmouth, and sailed from England on the 12th November of the same year. From the day of his embarkation to that of his return to England, he—notwithstanding his many official duties—kept a copious journal, which completely filled two small manuscript volumes. From these alone a full and graphic history of one of the most disastrous expeditions, that England ever embarked in, might easily be written. And surely with profit: for the study of defeats, by teaching us how to avoid them, is as profitable, though not as agreeable, as the study of victories is to teach us how to gain them. But as this work is not a history, but only the memoir of an individual, the quotations from these voluminous journals will be limited to such matters as regard the character, conduct, and fortunes of Captain Whittingham, although to do this clearly must entail the narration of many general details of the expedition.

The fleet and convoy touched at St. Iago, the capital of the Verde Islands, on the 14th December, 1806. There Captain Whittingham's knowledge of languages was very useful to the Brigadier-General, in official matters, and very agreeable to the donna and to her lovely daughters at whose house the Captain was quartered during the few days the fleet remained in the harbour. As the Staff Officer of the force, he had also to settle a serious affair, the result of the wanton midnight freaks of some wild British officers, who had finished by insulting the guard of the Governor Don Antonio Continho.* But the generous Governor was satisfied with an apology, interceded warmly in favour of the offenders, and finally ended by hospitably entertaining them and their mediator to dinner. 'Sorry I am to say,' says the journalist about this business, 'I never saw my countrymen appear to less advantage.'—

On the 11th June the expedition left the Islands. On

* The ring-leader of these rioters was the Hon. Captain ——, who was madly determined to force the Governor *into a bag*, which he had obtained for the purpose; and he was with difficulty dissuaded from carrying out his scheme.

the 29th, it passed the line, and reached the Cape of Good Hope on the 15th March. The secret of the expedition had been well kept even from the Staff Officer. But fresh instructions received at the Cape caused an entire change of the original plan. Meantime the stay at the Cape was enlivened by putting the troops ashore for some days; on one of which there was a grand review of the united forces under Generals Grey and Craufurd. The second of the two following extracts shows the penetration of the writer of the journal:—

'6th April [1807].—The gale having subsided about half past four in the morning, we got under way. The weather was beautifully serene, and a few hours took the whole fleet out of the harbour. In the evening we were becalmed.'

'7th April.—Yesterday evening the Admiral [Murray] made the compass signal to steer north-west during the night. This has decided my opinion as to our present destination: we are certainly going to St. Helena, and thence to Buenos Ayres.'

The fleet sighted St. Helena on the 19th April. On the 20th, Captain Whittingham left the 'Warre' transport to take the orders of the General, who was on board the Admiral's ship. He then proceeded ashore to call on the Governor, with whom he breakfasted; a clever crotchety man, who started a long and tedious discussion in the vain endeavour to prove to *the pupil of High Wycombe* the value of some very doubtful improvements in gunnery.*

On the 25th, the fleet and transports again started; and cast anchor near Montevideo on the 13th June, where they found Sir Samuel Achmuty (who had taken it by storm) with some 7,000 men. General Whitelocke

* The whole discussion is given in voluminous detail in the journal.

had also arrived; and now Craufurd's division was incorporated with the rest, and Captain Whittingham lost his Staff post. But General Whitelocke appointed him his extra aide-de-camp without delay, and ever afterwards treated him with kindness, and with a flattering appreciation of his abilities.'

'*16th June.* . . . At five, we were going to sit down to dinner at General Whitelocke's, when a flag of truce arrived. It proved to be an aide-de-camp of General Liniers, a captain of hussars, named Don Pedro Joseph de Pendo. He came to propose an exchange of prisoners . . . General Whitelocke rejected the proposal altogether. He [the captain] was invited to dinner; and in the course of the evening, the General desired him to say to General Liniers that he could not, after the abusive letters which had been addressed to his predecessor [Sir Samuel Achmuty], enter into any correspondence whatever.'

On the 18th June, the order of battle was given out to the troops as follows:—

In the first line Brigadier-General Achmuty was to command the left Brigade, consisting of the 5th, 87th, and 28th Regiments of Foot; Brigadier-General Lumley was given the command of the centre, composed of the 36th and 88th Foot, and a part of the 17th Light Dragoons dismounted. To the right Brigade, commanded by Brigadier-General Craufurd, were attached the 95th Regiment, and the Light Battalion.

The right of the first line was to be supported by two batteries of artillery of six guns each.

The second line, or reserve, was supported on its left flank by a six-gun battery. Then came, successively, the 9th Light Dragoons on foot, the 45th and 40th Regiments, the 6th Dragoon Guards on foot, and finally the remainder of the 17th Light Dragoons mounted.

The whole force considerably exceeded 10,000 officers,

non-commissioned officers, and men, from which might be deducted about 400 sick, and less than 50 absent.

The embarkation at Montevideo was successfully carried out; and the landing, 'a little to the westward of Barragan,' which began at ten a.m. on the 28th June, was effected without opposition.

Previous to leaving Montevideo (where Colonel Brown was left in command), General Whitelocke made an offer to Captain Whittingham, which, however kindly intended, and however flattering, yet proved how little he understood the character of his aide-de-camp. The journal records: —' He [the General] began by saying that, if my views in this country were those of pleasure and amusement, he feared that what he had to propose would not merit my approbation; but that, if, on the contrary, my desires and wishes were to render myself useful to my country, and to make unto myself a name, he thought he had an opportunity of placing me in a situation of honour, of emolument, and of much utility to the public good.'

'In a word, he wished to make me a sort of commandant, and to place under my care the police of Buenos Ayres, and of all the surrounding country, giving me the direction and control of all the force, whether native or English, that should be employed for that purpose. He did not entirely explain himself on this head, but as far as I understood him, he intended to appoint one officer under me, and he wished me to recommend another. Under the direction of the first the military branch might be immediately placed; under the orders of the second, the civil branch; both, of course, to be immediately under my command. Soon afterwards Major-General Gower repeated nearly the same offer. I told them both and more particularly General Whitelocke, that I could not sufficiently express my gratitude for the confidence with which he was pleased to honour me; that I felt highly honoured by the offer he had made me: but that, as he had condescended to enquire into my views and wishes as a soldier, I hoped he would excuse the liberty I took in stating that, if the employment he intended to confer on me must of necessity confine me to Buenos Ayres, and prevent my following the army to the field, I should feel myself called upon to refuse it, if left by him a right of election. "For, sir," I added, "I would rather be a common hussar in the outposts in an active campaign than enjoy the most honourable and the most lucrative situation which should deprive me of the chance of seeing service." I had the satisfaction of finding my sentiments were not disapproved of.'

In his journal of the 3rd July, Captain Whittingham narrates the first of the most important faults made by his kind but inefficient commander:—' It appeared that General Gower had passed the Richuelo [rivulet] the day before at the Paso Chico, had fallen in with the enemy's advanced guard at the Miserere, and had taken nine pieces of cannon and a howitzer. This trifling advantage unfortunately changed the original plan of attack; which was to have gained the north-west side of the town, and to have taken up a position from the Ricoleta to the Plaza de los Toros. From this commanding situation it would have been in the General's power to have laid the town in ashes, or to have dictated to the inhabitants the terms of a capitulation. It was now determined to attack the town from our present position, which was behind it, upon a line nearly parallel to the bank of the river.'

'4th July.—I was sent with a flag of truce to offer terms to General Liniers. They were refused, and the attack was ordered for the next day.'

He then gives in his journal all the orders for the attack in great detail. The chief mistake was the division of the troops into many separate columns, too distant to support each other, and having to penetrate narrow streets, the windows and housetops of which were crowded with armed militiamen. The troops were ordered to advance to the proposed point of union or post which they were to reach, not only without firing, but also unloaded. The wisdom of the latter part of this order at least may be doubted, but the General was acquitted at his court-martial of all blame in this respect; and this acquittal of part of one charge was the only exception to the universal verdict of guilty, on four charges. The words of the order in question were '*The whole to be unloaded, and no firing to be admitted on any account*;' an order not calculated to encourage troops exposed to murderous street-firing, and not sanctioned by the example of more recent times in Paris and elsewhere.

'*5th July.*—The signal agreed upon was made at thirty-five minutes past six. The Commander-in-Chief was stationed in the rear of one of the centre streets. The fire was very heavy, but more particularly on the left. In consequence of having observed some considerable bodies of the enemy's cavalry hovering about, I was sent to reconnoitre them with ten dragoons and a small body of infantry. I was joined soon after by Colonel Torrens, and we pushed our reconnoissance to some miles distance. However, in spite of every stratagem we could make use of, we could never get the enemy to stand the charge, though their numbers exceeded at one time 200. The dragoons came up with them once, and despatched five in less than as many minutes. On our return we found that the Carabineers had advanced up the centre street to take some guns, and that they had behaved with great gallantry, though they had not succeeded. Colonel Kington was wounded and taken prisoner, and Captain Burril killed. The 9th Dragoons had got into much confusion, and had lost some men. No account whatever had been received from either wing, and all communication with the right and left was entirely cut off. A little before three o'clock, General Whitelocke began to be uneasy at having heard nothing from Sir Samuel Achmuty, or from Brigadier-General [Robert] Craufurd, and [General Whitelocke] said that, although it was a service that he would not press upon any man, yet he should feel himself infinitely obliged to any of his staff who would undertake to penetrate to the Plaza de los Toros, and find out the state of Sir Samuel [Achmuty] and his Brigade. I immediately said I should be most happy to have an opportunity of rendering myself useful, and at three o'clock I marched off with a sergeant and ten dragoons, and thirty infantry. I neglected no precaution as to the proper distribution of my little force. The whole country about Buenos Ayres is intersected with hedges. I divided the infantry into two separate bodies, to act as flankers, one on each side of the road; and I had, moreover, a corporal and two mounted dragoons as an advanced guard, and two private dragoons at some distance as a rear guard. I had good reason to be satisfied with having taken these necessary precautions, for our whole route was one continual skirmish, and the enemy was constantly on the watch to surprise us.

'Captain John Brown, J.D. and A.D.C., joined me, as a volunteer. My directions for finding the Plaza de los Toros were to keep the Ricoleta on my left, and whenever this church should bear nearly west, the Plaza de los Toros would be nearly east. Notwithstanding, when we got within about a mile, being desirous to come to it by the most private road, I ordered the flankers, instead of firing upon the next armed people they should meet with, to endeavour to make them prisoners. They presently brought me three, and I gave them to understand that, if they wished to avoid the gallows, they must take care to conduct me safely to the Plaza de los Toros; where, in fact, I arrived after a march of one hour and a half.

'I found Sir Samuel Achmuty in complete possession of

the Plaza de los Toros. He had taken thirty-three pieces of cannon, an immense quantity of ammunition, and 607 prisoners. The slaughter of the enemy had been considerable. Sir Samuel had under his command . . . his own brigade, which had suffered considerably, and the 36th Regiment, which had joined him, under General Lumley. The 88th Regiment, which formed part of General Lumley's brigade, was missing. The communication with the navy was opened. Sir Samuel expressed his desire that the Commander-in-Chief should, if he thought proper, effect a junction with him without loss of time with all the force [which] he could draw from the centre. But, at all events, he requested that some artillerymen might be sent immediately to work the guns which had fallen into his possession. As it appeared of importance to communicate Sir Samuel's report as soon as possible to the Commander-in-Chief, I left the infantry at the Plaza de los Toros, and effected my retreat with the dragoons. I got to head-quarters in less than an hour, and, in consequence of my report, eighteen artillerymen were forthwith sent to Sir Samuel.

'We were still ignorant of the fate of General Craufurd's brigade, and of [that] of the 45th; and that of the 88th Regiment appeared very doubtful. It was very necessary that the General should know as soon as possible the state of affairs on the right, and I again volunteered my services to penetrate to the position which General Craufurd might be in possession of.'

'*6th July.*—At daybreak I was on horseback. My instructions were to make about one mile southing, and then three miles easting. At the moment of my departure, one of the *Peones** arrived with the intelligence that Colonel Mahon had passed the bridge with the column under his command of the 40th Regiment, the 17th Light

---

* Native scouts or spies.

Dragoons dismounted, two companies of the 45th Regiment, and one hundred men of the 88th, and waited for further orders.

'Colonel Mahon had been left at La Reduction, with the above-mentioned force, to act according to the orders he might subsequently receive. A letter had been sent to him to advance, but he had not received it, and had passed the bridge [only] in consequence of the firing he heard, and as concluding naturally that he should, at all events, make his force more disposable, by getting rid, as soon as possible, of the obstacle of the bridge.

'With the usual precautions, I advanced within half a mile of the Residencia, when, finding the enemy's parties falling back on the same point, and collecting in great numbers, I thought it right to endeavour to communicate to Colonel Mahon the order to advance to head-quarters, before I attempted to force the road to the Residencia. I inclined, therefore, to the right, and in about half an hour fell in with the advanced pickets, and waited upon the Colonel at his head-quarters. With Colonel Mahon, I left the party of thirty infantry I had brought with me, and received in return 100 men of the 40th Regiment, under the command of Captain Gilles. A little after one o'clock, I joined Majors Nicols and Tolly at the Residencia. Major Nicols had under his command seven companies of the 45th Regiment.

'Major Tolly, of the 71st Regiment, who was one of the prisoners under General Beresford's capitulation, but had made his escape, led this column on the day of attack, and had taken possession of the Residencia with the loss of only seven men. They had had no communication with General Craufurd. On the morning of the attack, an English flag had been seen flying about 700 or 800 yards in advance towards the north-west, or [the] direction where General Craufurd was expected to be. At three o'clock p.m. of the same day, it was struck.' (An almost sure proof of the surrender of that brigade and of its most gallant leader.)

'Colonel Gerard, of the 45th, had advanced with his company of grenadiers, soon after his regiment had taken possession of the Residencia, to endeavour to open a communication with General Craufurd, and had been seen no more. Whilst we were in conversation on the top of the building, a cannon-shot went over our heads; the guns were advancing up the street. In a moment, Major Nicols was at the head of his men, and in less than five minutes a howitzer, with the timbers, was in our possession. Major Nicols and Major Tolly having given it as their opinion that it would be in vain for a small force to attempt to penetrate in search of General Craufurd, and that a large force could not be spared without risking the safety of the Residencia, we were constrained to give up all hopes of opening a communication with the Light Brigade; and at four o'clock p.m. I began my retreat.

'At seven o'clock p.m. I arrived at head-quarters, without having lost a man; a little skirmishing had taken place on the road, and the enemy lost two men killed, and two taken prisoners. I found that the Commander-in-Chief and Major-General Gower had gone to the left, and that Colonel Mahon had occupied with his brigade our former position at the Miserere. I reported to the Colonel the strength of Majors Tolly and Nicols' position, the abundance of the provisions they had [found] in the convent and adjacent houses, and the two guns and the howitzer they had taken; the proximity of the river, which was not 300 yards distant, and the ease with which a communication might be opened with the navy. [I added] the want they had expressed of an artillery officer, and the advantage they would derive from a reinforcement. The Colonel immediately decided that a reinforcement of 300 men, under Major Gwyn, should be sent to them next morning, with an artillery officer.'

'*7th July.*—At daybreak, I was on horseback, to proceed with a small detachment to the Commander-in-Chief on the left; and the party for the support of Majors Tolly and Nicols was already paraded, when a flag of truce arrived with orders from General Whitelocke to suspend all hostilities till further orders!

'At nine o'clock, I joined General Whitelocke, and reported upon the state of the Residencia, Colonel Mahon's Brigade, &c. I then learned to my infinite sorrow that soon after my departure a flag of truce had arrived from General Liniers to inform the Commander-in-Chief of the capture of General Craufurd, Colonel Duff,* Colonel Gerard, Colonel Pack, and Colonel Cadogan, together with the 95th, the Light Battalion, and the 88th; and to offer all the English prisoners in South America to return if the General would agree to evacuate the territory of Buenos Ayres in ten days, and the river Plate in the course of two months. This offer was rejected without hesitation. The flag of truce was sent back, and the Commander-in-Chief and Major-General Gower repaired without loss of time to the Plaza de los Toros.

'On my return from Sir Samuel Achmuty on the evening of the 5th, I had reported the position of the Plaza de los Toros to be extremely good; that from it we might lay the town in ashes; that no force the enemy could bring forward would ever be able to take it from us; that the head-quarters of the army might be established in the Ricoleta, a short distance to the rear; that a few mounted dragoons would clear the country . . . and, consequently, ensure our *Peones* being able to supply the camp with beef; and that, finally, our communication with the navy being opened, we should be enabled to obtain an ample supply of salt provisions, biscuit and spirits.

---

* Younger son of the Earl of Fife and afterwards General the Honourable Sir Alexander Duff. He was brother to the gallant Lord Macduff and father of the present Earl of Fife.

'When the two generals came to the Plaza de los Toros, Major-General Gower's opinion of the position by no means coincided with my report, and I understand he expressed himself so strongly as to say that nothing more could be done, and that it would be better to accept General Linier's terms. I have since, however, had the satisfaction to find my report of the position completely supported, *in all its extent*, by the Chief Engineer, Captain Squire, and the commanding officer of Artillery, Captain Fraser.

'On the morning of the 6th, a very short time after his arrival at the Plaza de los Toros, Major-General Gower went himself with a flag of truce to General Liniers, and agreed upon the preliminaries of the treaty. This took place about the time I was returning from the Residencia.

'At twelve o'clock, the 7th of July, I was sent to General Liniers, who returned with me to wait on General Whitelocke. The preliminaries were finally agreed upon. In the evening, English and Spanish patrols of cavalry were established in the town. It was determined that the Residencia and Miserere should be evacuated, and that all the troops should reunite at the Plaza de los Toros. At eight p.m. the treaty arrived, signed by General Liniers. General Whitelocke signed it the same evening, and Admiral Murray the next day.'

The journal of Captain Whittingham contains many pages of sharp criticism and of indignant commentaries on the facts which led to this shameful surrender, which will not be dwelt on in this Memoir. One passage, however, is here given; and this chapter will conclude with a few more extracts from the journal, personally concerning its writer.

'(*7th July.*)—History will record, and posterity with difficulty will believe, that such an army as ours capitulated with the rabble of a South American town, and sold the interests of the country, and gave up the hard-earned conquests of their brother soldiers, in order to secure a retreat which it was most amply in their power to have made at their good pleasure; or, at best, to procure that liberty for their countrymen which under such circumstances was scarcely worth their acceptance. But enough of this subject. I am sick of it! Would to God the waters of Oblivion were as near at hand as are those of La Plata!'

'11*th July*.—Generals Whitelocke and Lumley, with their staff, dined with General Liniers at the fort. The dinner was excellent, and very well served. "God save the King" was played, and the healths of the Kings of England and Spain drunk. The meeting went off as well as the nature of the affair could admit, and certainly nothing could exceed the modesty and propriety of General Liniers's behaviour . . . Liniers is an emigrant, an ex-Baron, and a *ci-devant* captain of a ship of the line in the French Navy.'

'12*th July*.—I waited upon General Liniers for the last time relative to the hostages. They are three volunteers —Captains Stanhope, 6th Dragoon Guards, Carroll, 88th Regiment, and Hamilton, 5th Regiment. . . . . At two o'clock, [I] got on board the "Aurora" packet. We went under the stern of the "Nereide," and, having received the General's final instructions, made sail for Montevideo.

'14*th July* [Montevideo].—I cannot express what I have felt this morning, at having been informed by Brown, Blake, and Forster, that upon many of the corners of the streets was written, "General Whitelocke is either a coward or a traitor! Perhaps both!"

'All the English merchants are in an uproar. They say their losses will be immense; that upwards of three millions worth of property is on its way to this country, and that, if it is given up, half the merchants in England will be ruined. God knows what will be the result of this most unfortunate affair. It appears to me one of the most severe blows that England has ever received.'

'15th [*July*].—Lieutenant-General Whitelocke landed about seven o'clock A.M. [at Montevideo].'

By a return written by Captain Whittingham, but evidently copied from the official one, dated 5th July, 1807, there were 16 officers killed at the attack on Buenos Ayres, and 56 wounded; and of non-commissioned officers and men, 289 killed, and 592 wounded; 207 was the total amount of the missing.

The following extract from the journal is inserted from a feeling of justice and compassion to poor General Whitelocke, since many a man unfit for the trying post of a military commander in war may yet be excellent in other positions, and worthy of love and regard.

'17th *July*.—The head of the Cavildo* waited upon the General, to request he would sign certain papers relative to their justification, which the General promised to do. The head of the Cavildo begged leave to return his most sincere thanks to General Whitelocke for the honourable and generous treatment [which] the magistrates and people of Montevideo had experienced at his hands, and at those of his predecessors. He added that he was well aware that under the mild and benign influence of the British government alone could they have hoped to meet with such strict and impartial justice, tempered with mercy. He spoke of the mob of Buenos Ayres in much the same terms as I have done heretofore,† and seemed to think the period of a revolution not far distant.'

Before dismissing the subject of the Buenos Ayres expedition, it must be stated that the journal of Captain Whittingham contains a long and interesting conversation that he had on the 26th July, at Montevideo, with Captain Cormero, the aide-de-camp of General Liniers; or

---

* Local governing council of Montevideo.
† In a part of his journal not published in this work.

rather, it was the questions of the Englishman that drew out the information from the Spaniard. Captain Cormero (at the hospitable table of Captain Squire) appears to have been very frank in his communications. They were of a nature completely to confirm and verify the criticisms which had previously been entered in Captain Whittingham's journal; though also imparting much new and valuable information. One only of the answers will be here inserted.

'In possession,' said Captain Cormero, 'as you were, of the two important posts of La Plaza de los Toros, and the Residencia, we were convinced from the very instant that you indicated a wish to treat of a capitulation that your General must have been influenced by the tenor of his instructions, which, we conceive, must have directed him, in the most positive manner, to avoid all harsh measures with the inhabitants of South America. *In no other way could* we account for his conduct; though we had no idea at that time that the whole British force had ever exceeded 5,000 men, including all the losses in killed, wounded, and prisoners, sustained in the attack of the 5th.'

Captain Whittingham was eager to leave Buenos Ayres, and return to England. He had lost his paid Staff appointment, and was only an extra aide-de-camp to a General going home. He wished to obtain some new appointment, or, failing that, to rejoin the 13th Light Dragoons. Accordingly, having obtained leave from the General, and a passage from the Admiral, and taken leave of both those functionaries, he sailed from Montevideo for England, on the 30th July, 1807.

Whilst on the Staff of General Whitelocke, in South America, Captain Whittingham contracted many durable friendships amongst his brother officers, and more especially with Lieutenant-Colonel Henry Torrens, and Lieutenant-Colonel the Honourable Henry Cadogan. The former was destined soon to become the military secretary of His Royal Highness the Duke of York, and under the name of Sir Henry Torrens to acquire a reputation at the Horse Guards, honoured and respected in the army; the latter, a younger son of the Earl of Cadogan, gallant, chivalrous, and generous-minded, was destined to an early, but glorious, death, whilst leading his regiment to victory under the great captain of the age. But before this sad event was to occur, Lieutenant-Colonel Cadogan and Captain Whittingham were to renew their friendship in the Peninsular War, although their meetings there were to be brief and rare. The letters of Cadogan have not reached the author's hands. It is possible that they may have been returned to his friends at his death, although of this there is no proof. Fortunately, two copies of letters written to him by Captain Whittingham have been preserved, and will appear in their proper places. It is enough here to say that they give sufficient proof of a warm and almost romantic affection, rarely to be met with in these calm and civilized days.

It is probable that Captain Whittingham divided the few months that he remained in England (which were not occupied with the long trial of General Whitelocke) in doing duty with the 13th Light Dragoons, in which he was a captain, and in visiting his sister and brother-in-law. The famous court-martial commenced its proceedings on the 28th of January, 1808, at the Royal Hospital, Chelsea, under the presidency of Sir William Meadows, K.B.

Captain Whittingham was one of the most important witnesses; and to him (from the uniform kindness which he had received from the unfortunate prisoner) the task he was compelled to perform must have been truly painful to his feelings. The trial lasted till the 18th of March; about six weeks from which time Captain Whittingham re-embarked for foreign service, having obtained a new Staff appointment.

General Whitelocke was tried on four long charges,

most of them implying want of judgment and of capacity. The third charge was the most disgraceful, accusing him of being wanting in personal exertion, in a manner that appeared to comprehend a still graver charge, which it is needless to specify. The prisoner was sentenced to be 'cashiered,' and was declared to be 'wholly unfit and unworthy to serve His Majesty in any military capacity whatever.'

Short as was the time that Captain Whittingham had at his command, during his present stay in England, it is certain that he then had the high honour of attracting the notice of that great admirer of military merit, and indeed of all merit, His Royal Highness the Duke of Kent. This was, no doubt, due to the reputation which Captain Whittingham had acquired by the publication of his (and other corroborative) evidence on Whitelocke's court-martial.

The first of the following two letters was written by General Robert Craufurd, one of the best and bravest of soldiers, who was afterwards mortally wounded at the siege of Ciudad Rodrigo on the 19th January, 1812, and died on the 24th of the same month.

The date of the note, unfortunately, does not fix the time; but it must have been in the autumn of 1807:—

Brigadier-General Robert Craufurd to Captain Samford Whittingham.

'MICKLEHAM, *Sunday evening* [1807].

'My dear Whittingham,—A visit from a brother, whom I have not seen for a long time, and who can only pass two days with me, and some other circumstances, have occasioned my deferring this answer to your last letter, in which you expressed a desire that I would write to Gordon.* You may *perfectly depend* upon my sending

* Lieutenant-Colonel Gordon, Military Secretary at the Horse Guards, afterwards for very many years Quartermaster-General of the army, as Si Willoughby Gordon, G.C.B., and who survived to an extreme old age.

you, by *to-morrow's* post, a letter both to him and to General Brownrigg; and I beg you to be assured that to have an opportunity [of] expressing the very high opinion which I entertain of your military merit, or of proving my very sincere personal regard and friendship for you, will ever afford me the most real pleasure and gratification.

'Believe me always, your sincere friend,
'ROBERT CRAUFURD.

'[P.S.]—I hope my letters will not arrive too late. If you have not been with Gordon or Brownrigg, Tuesday will, I suppose, be as good a day as Monday. At any rate, pray send my letters to them if you do not get them in time to deliver them in person.'

Lieutenant-Colonel Gordon to Richard Hart Davis, Esq. M.P.

'HORSE GUARDS, 30*th September*, 1807.

'Sir,—I have the pleasure of your letter of yesterday, with its enclosures, which I will give to Mr. Murdoch as soon as he comes to town.

'It has given me great satisfaction promoting the views of Captain Whittingham, of whose good conduct every officer under whom he has served speaks in the highest praise. I remain, with great truth, sir,

'Your faithful servant,
'J. W. GORDON.

'Richard Hart Davis, Esq. M.P.
 'Clifton, Bristol.'

CHAPTER III.

1808.

APPOINTED TO THE STAFF OF THE ARMY IN SICILY—TAKES LEAVE OF THE DUKE OF KENT—ARRIVES AT GIBRALTAR—ACTS AS MILITARY SECRETARY TO SIR HEW DALRYMPLE—OBTAINS LEAVE TO JOIN GENERAL CASTAÑOS AS A VOLUNTEER—HIS BROTHER IN-LAW'S LETTER OF ADVICE—HIS APPOINTMENT TO THE STAFF OF SIR ARTHUR WELLESLEY—HIS 'RECOLLECTIONS' OF THE BATTLE OF BAYLEN—CASTAÑOS' GENEROUS SPEECH TO DUPONT—THE FIRST ENGLISHMAN WHO FOUGHT IN THE PENINSULAR WAR—SHARED IN THE VICTORY BY JOINING LA PEÑA'S ADVANCED GUARD—INTERVIEW WITH LORD COLLINGWOOD—WITH THE TRAITOR LA MORLA—SCENE AT SEVILLE IN THE JUNTA SUPREMA—CASTAÑOS' PATRIOTISM—WHITTINGHAM MADE COLONEL OF HORSE—THE ENGLISHMAN'S FALL—THE DUKE OF YORK'S PRESENT TO CASTAÑOS—COLONEL WHITTINGHAM'S LETTER TO HONOURABLE HENRY CADOGAN—HIS PROPHETIC ANTICIPATIONS OF SPANISH FAILURES—DON SANTIAGO WHITTINGHAM—FEVER AT TUDELA—A NEARLY SMOTHERED MEDICO—DISGRACE OF CASTAÑOS AFTER DEFEAT OF TUDELA—AN UNDISTINGUISHED RELATIVE OF THE EMPRESS EUGÉNIE—EFFECTIVE SPEECH TO A SPANISH MOB—'WHEN THE ENGLISHMAN SAYS IT, IT MUST BE TRUE'—THINGS MORE AGREEABLE AS RECOLLECTIONS THAN WHEN ACTUALLY OCCURRING—DUKE OF INFANTADO SENDS COLONEL WHITTINGHAM ON A MISSION TO SEVILLE—GLOOMY ASPECT OF AFFAIRS IN THE ABSENCE OF SIR ARTHUR WELLESLEY—FIRST MEETING WITH LORD WILLIAM BENTINCK.

CAPTAIN WHITTINGHAM was appointed in the spring of 1808 Deputy-Assistant-Quartermaster-General on the Staff of the army in Sicily. This was a post not at all to his taste, for he conceived himself much better fitted by his antecedents for service in South America; to which it was then believed that another expedition was soon to be despatched, to recover lost prestige by new and better organized plans. In 1806 his brother-in-law had been elected member for Colchester, and he was no longer in the friendless state in which he had entered the army;

whilst his conduct at Buenos Ayres had gained him some friends, who were attracted to him both by his military merits and by his agreeable manners.

Captain Whittingham to Richard Hart Davis, Esq. M.P.

(Extract.)*

'Sunday morning [*probably April* 1808].

'I dined yesterday with Colonel Gordon, who received me in the kindest manner. He has promised to endeavour to procure me a passage in a frigate which will sail in a few days. To-morrow I go to the Duke of Kent's, and from thence to Fulham, so that I shall not be able to see you. Tuesday I am to see the Duke of York and Colonel Gordon. But I will not fail to call upon you previously to my going to the Horse Guards.'——

As Captain Whittingham had no official connection whatever with His Royal Highness the Duke of Kent, his going to take leave of that Prince previously to embarking for foreign service is a proof of the favour he enjoyed in that quarter. Then, doubtless, was arranged that correspondence the existence of which will be proved; although the letters themselves, with one exception, are unfortunately lost or mislaid. This correspondence was a great and valuable tribute to the merit of a captain of brief standing in the army, and possessed of neither military nor aristocratic connections.

Captain Whittingham to his Brother-in-law.

'PORTSMOUTH, 28*th April*, 1808.

'General Oake's aide-de-camp has just been here to announce that we weigh anchor at eight o'clock to-morrow morning. I shall not, therefore, be able to receive your

---

* As nearly all the letters in this work from Samford Whittingham to his brother-in-law, Mr. Davis, will be extracts, the word *extract* will be omitted in future in *such* letters.

letter of to-morrow. There seems to be a strange kind of predestination in my going to the Mediterranean; and a soldier is more particularly bound to believe that whatever is, is right. It is to me most grievous to think that all my hopes of being once more employed where best I could have served my country are done away with. The die is cast, however, and there is no remedy. For as to my recall from Sicily to join the army in South America after the affair is over, I cannot even wish it. For that would be completely reducing one to the situation of a civil agent, whose knowledge of the language might be considered convenient.'——

Captain Whittingham, however, sailed without effecting his object of a change of destination. After his arrival at Gibraltar, (where, as in duty bound, he waited on the Governor, Lieutenant-General Sir Hew Dalrymple,) he wrote on the 2nd June :—' You will see by the enclosed letter for Mr. Murdoch the present state of things, and will judge of the heavy heart with which I shall, in a few days, embark for Sicily. When you have read it, have the goodness to send it to him. I have seen Maitland. He is well, and going into Spain with Captain Dalrymple. The King and Queen of Spain, the Prince of Asturias, and several of the first nobility have been arrested at Bayonne, where they went to meet Buonaparte, and have been sent into the interior of France.'

Captain Whittingham, it appears, now acted as Sir Hew's Military Secretary in the absence of Captain Dalrymple on leave. He thus discovered that the Governor was in correspondence with Lieutenant-General Don Xavier Castaños, commanding the Spanish camp near Gibraltar, relative to the plan of a projected campaign against the French. He, therefore, entreated Sir Hew Dalrymple to give him permission to join General Castaños as a volunteer. As his perfect knowledge of the language and people of Spain especially fitted him to cement the alliance of the two nations, the Governor does not appear to have thrown any difficulties in his way. How delighted this consent made him, let his own pen demonstrate :—

To his Brother-in-law.

'GIBRALTAR, *5th June*, 1808.

'My dear Davis,—It would be in vain to attempt to express to you the feelings of my heart upon this most delightful occasion. I feel thankful to God for all things; and I bless that fate which has been so singularly propitious to all my soul's best wishes. This very morning, my own dear brother, I proceed to San Roque, to meet the Spanish General Castaños, and to accompany him to the advanced guard of the Spanish army, which is at present near Ecija. I saw General Castaños yesterday, and he was highly pleased at Sir Hew Dalrymple's offer to send me to remain with him during the campaign. My instructions from Sir Hew are to send him a faithful and exact account of the state of the Spanish army, its numbers, its positions, the marches that may be made, and the battles that shall take place! This, of course, during His Majesty's pleasure; and I have now only to beg and entreat that you and my dear Mr. Murdoch will, *if Colonel Gordon approve*, use your utmost endeavours with Lord Castlereagh to get my present appointment from Sir Hew Dalrymple confirmed.'

He concludes a long letter by requesting his brother to get him put on half-pay, if his request could not otherwise be granted. The reply from the Horse Guards was long in reaching him, in his opinion; and yet the authorities could hardly have answered quicker, or, practically speaking, in a more flattering manner. But, meantime, he was exceedingly anxious on the subject. Full of hope, nevertheless, he joined General Castaños, whose headquarters were soon after established at Utiera.

The following extract from a letter speaks for itself. It is written with the kindness and in the spirit of an affectionate elder brother :—

Richard Hart Davis, M.P., to Captain Whittingham.

'[LONDON,] 12*th July*, 1808.

' My dear Samford, . . . Your most welcome letter of the 5th has come to hand. We share all your feelings in regard to your appointment . . . Prudence requires that your communications with Mr. Murdoch and myself should only embrace transactions that would be interesting to us in as far as you are personally engaged in them, and not embracing, as your letters to Government undoubtedly will, the secrets of the Spanish army, and the general policy of the country. In short, ours must be an interesting correspondence, because it regards you, but not as politically regarding Spain. *Trust no one* with information but through the regular channel of Government. Suspect all men around you; and depend alone on your own clear and unbiassed judgment. Inspire enthusiasm in others; but do not be led [into] acting by it yourself. Never push yourself unnecessarily into danger: *my caution shows how ready you will be to meet it.** Never send information home as certain and to be depended on but on the clearest evidence. Always speak *cautiously* as to future events, but without desponding. Recollect that it is a new system of warfare [that will be required] to make volunteers beat the troops that have conquered all Europe. Perhaps the Fabian system of delay, though the least magnanimous, will be of the most efficacy. I want in some degree to temper your enthusiasm, by suggesting that *you may be uselessly sacrificed by your ardour* in leading on young troops who may be panic-struck, and desert you.

---

* His relations ever feared that his chivalrous eagerness for distinction might lead him into acts of rashness.

Excuse this advice which may be, nay, probably is, unnecessary, but which the warmest affection for you suggests. You must, at all events, make up your mind to a long struggle, if Spain is to be successful; God grant that she may. If an early battle is fought, and the Spaniards are defeated, I fear that it will break the energy of their measures, and the unanimity of their councils. France has possession of the government, and the centre of the country, and can march to any part of the circle, and separate the force that is forming against her. She has, besides, possession of the passes into the country, and can, therefore, reinforce her army to any extent. The salvation of Spain, in my opinion, will not depend upon her own efforts only, nor on our assistance, powerful as it will be; but it must be connected with other hostile movements in other parts of Europe.*

'Be cautious in writing your dispatches. Use your own short and nervous language. Cultivate the good will of the Spanish Commander-in-Chief. You will be the link to unite the two armies, nay, perhaps the two countries; and to be successful, they must be harmonious. Besides, what the Spanish commander says of you in his dispatch will have great weight. I am most anxious to hear of the expected engagement with Dupont. Wellesley has probably sailed from Cork with his armament.'——

The following letter was not communicated to Captain Whittingham till some time after the battle of Baylen, though written more than a fortnight before it:—

Colonel J. W. Gordon to Lieutenant-General Sir Hew Dalrymple.
(Extract.)
'HORSE GUARDS, 2nd July, 1808.

'Sir,—Captain Whittingham, of the 13th Light Dragoons, having been appointed a Deputy-Assistant Quar-

* A true prophecy: for except for the invasion of Russia by Napoleon, the Peninsula could scarcely have been delivered.

termaster-General to the forces under the command of Lieutenant-General Sir Arthur Wellesley, I am directed to acquaint you that Captain Whittingham has the Commander-in-Chief's permission to remain with General Castaños.'——

Had this post been given to Captain Whittingham a few weeks sooner, he would undoubtedly have joined Sir Authur Wellesley without delay, and thus have been attached to that illustrious hero for the rest of the Peninsular War. In after years, he often regretted the decision that he now made to adhere to the career which he had, in the first instance, embraced mainly to escape proceeding to Sicily. He would certainly have been spared many disappointments and mortifications, occasioned by the misfortunes and misconduct of the Spaniards, if his service in the Peninsula had all been performed on the Staff under the eye of the great duke; and he would have personally shared in more of his victories. But, on the other hand, the very subordinate rank he would have held would have deprived him of the opportunity of displaying the military ability that he undoubtedly did display with the Spanish troops, the wretched condition of which ennobled the task of commanding them by increasing its difficulty. Still less, had he adhered to his English Staff Captaincy, could he have gained the confidence and respect of Marquis Wellesley, and of Lord Cowley, or have earned the flattering praises of an accomplished Marshal of France; all of which advantages fell to his lot in the service of Spain.

From Sir Samford's 'Recollections.' (Mentioned in the Preface.)

'The army of Castaños was composed of 10,000 regular infantry, 25,000 rabble, twenty-four pieces of horse artillery, and about 1,500 cavalry. The French force at that time in Andalusia exceeded 25,000 men.* Our first point of assembly was at Utiera, from whence we advanced to Baylen in four divisions, [the three first] commanded by Major-General Reding,† Lieutenant-General the Marquis de Compigny, and Lieutenant-General La Peña.‡ The fourth division formed the reserve. Previous to the memorable battle that took place some days afterwards, Reding and Compigny, by a flank movement, got to the rear of the French position; whilst Castaños, with two other divisions, attacked it in front. Dupont, in the battle, committed the fault of successively attacking the Spanish position at four different points, instead of concentrating and repeating his efforts upon one and the same point. The Spanish troops behaved nobly; and the Spanish artillery was eminently successful. Victory, after a hard-fought day, declared for the Spaniards; and the French *remained prisoners of war*. Nothing could excuse or palliate the conduct of Dupont; for he had not only surrendered himself and his army to a far inferior force, but he obliged General Vedel to countermarch on his route to Madrid, and to come to Baylen to be included in the capitulation.' [After describing how the disgraceful conduct of Dupont was mainly owing to his desire to save his effects, and the plunder he had accumulated, the ' Recollections' continue :] ' On the following day, when Dupont advanced at the head of his Staff to deliver up his sword to General Castaños, the Spaniard dismounted, and approaching the carriage in which Dupont and his Staff were seated, he addressed him in a kind and consolatory speech : calling his attention to the inevitable vicissitudes of human life, and attributing

* The French, however, at Baylen had only 17,500 men, including cavalry; but that number should have easily routed the undisciplined troops of Castaños.

† General Reding was a Swiss officer of considerable ability.

‡ This General was destined, at a later period, to be the involuntary cause of the greatest mortification that ever befell the subject of this Memoir.

his victory over one of the most renowned of Napoleon's generals more to his good fortune than to any superiority of talent. 17,500 men, of which 3,000 were cavalry, and a brilliant and numerous train of horse artillery, filed off before our ragged ranks, and laid down their arms.'

By joining La Peña, Captain Whittingham shared personally in this victory, and had thereby the honour of being *the first Englishman who fought for Spain in the Peninsular War.* Two days later, 20th July, 1808, Sir Arthur Wellesley, having preceded his troops, landed at Coruña, from His Majesty's ship 'Crocodile,' commanded by Captain the Hon. George (afterwards the late Earl) Cadogan, the younger brother of Lieutenant-Colonel Cadogan, the intimate friend and correspondent of Captain Whittingham.

In his 'History of the Consulate and the Empire,' M. Thiers says :—' Such was the famous capitulation of Baylen, the name of which, in our childhood, resounded in our ears as often as that of Austerlitz or of Jena.' *

In one of his letters to his brother-in-law, Captain Whittingham writes :—' General Castaños deserves the highest honour for his well-conceived plan, and for the cool determination with which he carried it into execution, in spite of all the popular clamours for an immediate attack upon the position of Andujar. The General was so kind as to allow me to advance with General La Peña's division.'

After Baylen, he travelled in various parts of Spain on General Castaños' missions, who himself, it appears, went to Seville.

* 'Telle fut cette fameuse capitulation de Baylen, dont le nom, dans notre enfance, a aussi souvent retenti à nos oreilles que celui d'Austerlitz ou d'Iéna.'—Vol. i. p. 205.

To his Brother-in-law.

'CORDOVA, 15*th August*, 1808.

' You forgot to enclose the note from Sir Thomas Plumer. I will not attempt to express the delight with which I have heard Sir Thomas's opinion upon my conduct. I will not run into unnecessary danger; but in the day of battle I cannot remain at head-quarters. General Castaños permitted me, with some difficulty, to move with the advanced guard at the affair of Baylen. I trust that he will never refuse his permission in future. It is the only point upon which I shall differ in opinion with my beloved General, whose kindness to me is that of a father to a son. Charles IV. has lost Spain for ever. He and his infamous Queen are detested, and the hopes and wishes of the people are fixed upon Ferdinand VII.

'. . . I have bought four horses, three for riding, and one as a bât horse; and a travelling carriage. I have made upwards of a thousand miles post since the battle of Baylen; and in this country we are obliged to travel with four horses. A number of little purchases made at Gibraltar for officers of General Castaños' staff I have requested them to accept, because even in the veriest trifle at present I would wish to see liberality the order of the day. . . . On the 29th July, I delivered my letter for you to Lord Collingwood.* I explained to his Lordship the reasons which induced General Castaños to grant such favourable terms to General Dupont, " namely, the impossibility of preventing the retreating of General Vedel upon Madrid." In the evening, I waited upon General Morla.†

---

* 'Lord Collingwood had not been satisfied with the terms granted to [General] Vedel. He was not sufficiently acquainted with the circumstances to understand why an inferior division should have been allowed to capitulate after the principal force had been defeated.'—Southey's *Peninsular War*, vol. i. page 390.

† Don Thomas de Morla, whose treacherous surrender, afterwards, of Madrid has covered his name with perpetual infamy.

31st July, I left Cadiz, and on the morning of the 1st August arrived at Gibraltar. Sir Hew received me with the greatest kindness. 3rd August, returned to Algeciras; 5th, to Cadiz; 6th, went again on board the fleet to see Lord Collingwood, where I learned the news of the augmentation of the British army of Portugal and the appointment of Sir Hew Dalrymple to the chief command. In the evening General Morla informed me that the French evacuated Madrid on the 31st July. On the 7th, I dined with Mrs. Gordon, at Xeres, and on the 8th, arrived at Seville at nine in the morning.

'I do not conceive I am wanting in my duty by communicating to you the very satisfactory conversation I had with General Castaños on my return to Seville.' [After mentioning a number of military arrangements that he had made in the province, Castaños added,] 'that he had sent the Chief of his Staff to General Moreno to Madrid, where he intended to go himself within a few days. The General then informed me that a battle had been fought in the neighbourhood of Rio-Seco between General Cuesta and General Bessières; the French force consisted of 15,000 men; the Spaniards, including the army of Galicia, amounted to 50,000. *The Spaniards had no cavalry. The battle was fought in a plain.* The French horse turned the left wing of the Spanish line; the defeat was complete; 5,000 or 6,000 men were killed, and the whole army dispersed. General Cuesta retreated to Salamanca, and General Blake, with the army of Galicia, to the frontiers of that province.

'If I might be allowed to give an opinion upon matters of such high importance, this battle of Cuesta, evidently fought without a proper attention to the nature of the ground, or the composition of the army, will ultimately tend to much good. In all probability it will lead to giving the chief command of the whole Spanish army to General Castaños, who will, I have no doubt, follow up the excellent system which he has begun, and prove himself the Fabius of Spain.'

'*11th August.*—I had a long conversation with the General, relative to the affairs of this Government. It appears that disputes had run high in the Junta Suprema of Seville upon the subject of Granada. Count Tilly threatened that a division of the army of Andalusia should march against Granada, and force them to obey the orders of the Junta of Seville. General Castaños then arose from his seat, and, striking the table with his hand, he said, "And who is the man that will dare to lead a division of my army, contrary to my orders? I do not consider the army I have the honour to command as the army of Andalusia, but as the army of Spain, and never will I stain the laurels which it has won by suffering it to become the vile instrument of civil discord. The affairs of Granada may be amicably and easily settled."

'As soon as the General had done speaking, Don Vincento Ori stood up, and, taking off his *banda*, threw it upon the table, saying that "he would never be a member of any body where such words as those which he had just heard from Count Tilly were tolerated."

'The discussion ended by an apology on the part of the Count for what he had said, and a recantation of his ideas upon the subject of civil war.'——

For his services at the battle of Baylen, Captain Whittingham was made a Colonel of Cavalry in the Spanish army by General Castaños, subject to confirmation by the Junta. Colonel Whittingham, soon after the above letter, accompanied his beloved and excellent chief to Madrid, and here we will quote from his manuscript 'Recollections:'—

'On our passage through La Mancha to Madrid, I was taken to the house of a woman, who had obtained great celebrity by the murder of a number of French soldiers. In the court-yard of her dwelling, there was a well of very good water, but the rope for drawing it up was very short, and you were obliged to stoop forward in order to be able to drink out of the bucket. Whenever an incautious soldier came to the well, and bent over to drink, she came behind him, and, seizing him by the legs, tumbled him into the well. She had, I understood, put eight men to death in this manner.

'The triumphant march of General Castaños to Madrid far exceeds my powers of description. On entering the gates of Atocha, our steps were directed to the chapel to hear mass. The crowd was immense; and at the church door, one of the *Manolas*, a stout handsome young woman, threw her arms round my neck with such affectionate violence that down we came at full length together on the floor, she exclaiming all the while, "God bless the Englishman, the delight of my soul."* The burst of laughter was not quite in harmony with church gravity, but Castaños long enjoyed the joke, and the Englishman's fall became a standing dish at his table.'——

To appreciate the joke, the reader must bear in mind that Colonel Whittingham was about six feet high in his boots, and stout and broad-shouldered, even more than in proportion to that stature; and he was a fine figure in the dress which he still wore, of Captain of the 13th Light Dragoons. He was, from early date, however, obliged to guard against a too great *embonpoint*, and at times lived very abstemiously for that purpose.

Whilst at Madrid, Captain Whittingham (for so by the Horse Guards authorities he was still styled) must have received the letter of which the following is an extract, and which was found amongst his papers :—

* Bendito sea el Inglesito de mi alma.

Lieutenant-Colonel Gordon to R. H. Davis, Esq. M.P.
(Extract.)
'HORSE GUARDS, 23rd *August*, 1808.

'You may assure Captain Whittingham that his conduct has given great satisfaction, and that, whenever the rules of the service admit of it, the Commander-in-Chief will immediately recommend him to the King for promotion.* He is in the meantime to continue with Castaños, and to hold his appointment as Deputy Assistant Quartermaster-General to the army, under Sir Hew Dalrymple. It is perhaps unnecessary for me to repeat to you the high opinion I have long formed of Captain Whittingham; but you may rely upon me for every aid in my power to the advancement of his interest, convinced that in so doing I am assisting an officer whose zeal and talents will be eminently useful to his country.'——

A letter from Samford Whittingham to his brother-in-law, dated Madrid, 2nd September, 1808, concluded with this commission:—' On the part of General Castaños, pray ask Mr. Knight to order one of the machines for making lint for the use of the army, to be forwarded immediately to Coruña. Adieu, God bless you. The French have pillaged Bilbao. The slaughter has been great.'

This commission for Mr. Knight led to a graceful act of courtesy on the part of the Duke of York to General Castaños, which Mr. Knight thus explained in a letter to Mr. Hart Davis, dated Weymouth, 30th October, 1808:
—' I accidentally mentioned to the Duke of York the commission of General Castaños, and His Royal Highness has taken advantage of the circumstance and the opportunity

---

* The Supreme Junta of Seville, by a decree in the name of King Ferdinand VII. of 20th July, 1808, had made Don Santiago Whittingham a Colonel of Cavalry, ' for the zeal and known valour with which you have distinguished yourself in the campaign of Andalusia, which terminated with the glorious battle of Baylen.'

to pay His Excellency a suitable compliment, by directing me to accompany the machine with a present from His Royal Highness of a portable medicine chest and complete set of instruments, finished after the manner in which they are furnished for service, for the Duke's personal use . . . I think this is a most handsome trait of the Duke, and it is like himself.'

It may be easily imagined what pleasure it gave to Colonel Whittingham to be the first to announce to his respected and kind chief the coming present from the Royal Commander-in-Chief of the British army.

General Castaños, whilst at Madrid, despatched Colonel Whittingham on a special mission, which the latter thus announced to Mr. Davis in a letter, dated Madrid, 7th September:—' I leave this town for Saragossa to-morrow. General Castaños sends me to examine into the real effective forces and condition of the armies of Aragon, Valencia, and Castile. I shall return with a faithful account of the state of things to our divisional head-quarters, which are about to be established at Soria. My old friend and commander, Lieutenant-General La Peña, commands there, and is extremely anxious to receive a report on the subject from me.'

On the 22nd September of this year, Sir Arthur Wellesley, unfortunately for the Peninsula, embarked at Lisbon to return to England. He arrived in London on the 6th October. There he was detained by the long enquiry into the convention of Cintra, and received the warm thanks of both Houses of Parliament. It was not till the 22nd of April, 1809, that he returned to Lisbon. During his absence occurred the defeat of the Spaniards under Castaños at Tudela, and the death of Sir John Moore at Coruña, followed by the abandonment of that coast of Spain.

In a long letter to Mr. Stuart, the Minister, dated Madrid, 22nd September, 1808, Colonel Whittingham defends the conduct of General Castaños after the battle of Baylen. The last sentence alone is here quoted :—

'The terms of the treaty, it is very clear, cannot be fulfilled. The Spaniards have neither ships, men, nor money to send these men to France, and by the capitulation they can only be sent home in Spanish vessels manned by Spaniards. They must, therefore, of necessity remain prisoners in Spain at least for some years.'

Colonel Whittingham to Lieutenant-Colonel the Hon. Henry Cadogan, 71st Regiment, 2nd Battalion.

'MADRID, 6th *October*, 1808.

'My dear Cadogan,—It would be difficult for me to express the pleasure which I have received from your truly friendly letter. Believe me, few things in this life could have given me greater satisfaction. I love to cherish the hope that you will be with us. We have much yet to do, and great indeed is the assistance which we stand in need of. I have been detained in Madrid longer than I had wished or expected. The proposed march of the English army to this country has been the cause of it. Everything is now settled, and to-morrow I go off to the army. We occupy the right bank of the Ebro, and the French the left. Their right is at Miranda, and their left at Milapo. Pampeluna is in their possession, and the other day they again entered Bilbao. They expect strong reinforcements by the 15th of this month. Their present force is 45,000 men. The centre of our army, commanded by General Castaños, occupies Logrono, Calahorra, Corella, Cascarte, and Tarragona. The left under Blake is at Frias and Orduña. The right, under Palafox, is at Saragossa, with a detachment advanced towards Sanguera. Our whole force may amount to 100,000 men. But at least 30,000 of them are not yet near the scene of action, having been detained by a complete want of clothing. Yet there is no time to be lost if we mean to attack the French before the arrival of their reinforcements. The orders to this effect from government are positive, and I shall probably have to communicate an account of a general action in less than ten days. *For the first time in my life,* my dear Cadogan, *my heart misgives me, and forebodes no good. I fear the result of this action.** The French are concentrated, and we are considerably scattered. Their troops are all equal; ours, some bad, and some good. They have the advantage of unity of command; we are directed by three generals, all independent of each other. I trust in God that nothing will delay the march of the English army to Burgos. It will be an excellent rallying point for us in case of disaster; but no time must be lost. The enthusiasm of the Spaniards is worthy of their cause, and their bravery such as you would wish your best friend to possess. But we are not yet organized; and as we are now to move in large bodies, and with combined operations, I cannot help entertaining some doubts of the issue of the first battle. As I shall probably not have time to write to anyone again before the action, I pray you, should anything happen to me, to let Colonel Gordon see this letter. It is not, however, with one or with twenty battles that Buonaparte will conquer Spain. Every town will become another Saragossa; and when his brother reigns in Spain, women and children will be his only subjects. I have General Castaños' order to join my old commander, General La Peña. His outposts are generally engaged with the French, and hitherto the Spaniards have uniformly had the advantage. When I returned about ten days ago from a reconnoissance of the line occupied by our troops, I sent my horses forwards; so that I have nothing to do

---

* The Editor has placed these words in *italics,* as proving that the victory of Baylen had not blinded the judgment of Colonel Whittingham to the inferiority of the Spanish to the French troops. The subsequent constant defeats of the Spaniards only too well justified his prognostications.

but to pass into the saddle of a good post-horse, and hasten to the scene of action. I have a famous stock of cigars, a pocket-compass, and some excellent horses. So that, you see, your old friend is well provided for the campaign. God bless you, and grant that you may soon be with us.

'Yours ever,
'SAMFORD WHITTINGHAM.'

His prophetic anticipations of failure were too soon realized, and the reputation of General Castaños was eclipsed on the 23rd of November at the fatal battle of Tudela. The blame, however, entirely lay with the Spanish Government. The battle was fought by order of the Commissioner, whom the Supreme Junta attached with full powers to the army, and who compelled Castaños, against his will, to assault the army of Marshal Victor. But by these remarks we are anticipating, and must now return to our story.

To his Brother-in-law.

'HEAD-QUARTERS, CALAHORRA, 30*th* October, 1808.

'Have the goodness to direct all your letters to me as follows :—

'" *Á Don Santiago Whittingham, Coronel de Cavalleria, en el Quartel General del Excellentísimo Señor Don Francisco Xavier de Castaños, Capitan General y General in Xefe del exercito centro. Adonde se halle.*" *

'I have paid every trifling debt, and I left Madrid without owing a shilling to anyone. On the other hand, my contingent account, which will be paid to me by the Commissary-General of the British army—at least so Sir Hew Dalrymple informed me—amounts to 708 dollars;

* From this time forth, he was usually addressed by his Spanish rank during the Peninsular War, except in official letters from the authorities in England, in which he was generally addressed by his rank in the British service.

all for expenses of different journeys and messengers on Government account. My carriage, horses, and personal expenses, of course, I have paid myself, and should not think of charging. Doyle has a carte-blanche for his expenses from Lord Castlereagh. You will see by the enclosed copy of a commission which I have received from General Castaños that they have made me a Colonel of Horse, with full rank and pay. But what I most esteem is the cause or motive which they state for having conferred the honour upon me, viz. my good services in the campaign of Andalusia. As His Royal Highness has approved of the rank given to Doyle, I flatter myself that he will have no objection to my holding the commission in the Spanish service. I understand that it is General Castaños' intention to give me the command of a regiment of hussars. This will not prevent his continuing me upon his Staff, and he has appointed me his first aide-de-camp. In regard to my promotion [in the British service], Lord Castlereagh has remitted to General Castaños a very handsome letter from His Royal Highness the Duke of York, in which he is pleased to say that His Majesty will be glad to promote me as soon as I have my standing.'—

On the 6th November, a week after the above letter was written, Colonel Whittingham was attacked in Tudela by rheumatic fever, which totally deprived him of the use of his limbs. He was thus compulsorily absent from the battle near that town which took place on the 23rd of the same month; and was saved the chagrin of witnessing the defeat of his gallant chief and comrades on that unlucky day. But let him speak from his 'Recollections:'—

'Before the battle of Tudela, I had been attacked by rheumatic fever, and confined to my bed for many days. Towards the close of the action, General Graham* called

---

* From this it would appear that General Graham (afterwards Lord Lynedoch) was present at the battle of Tudela; no doubt as a volunteer. No English troops were then in Spain, and Sir A. Wellesley was in London giving evidence on the Court of Enquiry regarding the Convention of Cintra.

on me to say that all was lost, and that I must be moved forthwith, or I should be taken prisoner. As all my horses were too gay and unsteady for a sick man, the General had brought one of his own, a strong steady horse, quite equal to my weight. A pillow was placed on the saddle, and I was carried downstairs, and lifted into it. But my sufferings were beyond human endurance; and after proceeding about three miles to the village of Ablitas, I was taken off the saddle, and thrown on a mattress.

'About ten o'clock at night, General Castaños and the principal officers of his Staff arrived. We had been completely defeated, were in full retreat upon Cuença, and the French pursuing. The General directed that I should be carried downstairs, and placed on a mattress in a little covered cart, which had been secured; and that, without a moment's loss of time, I should proceed on the road to Cuença. The whole of my body was at that time so inflamed with rheumatism that I could only be turned in bed by lifting up the sheets on which I was extended. Yet in this dolorous state I was forced to make a journey of three hundred miles in a cart without springs, in the depth of winter, and over abominable mountain roads.

'Castaños had kindly directed his principal medical officer to accompany me to Cuença; and one very cold morning before daylight, Doctor Turlan (that was his name) requested that I would permit him to enter the cart, and share my mattress with him. I readily consented. But we had not proceeded half a mile when the cart was overturned, and pitched down a precipice. In the fall, the unfortunate medico got under the mattress, and as Santiago (S. W.) with his *feather* weight remained upon it, the poor doctor was nearly suffocated. His cries and screeches were quite terrific. "For the love of God, Señor Don Santiago," shouted he, "I am stifled, I am suffocated! For the love of the most Holy Virgin, I be-

seech you to get up, or I shall die!" "Dearest Turlan,"*
I replied, "you see that I am totally incapable of movement; so that, if it should appear that your last hour is arrived, recommend yourself to God; for from human aid you have nothing to expect."

'The arrival of a few straggling soldiers put off the doctor's evil hour. They dragged me out by the feet, and again set the cart upright, but nothing could induce Turlan to re-occupy a share of my mattress.

'On the loss of the battle of Tudela, Castaños was superseded, and directed to appear at Seville before the Supreme Junta.*

'The Condé of Montijo, a grandee of the first class, but a man of infamous character, and a personal enemy of Castaños, preceded him by some days on the road to Seville, and spread the report throughout La Mancha that Castaños was a traitor, and deserved to die. At Miguel Turra, Castaños was billeted at the house of a curate, to whose firmness and presence of mind he owed his life. Deceived by the lies of Montijo, an infuriated mob assembled before the house of the curate, and demanded their victim. But Castaños had already passed through the garden by a back door, and had been conveyed to a secret spot; where his horses and servants were waiting.

'A few weeks after this occurrence, I was sent by the Duke of Infantado to Seville, and had to pass through Miguel Turra. An immense crowd was assembled in the Plaza, and I advanced on horseback into the midst. They asked, "What news of the traitor Castaños?" and I was happy to have an opportunity of speaking on the subject.

'" Gentlemen," said I, " I am grieved, astonished, and

---

* Queridísimo Turlan.

† The Junta performed the supersession gently and politely; pretending that they wanted the aid of General Castaños as a counsellor.

deeply afflicted, to see so many good and worthy men so easily duped and led astray by the lying inventions of one of the vilest of men. Castaños commanded the Campo de Gibraltar before the present struggle commenced. The French did everything in their power to gain him over to their party. But he met their intrigues by assembling the forces of Andalusia, and gaining the battle of Baylen. *I saw* 17,500 French soldiers lay down their arms, and surrender themselves prisoners of war to this very General Castaños. He then proceeded to Madrid, and organized and commanded the army which a superior French force has now defeated at Tudela. But, be it known unto you, gentlemen, that the General was obliged to fight this battle, against his own better judgment, by orders from the Supreme Junta. For he was well aware that an army of newly raised levies could ill compete with the veteran troops of Napoleon. This same Castaños, your best, your most devoted, friend, you, gentlemen, have wished to murder, because an infamous and lying coward, for such is Montijo, has fled from the field of battle to denounce him here."*

'The boldness of my address evidently surprised them. A murmur of consultation ran through the assembly; when a voice from one of the leading men exclaimed, "*When the Englishman says so, it must be true.*" † A tremendous shout of applause confirmed this opinion; and I was carried in triumph to my quarters, proud indeed of the honour done to my countrymen's integrity by so impartial a tribunal.'———

But many things which are agreeable as 'Recollections'

---

* If the conduct of the Count de Montijo was actuated by a partiality for the French, it has met with an unlooked-for reward to his family, in the elevation of the fairest and best of the Montijos to the throne of France.

† 'Quando el Ingles lo dice, verdad será.' No doubt, the fluency with which the English dragoon officer addressed them in their own language (by surprising and pleasing the mob of Spaniards) greatly facilitated the success of this well-timed oration.

are unpleasant enough when actually occurring, as the following letter, written at the period in question, will demonstrate :—

'HEAD-QUARTERS, CUENÇA, 16*th December*, 1808.

'My dear Davis,—A rheumatic fever attacked me on the 6th of last month in Tudela, and totally deprived me of the use of my limbs. I will not now enter into a detail of my sufferings. My escape was miraculous. In a covered cart, I have followed the retreat of the army. My servants were daily obliged to lift me in and out of the cart. I had no powers of motion, and the pains which I suffered were intolerable. The army retired to Calatayud, Siguenza, Guadalaxara, and Cuença. Our rear was warmly pursued by the French. Madrid has capitulated. Buonaparte is now collecting all his force to attack Sir John Moore. We shall probably soon advance towards Madrid. I can scarcely hold the pen. Let this plead in excuse for not writing to Colonel Gordon, to whom you will please to communicate this letter. I shall not abandon the Spanish army as long as I consider that my communications with Mr. Frere can be useful to the service of my country.'——

The prospect of affairs in Spain in the absence of Sir Arthur Wellesley, and with General Cuesta as chief of the principal Spanish army, were now gloomy enough to excite very serious apprehensions of many coming disasters and defeats.

At some period in 1808, which the Editor is unfortunately unable to particularize, Colonel Whittingham certainly met Lord William Bentinck for the first time at *Aranjuez*, and assisted his Lordship in certain negotiations with the Spanish Government in that town, for the fact (as the reader will find) is recorded by him more than twenty years afterwards, after having, for the third time, acted officially under that distinguished and excellent nobleman.

CHAPTER IV.

1809.

THE DUKE OF INFANTADO'S COMMISSION—THE DUKE'S RETREAT—THE CHIVALROUS DUKE OF ALBURQUERQUE—SURPRISE OF MORA—AN EXCITING CHASE—A FOX-LIKE RUSE—A HORRIBLE INCIDENT—A CUNNING COUNTESS—A COMPLETE HUMBUG—A MODEST TESTAMENTARY REQUEST—LETTER TO MR. J. HOOKHAM FRERE—BAD CONDUCT OF GENERAL URBINA—HIS DISGRACEFUL ROUT—ALBURQUERQUE'S TREATMENT OF TRAITORS—GALLANT CHARGE OF ALBURQUERQUE AND STAFF AT MEDELLIN—ALAVA'S HEROISM—REFORMING ROUTED CAVALRY UNFORTUNATELY LOST LETTERS—ALBURQUERQUE'S LAUDATORY LETTERS TO DUKE OF YORK AND LORD CASTLEREAGH—CONTRADICTORY ORDERS OF SPANISH GOVERNMENT—LETTERS TO MR. HOOKHAM FRERE—A PROPHECY DESTINED TO SPEEDY FULFILMENT—GENERAL CUESTA'S EARLIEST BRITISH CRITIC—A CONSTANT SOURCE OF ANNOYANCE—SIR A. WELLESLEY'S RETURN TO THE PENINSULA—BRIGADIER-GENERAL WHITTINGHAM'S LETTER TO DUKE OF KENT—HARMONY OF FRERE AND WHITTINGHAM—MARQUIS WELLESLEY'S OPINION OF WHITTINGHAM—DUKE OF KENT'S LETTER TO MR. DAVIS CONCERNING BRIGADIER-GENERAL WHITTINGHAM—LOST ROYAL LETTERS—INTERVIEW WITH SIR ARTHUR WELLESLEY—MEETING OF GENERAL CUESTA AND SIR A. WELLESLEY—WHITTINGHAM'S MISSION TO CUESTA—NARROW ESCAPE OF SIR ARTHUR WELLESLEY—HIS REMARKS TO WHITTINGHAM—COLONEL ROCHE'S LETTER ON TALAVERA—SIR A. WELLESLEY'S DISPATCH—A GLARING INJUSTICE—A TRUTHFUL COMPARISON.

THE commencement of a new year found Colonel Whittingham at Seville recovering his health, having been sent there by the Duke of Infantado. We continue the fraternal correspondence:—

To his Brother-in-law.

'SEVILLE, 13*th January*, 1809.

'I have the pleasure to inform you that my health is tolerably re-established, and that I shall again set off for head-quarters in a few days. You are not to imagine that I should have quitted the army for anything relative to myself. The Duke of Infantado requested that I would go to Seville on a particular commission, which, I am happy to say, I have executed to his satisfaction; and I have now no other anxiety but that of again entering the field of Mars with all possible expedition. I shall enter into no details upon our late unfortunate campaign, because I have to remit to Colonel Gordon by the next post General Castaños' defence of his conduct as laid before the Supreme Junta.'

To the Same.

'SEVILLE, 20*th January*, 1809.

'My dear Davis will rejoice to hear that this fine climate has operated a most favourable change on my health. I am, thank God, once again fit for the field; and I love to flatter myself that fate will throw in my way some opportunity to distinguish myself.

'21*st*.—On the 13th and 14th, the advanced guard of the Duke of Infantado, at Tarancon and Uccles, was attacked by the French in force, and obliged to retire upon Cuença, our head-quarters. For the last three days, we have received no news from the army. It is sadly to be lamented that the Duke had not quitted the position of Cuença long since. It was proposed and strongly urged that the army should immediately advance to Ocaña and Toledo as early as the 29th of last month. The advantages of this movement were clearly pointed out,* and the Duke appeared determined to advance. Cuença is in itself a bad position, and the retreat towards Andalusia impracticable, at least for the artillery. Twenty-six leagues is the distance from Cuença to Manzanares, the first town on the high-road to Seville. The road is so excessively bad and heavy that I was ten hours making

* By himself, no doubt. All his Spanish commanders appear to have listened to his counsels; but few, except the Duke of Alburquerque, followed them.

three leagues in a light carriage with five mules. I set off for the army on Thursday next. My health is quite re-established. Be assured, my dear Davis, that, however we may be beat for the present, we shall ultimately drive the French out of Spain. I cannot tell you with what delight I look forward to my return to the army. I really am never quite happy but in active campaign.'——

When the Duke of Infantado left Madrid on 2nd December, 1809, to join the army commanded, since the departure of Castaños, by Lieutenant-General La Peña, the latter most generously caused the Duke to be elected to the chief command. Infantado had been accompanied from Madrid by the young, patriotic, and chivalrous Joseph Maria de la Cueva Duke of Alburquerque;* a man beloved by his officers and soldiers, and having for enemies only the baser and meaner of his countrymen, who were governed by their jealousies or other malignant passions. If, as was the case with the Spanish nobility generally, his education had not been neglected, he might have made a greater figure in history; and as it was, he left a name second to none amongst his countrymen at that period. Colonel Whittingham, from the first, admired and loved him, and all the more because the Duke rarely displayed the obstinacy so common amongst his countrymen, and only required to hear in order to take good advice. What follows is from the already quoted 'Recollections:'—

'On my return from Seville, I was attached to the *corps d'armée* under the Duke of Alburquerque in La Mancha, where we had many affairs of cavalry, as the Duke had under his command 3,500 horse and two troops of horse artillery.

'At Mora, the French had a detachment of 600 cavalry.

* In this work the spelling of Spanish names by Colonel Gurwood is adopted, as that officer took much pains to acquire accuracy in that matter; whilst compiling the *Wellington Dispatches*.

The Duke advanced to surprise the post with 1,500 horse. We bivouacked a few miles from their outposts without being discovered; and before daylight we were upon them. The surprise was complete. They lost 160 men, and fled at full speed.

'Amongst the foremost of the pursuers was a servant of mine, a young Irish lad [named Charles], whom I had dressed up as a hussar. He fixed his eye upon a well-dressed middle-aged man, well mounted and apparently well fed. Charles was satisfied that he would turn out a good prize. Both horses were excellent; and both were urged to the top of their speed by the pursuer and the pursued. But my hussar had the advantage of a lighter weight, and was gaining fast upon his adversary, when the Frenchman turned round upon his saddle, and fired a pistol at him; which was soon followed by a second shot. Both shots, however, missed their object, and the old soldier was reduced to his last shift, which was, however, a good one. Judging from the appearance of his pursuer that his object would be plunder, he drew a knife from his pocket and cut the straps which fastened his portmanteau. The portmanteau then fell to the ground, and Charles immediately reined up, and secured his prize, which contained a brace of pistols and a good stock of clothes.

'Amongst the variety of incidents of this exciting day, an occurrence took place which we all deeply lamented. A remarkably fine young woman, apparently about seventeen or eighteen years of age, was making her escape from Mora in an open carriage, belonging to the French General commanding. Some of our cavalry attempted to arrest her progress. She immediately fired a pistol at the nearest soldier, and in return received from him a *coup de sabre* which almost divided her head from her body. In a moment she was stripped with that dexterity peculiar to soldiers, and her body left on the road.

'On our return to Mora, we were quartered in the house of the Countess de ——, whose previous guest had been the French General commanding. The enthusiasm of the lady was beyond description. She thanked the Blessed Virgin for her miraculous escape from perdition, and declared her determination to avail herself of the happy opportunity of returning to the paternal house, which our arrival afforded. Her gratitude to Heaven and to us knew no bounds. Orders were immediately given to pack up all her plate and jewels. A splendid dinner was prepared by the major-domo. The only carriage in the place and six mules were employed by the Duke's order for her conveyance, and the hour of departure was fixed for four o'clock on the following morning.

'Our party consisted of the Duke of Alburquerque, Alava,* and myself. The Duke retired to rest at nine. But I felt uneasy that our departure should have been put off till the morning, and I submitted to Alava that it was always a point of honour with the French to return a surprise with the least possible delay. [I added] that their force in cavalry and horse artillery in our immediate neighbourhood was very considerable; and that to effect our retreat, we must pass through a long and narrow defile, which commenced at the entrance of Mora, and that, if attacked during the passage, confusion and complete defeat would be the inevitable consequences, and the Duke's character as a soldier lost. I proposed, therefore, that we should awake the Duke, and submit to him the expediency of our commencing our retreat forthwith. Alava coincided in my view of our position. We awoke the General, and orders were immediately given to put the troops in motion.

* Afterwards General Alava (a favourite of Lord Wellington and on his personal staff); eventually Spanish ambassador in London about thirty years later.

'The chivalrous feelings of the Duke and of Alava did not permit their forgetting the perilous position of the disconsolate Countess. The carriage was ordered to the door, and her servants were directed to finish the packing with all expedition. But, alas! the Countess had fainted; and when she came to herself, she broke out into the most bitter lamentations against her cruel destiny. "Alas!" she exclaimed, " by this time to-morrow I shall have ceased to exist. For the French, on their return, will assuredly put me to death as a traitress and a spy. But, happen what may, how is it possible that a poor little delicate thing like me should be able to suffer the privations, the miseries, the hardships, of a camp follower? It cannot be. I am well aware of the cruel death that awaits me on the return of the French; but there is no remedy, and if my last hour is come, it is better for me to die in my own house and bed than in the fields!" A more complete humbug I never saw! Thus ended a comedy worthy of *Camilla* and *Don Rafael*; and the Countess, laughing [secretly] at the simplicity of our hearts and heads, dedicated herself forthwith to the preparation of an excellent breakfast for the French General on his return.

'Our accelerated retreat was fortunate. We had scarcely cleared the defile when our rear-guard was attacked.'

Thus was the gallant Spanish Duke and his party saved by the vigilance of their English comrade.*

On the 30th January, 1809, he relates to Mr. Davis the particulars of the defeat at Uccles of General Venegas, and adds, 'The Duke of Infantado's want of decision was the cause of this misfortune.' The Duke had been repeatedly advised to advance and support Venegas, who

---

* Doubtless this was one of Samford Whittingham's 'services in the early part of the war, the importance of which was passed over or little known.' —See the Earl of Fife's letter in *Preface*.

was sure to be attacked, but took no notice of the warning. In consequence he was ordered to join General Urbina, Count of Cartaojal, and to serve under him as part of the army of the Carolina. This supersession took place on the 18th February. But General Urbina proved to be a far worse commander than the Duke he superseded, as will be hereafter demonstrated.

To his Brother-in-law.

'HEAD-QUARTERS, LA CAROLINA, 12*th February*, 1809.

'The French are advancing against General Cuesta in force, certainly not less than 20,000 men. Their head-quarters on the 5th were at Oropesa. Their advanced posts occupied the bridge of the Arzobispo. General Cuesta had his head-quarters at Truxillo; his advanced posts at the bridge of Almaraz. A division of Portuguese and English was stationed at Alcantara, a force of from 12,000 to 14,000 men. Cuesta's army is about the same strength. A part of the French army from Galicia had directed its march upon Ciudad Rodrigo. On the 5th, they had arrived at Martin del Rio, distant from Ciudad Rodrigo ten leagues.

'The moment you cast your eye upon the map, you will see the danger of General Cuesta's position. Our advanced guard will march to-night upon Toledo, be supported by a second division, and followed by the whole army. The total strength of this army, now called the army of the Carolina, including the remains of the army of the centre, amounts to nearly 30,000 men. Our movement will call the attention of the French; and even if we arrive too late to save General Cuesta, it will prevent them following up the advantage which they have obtained. I have no comments to make on our probable success.

'As soon as I receive Mr. [Hookham] Frere's answer,

I intend to ask General Urbina's leave to join the advanced guard.*

'Adieu, my dear Davis, and as I once before told you, if we meet no more on this side of the famous river, don't forget to drink a glass of your best wine to my memory once a year.'

To the Same.

'Head-Quarters of the Advanced Guard,
'Ciudad Real, 13th *March*, 1809.

'Our head-quarters are changed from Manzanares to this place, in consequence of the movements of the enemy.

'I cannot account for the long silence of my friends in England. Your last letter was dated November. Since that period I have not heard one word from you, or any one on that side of the water.'—

There is too much reason to believe that a great number of letters addressed to Colonel Whittingham, in the course of the Peninsular War, never reached him. But at this time, after the departure of the army of Sir John Moore from Coruña, and during the prolonged absence of Sir Arthur Wellesley from Portugal, the means of conveying English letters into the interior appears to have been equally rare and hazardous.

Colonel Whittingham to the Right Hon. John Hookham Frere, H.M.'s Minister in Spain.

'Ciudad Real, Head-Quarters of the
'Advanced Guard, 17th *March*, 1809.

'Sir,—The repeated advices of all the confidential agents employed by the Duke of Alburquerque to watch the movements of the enemy confirm, beyond the possibility of doubt, the march of the French towards Talavera,

---

* This determination, to be always in front, never slackened. The risk, with such troops as the Spanish then were, was self-evident.

and the certainty that the expected attack upon General Cuesta will immediately take place.

'Our Commander-in-Chief, General Urbina, has rejected the proposition of the Duke [of Alburquerque] to allow him to advance upon Toledo with a division of 12,000 or 15,000 infantry, 4,000 cavalry, and twenty pieces of artillery. The General-in-Chief considers the organization of the main body of the army as an object of more importance, and the arguments of the Duke to convince him that this organization would be secured rather than impeded by his proposed movement have been of no effect.

You may rest assured, sir, that there is no time to be lost, and if the Junta Suprema does not come to a speedy determination, and immediately communicate decisive orders in consequence, it is sadly to be feared that General Cuesta will be defeated by the superior force which he will have to contend with, viz. from 30,000 to 35,000 men.

'You will recollect the effect produced by the expedition to Mora, and the retrograde movement made by the French troops in Estremadura in consequence. Surely, the same arguments which were then made use of by General Urbina, to induce the Duke of Infantado to consent to the advance of the Duke of Alburquerque, exist in the present case in even greater force, inasmuch as our means of offence are greater, and the dispositions of the enemy to attack General Cuesta more formidable.

'I shall only add that the confidence of the officers and men in the Duke of Alburquerque affords the best-founded hopes of the fortunate result of the proposed expedition.

'I have the honour to be, with the highest respect,
  'Sir,
    'Your most obedient servant,
      'SAMFORD WHITTINGHAM.

'P.S.—It is scarcely necessary to point out the advantages of the proposed movement, should the fortune of war favour General Cuesta, and the French be repulsed. The unexpected appearance of the Duke's division upon the rear or flank of a defeated enemy would probably prove as decisive as the combined march of the columns in the battle of Baylen.

'S. W.'

From the Same to the Same.

'Ciudad Real, Head-Quarters of the
'Advanced Guard, 20*th March*, 1809.

'Sir,—In consequence of the orders from the Junta Suprema, the whole of the disposable force of this army will immediately advance upon Toledo, in order to effect a diversion in favour of General Cuesta. The Count of Cartaojal [General Urbina], at the same time that he communicated this order to the Duke of Alburquerque, directed him to deliver up the command to Brigadier-General Don Juan Bernuy, and with the division of Brigadier Don Luis Bapcourt, and that of Don Pedro Echavari, to march immediately to Guadalupe to co-operate with the army of Estremadura.

'Thus, at the moment that the plan proposed by the Duke is about to be executed, he is deprived of the command of the vanguard, and exposed to risk his military reputation at the head of a small body of newly raised infantry without cavalry or artillery. It is to be feared that the absence of their favourite General may produce a bad effect upon the troops. At all events little or nothing can be expected in favour of General Cuesta from the small corps entrusted to the command of the Duke.

'I cannot avoid expressing my sentiments with freedom at this interesting moment. I conceive that the Duke has fallen a sacrifice to his too great popularity with the troops; and I sincerely lament that the army should be deprived of the valuable military talents of this officer. It is not to be expected, after what has passed, that the Duke will accept any command under the Count de Cartaojal.

'According to the advices received to-day from Sevilleja, the French had passed Estrella to attack a division of the army under the command of General Cuesta, which occupied the position of Valdevilacasa. It is therefore very possible that the movement upon Toledo may be now too late, and should General Cuesta be defeated, much evil, instead of good, may result from it.

'On the 13th of this month, the Duke proposed to the General-in-Chief to make this diversion in favour of General Cuesta. At that moment there could be no doubt that the army of Estremadura would have been saved by our advance upon Aranjuez and Toledo. At present the result is doubtful, and may be fatal.

'The Duke begins his march to-morrow towards Guadalupe, and I shall take care to inform you most exactly of everything that occurs.

'I have, &c. &c.
'SAMFORD WHITTINGHAM.'

The contemptible conduct of General Urbina was not long in bringing deserved retribution upon him, in the form of a disastrous and crushing defeat, which was followed by his supersession in the chief command by General Venegas :—

Colonel Whittingham to his Brother-in-law.

'SEVILLE, 4*th April*, 1809.

'You will see by all the enclosed papers the chain of evils, and the gross misconduct, which have completely destroyed our well-founded hopes of soon re-occupying the capital of Spain. General Urbina, Count of Cartaojal, has betrayed his country, and fled in disgrace with

30,000 infantry and 5,000 cavalry before 2,000 French horse.

'The Duke of Alburquerque has been sacrificed to the envy and jealousy of General Urbina. Cuesta has fought bravely, but unfortunately. I had the pleasure of being with the Duke in this action [the battle of Medellin]. At last the eyes of the Junta Suprema are opened. Urbina is deprived of his command, and the Duke appointed temporarily to the command of the army of the Carolina. Things do not look well. But if I can carry the point which I have in view, viz. that our total force, amounting to at least 40,000 infantry and 8,000 cavalry, shall be immediately concentrated, I have yet my hopes. If not, depend upon it, all is lost. We leave this place to-morrow at daybreak for the army. We have been here a few hours to make arrangements with the Government. Have the goodness to get Mr. Murdoch to translate the enclosed papers, and lay them before Lord Castlereagh and Colonel Gordon. I have not heard from you since January.'——

The battle of Medellin was fought on the 28th March, 1809, and was one of General Cuesta's numerous defeats. That stupid and obstinate, but very brave and indefatigable, old General fought the battle with his usual contempt of tactics and prudence, and yet had nearly won it by the bravery of the infantry but for the gross misconduct of the Spanish cavalry. Colonel Whittingham, being attached to the staff of the Duke of Alburquerque's division, shared his fortunes on that unfortunate day. We will now revert to his 'Recollections :'—

'Previous to the battle of Medellin, the Duke of Alburquerque was directed to join General Cuesta in Estremadura with two troops of horse artillery and 1,500 cavalry. On our route we came to a small town which had become notorious for receiving and concealing deserters. The

Alcalde and the Escribano* were deeply implicated, and the Duke was determined on making an example. They were, therefore, both laid hold of, and placed in the grenadier company of a leading battalion ' [to expose these compulsory soldiers to the greater danger in action]. 'I saw these men the next day, as we were moving upon the enemy in column of companies, and their faces are even at this moment completely before my eyes. I never had a just idea of the personification of Fear till then. Their countenances were literally horror-struck; their hair stood on end. They recognised me instantly, and, dropping on their knees, they shouted out, "Mercy, Señor Don Santiago, for the love of God and of the Holy Virgin, do not permit this sacrifice!" But the hard-hearted Santiago was implored in vain; and the butt ends of the soldiers' muskets soon brought them on their feet again. I never heard what became of them. At the battle of Medellin the defeat was complete; and as Victor gave no quarter, they probably perished with the rest.†

'When everything was lost, and the last battalion broken and dispersed, the French cavalry formed a chain in rear of the Spanish troops, and the slaughter commenced. The Duke of Alburquerque, Alava, Bigodet, Nazario Eguia, and *Santiago*, with a few orderlies and servants, formed a little group. The chain was closed around us. The Duke, turning to me, said, "Santiago, do you see that smart light dragoon, how vain he is? Now, be assured that before two minutes are passed, he will be under my horse's feet;" ‡ and putting spurs to

---

* The Alcalde, and Escribano, may be roughly translated into the Mayor and Town Clerk.

† This appears like a proof that even the gentle-hearted Duke of Alburquerque could steel his heart in active service; but the fact is that, at such a time, no Spanish General would have ventured to show mercy to traitors.

‡ These words (written from memory in 1840) slightly differ from those given by Southey, who at an earlier period doubtless obtained them from the letters written to Colonel Gordon, the Military Secretary at the Horse Guards, by the subject of this Memoir.

his fine Andalusian horse, he charged full speed upon the chasseur, followed, of course, by all his little party. The chasseur, being somewhat of Falstaff's school, held prudence to be the better part of valour, and taking ground rapidly to the right—with half a dozen soldiers who followed his salutary example—a hole was left in the chain, through which we instantly passed at full gallop. The chase after us was long, but vainly kept up.

'A wounded artilleryman whom we passed called out to Alava, "Señor Don Miguel, for God's sake, help me, or I am lost! I am badly wounded, and you see the French give no quarter." "Get up behind me," said the heroic Alava; "we will both be saved, or both perish together."

'It was about ten at night when we arrived at a solitary farm-house; and having made a bonnie fire, and got a dish of chocolate and a cigar, the Spaniards unanimously agreed, "The more we lose the more we gain; the Body Politic will yet require much blood-letting before its health can be perfectly restored!"*

'We lost at Medellin 14,000 men. An intimate friend of mine, a colonel of infantry, had two sons with him in the action. The eldest, under eighteen years of age, was most severely wounded by the dragoons late in the day. He was taken to Medellin, and to the quarters of the Commander-in-Chief, just as Victor was sitting down to supper; who graciously informed the young officer of the fate intended for him by saying, "If my orders had been executed, you would not have been here!"'

To his Brother-in-law.

'Cordova, 6th April, 1809.

'My dear Davis,—In the actions of the Duke of Alburquerque in La Mancha, the troops under his command

---

* 'Quando mas se pierde, mas se gana, y que muchas sangrias eran menester para restablecer la salud del cuerpo politico!'

were covered with glory. All the officers of his Staff, including me, were recommended to the Government for promotion.* In the last unfortunate action of Medellin, I had an opportunity of particularly distinguishing myself by reforming the routed cavalry and leading them against the enemy.† The Duke did me the honour to speak of my conduct in the field in the highest terms. You are yourself well aware that since the first shot was fired in Andalusia, I have been constantly with the army, and have sought every occasion of rendering myself useful. Yet I am the only officer to whose promotion the Government has objected. The reason is obvious: I was a friend of the unfortunate Castaños, and all his friends are persecuted.

'I entreat, therefore, that you will immediately apply to Colonel Gordon for leave to join my regiment. I can no longer be of service to a country to whose Government I am become obnoxious, nor am I accustomed tamely to suffer the insults of any man or class of men.'

To the Right Hon. J. H. Frere.

'CORDOVA, 11th April, 1809.

'Sir,—I observe by your letter of the 7th, which has been returned to me from the Carolina, that you consider the Duke [of Alburquerque] in command of that army, and ready to realize his projected plan of attack against the French force in La Mancha. I am surprised that the Junta Suprema should not have informed you that a division of 7,000 infantry and 3,000 cavalry began its march from the army of Sierra Morena on the 5th, and

---

* He was afterwards made Brigadier-General by the Spanish Government, with date from 2nd March, 1809.

† Here, no doubt, is another of those little known actions referred to by Lord Fife (*vide Preface*). This passing allusion to his having rallied the cavalry at Medellin is all the Editor knows on the subject. The lost letters to the Military Secretaries at the Horse-Guards might tell more of *what Lord Fife knew*.

will enter Seville the day after to-morrow. The force which now composes the army of Sierra Morena consists of 16,000 infantry and 2,000 cavalry, and is commanded by General Venegas.

'Had the Duke received the command of the army of Sierra Morena before the separation of the above-mentioned division, he might have defeated the French force in La Mancha, and immediately afterwards have reinforced Cuesta with nearly 10,000 men, by the same route which we before followed from Ciudad Real. At the same time that I received your letter, Mr. Ovalle communicated to the Duke the same information; and yet, previous to that date, General Venegas had taken the command of the army, and the division had already begun its march, with orders to the commanding officer, Major-General Count of Orgaz, to report daily to the Minister of War.

'I have, &c.
'SAMFORD WHITTINGHAM.'

Most unfortunately, all Mr. Hookham Frere's letters to Colonel Whittingham are lost. The above letter proves how necessary British agents were, from whom alone the English envoy could obtain reliable information and active assistance.

There is no doubt that Colonel Whittingham had the highest esteem for the Duke, as well as affection.* He had also had cause for gratitude, as will be seen in the following letter to his brother-in-law :—

'SEVILLE, 17th *April*, 1809.

'I enclose you two letters from the Duke of Alburquerque, the one addressed to his Royal Highness the Duke of York, and the other to Lord Castlereagh. I am

---

* These feelings were shared by Mr. Hookham Frere, and, subsequently, by Marquis Wellesley.

proud to receive these recommendations from the Duke, because as a soldier he stands unrivalled in this country.' [After detailing the ill-treatment that the Duke received from General Urbina and the Junta Suprema, he proceeds:] 'The Duke was further ordered to put himself at the head of a division of troops destined to march from the Carolina to the assistance of General Cuesta as soon as General Venegas should have taken the command of the army of Sierra Morena.

'Before the Duke joined the army, General Venegas had taken the command, and we are now on our route to join General Cuesta at Santa Olalla and Monasterio. The division commanded by the Duke is composed of 2,500 cavalry and 7,000 infantry.

'General Cuesta's army, after our junction, will exceed 25,000 infantry and 6,000 cavalry. The force left in Sierra Morena under the command of General Venegas is 16,000 infantry and 2,000 cavalry. In regard to the late shameful flight of the army of Sierra Morena from their cantonments at La Mancha, it is altogether too bad for description. Suffice it to say that folly, or more probably treason, sacrificed an army of upwards of 30,000 men, including 4,500 cavalry. The battle of Medellin, in Estremadura, was fought with bravery by all the troops excepting the cavalry on the left of the line. Their want of firmness lost the day. The right, where I had the honour of being with the Duke, behaved extremely well; and as our orders were positive not to retreat, the whole division of the Duke was sacrificed. When everything was completely lost, we opened a passage through the enemy, sword in hand.'——

The following are translations of the two letters which were enclosed in the above:—

The Duke of Alburquerque to the Duke of York.

'CORDOVA, 6th April, 1809.

'Sir,—The special merit which Colonel Santiago Whittingham* has displayed during the whole of the present war in Spain—and particularly the great degree in which he has distinguished himself in all the actions in which he has served under my command—affords me the opportunity of having the honour to make this known to your Royal Highness, for the satisfaction of this deserving officer. And for the same reason, I take the liberty of entreating your Royal Highness to make the same known to His Majesty.

'I take this occasion to present my highest respects to your Royal Highness, and I pray the Almighty to preserve your valuable life through many extended years.

'At the feet of your Royal Highness,

'THE DUKE OF ALBURQUERQUE.'

The Duke of Alburquerque to Viscount Castlereagh.

'CORDOVA, 6th April, 1809.

'Excellency,—I cannot do less than bring to the notice of your Excellency the distinguished services which Colonel Santiago Whittingham has rendered in the present war in Spain, and especially during the time he has been under my command, under which he still continues, with the most effective desire to distinguish himself daily more and more.

'I hope your Excellency will excuse the liberty I am taking in order that this highly deserving officer may obtain the satisfaction he so justly desires of being made known to your Excellency.

---

* Apparently, though the rank was dated back to 2nd March, 1809, either the Government had not yet gazetted Whittingham as Brigadier or the Duke had not known it so early as the 6th April.

'This occasion affords me the especial gratification of presenting my respects to your Excellency.

'May God preserve your Excellency.

'HIS EXCELLENCY THE DUKE OF ALBURQUERQUE.'

Brigadier-General Whittingham to the Right Hon. J. H. Frere.

(Extract.)

'OLALLA, 23rd *April,* 1809.*

'I enclose a copy of the Duke's letter of this morning to the Count of Orgaz, who commands the infantry of the division of Andalusia. You will observe by his answer that he does not consider himself under the orders of the Duke, and therefore declines sending him the returns he required. In consequence, the Duke has determined to proceed to Monasterio, where he will see General Cuesta to-morrow morning.

'These contradictory orders appear too nearly to resemble those of our last expedition to the Carolina. The country we have passed over to-day is not the least fit for the operations of cavalry. From Guillena to Santa Olalla the road is one continued defile; and cavalry, instead of being of use, would only serve, by a precipitate flight, to weaken the effects of the infantry. The total of General Cuesta's cavalry is very nearly 7,000. It appears that the French have attacked his advanced guard at Santos with a division of 6,000 men. Probably, this will prove a reconnoissance in force—an operation which they seldom omit previous to a general action. General Cuesta will, of course, defend the position of Monasterio as long as possible, fall back upon Santa Olalla, and finally occupy and defend to the last extremity the strong pass of the Herzadura, near to the Venta de la Cruz del Chapaxo, two leagues on the Seville side of Ronquillo. . . . . . .

---

* Sir Arthur Wellesley arrived at Lisbon, on his return from England, on the 22nd April, 1809.

'If 4,000 cavalry were sent immediately to the Carolina, and the command of that army given to the Duke, he would either enter into Madrid or force Victor to detach a considerable part of his army towards Toledo. This, in my humble opinion, is the only thing to be done in the present situation of affairs; and should General Cuesta offer to the Duke the command of the advanced guard, he would, I should think, do well to accept it. For upon the least further advance of the French, the cavalry at Santos must fall back to the rear of the Monasterio, and continue retreating to Seville; and thus the Duke, without the hope of victory, would only have acquired the fame of being a second time beaten.

'The present moment is so extremely critical that I feel it my duty to state it to you as my opinion that the salvation of the country will depend upon the success of your endeavours to change the theatre of war once more to La Mancha.

'Should this, however, not be approved of by the Spanish Government, they should, at all events, order a camp to be formed of 5,500 cavalry in the neighbourhood of Seville, which would be a rallying point for the infantry should the passes be forced, and might, possibly, if well directed, restore the fortune of the day. I am sure you will agree with me that the command of the force should be given to the Duke.'

From the Same to the Same.

'SANTA OLALLA, 24*th April,* 1809.

'Sir,—We have been to day to Monasterio. General Cuesta has finally determined that the Duke shall command only the cavalry of his former division, which he is to canton in the rear of the position of Herzadura. To-morrow the Duke will reconnoitre the ground, and determine upon the distribution of the force entrusted to his command. Major-General Echivari, with the advanced guard of this army, is at Fuente de Cantos, five leagues in advance beyond Monasterio. The outposts are daily engaged with the French. Two leagues in rear of this corps is situated Major-General Enesterosa with 3,000 cavalry; and he is supported by a strong detachment, at the distance of about a league, under the orders of Brigadier Zayas. General Cuesta's head-quarters are at Monasterio. I am convinced more and more by every day's experience that *General Cuesta is not the man to command an army upon which the fate of Spain may depend. His age, his infirmities, his excessive reserve, and his constant ill success, conspire to render him unfit for his situation; and the Junta Suprema will learn, when too late, that good intentions alone are a poor substitute for military talents.** Would to God it were possible to give General Blake the command of this army, and the Duke of Alburquerque that of the army of the Carolina! I am convinced that everything would go rightly, and, by a proper co-operation with the army of Portugal, affairs might soon be completely re-established.

'Will you have the goodness to send the Duke, if you can procure it for him, a map of the kingdom of Seville? I will thank you to direct your letters to me at Gerona, where the Duke's head-quarters will be established till further orders. He is very much hurt at what has passed, and has written to Mr. Ovalle upon the subject.

'I shall have the pleasure of writing to you as soon as we have finished the reconnoissance of the cantonment; and I have the honour to be, Sir,

'Your most obedient servant,
'SAMFORD WHITTINGHAM.

'The Right Hon. J. H. Frere.'

* Perhaps the retreat of Sir Arthur Wellesley, in August, from Talavera would never have been necessary had the advice of Colonel Whittingham in April been acted on, and the stupid and incompetent Cuesta been exchanged for a more rational and practical commander. The Editor has placed in *italics* a prophecy destined to such speedy fulfilment.

To his Brother-in-Law.

'GERONA, 25*th April*, 1809.

'You will see by the enclosed letters to Mr. Frere the position and strength of our armies. The head-quarters of General Victor are at Merida; his force about 40,000 men. General Sebastiani commands in La Mancha a division of 10,000 men. Of the division of Soult at Oporto and of that of Ney, in Galicia, I conclude that you are well informed.

'Our cause is sacred; and in spite of the errors into which we have fallen, we shall, I trust in God, with the cordial assistance of England, ultimately prevail. I am well aware that the conduct of the Government has been in many instances weak and ridiculous; but I love to hope that His Majesty's Ministers will forget and forgive, and only look to the great good that may ultimately result from the success of our endeavours.

'I did not lose my horses and baggage at Tudela. They afterwards appeared. But I lost at Madrid clothes, baggage, and a travelling carriage; the total cost of which exceeded £350. What most has grieved me is the loss of all my books and papers. The value of what I lost at Coruña you are exactly acquainted with.* I think, in the present state of affairs, you had better not send out the carriage for the Marquis of Benamigi.'†——

On the 28th April, Colonel Whittingham forwarded to Colonel Gordon, Military Secretary at the Horse-Guards, a copy of the following letter which he had addressed to the British envoy, the day before Sir Arthur Wellesley

---

* His baggage appears to have been lost in Sir John Moore's retreat having been sent to Coruña from England.

† This was, no doubt, some intended present from the too generous Englishman to some Spanish gentleman who had formerly shown him hospitality.

arrived at Villa Franca, and wrote the first batch of his dispatches in Spain :—

To the Right Hon. J. H. Frere.
(Extract.)

GERONA, 27*th April*, 1809.

'I had the honour to accompany the Duke of Alburquerque in his reconnoissance between this place and Santi Penni, and returned to Gerona this day by the way of Guillena. In Santi Penni the Duke has left three officers of Engineers to make a plan of the adjacent ground.' [He then enters into long local details, geographical and strategical, with his wonted accuracy and clearness, and continues :] 'The more I become acquainted with the Army of Liberation, and the major part of its generals, the more I am convinced that it is not in a state to cope with a French army, unless infinitely favoured by the strength of the position which it may occupy. General Cuesta would already have attacked the French again but for the instructions of the Supreme Junta. Upon so brave and respectable a character as that of the old General, I should not wish to be severe. But the times are too critical to admit of attentions of any kind which may lead to the smallest deviations from truth. The General is so extremely infirm that he is not in a state to fulfil the active duties of his profession, and at the same time so jealous of his authority, or so little accustomed to the treatment of organized armies, that he has no idea of delegating that proportion of his command to others without which the necessary and proper subdivision of labour cannot take place.

'In all the engagements which he has had with the French, his mode of attack has been below criticism ; and the consequences have been such as might be expected. At General Cuesta's time of life, men are little disposed to change ; and experience, however dearly bought, is not sufficient to correct errors, which by long habit have become second nature. Rest assured, sir, that, if General Cuesta is to direct the operations of this army, it is of the first importance to oblige him to remain upon the defensive; not only because he is at a distance of only a few leagues from the capital, and, consequently, the effects of a defeat may be fatal; but that it is almost impossible that he should ever be successful against the French, fighting his battles in the way that he has hitherto done. This being the case, the proposed expedition to La Mancha becomes doubly necessary. For, at the same time that the greatest good would of necessity result from the appearance of the Duke of Alburquerque at the head of a strong division in a province where his name is idolized, and where public opinion has so great an effect upon the people of Madrid, we should obtain, also, the much-to-be-desired advantage of obliging the Army of Liberation to remain on the defensive, at least till the co-operation of an English army should afford hopes of success.*

'I have, &c.
'Samford Whittingham.'

In another letter to Mr. Frere, dated Gerona, 1st May, Colonel Whittingham enforced the same views, adding more details on the state and positions of the Spanish armies.

The hero of the age had now arrived in Spain, and in a letter dated Villa Franca, 29th April, 1809, acknowledged to Mr. Frere the receipt of a letter from him, and of another from General Cuesta. Sir Arthur stated his intention of communicating with the Spanish Government only through Mr. Frere, and one sentence of his letter may

* In spite of the lost replies of Mr. Frere, there can be no question that the latter agreed, and sympathized, with his correspondent. It is a pity, however, that he did not send these letters to Sir Arthur, to acquaint him with what the latter learnt only after painful experience—the utter incapacity of Cuesta.

be appropriately quoted here, as confirming the wisdom of the advice given to Mr. Frere by the English captain who was serving so zealously in the arduous and hazardous post of a British agent, and at the same time of a Spanish colonel, in an ill-disciplined, disorganized, and badly commanded army.

'I hope,' writes Sir Arthur, 'that the Spaniards will adhere to their determination of acting on the defensive till I shall return to the eastward.'*

In a letter of the same date to Don Martin Garay, Sir Arthur writes:—' In the meantime, I cannot sufficiently recommend a strict defensive position in all quarters.'

If this advice had been strictly carried out, and General Cuesta at once removed from the command, much trouble would have been saved to the English commander. For although many of the Spanish generals were as incompetent as Cuesta, few were so impracticably stupid and obstinate as that old soldier, who, excepting courage, does not appear to have had a redeeming quality of any kind. To the subject of this Memoir he was destined to be a constant source of annoyance and disgust up to the very hour of his death, as Captain-General of the Balearic Islands.

The return of Sir Arthur Wellesley to the Peninsula, who was soon to take into his powerful hands the universal management of affairs, naturally lessened in some degree the personal influence of the military agent who was but a captain in the British army. He continued, however, to enjoy the full confidence of the Minister. To gain that of Sir Arthur was a work of time, especially as he had at first no direct communication with the Commander-in-Chief, but was considered under the orders of Mr. Hookham Frere in his capacity of agent. It may, however, be here remarked that, if the subject of this Memoir had not eventually obtained the complete confi-

* *Wellington Dispatches,* vol. iv. p. 281.

dence of his illustrious chief, these pages would never have been written; for, though the great Wellington was after all a mortal, and as such liable to error, still it is not too much to say that his opinion of those who served under him must be considered as final both for the present age and for posterity.

The jealousy of Cuesta against the Duke of Alburquerque vented itself in giving that gallant nobleman so reduced a command that 'nothing could induce him [the Duke] to remain but the expectation that a general engagement would take place as soon as Sir Arthur shall return from the attack of Soult.'*

Sir Arthur Wellesley to the Right Hon. J. H. Frere.†

'Oporto, 22nd *May*, 1809.

'My dear Sir,—My letter of the 20th will apprize you of all that has occurred in this quarter since I wrote to you on the 9th instant. I have returned here with the advance of the army, having done all I could, or had to do, northward, and having thought it necessary to move to the southward, in consequence of the invasion of Portugal by the attack and capture of Alcantara. . . . .

'I am much obliged to you for your letters of the 15th and 17th. I acknowledge that I do not consider Lord Wellesley's appointment a subject of congratulation to himself or his friends. I suspect that the task which will devolve upon him will be a most arduous one; and that some time will elapse before he will be sufficiently *au courant des affaires* to be able to form a judgment of its extent. I am truly concerned, however, that your removal should not be so consonant to your wishes.

'Believe me, &c.

'Arthur Wellesley.'

---

* Letter from Brigadier-General Whittingham to Colonel Gordon, (Military Secretary at the Horse-Guards), dated Zafra, 20th May, 1809.

† *Wellington Dispatches*, vol. iv. p. 353.

There can be no question that the new appointment did not, and could not, suit Sir Arthur Wellesley. The Marquis, his elder brother (and former patron, and official superior as Governor-General), was coming out as Ambassador Extraordinary to relieve the Minister, Mr. Frere. With such powers, and considering his past career, Lord Wellesley could not be expected to play any but the first part; and Sir Arthur would naturally hold a position relatively inferior to that which he possessed while Mr. Frere was Minister.

The advent of Marquis Wellesley in Spain, if no matter of rejoicing to his famous brother, brought with it one of the pleasantest episodes of Samford Whittingham's adventurous life, though his Lordship's sojourn in Spain was as brief as it was brilliant.

The following is the only copy in the Editor's hands of the several letters which its writer undoubtedly addressed to the illustrious father of Her Majesty the Queen :—

To His Royal Highness the Duke of Kent.*

'HEAD-QUARTERS OF THE SECOND DIVISION OF CAVALRY,
'COMMANDED BY THE DUKE OF ALBURQUERQUE,
'ZAFRA, 23rd *May*, 1809.

'Sir,—Since the battle of Medellin, which cost us the amount of 22,000 men, great changes have taken place. The efforts of this nation are in exact proportion to the difficulties which it has to labour under. Defeated at Medellin, put to a shameful flight in La Mancha, the French advanced to within fifteen leagues of Seville; the whole force which we at that time could collect in the passes of the Monasterio, and St. Olalla did not exceed 8,000 men. General Victor, who commands the French

---

* Only a very rough copy, difficult to read, and not apparently in the handwriting of Brigadier-General Whittingham, exists of this letter. The writer was, for the sake of the unhappy country he was so zealously serving, evidently trying to palliate the national errors.

army in Estremadura, lost the favourable moment for attack, and the energies of the nation were called forth. The present force and distribution of the Spanish and French armies are as follows:—

'General Cuesta, 24,000 infantry, 7,000 cavalry, and fifty pieces of cannon. His advanced guard at Merida, sustained by a body of 2,000 cavalry at Almendraligo; head-quarters at Fuente del Merthyr. His reserve at this place.*

'Opposed to General Cuesta is General Victor. His army is about 30,000 strong. He occupies Truxillo and Caceres, and has his advanced guard at Mortanchis. A small detachment of 300 or 400 men still occupy the old castle of Merida, but they are hourly expected to surrender.

'General Venegas commands the army of La Carolina, but subject to the orders which he may receive from General Cuesta. His force is 20,000 infantry and 3,500 cavalry, and a large and well organized force of horse artillery.

'General Blake is appointed Commander-in-Chief of Aragon, Catalonia, Valencia, and Murcia. *I understand* that he has advanced from Anton towards Cuença with 24,000 infantry and 1,000 cavalry.

'General Sebastiani, who commands in La Mancha, against General Venegas, has with him a body of 9,000 men.

'General Mortier marched a short time since from Saragossa to Burgos with a division of 11,000 men; and it is said that General Augereau has passed Irun from Bayonne with a body of 15,000 conscripts.

'General Ney with a small force occupies Ferrol and Coruña, but as the whole of Galicia is again in arms under the Marquis de la Romana, he may be considered as blockaded.

---

* Zafra, from which the letter is dated.

'General Soult has been completely defeated at Oporto by Sir Arthur Wellesley; but of this, I conclude, your Royal Highness is already informed.

'I have not sufficient details to be able to state accurately what is passing in Catalonia; but there is no doubt that affairs have there taken a very favourable turn.

'The result of this extension of the forces, and distribution of the Spanish and French armies, is that, should Victor fall back upon Madrid, and join Sebastiani, and should the divisions of Mortier and Augereau advance upon the capital, they will concentrate a force of 70,000 men. Cuesta, by effecting a junction with Venegas and Blake (which it is always in his power to do by a flank movement to his right, or by their making a flank movement to their left), will collect an army of 58,000 infantry and 11,500 cavalry.

'Sir Arthur Wellesley has promised to advance into Spain, following the right bank of the Tagus, and to cooperate with General Cuesta the moment that he returns from his expedition to Oporto; and he has requested General Cuesta not to compromise himself in any general action till his arrival. Sir Arthur's force between Coy and Portugal is estimated at 50,000 men. It is not for me to presume to give your Royal Highness an opinion on the issue of the present contest. But, at all events, whatever may be the issue, your Royal Highness may rest assured that as long as we can collect a dozen muskets we shall fight, and by dint of fighting, I trust in God, we shall become good soldiers.

'I have, &c.
'SAMFORD WHITTINGHAM.

'P.S.—I have the pleasure to inform your Royal Highness that the Junta Suprema has made me a Brigadier-General of Spanish Cavalry.

'S. W.'

*Brigadier-General Whittingham to the Right Hon.
J. H. Frere.*

(Extract.)

'ZAFRA, 26th *May*, 1809.

'The truth of what you have so often stated relative to the necessity of a diversion in La Mancha is now most strongly felt at head-quarters.* General Venegas has received repeated orders to advance and attack General Sebastiani, who has with him not above 12,000 men. But General Venegas pleads the want of spirit in his soldiers, and their reduced numbers. Under such an impression, it may perhaps be better for the country that he should do nothing. But it is sadly to be lamented that, at a moment when such important consequences might, and indeed must, arise from calling the attention of the enemy towards the right, the plan of the campaign should be exposed to ruin rather than employ, in the command of the army of the Carolina, the only man who possesses the full confidence of that army, and to whom the peasants of La Mancha look up with the most enthusiastic admiration.'†

The English Envoy and the military Agent were evidently working harmoniously together, though we can produce only one side of the correspondence carried on between them. He now meets again with an old friend:—

To his Brother-in-law.

'ZAFRA, 9th *June*, 1809.

'I am just returned from the vanguard, where we had a pretty little action, and carried off from the enemy 700

---

* Those readers who have observed how earnestly the Brigadier had suggested to the Minister this diversion in La Mancha will be struck with this passage. Anxious to have what is right properly done, he is indifferent about the credit of the original suggestion.

† He alludes to Alburquerque.

fanegas of corn. Lieutenant-Colonel Bourke and *Cadogan* are arrived at head-quarters from Sir Arthur Wellesley, at Alcantara. His whole force may be up in a few days. He has with him a force of 40,000 men, out of which 24,000 are English. General Cuesta has not less than 35,000 men. These armies co-operating must utterly destroy Victor if he awaits the attack. But if, as it is feared, he retreats from his present position in time, it will be absolutely necessary to pursue and harass him in his retreat with the whole body of the united arms.'

To the Same.

'Villaneuva de la Sirena, 15*th June*, 1809.

'The French abandoned Merida on the 13th. To-day they have retired from Miajadas; and it is evident that they are in full retreat by the bridge of Almaraz. Their position on the other side of the Tagus will probably be at Talavera de la Reyna.

'I cannot help expressing my opinion that, if General Cuesta crosses the Tagus, and follows the traces of Victor, we shall be reduced to the necessity of fighting a battle in order to obtain his further retreat; and, in the comparative state of the French and Spanish armies, the result of a general action is always to be feared; whereas by the plan which I have taken the liberty to propose, the desired effect would be produced by a war of movement without the smallest risk.

'I have taken advantage of Colonel Cadogan's[*] departure for the British army to send you these few lines.'

To the Same.

'Villar de Robledo, 25*th June*, 1809.

'You will see by the date of my last letter that we are within a league of the Tagus. We marched all last night

[*] Lieutenant-Colonel Cadogan was aide-de-camp to Sir Arthur Wellesley.

in order to attack the bridge of Arzobispo this morning. It has been delayed in consequence of the artillery not arriving in time. We shall probably cross the Tagus to-morrow. Sir Arthur is marching from Abrantes to Castel Branco, Rosminhal, Sigura, Zarza, Coria, Placencia —distance thirty-seven leagues.

'You will be much grieved to hear that the Duke of Alburquerque has left this army. He has been disgusted by the repeated ill-treatment which he has received; but I hope, when Lord Wellesley arrives, that everything will be set to rights. I remain with the vanguard, or rather with the cavalry of the vanguard, commanded by the Prince of Anglona. I think that we may probably enter Madrid in ten days.

'Sir Arthur Wellesley has appointed me to the Staff of his army as Deputy Assistant Quartermaster-General. This will give me eight shillings a day, and will not interfere with my plans here.'

The Marquis Wellesley to R. H. Davis, Esq. M.P.

'APSLEY HOUSE, 19th June, 1809.

'Lord Wellesley presents his compliments to Mr. Davis, and has the honour to acknowledge the receipt of his two notes under date the 4th and 17th June, together with the papers from Major* Whittingham, for whose character and talents Lord Wellesley entertains the highest respect. Lord Wellesley is extremely obliged to Mr. Davis for communicating to him these interesting documents, which he begs leave to return to Mr. Davis with many acknowledgments for his kind attention in permitting Lord Wellesley to peruse them.'

Thus, before ever seeing Samford Whittingham, Lord

* This arose from some mistake on his Lordship's part; Samford Whittingham was still only a Captain in the British service, but a Brigadier-General in that of Spain.

Wellesley, by the mere perusal of his letters and memoranda, had already imbibed a very high opinion of his character. If anyone was ever more ready to acknowledge merit, wherever it appeared, than this truly liberal-minded nobleman, it was the illustrious writer (a few days earlier) of the note which follows:—

His Royal Highness the Duke of Kent to R. H. Davis, Esq. M.P.

'KENSINGTON PALACE, 12th *June*, 1809.

'The Duke of Kent returns his best acknowledgments to Mr. Davis for his polite note of yesterday, and the obliging attention he has shown in taking the trouble of calling himself at Kensington with the letter from his brother-in-law, Brigadier-General Whittingham, that was sent to his care. The Duke conceiving it probable that the General may have instructed Mr. Davis through what channel to forward his letters to him, which he has omitted to do in his communication to the Duke, he hopes that Mr. Davis will forgive him for troubling him to take charge of the enclosed for that highly estimable officer, which he is peculiarly desirous should reach him in safety, as he has reason to believe other letters he has written to him before have not found their way to him, as in his last he makes no mention of having received any from the Duke.'

It appears, indeed, that none of these letters—not even the one which the Duke sent to Mr. Davis with the above—ever reached their address. At all events, they have all unfortunately disappeared, and it is, therefore, very satisfactory that another to Mr. Davis, in addition to the above, has reached the Editor's hands, which will appear in its proper place.

To his Brother-in-law.

'Coria, 5*th July*, 1809.

'I am just returned from Zarza la Maior, where I have been to see Sir Arthur, in consequence of his order. The first division of the British army marches into this town to-morrow morning!

'General Cuesta is at Almaraz, on the left bank of the Tagus. Victor occupies a position on the left bank of the Alberche river: his head-quarters at Ciboya. King Joseph is at Toledo. Sebastiani, reinforced by the greater part of the garrison of Madrid, has advanced against Venegas in La Mancha. Ferrol and Coruña have been evacuated. The Spaniards have taken possession of these towns; and the remains of the divisions of Ney, Soult, and Kellermann (in all 20,000 men), have evacuated Galicia and Asturias, and are directing their march towards this part of the country. It does not appear an easy or safe operation to attack Victor in his present position. Should the other divisions join him, we shall have occasioned the reunion of the French force, without having increased that of the Spaniards in the same proportion; and the truth of what I have before stated of the good effect to be expected from placing 60,000 men under Sir Arthur will be severely felt. Of course, everything I say to you upon these matters is in perfect confidence. If any military man can save this country, I think it will be Sir Arthur! His great abilities are aided by the most conciliatory manners. He is just the man to please the Spaniards; and, in my humble opinion, if he has the means, he will constantly prove victorious over the French. He is going to wait upon Cuesta in a few days.' *

---

* On the 13th July, Sir A. Wellesley writes to Mr. H. Frere:—'General Castaños having declined to send a large detachment to the quarter proposed by me, I, of course, have no opportunity of requesting that the Duke of Alburquerque should have the command to which I certainly should have

The following account of the battle of Talavera is extracted from the 'Recollections:'—

'A short time previous to Sir Arthur Wellesley's advance into Spain, I was directed to join his head-quarters on the frontiers of Portugal. Cuesta's army had been literally destroyed at Medellin; yet he had collected again a force of 35,000 men, of which 6,000 were cavalry, and had thrown a bridge of boats over the Tagus at Almaraz, of which he was very proud. It was agreed by the two chiefs that their meeting should take place near the bridge; and Sir Arthur advanced to the rendezvous escorted by a squadron of British dragoons. In consequence of this conference, Sir Arthur crossed the Tietar, and the combined armies advanced upon Talavera.

'A slight skirmish drove the French from the town, and they took up a commanding position on the left bank of the Alberche.

'Sir Arthur reconnoitred the ground carefully and minutely, and proposed to Cuesta that the attack should take place the next morning at break of day, in two columns. The right column, composed of Spaniards, and commanded by Cuesta, [was] to advance on the high-road leading from Talavera to Madrid; the left column, composed of British troops under Sir Arthur, [was] to march direct upon the position occupied by the French army, pass the Alberche, and storm the heights on the left bank. Cuesta's movement by the high-road would thus bring his whole army perpendicular to the left flank of Victor, whilst the front attack would be made by Sir Arthur.

'All Sir Arthur's orders were issued; but no decisive answer having been obtained from the Spanish General, I

been disposed, as well on account of your recommendation, as from his own character.' 'On the 22nd July, the outposts of the French army were driven in by the Spanish advanced guard under the command of General Zayas and the Duke of Alburquerque,' writes Sir A. Wellesley to Lord Castlereagh, on the 24th July, 1809.

was directed to wait upon him, and to ascertain what his intentions were. My conference with the old General and his Staff lasted till eleven o'clock at night; but I could bring him to no final decision, and I was obliged to return to the British head-quarters with this unsatisfactory result.

'Counter-orders were immediately issued, to suspend the projected attack; and an opportunity was lost of beating the French army in detail, and of immortalizing the opening career of the British General by a suite of brilliant and rapid successes, not surpassed at any period of the Peninsular War.

('See my memorandum on the battle of Talavera.'*)

'After much hesitation, Cuesta was at last brought to consent to the attack as first proposed, and a day having been wasted in talk, it was at length determined that the attack should take place next morning. We accordingly crossed the Alberche, and ascended the heights, but it was too late: the bird was flown. Victor had retreated upon Madrid the night before. In spite of the remonstrances of Sir Arthur, Cuesta and all his force set off in the pursuit of the French army, whilst the British General was occupied in reconnoitring the ground about Talavera, and in choosing the position where he should fight the battle which he foresaw must in a few days take place.

'Victor, having been reinforced by the troops of Madrid, was now at the head of 45,000 men, of which 6,000 were cavalry; and Cuesta was forthwith driven back to the entrance of Talavera. It was with the greatest difficulty that Sir Arthur obtained permission to speak to Cuesta (who at five p.m. was asleep in his tent on the left bank of the Alberche), to inform him of the immediate proximity of the enemy, and to request him to occupy, without a moment's loss of time, his position in the general

---

* This memorandum is too long for insertion, and, moreover, is (the Editor believes) embodied in Southey's *History of the Peninsular War*.

line. In the meantime the whole of the British cavalry was thrown out to cover his retreat on the Alberche. Colonel Elley,* and the Adjutant-General of the British cavalry, manœuvred the two lines in a most masterly manner, and so completely checked the rapid advance of the enemy that it was four P.M. before the last of the British squadrons repassed the Alberche.

'I had galloped to Talavera to report the result of the cavalry movements to Sir Arthur, when a Staff officer came in from General Mackenzie—whose division occupied a wood on our extreme left—to say that the division had been surprised; that one regiment had given way, and that all was confusion and dismay! In a moment, the General was in his saddle, and in full gallop towards the spot. We advanced into the midst of our skirmishers. The fire was hot, and the enemy rapidly approaching. Sir Arthur leaped off his horse, and scrambled up the wall of an old ruin close at hand. But he was obliged to throw himself down on his hands and knees, and to remount instantly; for the enemy's sharp-shooters had nearly surrounded the building, and a minute's delay would have constituted him a prisoner.

'A brigade of infantry was formed, at a short distance in our rear, on the right of which was the 45th [Regiment] commanded by Colonel Gordon. He was a little fat man, who had commanded the same regiment at Buenos Ayres. Whilst the General was speaking to him, a musket ball went through the blade of his sword, another took off the round knob of his hilt, and a third went through his cap! Sir Arthur then ordered the battalions to retire from the right of companies, [in order] to pass the wood in their rear. This manœuvre had scarcely been commenced, when the heads of the French columns showed themselves, and their artillery opened upon us.

* Afterwards General Sir John Elley.

'Our retreat to the position of Talavera was covered by the Spanish cavalry, and conducted with much order. The left of the Spanish line, in the position, rested upon the right of the British. An English battery of six-pounders, in the centre of the line, was removed to make room for a Spanish battery of eight-pounders; the fire of the six-pounders being found inadequate. I had no particular command in this action; but finding no commander with the Spanish division on the left of their line, I assumed the command, and found a ready obedience in both officers and men.

'About ten at night the French threw out parties of light infantry to open a light running fire down the line; probably to ascertain its direction. But our young Spanish soldiers, taking the alarm, commenced a fire so heavy and well kept up that Sir Arthur, who just at that moment came up, said—"Whittingham, if they will but fire as well to-morrow, the day is our own; but as there seems to be nobody to fire at just now, I wish you would try to stop it."—"I have been trying for some time in vain," I replied: and whilst I was speaking three battalions became so frightened at their own noise, that they fairly took to their heels, and fled from the field of battle. "Only look, Whittingham," said the General, "at the ugly hole those fellows have left. I wish you would go to the second line, and try to fill it up."

'Nothing could give a more correct idea of the superiority of Sir Arthur's mind than this little incident. He had advanced into the heart of Spain on his own responsibility. He was now in the presence of 45,000 Frenchmen. His whole force consisted of 18,000 British, and 35,000 Spanish troops; the latter hastily assembled since the defeat at Medellin; and, consequently, for the most part a mere rabble. Panic-struck by their own fire, a whole brigade had thrown down their arms and fled. At a moment so awful, when all was at stake, Sir Arthur coolly observed that the hole in the first line was an ugly one, and requested me to bring troops from the second line to fill it up.

'During the night a false alarm sent all our servants and baggage to the rear; they carried off our horses also, and I was glad to mount myself on a stray dragoon-horse, which chance threw in my way. We had had nothing to eat for the last forty-eight hours, and I was truly glad to fall in with General Zayas, who gave us an excellent breakfast of "*Bacallao con salsa*, (salt fish stewed in tomata sauce). About three p.m., July 28th, the French made a fierce attack upon the left of the Spaniards; but so marvellous is the effect of British courage that, like Falstaff's wit, it is contagious. The same troops who, a few hours previously had run away from their own fire, now fought like lions. The French were received in an echelon of battalions, the left thrown forward, and their attack failed altogether. A regiment of Spanish cavalry charged the French line with brilliant success. The Colonel who led the charge had his arm broken by a musket ball; but the effect was decisive. As I was giving an order to one of the battalions, a musket ball struck me in the mouth, carried away a large portion of my teeth, broke the jaw-bone, and came out behind the ear. I was stunned, but not dismounted, though instantly covered with blood.

'The attack on our left having ceased, I proceeded to the left of the line to report to Sir Arthur the result. On my way, I fell in with a party carrying Colonel Gordon to the rear,—he was severely, but not dangerously wounded, —when a shell burst immediately upon him, and killed the Colonel and his supporters. On the road to Sir Arthur, I stopped at the Blood Hospital, and had the wound examined, but nothing could be done even to stop the blood.

'When I ascended the rising ground on which the General and his staff were standing, Sir Arthur called out to me, " Ah, Whittingham, I wanted you to take a message to the Duke of Alburquerque:" but when he saw the state I was in, he turned on his heel, and said no more. I then sat down on the grass with Lords Fife* and Burghersh,† drank a tumbler of sherry, and smoked some good cigars with the sound side of my mouth.

'About seven in the evening, the French being in full retreat, Lord Fife, Lord Burghersh, and myself bent our course towards Talavera. We had not, however, advanced a hundred yards, when a shell fell just in front of our horses. Lord B. instantly dismounted, and laid himself flat on the ground; whilst Lord Fife, convulsed with laughter, kept calling to me to look at the extraordinary length of Lord B.'s figure, which he insisted was beyond all mortal bounds. The only wise man of our party was Lord B., for the shell burst and covered us with sand and dust, and our escape was wonderful.

'At Talavera my reception at the hospital of the guards was truly kind; but the surgeon wanted experience in gunshot wounds, and so completely mistook my case as to bind up my fractured jaw with a wooden splint, thereby driving all the splinters of the jaw-bone together with the pieces of the ball and teeth into the lacerated flesh. The pain was so exquisite, that before I reached my quarters,‡ I tore off and threw away the whole of the dressing.

'Sir Arthur gave me *carte-blanche* to go home viâ Lisbon, or to go to Seville, where Marquis Wellesley had just arrived as British Ambassador. I should have preferred remaining with Sir Arthur as one of his aides-de-camp, but he thought that I should be more useful with the Spanish army, as *major-general*, to which rank I had been pro-

---

* Then Lord Macduff, and who succeeded his father on 17th April, 1811, as Earl of Fife.

† Afterwards Earl of Westmoreland.

‡ It would appear (vide *Preface*) that Lord Macduff took him off the field and tended him at Talavera.

moted for my services at Talavera [by the Supreme Junta].'——

But we are anticipating, and, leaving the 'Recollections' for the present, must return to the correspondence of the period :—

Colonel Roche* to R. H. Davis, Esq. M.P.

'TALAVERA, 30*th July*, 1809.

'My dear Sir,—The 28th July will for ever remain memorable for the glory of England and the British arms. The French to the number of 50,000 arrived on the evening of the 27th upon the Alberche, and immediately commenced attacking our outposts, upon which occasion there was some loss on both sides. The following morning the whole line of defence was formed; the British, with their left resting upon a targe of hills, crowned with batteries, and extending across a plain, where it was joined by the left of the Spanish line, which had its right upon the Tagus. The battle, one of the most bloody and obstinate which was ever fought, commenced at five o'clock on the morning of the 28th. The attack was made with the whole French force upon the British, and lasted until half-past eight at night; and, notwithstanding we had not 17,000 men,† the enemy were defeated in all attacks and forced to retreat with immense loss.

'We have lost 5,000 men in killed and wounded, and, I am sorry to say, my excellent friend Whittingham is among the latter. His wound is however—I am happy to tell—in the most favourable way, and of no consequence. His

---

* Colonel Roche (afterwards Sir Philip Keating Roche) was a military agent like Whittingham. He was then Major in the British and Colonel in the Spanish service, and the senior officer of the two, and remained so till 1814, when Whittingham was made full Colonel in the British army.

† Colonel Roche alludes to the British numbers only, which was hardly fair to the Spaniards, to whom Sir Arthur Wellesley himself did justice, both in his dispatch home, and also in his letter to Mr. Hookham Frere.

escape, however, was miraculous. A musket ball entered his mouth, and came out at his left ear, without injuring or touching a bone or a tooth.* (?)

'He is in the same house with Lord Macduff and myself, and wants for nothing; and, in short, we expect he will will be on his horse in a week or ten days. He met with his wound *as he was bringing up a Spanish battalion† in the most gallant manner*, and I sincerely congratulate you and his family *on the distinguished part he has taken in* [the] most arduous and glorious day England ever saw. Excuse this hasty scrawl, which I could not deny myself the pleasure of writing, as well from my own inclination, as at the desire of my friend about whom you may be perfectly at rest. He is at this moment at my side, in high spirits.

'Believe, me, &c.,
'K. ROCHE.'

[P.S.] 'I forbear all details, as you will see the whole by the dispatches.

Extract from Sir A. Wellesley's Dispatch to Viscount Castlereagh, dated Talavera de la Reyna, July 29, 1809.

'At the same time he' [the enemy] 'directed an attack upon Brigadier-General Campbell's position in the centre of the combined armies, and on the right of the British. This attack was most successfully repulsed by Brigadier-General Campbell, supported by the King's regiment of Spanish cavalry, *and two battalions of Spanish infantry*, and Brigadier-General Campbell took the enemy's cannon.

'I also received *much assistance* from Colonel O'Lalor, of the Spanish service, *and from Brigadier-General Whit-*

---

* The wound would have been more miraculous than the escape, if it had really done no more injury than Colonel Roche at first supposed, deceived by the patient endurance of the wounded man.

† Colonel Roche should have written—*two* Spanish battalions.

tingham, who was wounded in bringing up the two Spanish battalions to the assistance of Brigadier-General Campbell.'——

This last sentence was the concluding one of Sir Arthur Wellesley's dispatch, and, therefore, very conspicuous.

On July 29, Sir Arthur writes to Mr. Hookham Frere :—

'I was well satisfied with the conduct of the Spanish troops who had an opportunity of assisting us.' And he gives the Minister some details in proof. However, as Cuesta still left the British troops without supplies, Sir Arthur was compelled to retreat, though that retreat did not take place immediately.

Lord Wellesley arrived on the 1st of August, but Mr. Hookham Frere continued to transact business for some days longer; and the first official letter addressed by Sir A. Wellesley to his elder brother is dated the 8th of August, 1809. The arrival of the Marquis was an event of some importance to the subject of this Memoir, already known to his Lordship by report, and soon destined to make his personal acquaintance, as will be seen in the next chapter.

After considering that extract from the duke's dispatch given above in *italics*, and also reading the letter of Colonel Roche on the gallantry of Whittingham—both the Commander-in-chief and the Colonel reporting his wound as well as his gallant action—the candid reader will understand how, at a later period, the utter silence of Napier's too partial history excited very natural indignation in the mind of the injured party.

That which was deemed worthy of especial mention in the brief dispatch of the victorious General, was surely entitled, in common fairness, to a place in a voluminous history, going into details far more extended than dispatches can ever admit of when written by victors from the field of battle.

CHAPTER V.

1809—1810.

TO SEVILLE FOR CURE OF WOUND—ATTACHED TO MARQUIS WELLESLEY'S EMBASSY—DR. KENNEDY'S TREATMENT—DR. KNIGHTON—GENERAL CUESTA RESIGNS HIS COMMAND—SIR A. WELLESLEY'S RETREAT—BRIGADIER-GENERAL WHITTINGHAM'S CONFIDENTIAL EMPLOYMENT UNDER MARQUIS WELLESLEY—DON PEDRO DE CREUS Y XIMENES, INTENDANT OF THE SPANISH ARMY—AFFECTIONATE LETTER TO COLONEL CADOGAN—LORD WELLESLEY'S CHARACTER—CADOGAN'S PRESENT TO WHITTINGHAM—A JUDGE OF WINE—WHITTINGHAM MAJOR-GENERAL IN SPAIN—INCONVENIENCE OF MARQUIS WELLESLEY'S AMBASSADORSHIP—SIR ARTHUR WELLESLEY'S CANDID CONFESSION OF ERROR—A SECRETARY OF LEGATION'S JEALOUSY—WHITTINGHAM AND FRERE DEEMED TOO PARTIAL TO ALBURQUERQUE—A JUSTIFIED PREFERENCE—LORD WELLINGTON'S ARISTOCRATIC PREJUDICES—CLOSE OF LORD WELLESLEY'S BRIEF EMBASSY—THE MARQUIS' EULOGISTIC FAREWELL LETTER—GENIAL SHADE OF ARISTOCRACY—LORD WELLINGTON'S ESTEEM FOR ALAVA AND WHITTINGHAM—LORD MACDUFF—LORD WELLINGTON'S LETTER TO GENERAL WHITTINGHAM—CASTAÑOS APPOINTS HIM GENERAL OF DIVISION—EMPLOYED IN ISLA DE LEON—ORGANIZES A SELECT BODY OF HORSE—IMPORTANCE OF THE BALEARIC ISLANDS—GENERAL WHITTINGHAM'S PROMOTION TO MAJOR IN THE ENGLISH ARMY—ALBURQUERQUE RELIEVES CADIZ—HIS RESIGNATION—PROCEEDS TO LONDON AS AMBASSADOR—DUNDAS TRANSLATED INTO SPANISH—MR. WELLESLEY AND GENERAL GRAHAM RECOMMEND WHITTINGHAM'S PROMOTION—INVITATION TO HIS NEPHEW—COLONEL CAMPBELL OF THE MAJORCA DIVISION—GENERAL GRAHAM'S VOLUNTARY TESTIMONY—MR. WELLESLEY'S OFFICIAL PRAISE—MARQUIS WELLESLEY'S KIND LETTER TO GENERAL WHITTINGHAM.

BRIGADIER-GENERAL WHITTINGHAM found his wound a more serious and tedious affair than he had at first anticipated; and he proceeded to Seville for change of air and completeness of cure. We return to his 'Recollections':—

'My journey to Seville was performed on horseback with pain and fatigue, for it was the height of summer, and I lived entirely by suction. At that time, and for six months afterwards, I could take nothing but tea and soaked bread.

'On my arrival at Seville, the Marquis [Wellesley] attached me to his embassy, for the time that I should remain there; and he wrote to the Admiral at Cadiz to request that he would send to Seville one of his best surgeons. Kennedy came; and, after examining the jaw, and hearing the account of what had been done, he laughed at the ignorance which had been displayed, and that very evening extracted seven pieces of bone, one of which was upwards of an inch long. Ten years afterwards he extracted, at Madrid, a piece of the ball twisted like a corkscrew, which had remained in the jaw-bone all that time.

'During my stay at Seville, I lived as one of Lord Wellesley's family; and there I formed my first acquaintance with that excellent man, Sir William Knighton. Our morning rides were a source of happiness to us both, and our friendship only ended with his life.'

In his first official letter, 8th August, 1809, to Marquis Wellesley, as Ambassador, Sir Arthur Wellesley writes: 'The plan of operations which I should recommend to the Spanish nation is one generally of defence. They should avoid general actions, but should take advantage of the strong points in their country to defend themselves and to harass the enemy.' This was good advice; but long before the hero of the Peninsula entered Spain, the subject of this memoir had (as has been shown) repeatedly urged the same advice. Well would it have been for Spain if it had been acted on from the beginning, and mere brainless fighters like Cuesta earlier removed from high command.

However, on the 13th of August, that stupid and infatuated old General sent in his resignation; and General Eguia succeeded to the command. But General Cuesta will, alas! re-appear again; no longer, indeed, to torment the great English chief, but to worry almost beyond endurance, the subject of this Memoir.

But the change of commanders not bringing supplies to the English soldiers, Sir A. Wellesley retreated from Spain.

Brigadier-General Whittingham to his Brother-in-law.

'SEVILLE, 22nd August, 1809.

'My dear Davis,—The fracture which has taken place in my jaw-bone will, I fear, protract very considerably the cure of my wound. I have lost all the back teeth on the left side of my face. But I am still gaily disposed, and only anxious to get quickly well, in order to take the field again.

'You will have been astonished at our retreat after our glorious victory of the 28th [July]; all owing to that old fool, Cuesta, who has done everything in his power to ruin his country. I thank God that he is at last removed; and if the Command-in-Chief be given to Sir Arthur Wellesley, things will yet go well.

'Lord Wellesley exceeds even the high idea that I had formed of him! The people here look up to him as their saviour.

'Venegas has fallen back upon the Carolina. There will probably be some change in the position of our armies upon the Tagus, of which I shall take care to inform you.'

To the Same.

'SEVILLE, 2nd September, 1809.

'My dear Davis,—You will, I know, be happy to hear that Lord Wellesley has attached me to his service for the present *in the most confidential manner*; and, as the state of my wound would not allow of my retaking the field for some time, I cannot be more profitably or more agreeably employed. As the first thing Lord Wellesley has encharged to me is the most profound secrecy, I feel myself called upon to be silent upon everything but simple matter of fact, even with you, the beloved friend of my heart.

'It is currently reported that the French are retiring, and even about to abandon Madrid. But I confess that I have strong doubts on this head. The British army appears to be taking up a strong position on the Portuguese frontier near Yelvas, where it will effectually cover the approaches to Seville, and at the same time refit and recover from its fatigues.

'My wound is going on very well. It will be a long time before my cure is completed; but my mind is at ease since his Lordship has been pleased to consider that my services may yet be useful.'——

At this time there was living at Seville, a Spanish gentleman named Don Pedro de Creus y Ximenes, an Intendant of the Spanish Royal armies. His family, originally from Catalonia,* had possessed property in Minorca ever since his ancestor, James de Creus, had, A.D. 1285, accompanied King James of Aragon to the conquest of the Balearic Islands.† Don Pedro was a widower, with two twin daughters, both remarkable for wit and accomplishments, and the elder distinguished by beauty and grace. Here the English Captain, become a Spanish General, lost his heart to the elder, Donna Magdalena; and some years later the younger, Donna Barbara, made a conquest of Mr. Bartlemy Frere, brother of Mr. Hookham Frere, and attached to the Embassy in Spain.

---

* The north-easternmost point of Spain, Cape Creus, gave its name to the family, say the Spanish genealogists.

† All this is duly certified by the Madrid heralds. Don Pedro's father, Don Francisco Creus, married a lady of the ancient family of Ximenes; thus the formal style of the military intendant was Don Pedro de Creus y Ximenes.

To Lieutenant-Colonel the Hon. Henry Cadogan.

'SEVILLE, 12*th September*, 1809.

'My dear Cadogan,—Had I not to plead illness as an excuse for not having sooner answered your truly affectionate letters of the 15th and 22nd July,* I should be ashamed to address a friend whose good opinion I esteem more, infinitely more, than I can express. I was, as you will have heard, wounded on the evening of the 28th July, at the battle of Talavera. I did not quit the field for upwards of two hours afterwards; and, as I remained during that time on the Hill with Sir Arthur Wellesley and his Staff, I suppose that this led to the conclusion that my wound was slight. It was, however, severe, which I only mention, in order to convince my friend that no trifling cause had prevented my writing to him sooner. The ball entered my mouth, carried off four teeth, broke the jawbone and took its exit behind the ear. Of the battle, I shall only say that Sir Arthur Wellesley surpassed everything that even my romantic fancy had formed him capable of. In the retreat to the position of the 27th, his timely presence and admirable dispositions saved General Mackenzie's division from utter destruction. Yet Sir Arthur, with a modesty unequalled, attributes the merit of the retreat to that unfortunate General, and from his dispatch, you would not know even that he was present.

'Lord Wellesley has displayed in his negotiations with this country such great talents, such a wonderful knowledge of men and things, that whenever his proceedings are made public, his character, high as it now stands, will rise much higher in the opinion of his countrymen. If it

---

* None of the letters written by Colonel Cadogan to General Whittingham have reached the Editor's hands. It is uncertain whether they were lost in the Peninsula, or returned to his friends after his heroic death on the field of victory at Vittoria in 1813.

be possible to save this unfortunate country, he will save it.* If he fails, all is lost. . . . .

'Knowing, as you do, how much and how truly I participate in all your joys and all your sorrows, I am not afraid to say that no event of my life has given me more pleasure than your ——'s being placed under your protection. May God grant you both as large a portion of happiness as my heart's best wishes would insure you.'

'A thousand thanks for your little box. It is a delightful present; and every time I open and shut it—which is very often daily—it brings recollections to my mind, which, I trust, I shall ever cherish as I ought to, and as I now do. Mr. Duff has promised me that your wines shall be of the very best quality that he can procure; the pale sherry, and Paxarete.† I trust that they have already sailed, but I shall write to him to-morrow on the subject.

'As Lord Wellesley's dispatches will probably be very soon laid before Parliament, I shall say nothing upon the unfortunate causes of our retreat after the battle of Talavera. The whole blame, however, rests with the Spaniards. Would that I could say that they had taken proper steps since that period to remedy the evils which arrested Sir Arthur's steps in his brilliant course of victory. But enough of this subject. You will see it ably, indeed, discussed by the pen of Lord Wellesley. You will, I know, be pleased at hearing that I am honoured by

---

* The Marquis had fully adopted General Whittingham's opinion of Alburquerque, as compared with other Spanish generals. On the 21st August, 1809, his Lordship wrote to Mr. Canning, then Secretary of State for Foreign affairs:—'The most proper person for the command in Estremadura would be the Duke of Alburquerque, who has been distinguished by several acts of gallantry and spirit in the last campaign. He is, however, an object of jealousy to the junta, and if he should be appointed to the command in Estremadura, attempts will be made to reduce the strength of that division of the Spanish army.'

† The subject of this Memoir was always—though a very moderate liver himself—noted for the excellence of his wines.

his Lordship's confidence. I consider this distinction as the finest feather in my cap. Have I not used a French expression? Adieu, my dear friend. My wound is getting well fast. Several bones have been extracted. But I cannot open my mouth; and I live like a woodcock— upon suction. In consequence of the battle of Talavera, the Spanish Government has been pleased to make me a Major-General.* I enclose the Spanish account of the battle of Talavera.

'Believe me, ever yours most truly,
'SAMFORD WHITTINGHAM.'

Mr. Frere had only been Minister, but the Marquis of Wellesley had come out as Ambassador Extraordinary. At that period only ambassadors had the title of 'excellency;' and, at all times, an ambassador is the only diplomatist who enjoys full and complete royal honours. But it was not only his superior rank, but also his fame and great abilities, that rendered Lord Wellesley's authority and position in Spain far higher than that of his predecessor, Mr. Hookham Frere. The latter had, however, evidently suited well with Sir Arthur Wellesley; and no candid reader of the dispatches, can fail to perceive that the great General was uneasy at his brother's advent into Spain. It was indispensable that one Englishman should have the preponderating authority of his country in Spain, and Sir Arthur alone could unite the civil and military power in the same hands. It was necessary, therefore, that the ambassador or minister should play a secondary part; and yet it could hardly be expected that the Marquis of Wellesley in such a situation, would entirely defer to the opinions of his younger brother, and late Indian subordinate.

The British agents attached to Spanish Generals (re-

* His commission as *Mariscal de Campo* (as Major-Generals are styled in Spain) was dated 12th August, 1809. Vide *Appendix* D.

porting previously to Mr. Frere) had been placed under the orders of Sir Arthur Wellesley. But Lord Wellesley brought out orders that these important and useful, though subordinate, officers should make their reports to His Excellency the Ambassador; which, as depriving Sir Arthur of the complete control, could not but be displeasing to him. One of the results of this unsatisfactory state of things, which, fortunately, was only temporary, was a series of snubbings to the military agents, both direct and indirect. The following extract, however, is quoted rather as a proof of the magnanimity of Sir Arthur, who could acknowledge an error most gracefully:—

Sir Arthur Wellesley to Marquis Wellesley, K.B.
(Extract.)
'BADAJOS, 17th *September,* 1809.

'My Lord,—I have the honour to enclose the extract of a letter which I have received from Colonel Roche, giving an account of the state of the Spanish army, which, I am sorry to say is, I believe, too well founded. In justice to Colonel Roche, I must add that, before I joined Cuesta's army, he wrote to me an account of its state, to which I was not inclined to pay any attention at that time, but which I afterwards found to be a true account in every respect.' *——

Thus Colonel Roche, at a later period, had confirmed, in letters to Sir Arthur Wellesley, the accounts which the then Colonel Whittingham had, months before, sent to the Minister, Mr. Hookham Frere. Even the greatest of mortals is liable to occasional errors. Sir Arthur had been somewhat too tardy, by his own confession, in appreciating the full demerits of Cuesta's command. Now, Cuesta was the jealous enemy of the gallant Duke of Al-

* *Wellington Dispatches,* vol. v. p. 162.

burquerque, and may for a time have injured the latter in the British Commander's opinion, and caused him to disparage the Spanish Duke to the newly arrived British Ambassador. Mr. Hookham Frere and General Whittingham both sympathized with Alburquerque, as against old Cuesta and the Junta of Cadiz; and the subsequent miserable conduct of Cuesta, and the gallant relief of Cadiz by Alburquerque fully justified this preference. But Cuesta and the Junta had then their partisans, and amongst these was evidently Mr. Charles Vaughan, the Secretary of Legation at Cadiz, who appears to have been at that time jealous of the influence which General Whittingham had with Mr. Frere, the Minister,* as well as with Alburquerque. Mr. Vaughan was, nevertheless, destined, a few years later, when Minister himself, officially to record his gratitude to General Whittingham for the aid of his influence.

On the 21st of September, 1809, Lord Wellington finishes a letter to Marquis Wellesley with this sentence: 'Although the Duke of Alburquerque is *proné* by many, amongst others by Whittingham and Frere, and is feared by the Junta, you will find him out.' †

It is certain that nothing worse was ever found in the gallant Duke of Alburquerque than a too sensitive mind, and that defective education which was then common to the Spanish nobility. His vigour, valour, and energy, as will be seen hereafter, astonished Lord Wellington himself some months later. How he was persecuted to death by the Junta is touchingly recorded in the pages of the honest and truthful Southey; one of the rare cases of a man

---

* The strong animosity of Napier to Frere has unmistakeably extended itself to his friend Whittingham; and he eagerly makes use of an expression of the Secretary to disparage the judgment of the Minister and of the Military Agent.

† If the reader refer to the note at page 84, he will see that some influence (probably that of General Cuesta) must have been used to change Lord Wellington's former good opinion of Alburquerque.

almost literally dying of a broken heart. Such sensitiveness was not, however, it must be confessed, calculated to win the confidence of that cold calm hero, who afterwards acquired the epithet of the *Iron Duke*. The confidence of Marquis Wellesley in General Whittingham continued, as will be seen, unshaken.

Lord Wellesley wished to assemble the Cortes. Lord Wellington acknowledged that he had 'a great dislike to a new popular assembly.'*

The liberal spirit of the Marquis was ready, not only to detect, but also to patronize merit wherever he found it united to integrity. Whereas, even a year later, in spite of the continuance of a bloody war, we find the illustrious, but too aristocratic hero of the age, urging upon that truly royal 'Soldier's Friend,' the Duke of York, the propriety of more speedily promoting 'officers of family, fortune, and influence in the country.'†—As if aristocratic officers were neglected in those days! But these remarks are wholly of the present age. No such thoughts occurred to the subject of this Memoir, then almost equally the devoted humble admirer of the two illustrious brothers; the younger not having as yet entirely eclipsed the elder, and the elder being decidedly the more amiable as well as the more liberal of the two.

General Whittingham passed a happy time in the house of the noble and genial Ambassador at Seville, and in visiting his future father-in-law, who then resided in that town. But the stay of Lord Wellesley in Spain was to be very brief, and ere long he was about to exchange his not very satisfactory position in the Peninsula for the higher post of a Cabinet Minister in England. But brief as his sojourn in Spain had been, it had been long enough to fully appreciate the merits of that English captain of

---

* Lord Wellington's letter to Marquis Wellesley of 22nd September, 1809.
† Vol. vi. page 325, of the *Wellington Dispatches*.

dragoons, who was now serving as major-general in the Spanish service.

Major-General Whittingham to his Brother-in-law.

'Seville, 4*th November*, 1809.

'I have been so long without writing to you, that I am almost ashamed to take up my pen. I wish that I could give you a good account of my wound; but it is very troublesome. Bones are continually extracting, and matter has repeatedly formed under my skin. There is, however, nothing in it, I believe, dangerous; and patience, the best of all remedies, must be my doctor.

'This morning we have accompanied Lord Wellesley to his audience of leave, and to the presentations of Lord Wellington and Mr. Bartlemy Frere. Lord Wellesley goes to-morrow to Cadiz, whither I should accompany him, if my health permitted. He exceeds every idea that I had formed of him. I think that the Marquis as a politician, and Lord Wellington as a general, will save Europe. It will give you great satisfaction to know that Lord Wellesley has treated me with the most marked attention during his residence at Seville, and is, I have reason to believe, well satisfied with me. Nothing connected with this mission has given me more heart-felt pleasure than the friendship which I have formed with Dr. Knighton,* the physician and confidential friend of Marquis Wellesley. I recommend him to you, my dear Davis, in the strongest manner. You will thank me for it hereafter; and I love to hope that I shall have laid the foundation of a lasting and mutually interesting friendship.† I have requested Dr. Knighton, who will deliver to you this letter, to introduce you to Sydenham. He was secretary to Lord Wellesley during his government in India, possesses his

---

* Afterwards Sir William Knighton, the well-known private secretary and confidential friend of George IV.

† And so it, literally, was the case.

confidence most completely, and well, indeed, deserves it. I have known few such men! You will thus become intimately acquainted with Lord Wellesley's character. He is the greatest man I ever knew, in the best sense of the expression. He has a power of attaching men to him that must be felt, for it cannot be described without apparent exaggeration. Notwithstanding, living with Lord Wellesley is more like living with an amiable monarch than with a private person. His good breeding is perfect; and so nice is his sensibility on this point, that the slightest deviation shocks and offends him. In short, you will, I hope, become acquainted with him, and form your own opinion upon this most wonderful man.

'I am at present translating our cavalry tactics into Spanish. So soon as my wound is well, I shall apply for the command of a division of [Spanish] cavalry.'——

Here follows Lord Wellesley's official acknowledgement of General Whittingham's services; a portion of which is placed in italics by the Editor:—

Marquis Wellesley to Major-General Whittingham.

'CADIZ, 10*th November*, 1809.

'Sir,—I have the honour to inform you that, having obtained His Majesty's leave of absence from Spain, the charge of the embassy has devolved on Mr. Bartholomew* Frere, with whom I request you to continue your correspondence, according to the directions which you have received from Lord Castlereagh.

'I have great pleasure in availing myself of this opportunity to communicate to you my sincere acknowledgements for the valuable information received from you since my residence in Spain. *On every occasion, your*

---

* Thus written in the original. Mr. Frere was so christened; though usually called Bartlemy or Bartle for the sake of brevity.

public conduct has been distinguished by the greatest zeal, ability, and integrity; and I discharge a most grateful public duty, in signifying to you my entire approbation of the satisfactory manner in which you have been employed both by the British and Spanish Governments in Spain. With great respect and esteem, I have the honour to be, Sir,

'Your faithful and obedient servant,
'WELLESLEY.'

To serve under Marquis Wellesley might certainly be called serving under the shade of the aristocracy; not, indeed, winter's 'cold shade,' but the genial and refreshing shade of summer. Only three months had General Whittingham served under him, and yet how warmly and ungrudgingly had that amiable and all-accomplished nobleman acknowledged his services and his merits.

In a letter to Mr. B. Frere, written a few days after Lord Wellesley's departure, and dated 17th November, 1809, Lord Wellington strongly, though indirectly, acknowledged the military talents of the officer, whose ability in civil matters his brother had so lately recorded. It must be premised that General Alava was already the friend of Lord Wellington, and afterwards served on his personal staff. The hero wrote: 'I do not understand the Duque's* retreat from his position. He never apprized me of it. It is very desirable that Alava and Whittingham—as soon as he is able,—should be sent to the Duque de Alburquerque, who, although he does not want spirit, is deficient in other qualifications for a commander, which his confidence in those officers can alone supply.'†

A sentence of the same letter reminds the Editor of one

* The Duke of Alburquerque.
† Vol. v., page 292, of the *Wellington Dispatches*.

of the most gallant of British nobles, who was a true and staunch friend to General Whittingham, namely, Lord Macduff, afterwards Earl of Fife. Lord Wellington wrote: 'I am most anxious about Areyzaga's corps, the fate of which must be decided before this time. If he should fail, the situation of the Duque del Parque will become critical.' Lord Macduff was fighting under the orders of General Areyzaga, whose army of La Mancha was totally defeated at Ocaña on the 19th November, 1809. Lord Macduff exhibited his wonted valour, and exerted himself in vain to retrieve the fortunes of the day. Though without a commission in the British, his Lordship eventually became major-general in the Spanish army. It does not appear, however, though so stated in the Peerage, that he really was wounded at Talavera.

The original of the letter addressed by Lord Wellington to Major-General Whittingham, and dated Badajoz, 22nd December, 1809, is not in the Editor's possession; and, from want of space, it is not copied at length from Gurwood's Dispatches.* An extract will suffice for this Memoir:—

To Major-General Whittingham.

'BADAJOS, 22nd *December*, 1809.

'My dear Sir,—I am concerned to hear that the state of your wound has obliged you to go to Gibraltar; but I wish that while you are in that part of the Peninsula, you would take an opportunity of seeing or writing to General Venegas on the subject of the defence of Cadiz.' [Then his Lordship enters into details of the military preparations required, &c., at great length, and the letter thus terminates]: 'These are the points to which, in particular, I would draw the attention of General Venegas if I were likely to see him; but as that is not probable, I beg you

* Vol. v., page 386.

either to see or write to him the sentiments which I have above written to you.

'Believe me, &c.
'WELLINGTON.

'Major-General Whittingham.'*

Thus Lord Wellington, in 1809, recognized Whittingham's rank in Spain as that of a general officer, and never wrote to him nor of him under a lower title till peace was concluded, and he reverted to his humbler position in the British Army. How ignorant of these facts must have been that historian who describes the major-general of 1809 as only a *colonel* of cavalry in 1811! To be sure, the Duke's dispatches generally were not then all available to the historian when he wrote as Colonel Napier, but those announcing victories had at least appeared in the 'Gazette.' As early as 1809, in Lord Wellington's dispatch of Talavera, that hero had called Whittingham brigadier-general, the Spanish rank taking full effect in the Peninsular War. But Napier's natural disgust against the Spaniards extended itself, apparently, even to the English who served with them, and his misstatements must be compared (by all lovers of impartiality) with the more correct statements of Southey, and especially with the facts narrated in the Wellington Dispatches.

But it is necessary to revert here to General Whittingham's private correspondence:—

To his Brother-in-law.

'SAN ROQUE,† 8*th January*, 1810.

'I love to hope, before I sail for the new world,‡ to pass a few months with you and my dear Mrs. D.; and I

---

* In a note to this letter, Gurwood represents Whittingham as then a *Lieut.-Colonel* in the British Army, whereas he was only a *Captain*, and gazetted a *Major* only on the 12th March, 1810. Gurwood was misled, perhaps, by Napier's history. (See *Appendix* D.)

† Near Gibraltar.

‡ There was at that time a plan for sending an expedition to South America, to recover the revolted colonies for Spain.

have now a double interest in this wish, as it will give me an opportunity of introducing my dear Mrs. W., to whom I was married on Friday last at Gibraltar. General Castaños gave her away. We are now at San Roque, and as soon as my wound, which is still very troublesome, will permit, I shall go to Cadiz, where I have some very interesting affairs to canvass with the Governor, General Venegas, by the express desire of Lord Wellington.

'I pay the greatest attention to my papers. I keep copies and originals, as circumstances permit, and when I have the happiness of seeing you, I shall deposit the whole in your hands.* I have never had so delicate a part to play as at this moment. I am consulted by the leaders of the different parties, and they trust me with their secret views and intentions. I communicate everything to Lord Wellesley, and I am now anxiously waiting his orders.† The Spanish Government will employ me as major-general the moment I return to Seville. I have received a very pressing letter on the subject. But in the present situation of their army, I will not risk the little fame that I may have acquired by taking the command of a division of cavalry. But I will request to be employed as a major-general attached to the staff of the army of the Duke of Alburquerque. This will, in fact, make me second in command, at the same time that I avoid the dreadful responsibility of directly commanding ill-disciplined and disheartened troops.'

To the Same.
'GIBRALTAR, 22nd January, 1810.

'General Castaños is appointed Captain-General of Andalusia, which gives him, in fact, the supreme com-

---

* Though much of his correspondence has been lost, yet a great deal has been preserved, which would fill volumes.
† Lord Wellesley was now Minister for Foreign Affairs.

mand. He takes me with him as one of his generals of division. We leave this place to-morrow. Mrs. W. will remain at Cadiz, and I shall immediately take the field with the General. The French are about to attack the Sierra Morena on three points. I think that their grand attack will be by the road of Almadin de la Plata. I fear that Andalusia will be lost. But the Isla de Leon may be occupied in great force, and will protect the advances to Cadiz, and give time for any combined operations in the rear of the French army. I pray you don't lose sight of my Majority.*

'The Junta retire to the Isla de Leon, and the Junta of Seville are entrusted with the defence of the kingdom of Andalusia. My wound is, I hope, well.'——

On the 2nd February, 1810, after a very rapid march of 260 English miles, Alburquerque entered the Isla de Leon with 8,000 men, and thus saved Cadiz. He was afterwards made Governor of the City and President of the Junta. On the 7th of same month,† Lord Wellington writes from Mafra to the Hon. General Stewart: 'I cannot sufficiently recommend you to endeavour to keep up a good understanding with the Spanish officers. You will find General Castaños, who is at present at the head of the Regency, and General Venegas, who is Governor of Cadiz, highly deserving your confidence; as well as General Whittingham, who is an English officer, and who is, I understand, at present at Cadiz.'‡

---

* He had applied to be promoted to be Major in the British army, being still only a Captain.

† *Wellington Dispatches*, vol. v. p. 489.

‡ Two days later, Lord Wellington wrote to Lord Liverpool: 'I have received intelligence, which I believe to be true, that the Duque d'Alburquerque's corps which had been at Carmona on the 24th January, and was supposed to have retired across the Guadalquivir, had retired upon Cadiz, and actually arrived at Xeres on the 1st instant.' Vol. v. p. 494.

To his Brother-in-law.

'ISLA DE LEON, 1*st March*, 1810.

' I am occupied from morning till night. The Regency place an unlimited confidence in me. The Duke [of Alburquerque] consults me upon everything, and has honoured me by the command of the cavalry, with full powers to organize as I may think proper. I have translated Dundas, and formed a corps of carabineers chosen from the different regiments for instruction. The officers assemble every evening at my house, and the practice of the day is rendered familiar and easy by the theory clearly explained at night. The Duke wishes me to take the employment of *Chef de l'Etat Major.* I have no objection to it. It is the next [post] to the Commander-in-Chief.'*——

General Whittingham, it is plain, commanded all the Spanish cavalry at Isla de Leon, although he there chiefly dedicated himself to the organization of a select number. He did not thereby (as some have apparently ignorantly imagined) become again a simple colonel of cavalry.

In the beginning of March, the Right Hon. Henry Wellesley arrived at Cadiz, as His Majesty's Minister in Spain, and from this time it was with him that General Whittingham habitually corresponded.

In a letter from Lord Wellington to Mr. Wellesley, dated Viseu, 27th March, 1810, there are two sentences that bear connection with the future proceedings of General Whittingham in Spain, and are, therefore, here inserted.

' Whether the fleet is, or is not sent to Minorca, the security of the Balearic Islands is a consideration of the utmost importance, which must not be lost sight of. You and I (I probably more than you) will be considered re-

* The rest of the letter is filled with military speculations and projects regarding the future campaigns.

sponsible for everything that occurs, although we have no means in our power, and no power to enforce the execution of what is necessary.

'It is desirable that we should advert to everything, and should recommend to the consideration of the Spanish Government those measures which appear to us to be necessary. Accordingly, I suggest to you to pass a note to the Regency, recommending to their serious attention the security of the Balearic Islands, Minorca particularly; they should send there, in the first instance, the Viscomte de Gand's corps which is now in Algarve; they should, besides, endeavour to raise men in Cadiz, where, by proper measures, they could get thousands.'

Venegas's politics were considered of a doubtful character, but he was junior to the Duke of Alburquerque, and therefore Lord Wellington writes in February that he considered his opinions immaterial, ' particularly recollecting a letter which I wrote to General Whittingham in December upon this subject, which I know was shown to Venegas, and which was certainly calculated to inspire confidence rather than mistrust of our designs in regard to Cadiz.'

On the 12th March, 1810, Samford Whittingham's name appeared in the 'London Gazette,' as promoted from Captain in the 13th Light Dragoons, to be Major of Infantry on half pay. In a letter dated *Isla de Leon*, 1st April, 1810, he writes, introducing Mr. B. Frere, then about to proceed to England to his brother-in-law, Mr Davis.

To the Same.

'ISLA DE LEON, 8*th April*, 1810.

'I believe that I mentioned to you, that the Duke of Alburquerque has resigned the command of this army, and is going as ambassador to England. The Regency wished me to have accompanied him, and proposed giving me a special commission for the arms and accoutrements of the cavalry; but this plan was objected to by Mr. Wellesley and General Graham, who were pleased to consider my presence here as absolutely necessary!

'I have, you know, undertaken to introduce a new system of tactics in the Spanish cavalry. My day is at present thus divided: From eight in the morning till eleven, I exercise three squadrons on foot, which I have selected for the purpose of instruction. From twelve to three, I am occupied in correcting the translation of Dundas on "Cavalry Movements." From three to five, exercise of a troop on horseback. From seven to nine, academy of all the officers of the three squadrons of instruction at my house, where the principles of cavalry movements are explained to them. Add to all this the visits that I have to make to the Commander-in-Chief, General Castaños, and the various conferences with Mr. Wellesley and General Graham, and you will, I think, agree with me, that my time is tolerably well taken up.

'On Sunday next, the Regency, the Minister of War, Generals Graham and Stuart, General Giron, and all the officers of high rank in the island are to be present at the review of the regiment which I have formed on the new system. The regiment will go through all the principal manœuvres, and the Government will determine whether the new system is to be adopted or not! Notwithstanding the acknowledged necessity of a system of tactics for the cavalry, and the beauty and goodness of that proposed, I am by no means confident of success. The Inspector-General of the cavalry is the declared enemy of my undertaking, and as all recommendations for promotion are made through him, *almost all* the officers of cavalry follow his opinion. Whatever be the result, I have done my duty; and I am perfectly satisfied that, unless a change of system takes place, dishonour and disgrace will ever attend the Spanish cavalry.

'In losing the protection of the Duke [of Alburquerque], I have, I fear, lost a great support; but be it as it may, nothing would induce me to retain the command of the Spanish cavalry, unless I should be permitted to give it that degree of mobility absolutely necessary for its success in the day of action.

'I have entered more into detail than may appear necessary, because if the system of reform be not adopted, I shall request General Castaños to relieve me from this command, and to make me Inspector-General of the troops of the Balearic Islands.

'I pray of you to wait upon the Duke of Alburquerque as soon as he comes to town. One of his aides-de-camp speaks English very well. I am sure I need not say that anything you can do to serve or to amuse the Duke will infinitely oblige me; for no one is better acquainted than yourself with the favours he has conferred on me.

'The Duke has left the command of this army in consequence of a dispute with the Junta of Cadiz. It was proposed to him by the Regency (when the Duke determined to resign his command here) to make him Captain-General of the Balearic Islands! I was to have gone with him as head of his staff. This idea was highly approved of by Mr. Wellesley. The Duke was to have full powers to recruit in Spain for the army which he was to form at Majorca and Minorca; and I have no doubt that in less than four months we should have collected 20,000 men. In my humble opinion, this, of all others, was the situation for the Duke. At first he thought so himself, but the advice of light and interested men altered his mind, and he determined not to accept it. The embassy was then thought of. It pleased him, and everything was forthwith fixed. The Duke has committed a capital error, and of this he will sooner or later be convinced.'*

* Southey has recorded the sad death of Alburquerque at the Spanish Embassy in London.

To the Same.

'Isla de Leon, 26th *May*, 1810.

' As Mr. Wellesley and General Graham have both written to request that I may be made Lieutenant-Colonel in Spain, I am in hopes, notwithstanding the difficulties which at first appear, that the affair may be carried through.'*

' It was settled for me to accompany the Duke on his embassy to England; but Mr. Wellesley and General Graham objected to it so strongly, that I was obliged to request General Castaños to state to the Duke that it could not be. I still remain in command of the cavalry, and I have every reason to believe that I shall have the honour of introducing a complete new system of tactics for the cavalry of this country. It is incredible the opposition that I have met with, but, thanks to the steady friendship of the Duke in the first instance, and subsequently of General Castaños, I am in a fair way of conquering all difficulties. Nothing would enable me to do the Spanish cavalry so much good as clothing, arming, and equipping one corps in the English style. Mr. Wellesley would send out a complete equipment for 400 hussars, which compose the corps d'élite that I have taken from the whole of the cavalry. This corps would serve as a model for clothing, arms, and furniture, and would, I am convinced, induce the Spanish Government to make further contracts in England for the future clothing and arming of their troops.'

To the Same.

'Isla de Leon, 28th *July*, 1810.

' The enclosed letter for Torrens, I will thank you to seal and forward as soon as you have read it. You

---

*He was not promoted to a Lieutenant-Colonelcy till the autumn of 1811, but the Lieutenant-Colonelcy was afterwards dated back to 30th May, 1811.

will see by its contents my opinion of the present state of affairs. Be assured (but this is entirely *entre nous*) that unless the work at Santi Petri is finished in a proper manner before the French can attack us in force, the island will be lost, and if this unfortunate event should take place, Cadiz must at last fall!

'For my own part, as soon as the clothing complete arrives, I shall present the regiment of cavalry that I have formed to the Government; and I may venture to assert that Spain has hitherto possessed no such corps. I have laboured day and night, and I flatter myself that I have succeeded. But as the scale of cavalry in this island is infinitely small, it is my intention to propose to Government to raise a corps of two thousand cavalry in Majorca; and I shall endeavour to have the clothing, arms, &c., from Mr. Wellesley.'

[After using much persuasion to induce Mr. Davis to let his son visit him in the Isla de Leon, he adds:—]

'He will in me find not only an affectionate uncle, but his father's oldest and best friend. Mrs. W. joins with me in this wish; and I really do think that a few months so employed might be of the greatest utility in his future career.* He might come here with Major Armstrong, who is about to return, and there can be no danger of a warlike nature at present, as it is totally impossible for Buonaparte to attempt anything against this place till he has driven Lord Wellington out of Portugal—an event his Lordship conceives to be far distant.'———

On the 25th September he writes again to his brother in-law to express his delight at learning that his nephew is coming out, and promises that he shall not enter the service, and also to take good care of him.

* As a member of Parliament.

To the Same.

'Isla de Leon, 10*th November*, 1810.

' This letter will be delivered to you by Colonel Campbell, who goes to England on the subject of the clothing and appointments of the force to be disciplined, organized, &c. &c. in Majorca by me. I am to have the sole direction of the corps, and to be general, head of the staff, and inspector. It is a great undertaking. Everything is to be created anew; but I trust in God and in my good fortune.

' Colonel Campbell is one of my most intimate friends. We have long been in the habit of the greatest intimacy, and I can safely and cordially recommend him to your warmest attentions. I am delighted that Hart is coming.* Pray would you choose that he should accompany us to Majorca? I think he might pass a month there pleasantly. He cannot fail to learn Spanish with us. English is hardly ever talked at our house, and Mrs. W. will be happy to give him lessons in her native tongue. He will find an old and intimate friend of his here attached to the Embassy, I mean Mr. Clive.'——

At the Isla de Leon occurred the first trial of Spanish military organization on a very small scale. How he laboured at this work, limited as it was to 400 cavalry (officers and men) has been shown in his correspondence with Mr. Davis, his brother-in-law. As to its results, the two subjoined letters will testify :—

* Mr. Hart Davis, junior, General Whittingham's nephew, remained a few years in Parliament, and eventually became Deputy Chairman of the Board of Excise, in which post he established the reputation of great ability and unwearied industry in the public service.

*Lieut.-General Graham** to Major-General Whittingham.*

'ISLA DE LEON, 1*st December*, 1810.

'My dear General,—Having just heard that you are soon to leave this on an important commission to the Balearic Islands, I am anxious to take this opportunity of testifying my sincere satisfaction at the complete success which has attended your exertions here. I am free to confess that the task appeared to me to be so difficult a one that I much doubted that even your perseverance and skill would have produced the desired effect. For I should have considered it less arduous to have begun with recruits than to instruct on an improved system officers and men who at first probably imagined they required no instruction.

'But the readiness and precision with which these squadrons executed every formation, and performed every evolution that can possibly be required of cavalry, convinced me that you had been able to overcome all prejudice, and to bring these squadrons in a very short time into a high state of discipline, that cannot fail to make them a valuable corps. The principle of good instruction and practice is common to both infantry and cavalry; and the advantages resulting from that uniformity must strike forcibly the mind of all military men who give themselves the trouble of thinking on professional points. But cavalry, above all, requires such a variety of attention that the system of the greatest simplicity must be the best; according to the state of discipline, this arm is formidable to their enemy or dangerous to their friends; and till cavalry has acquired confidence in itself by a thorough knowledge of its powers, by being capable of acting without confusion, one would rather go into action without it.

* Afterwards Lord Lynedoch.

' But I forget myself ; for least of all to you can it be necessary to make such reflections.

' I am happy to think that you will now have it in your power to exert your talents on a more extensive scale for the benefit of a country and a cause in which our hearts are so warmly engaged. Do not think me vain for thus offering you my tribute of applause. I am merely doing justice to my own feelings. Believe me ever, my dear General,

' Most truly and obediently yours,
' THOMAS GRAHAM.'*

The Right Hon. Henry Wellesley to Major-General Whittingham.

' ISLA DE LEON, 16*th November*, 1810.

' Sir,—I cannot avoid expressing to you the satisfaction [which] I felt at witnessing, this morning, the complete success of your exertions to bring into the field a corps of Spanish cavalry, formed upon the model of a British regiment, and in a perfect state of discipline and efficiency. You may reasonably take to yourself the credit of having introduced into the Spanish cavalry a system of discipline, which, if adopted by the other corps, cannot fail to render them equal, if not superior to the cavalry of the enemy.

' The steadiness and temper with which you have resisted all the attempts to defeat this object, and the perseverance and skill which you have manifested in bringing it to perfection, are highly creditable to you, and justify a confident expectation that your efforts will be equally successful in the attainment of a still more important object, which, with a view to the im-

---

* In the British Service, Graham was then a Major-General, and Whittingham only a Major, a fact which renders the tone of deference and respect employed in this letter equally honourable to the modesty of the superior, and to the merits of the subordinate officer.

provement of the Spanish army, you are now about to undertake.—I have the honour to be, Sir,

'Your most obedient, humble servant,
'H. Wellesley.'

The expectations of Mr. Wellesley were destined to be realized in due time; but in the meantime a great mortification was being prepared by destiny for General Whittingham. But this year closes with a friendly letter from the head of the house of Wellesley:—

Marquis Wellesley to Major-General Whittingham.
(*Private.*)
'Apsley House, 9th *December*, 1810.

'My dear Sir,—I am apprehensive that my silence may have inclined you to suppose that I have not remembered, with sufficient attention, your valuable services at Seville, and my estimation of your talents and character. But I flatter myself that when you reflect on the sudden manner in which I was cast on the turbulent flood of politics in this country, and on the nature of the crisis in which I have been required to act, your indulgence will furnish some excuse for my apparent negligence.

'You may be assured that I have used every endeavour to forward every point connected with your most useful plan for raising a corps in Spain, although, from some accident, I have not yet seen Colonel Campbell.

'I shall always feel a deep interest in whatever regards your welfare and honour. I hope that you will apprize me at the earliest moment of your wishes on all subjects of importance; and that you will continue to afford me the advantage of your correspondence, and to believe me to be, my dear Sir,

'Your faithful friend and obliged humble servant,
'Wellesley.'

CHAPTER VI.

1811.

THE GREAT DIFFICULTY OF GENERAL WHITTINGHAM—NAPIER AND SOUTHEY ON THE BATTLE OF BARROSA—GRAHAM'S ASSUMPTION OF COMMAND—HE IMPUTED NO BLAME TO WHITTINGHAM—GENERAL WHITTINGHAM COMMANDED INFANTRY AS WELL AS CAVALRY—DISADVANTAGE OF TRUSTING TO MEMORY—WHITTINGHAM'S OFFICIAL REPORT TO LA PEÑA—ORDERED TO RETREAT ON MAIN BODY—GRAHAM'S SUCCESSFUL CHARGE—WHITTINGHAM'S REPORT INDIRECTLY BLAMES LA PEÑA—ACCIDENTALLY DELAYED ADVANCE—AN EGREGIOUS MISREPRESENTATION OF FACTS—GENERAL WHITTINGHAM'S LETTER TO MR. DAVIS ON BARROSA—*THE DUKE'S* COMPREHENSIVE TESTIMONY IN FAVOUR OF WHITTINGHAM—THE DUKE OF KENT'S SPONTANEOUS TRIBUTE TO HIS MERITS.

IN casting in his lot with the Spanish army, the great difficulty of General Whittingham had ever been to find good opportunities for distinguishing himself, whilst serving with raw and undisciplined troops under more or less incompetent generals. These premises duly weighed, it may perhaps be considered fortunate that only on one day of his long career has his military conduct been made the subject of hostile criticism, and this not by any official superior—either English or Spanish—but by the pen of an able, eloquent, and gallant, but also prejudiced and partial historian, who himself held a very subordinate position in the Peninsular War, and whose bias against the Spaniards, and against Englishmen who were employed with them, appears to have been indiscriminate and unbounded.

The battle of Barrosa, fought on March 5, 1811, was certainly an unfortunate day for General Whittingham;

but few officers who have seen much service have wholly escaped such days. Even the great hero of the age had had his Seringapatam and his retreat from Burgos. The hero of Barrosa, Graham, also, was not always, though very generally fortunate; but that excellent officer never himself attributed any blame to General Whittingham, much as he found fault with the Commander-in-Chief, La Peña.

The reader must be reminded, that to this day the battle of Barrosa is a difficult and complex question to all who take the trouble impartially to study its details in the works of the various historians who have undertaken to describe them. Putting the Spaniards aside, do Frenchmen and Englishmen agree? Is Napier corroborated by Marshal Victor's dispatch, or by Thiers's history of the French empire? But, what is still more important, do the English themselves agree together? Is not the account of the patient and pains-taking civilian, Southey, diametrically opposed to that of his impetuous military rival? If few persons of judgment will deny that the work of the military historian is a far more brilliant production than that of the civilian; yet on the other hand few will maintain that Napier was as impartial or as desirous to do justice to all parties and to all nations as was the historian Southey. The latter neither felt personal hatred against the Spaniards, nor could be jealous of those military agents attached to the Spaniards, who obtained higher, but temporary and local rank. This temporary rank they obtained in return for the sacrifice of serving with wretched and undisciplined troops, instead of fighting by the side of those British soldiers who so often, by their valour and stubbornness, more than make up for the ignorance and incompetency of their leaders.

General Graham won the battle of Barrosa by suddenly taking the command, and setting aside the Spanish Commander-in-Chief under whom he had himself agreed to serve. The partial success—as to results at all events—that followed the battle, and the *prestige* of a victory (then much wanted, after the retreat of the army to Portugal), caused the military insubordination of Graham to be converted into a patriotic virtue. But General Whittingham was on that day in a different position from that of Graham, who was only temporarily under La Peña's command, and that by his own desire. Whittingham was under the immediate orders of La Peña as a Spanish general officer, and he was also acting as a British military agent, whose business it was to keep on good terms with the Spanish Commander-in-Chief. By every principle of duty and policy, and conscience, therefore, he was bound to obey La Peña, as his own Commander, as well as the Commander of the allied armies. On the other hand, he had every reason to love and respect Graham, who had lately recommended him for promotion, and praised his military talents in a most flattering letter.

General Whittingham ever maintained that he was, and very naturally so, most anxious to be allowed, and had requested in the first instance, to join himself to, Graham's division; but he was refused. But what impartial person could blame La Peña for not consenting to deprive himself of the immediate aid of those 400 Spanish horsemen, who had been trained to unusual excellence of drill and discipline, by the voluntary confession of Graham himself?

Certainly, it was most unfortunate, that the chief command had not originally been invested in General Graham. But La Peña was the senior, and would not waive his rights; for it had been agreed between Lord Wellington and the Spanish Government that when English and Spanish forces were united, the senior officer of either nation should command the whole army.

From the false statements of the French Marshal Victor (as narrated by Southey) that the English had purposely exposed the Spaniards to the first attack, it does not necessarily follow that the first demonstration of the French was not directed at La Peña's advanced guard. Victor may have been right in his facts, though wrong as to the motives he suggested.

General Graham imputed no blame to 'General Whittingham,' whom he in his dispatch correctly names by his Spanish rank; and who, whilst reserving for La Peña the official report of his proceedings as commander of the Spanish advanced guard, appears to have communicated verbally to Graham after the action the reason why he had been prevented joining him in time with his cavalry. In his dispatch to Lord Wellington, General Graham writes: 'I understand, too, from General Whittingham, that with three squadrons of cavalry, he kept in check a corps of infantry and cavalry that attempted to turn the Barrosa height by the sea. One squadron of the 2nd Hussars, King's German Legion, under Captain Busche, and directed by Lieutenant-Colonel Ponsonby (both had been attached to the Spanish cavalry), joined in time to make a brilliant and most successful charge against a squadron of French dragoons, which were entirely routed.'

Unfortunately, General Whittingham, not being under General Graham's orders, did not send him a copy of his dispatch to General La Peña. If he had done so, Graham would have seen that the Spanish advanced guard, which checked the threatened attack of the French on the right, consisted of *infantry as well as cavalry*, and that General Whittingham was not that day a simple commander of cavalry. To explain to General Graham why the Spanish cavalry had not joined him, was of course the only object of General Whittingham's communication to that officer. It was to his own General, the Commander-in-Chief, that he had to send the full details of his proceedings. This report he wrote in Spanish with the usual forms employed by Spanish officers. Of this document he, fortunately (the day after writing it), sent a copy in the original language to his beloved brother-in-law, who was himself a good Spanish scholar. Finally, this document only a few months back (with the rest of Sir Samford Whittingham's long packed-away papers), reached the Editor's hands. It had never been seen by Sir Samford since March 8th, 1811, when he dispatched it to his brother-in-law, and consequently, when twenty-two years later he found himself, whilst in India, unexpectedly attacked in Napier's history, he had only his memory to rely on for his defence. That memory, ordinarily good, the inscrutable wisdom of providence permitted on this occasion to be materially, to his own great discomfiture, defective; the sad consequence of which was that the injured veteran was deprived of his invulnerable arms—like Patrocles in his combat with Hector. The box of papers, left at the bottom of a cellar in the public offices of London, was not available to refresh the memory of the veteran wearing away his life in a tropical climate, in the unceasing service of his country!

The following is a translation of Major-General Whittingham's Official Report to the Commander-in-Chief La Peña, of his share in the battle of Barrosa:[*]—

'Excellency,—At two o'clock p.m. of the 5th instant I received orders from your Excellency to take post, with three squadrons, and two troops of cavalry, *and 1,350 infantry,*[†] commanded by Brigadier Don Antonia Begines de los Rios, at the camp of the Cerro del Puerco. Consequently, I was proceeding to take up my position by joining the infantry, when Colonel Don Louis Michelena

---

[*] Vide *Appendix* A for the original Spanish copy of the Report, as sent to Mr. Davis.

[†] The Editor has placed in *italics* those portions of the Report to which he desires to draw the special attention of the reader.

informed me that troops were in sight, which appeared to be enemies, by their marching towards us. I hastened the junction' [*with the infantry*], 'and reconnoitred the enemy, who marched in two strong columns; having with them a battalion of light infantry, which formed their vanguard. The one marched directly on my position; the other extending itself to its left for the purpose of outflanking us. I ordered the infantry to form in squares, and placed the cavalry on the left in echelon, to maintain the position. At this moment I received *your Excellency's order to fall back on the main body of the army;* and I discovered, besides the two hostile columns already mentioned, another stronger one approaching rapidly on my left to occupy the pine wood, between my camp and that of the main army, the only passage by which I could accomplish *your Excellency's latest instruction to fall back.* The enemy's force was at least quadruple that which I had with me. I determined, *in conformity with the said order*, that the infantry should commence a retreat covered by the cavalry. The English battalion under the command of Colonel Brown opened the march, followed by the Spanish troops. I took the detachment of Royal carabineers, and one troop of English hussars[*] with me, to cover the right flank of the line of march in the retreat—interposed between the right flank and the enemy—continuing the retreat up to taking possession of the wood, where I immediately posted Don Juan de la Cruz; ordering him to cover the right flank of the position, which the enemy were already endeavouring to surround. In compliance with my orders, Major Busche with the English hussars, Lieutenant-Colonels Don Francisco Ramonet, and Don Francisco Serrano with a squadron of grenadiers, and, of the same rank, Don Santiago Wall with two troops under his command, and some guerilla

---

[*] These were hussars of the German Legion, in the pay of England.

infantry, maintained themselves *till the retreat of the infantry was accomplished, of all the baggage of the army, and of the two pieces of artillery;* * which up to the last moment of being sharply attacked, had maintained unflinchingly a very well-directed and vigorous fire upon the enemy.

'The cavalry covered the retreat perfectly and in good order, notwithstanding the continued skirmishing, which the enemy's cavalry kept up, throughout the whole of their advance, closing their ranks as they debouched, and stronger by one-third, against ours, separated at that time at several points.'

'At this moment, I perceived the corps of General Graham issuing out of the wood, and moving towards their former position on the heights now occupied by the enemy. It would be difficult to give a just idea of the impetuosity with which the common enemy was driven back from all the heights by the English bayonets; the same enemy who had charged us with such insolence and confidence as if he had already gained the victory. His force was double that of the English; but the victory, though costly, was complete, and decided by the point of the bayonet. The fruits of this distinguished day would have been gathered beyond the principal object, *if the enemy*—who in their precipitate retreat abandoned their wounded of all ranks and descriptions, three guns and two ammunition waggons—*had been charged in flank and threatened in the rear.*†

* To represent as a mere Colonel of a small body of horse a *General*, who had infantry, artillery, and baggage under his orders *as well as cavalry*, was assuredly a wonderful specimen of ignorance in the popular historian. If, denying him the Spanish rank in which he was then employed, the historian intended to call him by his English rank, he was equally wrong. Whittingham was not even *Lieutenant-Colonel*, but only Major, at the battle of Barrosa, yet Napier styles him 'Colonel.'

† The officer who ever considered obedience as the first and last duty of a soldier, could, nevertheless, not resist on this occasion hinting to the Commander-in-Chief how, instead of ordering his advanced-guard to retire, he might have advanced himself with the main body and completed the victory.

'A squadron of English hussars, which were under my command attacked the guard of Marshal Victor, routed and dispersed it. This squadron of English hussars, jointly with the one already mentioned of the Spanish grenadiers, under the command of Baron Carondelet, and the two troops of Don Santiago Wall, covered the right wing; and supported by the troops of brigadiers Don Antonio Begines, and Don Juan de la Cruz, prevented the enemy, by their gallant conduct and manœuvres, from surrounding us along the shore, as they had twice attempted to do. These two troops behaved with gallantry; retiring from and advancing upon the enemy, at the right moment, as equally did the detachment of the Royal carabineers. All the cavalry in short brilliantly fulfilled their duty.

'The enemy, after finding himself repulsed from the heights, commenced his retreat in an orderly manner, covered by his cavalry. This was the moment in which I proposed to myself to collect together and act on the offensive with my 400 horse, which I had under my orders.* With this view I had desired Ramonet and Serrano, in union with Wall, to observe and to co-operate with the movements of the English hussars and the Royal carabineers, which I kept with me; when, upon the right of the whole line, there appeared a column of infantry of about 500 men, preceded by a party of horse, and moving as if to turn our flank. It was indispensable to manœuvre so as to keep them under observation, whilst a sergeant and six men of the squadron of carabineers reconnoitred them; *and the opportunity thus escaped me of charging*, with the whole of my disposable cavalry, the enemy who was retiring rapidly. At the head of the English hussars

* This corps, which he had himself trained and organized, to the admiration of General Graham and Mr. Wellesley, was under his *special orders*; though as General (as his dispatch clearly proves) he on that day commanded, under La Peña, the whole Spanish advanced-guard—amounting, apparently, to about 2,500 of all ranks—a small force against such an enemy; but still no *Colonel's* command.

I followed them, resolving to attack a body of cavalry, posted at the side of a lake, which covered their left flank. But on my advance, I discovered that the whole of the enemy's infantry were collected on their right, supported by the artillery, and covered by the pine wood; a situation which did not allow of a partial or isolated movement against the above mentioned force, so well protected. In this situation, two pieces of artillery were placed in position by General Graham which by a well directed fire obliged the enemy to continue his retreat between the lake and the pine wood in the direction of Chiclava.

'I cannot do less than entreat your Excellency to make known to their Serene Highnesses,* the particular merit evinced in all circumstances, by the commanders, officers, and troops in this action, without being able to select or individualize any to your Excellency, where all have emulously and honourably fulfilled their duty, on this happy occasion thus offered to them, of showing themselves to the nation as its defenders.

'God preserve your Excellency.

'His Excellency [Major-General] Senor Don Santiago Whittingham, to his Excellency [Lieutenant-General] Senor Don Manuel de la Peña, General-in-Chief.

'Camp of Cerro del Puerco, 7th March, 1811.'

This dispatch demonstrates that notwithstanding La Peña's orders to retire, it was simply an accident over which he had no control, that delayed the advance of General Whittingham, after the successful charge of the British under General Graham.

That some of these details, as well as those regarding his rank and position, should have escaped his recollection after about a quarter of a century had elapsed—a period passed in nearly ceaseless laborious duties and occupations—is less extraordinary than that an historian

* The Regency of Spain.

sitting at home at ease should have made so many mistakes, and egregiously misrepresented the proceedings of that small part of La Peña's army which took part in the battle of Barrosa.

As usual, so on this occasion, General Whittingham was with the advanced guard of the Spanish army. The fatiguing marches which the Spaniards had undergone, may have palliated the tardiness of La Peña, who had also perhaps a just right to complain of the disobedience of his subordinate General Graham. But certainly La Peña was not in sight of the action that day, and interfered only to order the retreat of his advanced guard, on to the main body.

It may be that Southey is too severe on Graham, under the circumstances; but at least he appears to have discussed the question with studied calmness and impartiality, as well as with a fullness of details, which may have exhausted the patience of some of his readers. But most assuredly if truth and accuracy are the most important points in a history, in that respect Southey has borne the palm from his military rival, even though it is probable that some errors also exist in his pains-taking accounts of Barrosa.

The painful uncertainty of history, of which many examples have been furnished in the present century, was never more patent than in the conflicting testimonies, regarding that battle, in acting in which, General Whittingham appears to have done his duty under most trying circumstances. That he was indignant with the Spanish Commander-in-Chief, and that all his sympathies were with General Graham, is proved by the following private letter written three days after the action, more plainly than etiquette would admit of in the official dispatch:—

Major-General Whittingham to his Brother-in-law.

'ISLA DE LEON, 8*th March*, 1811.

' My dear Davis,—The time is so short, that I have scarcely time to send you a copy of my report* to the Commander-in-Chief La Peña of the part I had in the action of the 5th. If the English had been supported by an advance movement of the Spaniards in the wood, the siege of Cadiz must have been raised, and the whole business would have been most glorious. As it is, the British army gained a most complete victory against double the number of French, and covered themselves with immortal honour.

' The loss of the English exceeds 1,200 men, and after such a specimen of Spanish generalship, it is not to be believed that General Graham will again engage in offensive operations, unless he has the command-in-chief. The Spaniards still keep the bridge of boats upon the river, and talk of undertaking offensive operations alone. As everything relative to my expedition to Majorca is settled, I shall give up [my command] here, as soon as they may choose to take away the bridge of Santi Petri. Colonel Macdonald will do me the favour to deliver this letter. He is Adjutant-General of the British forces here, and I beg to recommend him to your particular attentions. My best love to Mrs. Davis and all the family, as well as to James [Whittingham] and his family, and believe me,

' Ever yours most affectionately,

' SAMFORD WHITTINGHAM.'

If Napier had delayed his history till after the publication of the 'Wellington Dispatches' (since the Duke refused him access to them), he would probably have done more justice to General Whittingham, of whom so much

---

* He means, *scarcely time to do more than send a copy of his report.*

honourable mention is therein made. Above all he would have read the Duke's all-comprehensive testimony to the merits and services of Sir Samford Whittingham, from the commencement to the close of the Peninsular war. Three years after Barrosa the Duke wrote in favour of the subject of this Memoir that he had 'served most *zealously* and *gallantly*, from the commencement of the war in the Peninsula, and I have had *every* reason to be satisfied with his conduct, in *every* situation in which he has been placed.'*

Let the reader mark the two *everys* employed by one who weighed his words; and was not Barrosa one of the situations in which the subject of this Memoir had been placed?

A month later the Premier, Mr. Perceval, thanked Mr. Davis for a copy of General Whittingham's translation of Dundas's Cavalry Tactics, and expressed the 'most sanguine hopes of the benefit the Spanish cause will derive from his being entrusted with the formation of a considerable body of their army.'

But the following letter must have given General Whittingham greater pleasure than all the other acknowledgements he received of the copies of his military Spanish publication:—

H.R.H. the Duke of Kent to R. H. Davis, Esq. M.P.

'Kensington Palace, 16*th April*, 1811.

'The Duke of Kent does himself the honour of acknowledging Mr. Hart Davis's polite note of yesterday, enclosing a copy of General Whittingham's translation of Dundas's Cavalry Tactics into Spanish; and the Duke begs to assure Mr. Davis that he values most highly the General's attention, as well as the very handsome manner in which Mr. Davis has become the instrument of imparting it.

* This letter will appear in its proper place.

'*The Duke cannot resist, upon this opportunity, paying what he considers a* JUST *tribute to the merits of General Whittingham, by observing that he views him as a high ornament to the British service, and a most efficient aid in the prosecution of the Spanish cause.*'[*]

'Hart Davis, Esq.'

At this time, as the 'Wellington Dispatches' testify, General Castaños, who had been appointed a member of the Regency, as well as Commander-in-chief, was fast gaining the confidence and friendship of Lord Wellington, to the great delight of his former aide-de-camp, who was now starting to undertake the very difficult task of raising and organizing a large Spanish division, with at first one only other British officer to assist him, and to the very last obtaining little aid from any but Spanish officers trained by himself.

[*] The Editor deems such spontaneous praise from the excellent father of Her gracious Majesty, worthy of being placed in *italics*.

CHAPTER VII.

1811—*continued.*

GENERAL WHITTINGHAM'S ARDUOUS TASK AT MAJORCA — FINANCIAL DUTIES—A PUNCTILIOUS GOVERNOR—LANDS AT PALMA—FRENCH AND GERMAN PRISONERS—GENERAL DON GREGORIO CUESTA AGAIN—LETTER TO COLONEL TORRENS—LETTER TO RIGHT HON. HENRY WELLESLEY—TREATISE ON MAJORCA—LETTER TO HON. CAPTAIN BLACKWOOD, R.N.—LETTER TO ADMIRAL PELLEW—COLONEL TORRENS'S OPINION OF WHITTINGHAM—LETTER TO COLONEL TORRENS—PROMOTION TO LIEUT.-COLONEL IN BRITISH ARMY—LETTER TO MR. DAVIS—CAPTAIN BRIARLY'S MISSION TO CADIZ—OFFICIAL DELAYS—GENERAL WHITTINGHAM DESIRED AS GOVERNOR—SOLICITATIONS FROM ENGLISHMEN—SPANISH JEALOUSIES AND INTRIGUES—A NEARLY EXHAUSTED PATIENCE—GENERAL CUESTA'S ENMITY AND INSULTS—GENERAL CUESTA'S DEATH.

THE arduous task undertaken by General Whittingham—to raise, organize, pay, clothe, feed, drill, and instruct a large division of Spanish troops in Majorca, is now partly represented by a large manuscript folio volume, containing the written copies of the correspondence which such an Herculean task necessarily occasioned. The word *partly* is used advisedly, as much of his personal active military exertions were never represented on paper. His financial duties especially weighed on his mind; no English paymaster having been appointed to assist him, whilst in the Spanish paymasters he could not feel complete confidence. Colonel Patrick Campbell, indeed, of the Majorca division, acted voluntarily as his deputy paymaster; but the entire responsibility rested with himself, and became the greatest, as it was the most unjustifiable, of the burdens he had to bear in the island.

The chief advantage of having a deputy arose from the

fact that the actual money did not pass through the General's hands, though disbursed by his orders; and this arrangement, without lessening the legal, of course diminished his moral responsibility; which rested chiefly with Colonel Campbell, who had charge of the monies.

It is of course but a small fraction of his voluminous Majorcan correspondence, that will now be laid before the reader; but sufficient to show the nature and extent of his task.

The Right Hon. Henry Wellesley to Major-General Whittingham.

'CADIZ, 8*th June*, 1811.

'Sir,—Upon your arrival at Gibraltar, you are to consider this letter as sufficient authority for you to draw from that place, on His Majesty's Treasury in London, for one hundred and fifty thousand dollars.

'I am, with much respect, Sir, your most obedient and humble servant,

'HENRY WELLESLEY.'

On June 13th, 1811, General Whittingham landed at Gibraltar. When three years earlier he had first landed on the rock, as Captain Whittingham, kind and courteously had he been received by Sir Hew Dalrymple. This time it was different. The pompous Governor was difficult of access, and the new arrival was anxious to arrange without loss of time, the cashing of his Treasury order, and to proceed on his mission to Majorca. He, therefore, armed with the above-mentioned authority, proceeded to negotiate with the merchants of Gibraltar; Mr. Wellesley not having authorised him to consult anyone whatever, and having limited his powers as to rate of exchange, so that the utmost secrecy was necessary, in order to raise the money on the required terms. But the

Governor discovering the negotiations, and more mindful of his own dignity than of the efficiency of the public service, flew into a violent passion, and commencing a most harsh correspondence with the unintentional offender, ended by ordering him to proceed 'on his mission with the least possible delay.' The matter was reported on both sides to their respective superiors, and entailed plenty of correspondence; but apparently the various departments concerned never came to any positive understanding on the matter. At all events it does not appear that it was ever satisfactorily settled. General Whittingham, however, effected his business in a few days. Before leaving Gibraltar he wrote to Mr. Wellesley and to Marquis Wellesley; to the former, a justification of his conduct, as his official superior, to the latter an account of the affair as to his friend and protector, and to his brother-in-law he of course explained everything. Assuredly this dispute was forced upon him, without any fault of his own; as he was denied all opportunity for amicable explanation. The details of his financial proceedings at Gibraltar are recorded with the accuracy of a counting-house. He succeeded so well that Government made a better bargain than could have been made at Cadiz, all which he explained to Mr. Wellesley for the information of the Treasury.

On the 28th June, he landed at Palma in Majorca, where he immediately hired a house for his stores, and commenced disembarking the clothing and arms which had arrived for the use of the army of reserve about to be raised in the island; of all which proceedings Mr. Wellesley and Admiral Sir Charles Cotton were duly informed in clear and ample details. Long letters follow on the statistical state of the island and of its intricate politics, and regarding the French leanings of some of the inhabitants.

A serious danger was the number of French prisoners

in the Balearic Islands, whom, especially the officers, it was difficult to keep from intriguing with the inhabitants, on whose loyalty the retreat of Lord Wellington to Portugal had had a bad effect. Many of the first families in Majorca were more than suspected of conspiring with the French officers on parole with a view to a revolution in the interest of Napoleon. In communicating these and other facts to Admiral Sir Edward Pellew, Bart.,* on the 14th July, 1811, General Whittingham adds, amongst his postscripts, this curious sentence : ' I should think it would be highly advisable to remove the French officers, at least, from this place to Mahon for the present, and that without losing a moment's time. My information comes from the Church, *through means which they alone possess*, and therefore cannot be doubted.'

Amongst the prisoners were some Germans, who had only reluctantly served with the French, and these after some correspondence, General Whittingham was allowed to enlist into his Majorca division ; and they were found to be a valuable acquisition.

On the 13th July he reported his arrival and proceedings to Marquis Wellesley, who it appears had used his influence with Ministers in England to cause the adoption of General Whittingham's plans of raising troops in Majorca. With the Spanish authorities he corresponded in their own language, as his Majorca letter-book testifies.

But of all his worries and misfortunes in Majorca (and their name was legion) the greatest was undoubtedly the fact that Don Gregorio Cuesta (the man whose stupid obstinacy, dislike of the English, and utter incompetency, General Whittingham had exposed and denounced to Mr. Hookham Frere, before the arrival in Spain of Sir Arthur Wellesley) was at this time, Captain-General of the Balearic Islands, with full and unlimited powers!

* Afterwards the celebrated Viscount Exmouth.

Now that he could no longer worry the hero of the age he vented his malice on the British officer now serving as a Major-General in the province he commanded as Captain-General. It is very probable, also, that he was not wholly unaware of how the friend of Alburquerque had formerly thought, spoken, and written of Cuesta's jealousies and incapacity, and that he was glad of an opportunity of revenging himself. But of Cuesta more hereafter.

Major-General Whittingham to Colonel Torrens.*

'PALMA, 5th July, 1811.

'My dear Torrens,—I hasten to inform you of my arrival here, and to assure you that I shall lose no opportunity of giving you an exact account of everything that occurs, and particularly relative to this army of reserve. In the meantime I must inform you that your friend, Captain Clarke, having gone as a volunteer with General Blake to Estremadura, it was not in my power to take him with me when I left Cadiz; but I sent him a message by Lord William Russell,† desiring him to join me as soon as possible, and offering him a troop of Hussars. . . .

'The unfortunate loss of Tarragona has deprived me of 200 Catalans, who were upon the point of being sent here; but the number will be easily made up in Valencia and Murcia. I am extremely anxious to organize a few battalions, as the force at present on the island is so very small that we cannot by any means be considered in a state of security. We have in the island of Cabrera, 4,000 prisoners; a considerable part of them Germans from Westphalia and Hesse Cassel, and consequently good soldiers, and not attached to French principles. If I had

---

* Military Secretary to H.R.H. the Duke of York, afterwards Sir Henry Torrens, who died as Adjutant-General at the Horse-Guards in 1828.

† Elder brother of Earl Russell, afterwards Major-General, and in 1836 Envoy at Berlin.

the power of selecting, I could get some excellent recruits. There are also eighty officers prisoners, belonging to these men in this island, and it certainly would be very much for the good of the service that they should be removed elsewhere without loss of time, as they are daily forming to themselves an interest with the inhabitants.

'I remain, &c.,
'SAMFORD WHITTINGHAM.'

Major-General Whittingham to the Right Hon. Henry Wellesley.

(Extract.)

'PALMA, 1st *August*, 1811.

'I have the honour to enclose a copy of my letter of this day's date to Mr. Bardaxi,* being also a copy of that which I have written to the Minister of War, relative to certain points of service, which if they are not finally and satisfactorily settled, must lead to the most unpleasant disputes between myself and General Cuesta. You will have the goodness to observe that I rest my argument upon the Spanish *ordenanza*, which provide, that whenever a reunion of troops be ordered in any province of the monarchy, and a General appointed to command them, all military command of these troops is vested in him, and the Captain-General of the province has only to direct with regard to the civil jurisdiction, destination of quarters, &c.

'I have already experienced a sufficient degree of opposition from General Cuesta to alarm me at least for the future; and I am, therefore, extremely anxious, that by a complete and total separation of command, every possible disagreement should be avoided. . . .

'The conscription and war contribution may meet with

* A member of the Junta, well-disposed to the English. The enclosures are all in Spanish, in which language he carried on his correspondence with all the Spanish authorities ever since his arrival in the country, as he wrote and spoke it as fluently as English.

those obstacles which originate in intrigue; but I am satisfied that they may, as far as concerns the people, be carried into effect without difficulty or danger.

'I beg to call your attention in the most earnest manner to the settling of the points of service mentioned in the enclosed letter; as I am convinced that there can be no other way of avoiding disputes which must inevitably in the end ruin the plan altogether.'——

To prove what difficulties General Whittingham had to contend with in his dealings with General Cuesta, Lord Wellington's remark to Mr. Wellesley in his dispatch of the 29th August, 1811, is worthy of record; viz. 'I am quite convinced that the majority of the officers of the Spanish army would prefer submitting to the French, to allowing us to have anything to say to their troops.'*

On the 23rd August, 1811, General Whittingham dispatched a letter, containing four foolscap pages, to Mr. Wellesley; sending on the same day a similar letter to Marquis Wellesley in London, and a copy besides to his brother-in-law. It was a brief treatise on the Island of Majorca, under three distinct points of view. *First*, as to its intrinsic value. *Secondly*, as to the security it affords Port Mahon. *Thirdly*, as to the best means of deriving from it every advantage, with the least possible expense. At that time, as we have seen, Lord Wellington attached great importance to the possession of the Balearic Islands. But the interest of this subject having wholly passed away, it is unnecessary to make any extracts from this document.

On the 20th September, in a friendly letter to the naval officer then at Palma, the Honourable Captain Blackwood, he rejoices at the departure of the French prisoners, whose presence and machinations had given him so much trouble; adding, 'The friends of the good cause hold up their heads

* *Wellington Dispatches*, vol. viii. p. 244.

and begin to fancy themselves out of danger; and, on the other hand, the French party are become circumspect and silent.' After alluding to some consular intrigues, he adds: 'I am sorry to inform you that the Captain-General [Cuesta] has taken possession, for his own riding, of the horse which I intended for you. I am not surprised, though the enemy was, at your having taken up an anchorage at Hare's Bay. Sir Edward [Pellew]'s character is too well known to allow of a supposition that he would leave anything undone which could be done.' . . .

On the 20th September he writes to Admiral Sir Edward Pellew, amongst other matters, as follows: 'I cannot help expressing how much service it would be rendering the division, if you could possibly allow the "*Guadalope*," or any other small vessel, to go to Oran, to take the money for the purchase of the barley, and to bring the vessel loaded with that grain.* The Junta superior of this island has positively refused to provide me either with barley or straw. And, although I conceive that their conduct will not be sanctioned by the Regency, yet, as it is impossible to wait in these cases for distant decision, I have directed a person of confidence at Oran to buy, for the use of this army, 7,000 fanegas of barley. But I am totally without the means of bringing barley here, or of sending him the money which he must have advanced for the purpose. I enclose a fresh return of the force under my command, which you will see is gradually increasing.'

It is quite impossible to give in this work an adequate idea of the labours and difficulties which General Whittingham had to contend with in Majorca. Their contemplation fills the Editor's mind with astonishment, that such a burden of responsibility, care, labour, and ceaseless annoyance, should have been not only endured with temper and patience, but carried out to a triumphant con-

* Thus he acted as the commissary, as well as the paymaster of the division which he had to *raise, organize, discipline, instruct, and command.*

clusion, by an almost solitary Englishman in the midst of half-civilized Spaniards.

Colonel Torrens, Military Secretary, to Mr. Davis.*

(Extract.)

'Horse-Guards, 22*nd September*, 1811.

'My dear Davis,—I return you the interesting papers enclosed to me in your letter of the 20th instant; and I am most thankful to you for the perusal of them.' [After alluding to the interesting command now held by Whittingham, he adds], 'He will have many difficulties to encounter; but I know no person so well calculated to overcome them.'——

On the 1st October, General Whittingham wrote a long letter to Lieutenant-Colonel Torrens, detailing his proceedings in the raising and organization of his Division; a few extracts from which may be interesting:—

'I expect, in a short time, 300 horses from the coast of Africa. The requisition in this island will give me at least 200 more; and the officer employed on that service in Sardinia, informs me that he can purchase for me on this island from 600 to 700 more, as soon as I furnish him with the pecuniary means. So that, as to mounting my two regiments of cavalry, I am under no alarm, and you may be assured that they shall not be wanting as to discipline. Still, however, there is always a shade of doubt upon my mind; inasmuch as they will be wholly composed of new levies, and, consequently, at first they must be incapable of comprehending the full extent of their own powers. Even the oldest and best of the Spanish troops never fight [by themselves] as they do in the presence of the British. How much stronger, therefore, must

---

* This letter is written on the back of the docket enclosing the returned papers.

this necessity be, when the troops in question have never been under fire!' The concluding sentence of this letter refers to a most gallant Irishman, doomed to an early but glorious death. 'If it be possible, I should much wish that Captain O'Reilly, of the 13th Foot, should be sent to me with leave to serve in the Spanish army, I knew him well at [High] Wycombe, and he would be particularly useful to me in the Quarter-master-General's Department.'

On the same day (the 1st October) General Whittingham describes to his brother-in-law, his joy at the news of his promotion to Lieutenant-Colonel, which had evidently taken place only in August; but was afterwards back-dated to 30th May, 1811.

On the 7th October, General Whittingham writes to Mr. Davis a long letter regarding the struggles carried on in Majorca, between the patriotic party, anxious in order to further the organization of the Division of troops, to increase General Whittingham's powers, by causing him to be made Governor of Majorca; and the opposite faction, which from jealousy of the Englishman, and from love of intrigue, violently opposed the project. To his brother-in-law the General writes:—' In respect to the Government of Majorca, it is to me a matter of perfect indifference, although the person actually holding that employment is certainly a very improper man [to hold it], from his too well-known attachment to French principles. But I should wish to be acquainted with the sentiments of His Majesty's Ministers on that head, in case General Valdes, who is now appointed Captain-General of the Balearic Islands*, instead of Cuesta, should press the employment upon me.'

Enclosed in this letter to Mr. Davis was a copy of the Report of a certain very intelligent Captain of the Spanish

* Either this was a false report, or the appointment was afterwards cancelled.

Royal Navy, who had been sent by General Whittingham, on a special mission, to Cadiz, to defend his interest and the good of the cause, with Mr. Wellesley and the Spanish Junta. As a graphic description of some of the difficulties in the way of carrying out the Majorca scheme, and also as a picture of Spanish intrigue, it may amuse some readers, and is therefore inserted here :—

'*Remarks and Occurrences, in a Voyage from Majorca to Cadiz and back, by A. Briarly, Captain Spanish Navy, 1811.*'

(Extract.)

' General Whittingham observed to me on the 22nd July, that a foul plot or conspiracy has been entered into by a French party in this island, for the purpose of giving it up to the French ; and that they were in communication with the French officers, [who were] prisoners in the Castle of Belver. He at the same time urged the necessity of my going to Cadiz with the dispatches; as the Junta had applied to him for an officer of confidence. He also observed that there were many things of great consequence, necessary for the use of his Division, which I could at the same time apply for. I consented to go ; but there was no vessel of any kind except a schooner of eight guns, which had been taken [whilst] smuggling a cargo of tobacco. This vessel lay empty at the Quay ; and was offered to me, provided that I would man and victual her ; as they were not able. This I consented to do ; and on the morning of the 27th July I sailed from Palma with thirty-six seamen on board.

' I arrived at Cadiz, on the 7th August, and immediately waited upon the Regency with my dispatches ; next upon the Secretary of War, Heredia ; and, finally upon the British Minister, Mr. Wellesley, who promised me that he would do everything in his power to have me dispatched as soon as possible; and that he would see about having the prisoners removed from Cabrera, and, at all events, the officers from the island of Majorca immediately.

'The Secretary of State [for War] assured me that he would do everything in his power for the safety of the island; and that all General Whittingham's wants should be paid attention to immediately. At the end of the first week, however, I found that the only thing done to forward me was the taking the schooner from me, in consequence of a requisition made by the British Admiral and [the British] Minister.

'I found that the promises, which I had obtained from every part of the Government, were nothing more than words of course. For at the end of August, although I had not missed a single day without paying a visit to every one of the Ministers upon the subject of my dispatches, I was just where I started. The Bishop of Majorca, Llaneres, and the two deputies in the Cortes for the island, exerted themselves as much as possible also, and were it not for their interference nothing would have been accomplished.

'Mr. Wellesley observed to me, that General Whittingham must not purchase provisions of any kind with the money given to him; as when that should be expended he would not give him any more. He also desired me to tell General Whittingham, that he was not to interfere, in any way whatever, with the Government of the island, nor in any of their political discussions; that he was solely to organize his division; and not to have anything, directly or indirectly, to do with anything that did not concern it. This last observation was stated, no doubt, in consequence of the dispatches of the Cortes for the island having insisted on both the Captain-General [of the Balearic Islands], and the Governor of Palma being re-

moved; and the Bishop of Majorca and the others*
wishing to put in Admiral Valdes as Captain-General;
and I am sure that it was, and is their intention still, to
have General Whittingham appointed Governor of
Palma.† And there can be little doubt of their succeeding in their wishes, when they have got Valdes appointed
Captain-General.‡

'On the 2nd September I called upon the British Vice
Consul, Mr. Archdeacon, to inquire if any of the transports loaded with clothing for General Whittingham had
[arrived], or were likely to arrive. On looking over his
books he told me, that there was a transport the
"*Wellington*," loaded with clothing for the General,
which had arrived and been in Cadiz for two months: and
that Mr. Wellesley had been informed of it on that
vessel's arrival. I went and told Mr. Wellesley, and he
observed that I might take her up to Majorca if I would
get a convoy for her. I applied to the agent of transports,
who wrote to the Admiral, he being out cruising off the
Gulf of Gibraltar; and finally on the 10th [September] a
convoy was appointed.' Captain Briarly arrived in Palma
with his supplies on the 28th September, to the great joy
of his General, as may be well supposed.

General Whittingham was often applied to by half-pay
British officers, and even by civilians, who wanted commissions in some regiment of his division. Some of them
came out strongly recommended. But as he had only a
few posts reserved for Englishmen (for fear of giving
great and impolitic offence to the Spaniards), so he was
generally compelled to decline such applications; and
thus unintentionally to multiply his enemies, and to aug-

---

* The two deputies from Majorca.

† He means of Majorca, of which Palma is the capital.

‡ Valdes never was appointed Captain-General, and so the well-meant
scheme of the good Bishop and of the patriotic island deputies to increase
the powers of the English General, and thereby facilitate the formation of
the division, was frustrated.

ment the feelings of jealousy to which his high position in the Spanish army often exposed him. But he kept his temper, and continued with patient perseverance to fulfil his onerous duties to the best of his power and judgment.

On the 29th of October, 1811, General Whittingham pointed out to Mr. Wellesley in a long dispatch the breach of faith on the part of the Junta, and especially of the war minister, in regard to the stipulations originally made as to the recruiting and organization of the Majorca division; one sentence in which is interesting, from certain circumstances which eventually caused the interference of Lord Wellington himself. 'By the enclosed copy of a letter from General Valcarcel of the 24th September, you will see an attempt made to take the inspection, and consequently the proposal of officers out of my hands. For if all my *propuestas** are to be submitted to the opinion of the Inspectors in Cadiz, it is a perfect joke to decorate me with the title of Inspector-General of this division.'

The jealousy of General Whittingham imbibed by some of the Spanish ministers, vented itself in various annoying ways, on which there is no space to dwell.

No wonder that at last, the patience which Mr. Wellesley had admired, when displayed in the lighter work at Isla de Leon, was nearly exhausted by the heavy burden at Majorca, and that to his brother-in-law he began to display his half-formed wish to retire from the Spanish service.

On the 2nd November, after passing nearly five months on the Island, he pours out all his feelings on the conduct of those ' whose dearest interest it should be to protect the formation of a division, which might lay the foundation of the salvation of the Spanish monarchy; but which, at all events must ensure the safety of the Balearic Islands.

---

* Proposals or recommendations for promotions and appointments.

The Minister of War is at the head of the whole intrigue;* and not a day passes without orders being given directly contrary to the basis of the agreement between Mr. Wellesley and the Spanish Government; and tending only to a repetition of insults to induce me to throw up the command, and leave the island.

'Had I only to do with the Spanish Government, I should not have hesitated a moment; but I am now held by other ties to me ten thousand times more strong. I am compromised with the British Government, and therefore whatever may happen, I shall not take a single step without its being first sanctioned by its approbation.'

On the 10th, 11th, and 12th November, three more letters, long and full, are dispatched to Mr. Wellesley, exposing the conduct of the Spanish authorities and the defenceless state in which they had left Majorca and the injurious treatment which he had met at their hands. The letter of the 12th commences thus: 'Every day brings fresh proofs of the decided enmity borne by General Cuesta to everything English, and of his particular hostility to me.' The letter continues:

'Conceiving it of importance to forward my dispatches to you of the 11th and 10th of this month, by a safe conveyance, I sent an officer of my staff to General Cuesta's secretary's office to ask for a passport to Cadiz, for Lieutenant Niel Macdoudel of His Majesty's 75th Regiment of infantry. The reception which this officer met with is too scandalous to be related. The Captain-General made use of language to him, which ought only to be used by porters;—asked him who had constituted him the defender of Englishmen, and threatened him with punishment if he again interfered in such like commissions.

---

* This was the man who scrupled not officially to worry and insult Lord Wellington himself.

'Aware that this behaviour, on the part of the Captain-General could only proceed from a desire to irritate me, and, by throwing me off my guard, induce me to commit myself by some act of violence, I abstained from seeing him on the subject, and contented myself with sending him an official letter requesting a passport for a British officer to go to Gibraltar.

'The passport, which Lieutenant Macdoudel, who is nephew to Colonel Campbell, will have the honour to show you, was the answer. I beg leave once more to state, that my stay here cannot but lead to the worst consequences, unless the Captain-General be removed, and unless the independence of my command be fully and decidedly established.'

On the 13th and 25th November he again impresses on the Minister the state of his relations with the Spanish officials, and the difficulties he has to encounter in obtaining necessary supplies for men and horses. In that of the 25th, he reports on the enlisting of some Germans into his division: 'Baron Halberg, an Austrian officer in the service, was sent by me to Cabrera to choose out the Germans only, and not even to take Italians or Poles. He in consequence brought with him 133 men, all Germans, and who have since conducted themselves with the greatest propriety.'

In a letter dated 7th September, 1811, Mr. Wellesley writes: 'I am informed by M. de Bardaxi that the Junta has consented that your troops should be supplied with rations from the island; that the necessary buildings will be allotted for their accommodation, and that you are to be allowed to recruit from the German prisoners at Cabrera to the extent of 600 men.'

On the 20th December General Whittingham congratulates Mr. Wellesley upon his appointment, from simple minister and envoy, to the post of ambassador extraordinary, but accidentally omits entirely the title 'excellency' which was now Mr. Wellesley's due. One sentence in this letter, *without comment of any kind*, records a fact, which must nevertheless, have afforded unspeakable relief to the writer: 'I have only now to communicate the news of the death of the Captain-General Don Gregorio de la Cuesta.'

CHAPTER VIII.

1812.

LETTER TO SIR HENRY WELLESLEY—GENERAL WHITTINGHAM'S VISIT TO MINORCA—COLONEL SERRANO'S REPORT OF THE ALARM IN HIS ABSENCE—MILITARY COLLEGE ESTABLISHED BY GENERAL WHITTINGHAM—A GENEROUS AND LIBERAL SPANISH BISHOP—VOLUMINOUS DISPATCH TO MR. WELLESLEY—IMPORTANCE OF THE MAJORCA DIVISION—ITS NUMERICAL STRENGTH AT THIS TIME WEAK—SHOCKING STATE OF SPANISH OFFICERS IN PALMA—CONDITIONAL RESIGNATION OF COMMAND—MAJORCA DIVISION TO OPERATE ON EASTERN COAST UNDER LORD WILLIAM BENTINCK—LETTER TO SPANISH MILITARY INTENDANT—A JUSTIFIED ASSURANCE GIVEN TO THE ADMIRAL—URGENT REQUEST FOR A PAYMASTER—GENERAL WHITTINGHAM EMBARKS WITH HIS DIVISION—RESIGNS HIS COMMAND PROSPECTIVELY—IS FLATTERINGLY REQUESTED TO RELINQUISH HIS DESIGN—HIS GRATEFUL REPLY TO THE AMBASSADOR—SUCCESSFUL AFFAIRS OF POSTS—A MILITARY DIVERSION—THE PAYMASTER DIFFICULTY—A PROSPECT OF RELIEF.

ONE of the great disadvantages under which General Whittingham laboured was that the unpopularity of the Spaniards with the English army abroad, and with Englishmen at home, extended itself to the English officers employed in the Spanish service. The extra army rank of these agents, though for the most part only local and temporary yet, perhaps not unnaturally, excited the jealousy of the regimental officers. Lord Wellington, however, very early in the war, recorded his opinion that no officers more deserved their promotion than the British agents with the Spanish army; whose duties, indeed, were arduous and hazardous, and required much exertion and intelligence to perform them efficiently. Lord Wellington was not always satisfied with all of them, but all the readers of his dispatches knew that he recorded his complete satisfaction at the close of the war, with the conduct of General Whittingham, who, whilst only a Captain in the British army, had been addressed by his Lordship as a Spanish Major-General. Nevertheless the year 1811 had not on the whole been a fortunate one to the Major-General. But 1812 opened more cheerfully; the death of General Cuesta having removed one great enemy to the raising of the Majorca division under the command of an Englishman.

Major-General Whittingham to the Right Hon. Henry Wellesley.

(Extract.)

'PALMA, *6th January*, 1812.

'Enclosed I have the honour to send you a return of the force under my command, by which you will see its gradual increase. The state of discipline of this small corps is so far advanced, that they manœuvre in line without difficulty, and the interior of regiments will bear the minutest inspection.

'I beg leave to submit to your better judgment the good effect that would be produced by the naming Brigadier Marquis de Vivot my second in command. He was wounded in Catalonia, but he is now well enough to mount on horseback. The Marquis is the head of the nobility of this island, has very considerable estates here, and is particularly attached to the English. It is at his express desire that I take the liberty of soliciting this favour.'*——

About the 24th of January General Whittingham embarked for Minorca on some military business, returning to Palma in fifteen days. The following is the translation

---

* Mr. Wellesley's answer is not extant, but there can be little doubt that the request here made was complied with.

of an official letter written to him by his Chief of the Staff during his absence.* It proves how necessary to the peace and security of Majorca was the presence of the energetic English commander:—

Colonel Francisco Serrano to Major-General Whittingham.

'PALMA, 6th February, 1812.

'General,—From circumstances, which have occurred here during the thirteen days of your absence, I am very anxious for your return; and have determined to dispatch Captain Dominguez to you with this letter, giving a detail of the events most deserving your attention.

'Shortly after your departure reports were circulated of a rising and assembling of the people; and some attempts were made to seduce the soldiers of the division, who immediately communicated the fact to their officers; and from other circumstances that occurred, I conceived it prudent to assemble the commanding officers. I issued out ammunition; secretly reinforced the guards; and pointed out their alarm-posts to the different corps, in such a manner that, at the least commotion, they should assemble and occupy the most important posts, to support the public authorities, and to quell any tumult which might arise.

'I conceived it prudent to take these necessary measures of precaution, as the alarm had been very general, and had extended itself to all the constituted authorities. The commanding officers of corps have behaved as you could wish, and may be fully depended upon in case of need.

'I have, &c.,
'FRANCISCO SERRANO.'

* It appears that the letter was written only two days before the return of the General from Minorca, and was probably delivered to him on landing.

The following letter speaks for itself:—

To Vice-Admiral Sir Edward Pellew, Bart.

'PALMA, 14*th February*, 1812.

'Sir,—I have the honour to enclose the prospectus and regulations of a college for the officers and cadets of the division under my command, which I have established in this town.

'From the entire neglect of education in Spain, during the last twenty years, and more particularly since the Revolution, most of the young men commencing their military careers as cadets scarcely know how to read and write. The expense of the establishment at the present moment would have been a serious objection, had it not been done away with by the zeal and patriotism of various individuals.

'The Bishop of Majorca [Llaneres]—independently of a donation of 20,000 reals vellon*—has given up a house for the academy. The masters have all undertaken their employments gratis; and as the officers and cadets all belong to the division, I have the satisfaction of seeing my ideas realized, without the smallest expense, either to the British or Spanish Government.

'I have, &c.,

'SAMFORD WHITTINGHAM.'

Major-General Whittingham to the Right Hon. H. Wellesley.

(Extract.)

'PALMA, 18*th February*, 1812.

'Sir,—I have the honour to inform you of the arrival of Colonel Campbell on the 8th instant, and beg leave to offer you my warmest thanks for your very zealous

---

* £200. So generous and liberal-minded a bishop in Spain was truly a wonderful phenomenon.

interference and support in obviating the many difficulties under which I have hitherto laboured; the result of which will, I feel assured, prove highly beneficial to this division.

"I beg leave to enclose for your information the following papers :—

' No. 1. The translation of my exposition to the Junta; which I felt myself imperiously called upon to make, from the critical position this island is placed in, owing to the late success of the enemy on the opposite coast.

" No. 2. My letter to the Admiral.

" No. 3. Copy of a letter to me from the Chief of my Staff during my absence.

" No. 4. General return of the strength of the division.*

" No. 5. Translation of my observations on Puerto Pi, a small port in the Bay of Palma; and the advantages which might be derived from employing the French prisoners in its enlargement."

' I found it necessary to go to Minorca, for the purpose of personal communication with the Admiral, relative to the prisoners here, and other important points, and my absence was prolonged by contrary winds to fifteen days.

" The Admiral was pleased to express his unqualified approbation and concurrence in the proposed system of pontoons; and offered to fit them out, and equip them completely, and to send a frigate and brig to guard them. He also expressed his earnest desire that I should establish the telegraphs as soon as possible.

' The excellent disposition and the zealous support which I have experienced from the [*acting*] Captain General Gregory will make me regret the loss of one

---

* No copy of this return has reached the Editor's hands.

so every way qualified for this important command; as he combines discernment and judgment with energy, and decision, and has given me his most decided support in everything relative to the division, and, as you will see, by No. 3, we require here one of his firm and determined character.

'A levy of all the idle strangers takes place to-morrow; and the *Alistamento Generale* immediately follows. The volunteers of Colonel Campbell's battalion, not having presented themselves within the period allotted, the privilege of limited service is done away with, and no exceptions are to be permitted in the conscription.

'On referring to No. 3, you will perceive that the disaffected party here were in movement during my absence; tampering with the troops, posting placards, &c. But their attempts were rendered abortive by the excellent disposition of the officers, whose conduct it is impossible to praise more forcibly, than by stating that they obeyed the orders of the Chief of my Staff, (although there were several of superior rank) with the same zeal and promptitude as though I had been present. The same excellent dispositions were manifested by the soldiers of the division.

'I must beg leave to call to your attention our financial necessities, and to submit to your better judgment the importance of the Balearic Islands, whose safety, at this critical moment, may be confidently said to depend on the existence of this division, the resources of which must entirely depend on your countenance and support.

'Convinced that nothing is so much wanting among Spanish officers as the means of the acquiring military information—and satisfied of the necessity of giving to the cadets a military education,—I have established a college here on the basis of the enclosed prospectus.

It was opened yesterday, in the presence of the Captain General, several Bishops, and all the principal officers and people of rank in the Island.

'It is not a trifling consideration, at the present moment, to be able to say that the establishment will be of no expense. The generosity of the Bishop has furnished us with a house, and 20,000 rs. vn. to purchase books, &c., and as all the masters attend gratis, and the officers and cadets belong to the division, no disbursement of any kind will be necessary.'———

The safety of the Balearic Islands was considered of great importance at that time by Lord Wellington; and General Whittingham was in constant correspondence with the Admiral and Ambassador, upon the defence of the Islands, and upon plans for future aggressions against the enemy on the main-land. These letters display a consummate military knowledge both in theory and in detail; but the extracts must here be limited to a few of the most interesting particulars.

To the Right Hon. H. Wellesley.

(Extract.)

'PALMA, 21st *February*, 1812.

'The force at present under my command is only 2,200 men;* but if I may judge from the firm measures adopted by General Gregory, this number will be more than doubled in less than two months: and nothing would give me so much pleasure as to be employed in any plan of attack which might merit Sir Edward [Pellew]'s approbation.

* Hitherto the comparatively slow growth of the division had been caused mainly by the hostilities of old General Cuesta, and by the jealousy of the Minister of War, and the neglect of provincial Juntas to fulfil their engagements.

'As the difficulties we have hitherto met with will probably cease now that a Regency is appointed, so every way deserving of the national confidence, and which appears so completely to merit your approbation, I have not the smallest doubt that a few months will enable me to repay the confidence with which you have honoured me, by efficient co-operation [on my part], with the Admiral in his plans of attack; at the same time that I may be able to answer for the safety of these valuable Islands.

'However, the finances of Majorca are in such confusion, as to make it wholly out of its power to meet the expense of paying the troops; and indeed, to such a state are they reduced that the officers of the 2nd and 3rd battalions of Cordova and Burgos are *literally begging charity; and a few days ago, one of them fainted away in the coffee-room from absolute want.** Foreseeing, as I must of necessity do, the situation in which I shall see myself, with the troops under my command, should my pecuniary resources entirely fail, I take the liberty of earnestly entreating you—not only as British Ambassador, but as a friend, to whose kindness I have been indebted for many favours,—that, should the British Government consider the existence of a division of 4,000 or 5,000 men in the Island of Majorca, as not necessary either for co-operation in the plans of attack of Admiral Sir Edward Pellew, or for the defence and security of the Balearic Islands,—and should therefore determine to lend it no further assistance —you will have the goodness to obtain an order to have all these troops sent immediately to any part of the continent that may be judged proper; and, at the same time to give in my resignation to the Spanish Government, in order that I may proceed without loss of time to join the

---

* In the original the words (judging by the book into which the letter was copied) do not appear to have been underlined, but the Editor deems them worthy of *italics*.

British army in Portugal. It will be the last time, my dear sir, that I shall be troublesome to you; but I do most earnestly beg and entreat, that you will add this favour to the very long list, and enable me to avoid the wretchedness of witnessing the misery of those we esteem, without [having] the power of applying any remedy.'——

In a letter from Lord Wellington to Sir Henry Wellesley, K.B., dated 'Badajoz, 11th April, 1812,' there occurs this sentence, 'Fourthly; that 3,000 men of General Roche's division at Alicante, and 3,000 men of General Whittingham's division at Majorca, should be prepared to be embarked early in June, in order to join and co-operate on the eastern coast, with the troops under Lord William Bentinck, which will come from Sicily.' In another letter from the same to the same, dated 17th May, Lord Wellington appears to have rightly estimated the future strength of the Majorca division, which (after the death of General Cuesta and the change of Regency in Spain) had already considerably augmented in numbers. 'There are other points for consideration,' (writes Lord Wellington), 'First; how many men is it expedient to leave in Majorca for the defence of the Island, of the 7,000 of which it is supposed General Whittingham's division will consist? Secondly, General Whittingham's division will have been newly raised, excepting 3,000 men. How many of the 7,000 men would it be expedient to leave behind, as being recruits and unfit for service?'

On that same date (and the day following) General Whittingham was corresponding with the Admiral and the Ambassador, on the details of the expedition, embarkation, &c.

He had also to correspond semi-officially with his father-in-law, who was military intendant of Majorca in the service of the King of Spain :—

Major-General Whittingham to Don Pedro Creus.

'PALMA, 18*th* May, 1812.

'My dear Sir,—The extreme distress in which I have found this island at my return from Cadiz, in spite of every effort of the Marquis of Compigny * to provide against the growing difficulties, makes me particularly anxious to call your attention to this important point, in the hopes that you will use your best endeavours with Sir Edward Pellew, to induce him to aid and assist us in our manifold wants.

'The Marquis is ready to give me 2,000 conscripts immediately, which will complete the division to 5,000 men. But as even for the existing force it is almost impossible to find bread, he will, I much fear, be induced to delay the levies of men till after the harvest, which would be too late to be of any service to the division. If it were possible for Sir Edward Pellew to furnish me with a sufficient quantity of flour to supply the rations of 5,000 men at one and a half pound of bread [per day] for one month, the harvest would be got in, and our difficulties would be at an end. But without this assistance I am too well convinced that I shall not be able to effect the organization of the proposed division as speedily as I would wish, and as the service I know will require.

'Should it be in Sir Edward's power to furnish us with the proposed supply, the 4,000 conscripts will be given me immediately; and the Marquis will give bills on the Spanish Government for the supply. Have the goodness to state the extreme necessity of our case to Sir Edward; and believe me to be, &c.,

'SAMFORD WHITTINGHAM.'

He wrote also direct to Sir Edward, on the same

---

* Now Captain-General of the Balearic Islands.

subject, and estimated the force he proposed to embark, including some expected troops from Alicante, at upwards of 4,200 men.

The following letter is worthy of record, for it contains a prophecy which was destined to be no idle or sanguine boast, but a fact established on undeniable testimonies :—

To Vice-Admiral Sir Edward Pellew, Bart.

'PALMA, 24*th May*, 1812.

' My dear Sir,—The extreme anxiety which I feel to get the division in a perfect state to meet your's and Lord William [Bentinck]'s wishes by the end of next month, makes me, I fear, very troublesome. But your well-known zeal for the service will plead my best excuse.

' For God's sake press Compigny not to lose a moment's time; and you may rest assured *that the troops of this small and gallant division will prove themselves worthy of fighting by the side of Englishmen.*

'I have, &c.,

'SAMFORD WHITTINGHAM.'

On the 28th May he sends to Sir Henry Wellesley his accounts of expenditure and receipts, and trusts that by the end of June his division will amount to 4,000 effective muskets, exclusive of cavalry and artillery; and he repeats the promise of their future effectiveness in the field in nearly the same words as he had lately addressed to the Admiral.

To the Right Hon. Sir H. Wellesley, K.B.

'PALMA, 20*th June*, 1812.

'Sir,—The division being now paid by the British Government, according to the existing agreement between the allied courts, I beg to submit to your Excellency's consideration the necessity of appointing a British paymaster-general, or other officer, who will be responsible for, and charged with the accounts of the division.

'Hitherto those accounts have been kept by persons appointed by the Spanish Government for that purpose; and I have taken the precaution to have them regularly examined, and made out in triplicates. But it is utterly impossible that in the midst of active duties, I can remain charged with such a weight of responsibility, and with accounts of so complicated a nature.

'I trust that you will perceive the necessity of calling the attention of His Majesty's Government to this important object; and that until a person so authorized can come from England, you will be pleased to send an officer of the Paymaster's department to take charge of the accounts of this division, which will be more satisfactory to your Excellency. Besides, should any accident happen to me, the presence of such a person would obviate every difficulty, which would otherwise arise. And I trust that your Excellency will pardon my pressing this subject, and urging the speedy departure of the person you may appoint, when you consider the very great responsibility attached to the families of persons entrusted with public monies.

'I have, &c.,
'SAMFORD WHITTINGHAM.'

On the 24th July, 1812, the Majorca division embarked at Palma: the infantry portion of which consisted of 159 officers, 3 chaplains, 8 surgeons and 4,180 non-commissioned officers and men.*

From, 'on board the "Romulus" at sea off Alicant' on the '8th August,' General Whittingham, amongst other

* Of the cavalry and artillery that embarked, no returns are extant.

matters, again urges the affair of the paymastership on Sir Henry Wellesley. What led him the day following to send in his resignation of his Spanish command can only be surmized, as Sir Henry's letter which induced the resignation is not forthcoming.

Major-General Whittingham to his Brother-in-law.

'MUCHAMIEL, 2nd *September*, 1812.

'By the enclosed letter for Colonel Gordon, you will see the state of the force which I brought with me; [of] that [which] I left at Palma, and Mahon; and the total strength of the division. The detail of our military operations is also enclosed.

'The troops under my command have conducted themselves with so much order and discipline, and have made their marches in so military a manner, that they have merited the approbation of everybody; and I have not the smallest doubt, that whenever we come into action, they will do themselves much honour. But unless things are put upon another footing, it is impossible for me to continue in this command.' [He then repeats his paymastership grievances and adds] 'I have repeatedly written to Sir Henry Wellesley requesting to have a paymaster of the division appointed, but without effect. And I have finally written to him to say that as soon as a general action will allow me to retire with credit, I shall give up the command of the division and return to England. I am sure that you will see the extreme necessity for taking a speedy determination.'——

However, Sir Henry Wellesley was in no hurry to accept of the resignation of such an officer:—

Sir Henry Wellesley, K.B. to Major-General Whittingham.

(Extract.)

'CADIZ, 6*th September*, 1812.

'I have the honour to acknowledge the receipt of your letter of the 9th August, which only reached me last night.

'I can hardly bring myself to believe that the contents of my letter of the 25th July can have given rise to the resolution which you have announced to me of resigning your present command. There was nothing in that letter which was intended to hurt your feelings, and if you will recollect that I am personally responsible for every shilling of public money placed at my disposal in the service of Spain, you cannot be surprised that I should have adverted to the expenses of your corps, and the necessity of confining these expenses within certain limits.

'If your resolution to resign was occasioned by the contents of my letter of the 27th July, I hope that this explanation will satisfy you that it was written in the mere performance of my duty, and that it was not intended in any way to reflect on you personally.

'I believe that I might venture to add, that from the moment of my arrival in Spain, I have given you all the assistance and support in my power, and I am sincerely disposed to continue them to you, as long as the means of doing so shall be entrusted to me. I cannot therefore but hope that you will be induced to relinquish your intention of resigning.'——

No doubt the fact of his being still left without the assistance of a paymaster had, in the confinement of a ship, preyed with additional force upon the mind of General Whittingham, and caused him to feel acutely those criticisms as to his official expenditure, to which all officers in command are liable. Perhaps also his anxious desire to provide for the comfort of his officers and men inclined him to greater liberality than governments are usually prepared to sanction.

On the 21st September General Whittingham writes a long and grateful letter to Captain General O'Donnell the hero of Catalonia, who had written to him a very complimentary epistle on the state of the Majorca division.

Major-General Whittingham to Sir Henry Wellesley.

(Extract.)

'MUCHAMIEL, 3rd October, 1812.

'Dear Sir,—I have the honour to acknowledge the receipt of your letter of the 6th September; and I beg leave to return you my most grateful thanks for this fresh proof of your kindness and attention. I should be the most ungrateful man alive were I even for a moment to forget the many and great favours which I have received at your hands; and it will ever be the first wish of my heart to acknowledge publicly and privately my sentiments of gratitude and respect towards you. It is quite sufficient for me to know that you wish me to continue in the command of this division, to do away with every idea of giving it up. But at the same time I wish with all respect to call to your mind the delicacy of my situation. The only thing that I ever had a dread of was to become a public accountant! As long, however, as the troops were in garrison I conceived, that by the greatest care and attention, and with the assistance of Colonel Campbell, I might have every account, with all the requisite receipts, arranged monthly, and thus be always in a state to meet examination. But now that the troops are in campaign, and that I am unavoidably exposed to lose my papers by any of the very many accidents that so often occur in war, I tremble at a responsibility that may not only ruin my own private fortune, but, what is infinitely worse, compromise my good name and place my honour in doubt in the public opinion. Allow me to say, my dear sir, with the freedom which your friendship entitles me to use, that you are not in the same situation. It is true that you are answerable for the public monies entrusted to your charge: but there can be no difficulty in showing the sums that you have entrusted to me; and for the expenditure I alone am answerable. I have ever been of opinion that it is not sufficient for a man to be most honourable in all the transactions of life, [but that] it is indispensable that he should never be stained by even the shadow of a doubt. Having said thus much, I shall forbear in future to return to this unpleasant subject.'

To his Brother-in-law.

'MUCHAMIEL, 20*th October*, 1812.

'The Majorca division has the honour of occupying all the outposts of the army. I am just returned from them, and avail myself of the opportunity of a vessel going to Cadiz to let you know what is going on. We have had since our arrival a great number of affairs of posts, in all of which my troops have been successful; and have in consequence begun to form a character which I hope and trust will soon be established. My force at present is rather more than 6,000 men; but I expect another battalion from Minorca in a few days, which will complete my force to 7,000 men.* I have besides two strong battalions in Majorca clothed and formed by me, which the Captain-General, Marquis de Compigny, has refused to send to me. But I have written to Sir Henry Wellesley

* He was only a Lieutenant-Colonel in the British service then, and in that capacity could not have expected a command of more than six or eight hundred men.

and the Spanish Government on the subject, and daily expect their positive order to bring them here.

'On the 18th, the French of the army of Suchet fell back from Sax, Villena, and Biar, upon Fuente la Higuera; and from Alcoy upon Concentayna, Albayda, and San Felipe. In consequence of this movement, my advanced posts are now at Sax, Biar, and Alcoy.

'If you should be able to procure me a good strong hunter, and send him out to me at Cadiz, or at Alicante, you would do me the greatest favour. I have several good horses, but not one of right good confidence for a long day's action. Hart would, I dare say, undertake the commission. I wish you both joy of your success. I have read Hart's maiden speech with delight.'——

Mr. R. H. Davis had just been returned for the first time as member for Bristol, and been succeeded at Colchester by his eldest son, whose very great abilities gave promise of a brilliant parliamentary career, which was too soon frustrated, by the state of his health compelling him to retire from parliament.

General Whittingham soon afterwards cancelled the commission for another horse, as finding the expenses of a General of Division were already beyond his means, both public and private.

To the Same.

'MUCHAMIEL, 18*th December*, 1812.

'I advanced a few days since with the whole of my division on Alcoy, to make a diversion in favour of General Elio, who was to have attacked Requena. His movement did not take place; and, after occupying Alcoy some days, I received orders to break up, and to reoccupy my former cantonments. My troops have in charge the whole of the outposts of the army.'

To the Same.

'MUCHAMIEL, 29*th December*, 1812.

' As Sir Henry Wellesley has not engaged to supply me for the present with more than 35,000 dollars monthly—which I understand he gives me out of the money at his disposal for the service of Spain—I much fear that nothing will be done in regard to the paymaster, unless the British Government should agree to take a certain number of battalions and regiments of cavalry into their pay; and this, I should suppose, they would not do without consulting Lord Wellington. I am not aware that Sir Henry has ever officially desired that a paymaster should be appointed to this division. I should think that he had not. But as far as I am concerned, I should prefer very much giving up the command altogether to the continuing a responsibility which sooner or later will in all probability reduce me to beggary! You well know the money I have spent in Spain.* . . . Thus, whilst others have been making fortunes, I have been spending more than I could afford, without any security that, at the winding-up of the peace, the complication of long and difficult accounts may not ruin my character and my fortune.'——

On the 30th December, he states that he had forwarded to Mr. Wellesley an application for the paymastership of the division from Captain Foley, and a prospect of relief from an unjust and intolerable burden closed the year 1812.

* Out of his private fortune he means, having got into debt, besides spending all his private income, in the country. He had afterwards to sell out some of his original capital.

CHAPTER IX.

1813.

LORD WELLINGTON'S INSTRUCTIONS—LORD WELLINGTON REFUSES THE INSPECTORSHIP TO GENERAL WHITTINGHAM—THE FRENCH ATTEMPT TO SURPRISE XIGONA—TREACHERY OF AN ITALIAN REGIMENT—COLONEL WALKER AND OFFICERS OF H.M.'S 58TH REGIMENT—LORD WELLINGTON GRANTS THE PREVIOUSLY REFUSED INSPECTORSHIP—HIS RELUCTANCE TO THE MEASURE—DIFFERENT STYLE ADOPTED TO ANOTHER AGENT—GALLANT CONDUCT OF THE SPANISH CAPTAIN RUTI—GENEROUS CONDUCT OF THE FRENCH CAPTORS—A SUCCESSFUL RUSE—A BRAVE SPANISH LIEUTENANT — THE FRENCH DRIVEN BY GENERAL WHITTINGHAM THROUGH THE PASS OF ALBAYDA—GENERAL MURRAY'S TWO GENERAL ORDERS—LORD WELLINGTON'S DISPATCH—GENERAL WHITTINGHAM'S REPORT TO THE AMBASSADOR — CONCENTAYNA COMBAT — SIR HENRY WELLESLEY'S CONGRATULATIONS—LORD WELLINGTON'S PROOF OF CONFIDENCE—THIRD GENERAL ORDER PRAISING WHITTINGHAM'S DIVISION—GENERAL WHITTINGHAM'S REPORT TO SIR JOHN MURRAY—BATTLE OF CASTALLA—SIR JOHN MURRAY'S DISPATCH TO LORD WELLINGTON—AT CASTALLA SPANIARDS RIVALLED THE BRITISH—ANECDOTE FROM THE 'RECOLLECTIONS.'

IN the 10th volume of the 'Wellington Dispatches' there is a long letter from Lord Wellington to Major-General Whittingham, dated Cadiz, 8th January, 1813. Amongst Sir Samford Whittingham's papers there was found a kind of condensed extract from this letter (probably made with the view of translating it for the benefit of the officers of his now considerable division) comprising all that he thought necessary to publish, and which will doubtless also be sufficient for the reader. Lord Wellington was a Spanish grandee,* and Commander-in-Chief at this time, of the Spanish, as well as of the British, army :—

---

* He had been created Duke of Ciudad Rodrigo.

Copy of the Order of His Excellency the Duke of Ciudad Rodrigo to General Whittingham, dated Cadiz, 8th January, 1813.

'The corps of troops under your command in the Peninsula is one of those which I am desirous should be paid out of the funds set apart by Great Britain for the support of the Spanish cause. The clothing, arms, and furniture of the corps under your orders being for the account of Great Britain, the said funds must by no means be applied to the liquidation of those charges. Nor must they be expended in provisions, hospitals, or means of transport, as these branches are to be provided for by the Spanish Government, in the same manner as for the other Spanish troops. The pay of absent officers and privates must likewise be for the account of the Spanish Government; for it is my intention that nothing be paid out of the said funds to any officer or private not appearing on the monthly returns to be in the actual discharge of his duty. The pay of the general and other officers and privates of your division present, and in the actual exercise of their duty, is all that should be supplied out of those funds.

'You will send on the 20th of every month to His Excellency Sir Henry Wellesley, an estimate of the money wanted for the payment of the officers and privates under your command for that month, on the principles before expressed; and on the receipt of the month's pay, whether the produce of bills or otherwise, you will distribute it in the proper proportions to the individuals entitled thereto, taking their receipts, which will be your discharge for the amount received. You will, however, adopt all necessary means to ensure the just application of these allowances to officers and privates, according to the regulations of the Spanish service.

'You will appoint Patrick Foley, Esq.,* to be Paymaster-General of your division. He will take the detail of this service under his direction and responsibility; and as all payments are to be made one month in arrear, you will take care that the money be distributed as soon as received, as beforesaid.

'I do not wish the division under your orders to exceed 6,000 effective men in the field. In order to keep up this, you must establish a depôt at Alicante; and I will take care that you shall receive the pay of 7,000 men, inclusively of such as are in hospital; for whom, as I said before, the Spanish Government must provide.'——

The appointment of Captain Foley was a truly great relief, for which General Whittingham felt grateful. But a few days later he received a letter from Lord Wellington which caused him much vexation, as threatening to nullify that independence of subordinate Spanish authorities, which from the incompetency of the latter, he considered to be indispensable to the efficiency of his division :—-

The Marquis of Wellington to Major-General Whittingham.

'FRENEDA, 19*th February*, 1813.

'Sir,—Sir Henry Wellesley has transmitted to me your letter of the 3rd January, in regard to your holding the office of inspector of the division of Spanish troops under your command, and to the abuses and inconveniences to which your troops would be liable in case your expectations in this respect were disappointed; and having conversed with the Chief of the staff, and with the Inspectors-General of cavalry and infantry on this

* It would appear that Captain Foley was no longer in the regular army, when he obtained his new appointment.

subject, I have been informed by each of those officers that it was particularly settled with you, that when the troops under your command should serve in the Peninsula,* they were to come under the control of the Inspector's office, and were to have [Deputy] Inspectors attached to them in the same manner as other [Spanish] troops.

'This being the case, it remains to be considered whether, adverting to the inconveniences to which you refer, it is proper I should now exempt the troops under your command from this control. Upon this point I have to observe, first, that I hope to be able to prevent the abuses of which you complain, as well as of others; secondly, that even if I should not succeed entirely, it is not worth while to enter into the disputes and complaints which a partial departure from a system long established in the Spanish army would occasion.

'I have therefore desired the Inspectors-General of infantry and cavalry to appoint Deputy-Inspectors for your division, and I beg you to submit to their control.'†

'I have the honour to be, &c.,
'WELLINGTON.

'Major-General Whittingham.'

This letter was a truly discouraging one to General Whittingham, but, as will be seen, it was soon rescinded.

To his Brother-in-law.

'SAN JUAN, 22nd *February*, 1813.

'Your truly amiable and excellent friend General Clinton remained only a very short time in command here. Major-General Campbell, Adjutant-General to the

---

* In Majorca he had had the full powers and offices of Inspector, both of cavalry and infantry, according to previous agreement.

† These orders were given by Lord Wellington, as Commander-in-Chief of the Spanish armies.

army in Sicily, arrived soon after him and being his senior, the command, of course, devolved upon him.

'In respect to the operations of the ensuing campaigns, in my humble opinion, Lord Wellington himself must open it before this army can do anything of consequence. I beg leave to call your attention to the judicious position taken up by Soult at Toledo, where he has his headquarters. He is in the centre of Lord Wellington's two lines of operations; and as his force is extended over La Mancha, he would, in case of our moving forward upon Valencia, be upon our left flank and rear before any assistance could be received from Lord Wellington! It is therefore my opinion that his Lordship must open the campaign himself, and, by drawing towards him the mass of the French force enable us to make a brilliant and decisive attack upon what remains.

'The French attempted a few nights since to surprise Xigona, which is one of our outposts. One of the Italian regiments raised by Lord William Bentinck in Sicily, and composed from deserters from all parts of the world, formed part of the garrison of Xigona. In the course of forty-eight hours upwards of 86 men from this regiment had passed over to the French; and Colonel Grant assured me that it was his opinion, and that of all his officers, that none of the men could be depended on; and that it was his and their opinion that if they were ordered to march to Alicante, the greater part of them would desert on the road. The last party [of deserters] had taken their officer with them; and had spared his life only in consequence of the intercession of one of the corporals.

'All circumstances considered, I determined to send off an orderly dragoon to General Campbell, requesting his instructions how to proceed. The general came in the course of the morning to Xigona, and directed me to disarm the regiment, and to send them as prisoners to

Alicante. The garrison of Xigona consisted of my battalion of grenadiers and of this Italian regiment. On the first alarm I had directed the battalion of Murcia to march to Xigona; and General Campbell had ordered the 1st battalion 27th [Regiment] to follow them, together with a squadron of the 20th Dragoons. About half-past five p.m. the British troops came up. The Italian regiment was marched into an open space, and disarmed without the smallest difficulty, and immediately afterwards marched off to Alicante, escorted by the 27th [Regiment], the squadron of dragoons, and my battalion of Murcia. On their arrival at Alicante they were all sent on board ship.

'I remained at Xigona with my battalion of grenadiers; and about eight p.m. the 1st battalion of the 58th [British Regiment] marched in by Palomos, by General Campbell's orders, to strengthen the post. The French (who were undoubtedly in concert with the Italians, but who knew nothing of what had passed) determined upon attacking Xigona that night; and at seven p.m. Generals Hubert and Gudin marched from Alcoy with 1,500 infantry and 150 cavalry.

'At half-past two a.m. the firing of the outposts began. The troops, both Spanish and English, were under arms with admirable celerity; and every disposition was taken to make it impossible for the enemy to force the post. Our outposts were after some time driven in, and the French descended to the ravine; which they could not, however, pass from the briskness of our fire. They then extended themselves by their left to endeavour to open a communication with the Italian barracks' [which they still believed to be occupied by their friends].

'Upon the first glimpse of day we crossed the ravine with the light companies; and, upon ascending the hill on the other side, we discovered the French columns more than half-way up the mountain, and their light troops covering their rear. They had probably discovered the change which had taken place in the troops, and in consequence [had] begun their retreat an hour before daylight, leaving only a few light troops on the borders of the ravine, being well assured that we should not quit the strong position we occupied to attack them till daylight should enable us to examine their force, and make our dispositions in consequence. I had the satisfaction of being told by Lieut.-Colonel [David] Walker and the officers of the 58th [Regiment] that he and they should be at all times most happy to serve under my orders, and that they were all satisfied and delighted with the dispositions that I had made that night.* We took six prisoners, and thus ended an affair which I should not have thought worth relating to you, but for the providential escape we all had, in consequence of having removed the battalion of Italians that day.† For, had the French been aided, as they expected, by these people, the battalion of grenadiers and I [myself] must have been sacrificed without the possibility of avoiding it. The worst of all would have been the moral effect which it would have produced in the country; where it would have been generally believed that a British battalion (for, being dressed in scarlet, they would have been supposed to be British) had fired upon the Spaniards and joined the

---

* What enhances this compliment is the fact that Col. Walker was considerably the senior in rank in the British service, and so continued.

† In the *Recollections*, it is said that 'Major Bourke, an Irish Austrian officer of twenty-five years' service,' commanded the first battalion of Italians in General Whittingham's division, and that 'his *tact and judgment* made him the glory and pride of his men.' The main cause on the other hand, of the infamous behaviour—as recorded in the text—of the 2nd battalion of Italians, was attributed to 'Grant's want of those qualities,' which 'induced him to adopt all the minute worry of the old British school, and made him cordially detested by all the men of his regiment.' Unfortunately the second regiment and not the first had garrisoned Xigona, on this occasion.

French. To do away such an impression would have been a work of time and difficulty.'——

How admirably the details of the Majorca division were carried on in active service is shown by eight documents in the Editor's possession. Of these Spanish returns, six are dated Concentayna, 31st August, and the other two dated 12th August, 1813. All appear to be monthly returns, and are made out with a neatness and precision that could not be exceeded by the orderly room of the smartest British regiment at the present day.

Colonel Serrano, General Whittingham's able and trusted chief of the staff, was dispatched to Freneda, with a packet of letters, to undertake the by no means easy task of persuading the victorious chief of the British and Spanish armies to rescind the order which he had given that the Majorca division was to submit to Spanish deputy-inspectors; and thus to transfer to these officers from the hands of General Whittingham not only the power of rewarding and censuring officers and men, but also of recommending them for promotion in, or appointments to, regiments both of cavalry and infantry.

The copy of the 'duplicate' original of Lord Wellington's reply is now before the Editor. It is written in a fair clerk's hand; and though an important letter (reversing a previous decision), is merely signed by Lord Wellington, though doubtless he either wrote out the original draft, or at least dictated every word of it:*—

* Some readers will consider this explanation unnecessary. But the writer has met with civilians of intelligence who have believed that all the correspondence Lord Wellington signed was sent in his own handwriting; a task which would have put to shame all the labours of Hercules!

The Marquis of Wellington to Major-General Whittingham.*

(Duplicate.)

'FRENADA, 1st March, 1813.

'Sir,—I have had the honour of receiving your several letters to the 1st February, by the Chief of the Staff of your division, who arrived here yesterday.

'In answer to your letter of the 26th January, I have to inform you that Captain Grey being employed on the eastern coast of Spain, on the service of the regiment to which he belongs, I cannot allow him to serve in the Spanish army.

'I have settled with the inspectors-general of cavalry and infantry, *that you shall be appointed the inspector of both arms in the division of troops under your command*; and you will carry out that duty according to the orders and regulations of the Spanish Government.

'I have settled with the inspectors of the cavalry to draft the Hussars of Aragon and the regiment of Cuença into the regiment of Almanza and Olivenza. This draft will make those regiments over complete in men; but you will dispose of the horses as you may think proper among the trained men of the regiment as already formed; and the others you will have trained either in Spain or Majorca, until I shall send orders for the disposal of them. —I have the honour to be, Sir,

'Your most obedient servant,
'WELLINGTON.

'Major-General Whittingham.'

Lord Wellington, who, as their Commander-in-Chief, naturally studied to please the Spaniards, gave the above consent most reluctantly, and afterwards refused permission to act on it as a precedent in the case of others, to Lord William Bentinck, on his Lordship's application for

---
* *Wellington Dispatches,* vol. x. p. 153.

that purpose. Could Lord Wellington have given a greater proof of the confidence and esteem which he entertained for General Whittingham?

The manner in which Lord Wellington yielded on this occasion, was the more remarkable from the impatience with which he received the suggestions and remonstrances of another British Agent, who was senior in rank to General Whittingham. To the officer in question he wrote a few days later as follows:—

'If you dislike your situation, or make any further difficulties about obeying the orders you receive, or fail to carry on the service, you must either resign your command, or in the latter case, I shall recommend to the Government that another officer may be appointed to it.'*

Sir Samford Whittingham's 'Recollections' contain a dramatic account of the surprise which the French attempted at Xigona. But there were some (though trifling) inaccuracies, chiefly of names of persons, which occasioned the preference which has been here given to the matter-of-fact letter, written at the period to his brother-in-law, over the more picturesque account written for the amusement of the General's nieces. But the gallant action of one of his own trained Spanish officers is now given from the 'Recollections,' in which alone it is recorded:—

'My head-quarters were at a place called Muchamiel, about three miles from Alicante. At Xigona I had a strong detachment: but the commander of the forces directed me to occupy Tibi, a village on the farther side of the mountain, and about ten miles in advance of Xigona. I obeyed much against my will. For Tibi was an insulated post, totally unconnected with my chain, and exposed to be attacked by two battalions of French

---

* Vol. x., page 184, of the *Wellington Dispatches.*

infantry at Onteniente on the right, and by 300 cavalry under the Baron de Lort on the left.*

'I selected for the command of this dangerous post, Captain Ruti, a young aide-de-camp of mine of great promise, to whom I was much attached; and I placed under his orders 200 infantry, and 50 hussars of his own regiment of Almanza. I went over the whole ground with Ruti; and pointed out to him the danger of his position, and the line of retreat that I wished him to follow, and the manner in which it should be conducted.

'Many nights had not elapsed when the infantry outposts were driven in by a very superior force. But the retreat was conducted with great order and regularity to the plaza of Tibi, where Ruti waited to receive them at the head of the troop of the Almanza Hussars. As had been previously arranged, the infantry then retired to the entrance of the pass in the mountains, which led to Xigona, where they halted and formed to cover the retreat of the cavalry through the defile.

'In the meantime Ruti had detached a subaltern and ten hussars on the road by which de Lort and his cavalry must come, with orders, on falling in with the enemy, to take ground to his left, to open a desultory fire to detain the movement, and to dispatch a trusty soldier to him (Ruti) at Tibi. The order was perfect: not so, the execution! The young subaltern in command of the party fell in with the enemy as expected, remembered to take ground to his left, but forgot everything else—for he sent no report to Ruti, and he never halted till he arrived at Tibi, several miles distant. Ruti, with the rest of his cavalry, forty hussars, remained formed in the Plaza till daylight; when despairing of receiving any report from his detachment, he determined upon commencing his re-

* Although on military grounds he considered the order unwise, yet he obeyed it without any expostulation. He always taught that the *first*, *second*, and *third* duty of a soldier was obedience!

treat upon his infantry. Scarcely, however, had he cleared the village when he saw, drawn up across the only road he could take, four lines of the 24th French dragoons, to intercept his retreat upon Xigona.

'Ruti was a second *Chevalier Bayard*.* He saw the extent of his danger, but he felt how greatly his honour would be compromised by suffering his post to be surprised, when he had been especially selected by the General, as peculiarly trustworthy. He did not hesitate, but, briefly addressing his men, told them of his determination to charge, and asked them whether they would dare to follow him. They all shouted *Santiago, y à ellos!* [the Spanish war cry, " St. James, and have at them "] and Ruti, at the head of his forty hussars, charged and broke through the first line of French dragoons with little or no loss. The second line was broken through in a similar manner, but with considerable loss; and in the charge against the third line, Ruti fell covered with wounds. His head was dreadfully cut up; and a sabre had passed through his body. Still the charge was continued; and ultimately eleven out of the party joined me at Xigona!

'The French were so enchanted at the daring bravery displayed by Ruti, that they carried him on a litter to Onteniente, the head-quarters of their commandant; procured for him the best medical aid; and when miraculously cured of his wounds they sent him to my head-quarters. I returned the compliment by restoring to liberty two of their [the French's] comrades, who were in my power. For this action Ruti was made a knight of the military order of San Fernando,† and shortly afterwards promoted to the rank of Brigadier of cavalry.'——

---

* That is, '*sans peur et sans reproche*,' the very words applied to Sir Samford Whittingham himself by an able reviewer.

† This order consisted of Knights; Knights-Commanders; and Knights-Grand-Cross.

The affair of Concentayna will next be given from the 'Recollections':—

'Not long after this splendid skirmish, a general advance took place; and my head-quarters were stationed at Alcoy. Sir John Murray had now taken the command of the army at Alicante; and a general reconnoissance to our front was determined on. I had with me at Alcoy five battalions of infantry, a squadron of cavalry, and some mountain guns carried by mules; and on the morning of the reconnoissance I assembled the five battalions, the squadron of cavalry (Cazadores de Olivencia) and two guns, in contiguous close columns, near to Alcoy: and gave verbally the necessary orders for the advance.

'My advanced guard consisted of the whole of Colonel Campbell's regiment of light infantry 1,500 strong, a troop of cavalry, and two guns; and was supported by three battalions of infantry, a troop of cavalry, and two mountain guns.

'Before the day had well broken we fell in with the French advanced posts, which occupied a wood in front of Onteniente. They were immediately driven back, but rallied on their reserves. As I wished to ascertain the strength of the French force before me, I determined to appear to give way, and sounded the retreat. This brought the French on, hand over hand—and as the whole of Campbell's battalion was at the time in extended order supported by the three battalion columns, the length of the line was immense; and the left being too much thrown forward was in some danger of being cut off, on the rapid and sudden advance of the French.

'To provide against this evil I directed the troop of Chasseurs under Lieutenant Fernandez to charge the centre of the French line, whilst my bugles sounded: *Change front on the centre the left thrown back.* This movement was executed as beautifully and correctly as it could have been done on parade, whilst the sabre of Fernandez almost divided in two a soldier who ventured to oppose him. Every little error being rectified we continued our retreat to where the attack had commenced.

'Having thus led the French to show what their force really was, I determined to drive them from their present position and beyond the pass of Albayda. Accordingly we again advanced with the whole of the light infantry in extended order, supported as before stated; and we drove the enemy at double quick [time], from tree to tree, till he was clear of the wood, at the extremity of which his line was formed.

'A momentary halt, which I unavoidably made, to give orders as to the occupying a road on our right, which led to the head-quarters of General Abert, enabled one of the French sharpshooters to take good aim at my head and to hit me on the right side of my mouth. My former wound was on the left side. This last, however, was only a flesh wound, and I had no time to attend to it. Our advance through the wood was most brilliant and as soon as we had cleared it, our guns were instantly in position; and the two first shots directed by Captain Arabin* plunged into the centre of the French line, and created considerable confusion. I forthwith ordered a general advance of all the troops under my command; nor was there any further check till we had conducted the French through the pass of Albayda.

'[General] Abert's force and mine were nearly equal, each consisting of about 4,000 bayonets.'——

Here at last Spanish troops, unaided by British soldiers (except their English chief, and the Scotch Colonel), had under skilful guidance, proved more than a match for veteran French warriors. The disgusts and the labours

---

* Captain Arabin died as Colonel Arabin, in command of the Royal Artillery at Bermuda, on the 17th August, 1843. On the 8th April, 1847, the eldest son of Sir Samford Whittingham, married Eliza, the eldest daughter of Colonel Arabin.

experienced at Majorca were here at last repaid by undeniable fruits on the two occasions narrated; and which were to be officially acknowledged without delay :—

'*General Order.*

'Head Quarters, ALCOY, 8*th March*, 1813.

'In the attack which took place yesterday, Lieutenant-General Sir John Murray received particular satisfaction from observing the brilliant conduct of the Spanish troops engaged; and he begs General Whittingham will make known his approbation in the strongest terms to the officers, and desire them to communicate his sentiments to the troops.

'THOMAS MOLLOY,
'Assistant Adjutant-General.'

The above referred to the Xigona affair. That of Concentayna, or the Puente de Albayda, deserved and received warmer acknowledgment :—

'*General Order.*

'Head Quarters, ALICANTE, 17*th March*, 1813.

'No. 2.—Lieutenant-General Sir John Murray has again to draw the attention of the army to the spirit and gallantry with which the Spanish division of Major-General Whittingham conducted itself on the 15th instant.

'The attack on that side was much more serious; but by the able dispositions of Major-General Whittingham, and the bravery with which he was supported, the enemy was driven from his positions, and pursued with great loss as far as the Major-General thought expedient.

'Lieutenant-General Sir John Murray requests Major-General Whittingham to acquaint the corps engaged, how much their steadiness and general good conduct is approved.

'G. A. HARZENBUHLER,
'Assistant Adjutant-General.'

The Marquis of Wellington to Earl Bathurst.*
(Extract.)

'FRENEDA, 7*th April,* 1813.

'Since the movement made by Lieutenant-General Sir John Murray, of which I enclosed the report in my last dispatch, it appears that Marshal Suchet has collected his troops on the right of the Jucar, and has established his head-quarters at San Felipe de Xativa. General Whittingham's division of Spanish troops had driven the enemy's advanced guard beyond the Puente de Albayda.'†——

As military agent General Whittingham wrote an official account of the action of Concentayna to the Ambassador:—

His Excellency the Right Hon. Sir Henry Wellesley, K.B.

'ALCOY, 16*th March,* 1813.

'Sir,—I have the honour to inform your Excellency that, in consequence of orders from Lieutenant-General Sir John Murray directing me to make a strong reconnaissance on the enemy's force near Concentayna, I advanced from this at 3 o'clock yesterday morning, with the greater part of the division of Majorca.

'I also directed Lieutenant-Colonel Bourke commanding the 1st Italian Regiment, which was in La Sarga, to occupy Alcoy with his battalion at daylight; and having situated the regiments of Murcia and Cordova with two four-pounders, and a howitzer in a position previously marked out, about half a league beyond Alcoy on the Concentayna road, in front of a ravine (on which we had constructed some rough breastworks, and cut the bridge across it so as only to allow one man at a time to pass);

---

* *Wellington Dispatches,* vol. x. p. 272.
† Except an allusion to General Donkin's successful reconnoissance this little dispatch of the Duke's is all in honour of General Whittingham's two successful affairs previously to the battle of Castalla.

I marched out with the remainder in the following order :*—

ADVANCED GUARD.

3 companies of Cazadores de Mallorca Light company of Murcia Light company of Cordova 1 Subaltern and 10 Dragoons of Olivencia	*Commanding Officer,* Lieut.-Colonel Mouet, of Cazadores de Mallorca.

COLUMN.

5 companies of Cazadores de Mallorca 2 English mountain four-pounders 5th battalion of Grenadiers 1 Cap. 1 Subⁿ. and 25 Dragoons of Olivencia	*Commanding Officer,* Colonel Campbell.†

'On arriving near Concentayna, I posted the grenadier battalion on a rising ground commanding the entrance to the town; the advanced guard entered it; and Colonel Campbell formed the rest of his regiment in close column in the road leading into Concentayna.

'Lieutenant-Colonel Mouet passed through the town, and proceeded on by the high road to Albayda; and, a few minutes before sunrise, fell in with an advanced post of the enemy at the Cruz de Valencia, about half a mile from Concentayna. This advanced [French party] fell back on the next post, followed by Lieutenant-Colonel Mouet's skirmishers; and the enemy, having sent forward reinforcements, there was a very warm fire kept up on both sides, during which Mouet drove the enemy before him for more than a mile; when the French having considerably reinforced their skirmishers, and having drawn up, in position, a battalion of about 600 infantry and 150 dragoons, I directed Lieutenant-Colonel Mouet to retire slowly towards Concentayna, in the hope of drawing the enemy from his position.

'Colonel Campbell at the same time moved forward with the five companies of his regiment in close column and [with] one of the mountain four-pounders under the

---

* Official military letters are apt to scorn full stops, and to prolong sentences into pages, that they may be both written and read with rapidity.

† Patrick Campbell, then Colonel in the Spanish service.

command of Captain Arabin of the British artillery. The dragoons of Olivencia, with some light infantry moved by the right flank along the road to Muro, and occupied Alcudieta; where the commanding officer was informed that, as soon as the firing began, the [French] troops which were in Muro and the neighbourhood, had posted themselves at the bottom of the hill near the Puerto de Albayda.* The column having come up near the rear of the advance, Lieutenant-Colonel Mouet again drove the enemy before him, followed by the column, which, with the four-pounders, having arrived within five or six hundred yards of the enemy, halted; when Captain Arabin opened a well-directed fire on the enemy's battalion, which, after a few rounds, retired towards the Puerto de Albayda. Having thus fulfilled Sir John Murray's instructions, I directed Colonel Campbell and Lieutenant-Colonel Mouet to fall back on their former position, which was done without the least molestation on the part of the enemy. The firing began about six in the morning, and lasted till half-past ten in the forenoon.

'The enemy's loss, as I understand from different deserters who have since come in, is about sixty men, and two horses killed and wounded. We have counted fourteen dead bodies and two horses. On my part not a man killed,† [but] one captain and five privates of the Cazadores de Mallorca, and two privates of the light company of Murcia are wounded; and I have received a musket-shot in the right cheek.

'I have every reason to be highly satisfied with the gallantry and coolness of the officers and soldiers of the

---

* *Puente* de Albayda it is called in the *Wellington Dispatches*; that is, *bridge* instead of *gate*. Gurwood took such trouble and pains in fixing the proper spelling, and general correctness of the Spanish words, that probably *Puente* is right.

† No doubt the rapidity of the attack and pursuit (leaving the enemy little of the leisure and coolness necessary for good firing) was the cause that the victors suffered so little. But of the few wounded the General was one.

division under my command; who, on this as on every other occasion, have most completely acted up to my expectations, and fulfilled the duty [which] they owe [to] their country.

'I have the honour to be, your Excellency's most
'obedient and humble servant,
'SAMFORD WHITTINGHAM.'

To conclude the Concentayna affair, the Ambassador's reply is here inserted at once:—

Sir Henry Wellesley to Major-General Whittingham.
'CADIZ, 1st *April*, 1813.

'Sir,—I have the honour to acknowledge the receipt of your letters of the 16th and 19th ultimo, which reached me this morning; and it is with the most sincere satisfaction that I now congratulate you upon the signal proofs afforded by the conduct of your corps in the several affairs in which it has been engaged, of the efficacy of your exertions to bring it to perfection. I shall not fail to transmit to Lord Wellington a copy of your letter to me, and another copy for information of the Government of His Royal Highness the Prince Regent.

'I am very happy to learn that the wound which you have received is not of a nature to deprive the country of your services in the field for any considerable time.

'I will endeavour to obtain an order to the Marquis of Compigny to the effect mentioned in your letter of the 19th March.* I will also use my utmost endeavours to procure the confirmation of Colonel O'Reilly in the command of the 5th battalion of Grenadiers.

'I have, &c.,
'H. WELLESLEY.'

---

* The letter of the 19th is one of many letters too numerous for insertion in this work. It complained that the Marquis, then Captain-General of the Balearic Islands, kept back in Majorca troops of General Whittingham's division that should have been sent to join the latter.

'At page 297, vol. x., of the 'Wellington Dispatches,' there is a long memorandum written by his Lordship, (dated '14th April, 1813'), regarding the coming operations on the eastern coast, which frequently refers to the Majorca division: but of which only one sentence will here be quoted, namely—the last paragraph:—

'If General Sir John Murray's allied British and Sicilian corps, and the whole or part of General Whittingham's division should embark, General the Duque del Parque will direct the operations ordered in this memorandum to be carried on in the kingdom of Valencia; but, in either case, the general officers commanding the first, second, and third armies, and General Whittingham, must command each their separate corps.'

This was putting a General of division on the footing of a General commanding an army, as subordinate only to the actual Commander of the Forces—a strong mark of confidence. This was written a fortnight before Lord Wellington received Sir John Murray's report of the battle of Castalla, which established yet higher the reputation of the Majorca division.

To his Brother-in-law.

'*Division, Majorca Head Quarters,* ALCOY, 19*th March,* 1813.

'My dear Davis,—I enclose an account of an affair which took place on the 15th. You will see with pleasure that the division has been twice thanked in General Orders.

'As my wound is painful, though not in the least dangerous, pray send a copy of the enclosed to Colonel Torrens, and beg him to excuse my writing.

'The French have fifteen battalions in my front, at Albayda and San Felipe. Our army is concentrating itself, and a few days will, I hope, bring on a general action, at which, I thank God, I shall still be able to play my part.

'Best love to all, and believe me, ever yours,

'SAMFORD WHITTINGHAM.'

BATTLE OF CASTALLA.

The battle of Castalla was fought and won on the 13th April, 1813, by the allied English and Spanish troops; but mainly by two corps of that army; namely, one of Englishmen under Colonel Adam,* which gained the chief honours of the day; and the other of Spaniards under Major-General Whittingham, who proved themselves worthy of fighting with British soldiers, and contributed largely to the successful result.

But let the Commander-in-Chief on that day have, as is right, the first word: —

'*General Order.*

'*Head Quarters*, CASTALLA, 14*th April,* 1813.

' Lieutenant-General Sir John Murray congratulates the army he has the honour to command, on the result of the action which took place yesterday. Marshal Suchet collected his whole force, for the express purpose of destroying this army; trusting to the good fortune which had hitherto attended his arms. He has been defeated, and forced to retreat, by a small portion of it.

' The Lieutenant-General requests the officers and soldiers of the corps engaged to accept his best thanks for their gallantry; and assures them, that he will not fail to draw the attention of his Royal Highness the Prince Regent, and of the Spanish Government, to the bravery, spirit, and discipline displayed.

' As the reports from the officers commanding divisions, of what immediately passed under their direction, have not yet reached the Lieutenant-General, he is obliged to defer the just tribute of applause to those corps and in-

---

* Colonel Adam, of the 21st Foot, (afterwards Sir Frederick Adam, K.C.B., G.C.M.G.,) was far senior *in the British army* to Lieutenant-Colonel Whittingham; for on the same 4th of June, 1814, on which the latter was made a Colonel, the former was gazetted a Major-General. It was not till 1825, that Whittingham became a Major-General in the British service. Sir F. Adam was the second Lord High Commissioner of the Ionian Islands.

dividuals who have been fortunate enough to find an opportunity of distinguishing themselves. But, from Sir John Murray's own observation, he is fully authorized to hold up to every army in Europe the conduct of Colonel Adam and his brave corps, on the 12th and 13th instant, as an example worthy of applause and imitation; and he has the satisfaction of expressing a no less degree of approbation of the conduct of Major-General Whittingham and his gallant troops in the action of the 13th.*

'The Lieutenant-General has much satisfaction in conveying his approbation of the spirit displayed by every other part of the army on the 12th and 13th instant. They had not the fortunate lot of the advance, and of General Whittingham; but it was evident that had the enemy waited the attack on the 13th, in the plains of Castalla, that he would have found the same spirit to have existed throughout the whole allied army.

'The Lieutenant-General has experienced, ever since he has held this honourable command, every support and assistance from the general officers and brigadiers † of the army; and he is happy that an opportunity has been afforded him of expressing that gratitude which he deeply feels. Nor is he less indebted to the general staff of the army, for their cordial support, and the cheerful alacrity with which every part of the service is performed. In mentioning the general staff of the army Sir John Murray feels that he would be wanting in justice if he omitted the name of Major-General Donkin, to whom he is more particularly indebted. The Lieutenant-General has now only pointedly to express his approbation of the artillery corps engaged in every part, and to assure Captain Arabin

---

* Thus three times in five weeks was the Majorca division praised in General Orders.

† Colonel Adam appears to have been one of these Brigadiers, as he is described as commanding a body of troops. He was Lieut.-Colonel of the 21st Regiment of Foot, the North British Fusiliers.

that, so far from finding the slightest grounds of censure for the loss of the two mountain guns, he highly approved the spirit and motive which induced him to keep them in their position, till it became impossible, in their crippled state to remove them.

'Deeply as every soldier feels the loss of a brave comrade who may fall, it is a consolation to think that the allied army has, in comparison with that of the enemy, suffered, in numbers at least, a trifling loss.

'THOMAS KENAGH,
'Assistant Adjutant-General.'

General Whittingham's official report was as follows:—

To His Excellency the General-in-Chief of the Allied Army.

'CAMP OF GUERRA, 14*th April*, 1813.

'Sir,—Yesterday the 13th, in consequence of your Excellency's orders communicated to me by Lieutenant-Colonel Catinelli, I marched at mid-day by my left, from my position on the heights of Guerra, with the 5th battalion of Grenadiers, the 2nd of Murcia, and that of the Cazadores of Majorca, by the road of the Montaña, which joins that of Sax; prolonging the left of the line, and leaving in my position the 1st battalion of Cordova and the 2nd of Burgos, under Colonel Juan Romero.

'After marching about half an hour I received a message from Major Guerra (whom I had left with two companies covering the heights of Nadal) informing me that three columns of the enemy were forming at the foot of his position, and were preparing to attack him. I immediately ordered Colonel Serrano, chief of my staff, to march rapidly and place the 2nd Regiment of Murcia [so as] to support Major Guerra; giving positive orders to Colonel Casans that the post should be defended at whatever cost, and that he should proceed to the heights of Guerra, and acquaint me with the state of that point. The fire was already general along the line; and observing that the enemy was possessing himself of the last height on the left—from whence he might flank those on the Nadal, I ordered Colonel Campbell, of the Majorca Cazadores, to obtain possession of that height with two companies; which he accomplished most promptly at the point of the bayonet. Leaving the remainder of this corps on this part of the line, I hastened with the 5th Regiment of Grenadiers back to the position on the heights of Guerra, which was now vigorously attacked. On my march I received a verbal communication from Colonel Serrano, informing me that it was absolutely necessary to strengthen that point with more troops, as Colonel Romero, with the Cordova and Burgos Regiments, was sorely pressed, and required support. The moment I arrived, I formed the grenadiers into two columns on the flat on the top of the heights of Guerra, fronting the two most accessible points, and against which the attacks were principally directed. A strong column of French grenadiers had taken the height of Sarratella, with another still stronger [column] of fusiliers on their right. I ordered the reserves to advance. Romero maintained himself on the first line with great firmness. After a very obstinate fight on both sides, the enemy determined to attack with the bayonet; his first column [advancing] by the crest of the mountain; the second, lower down, by the opening of Palliser.

'I immediately directed Lieutenant-Colonel Ochoa to advance with our reserve, and sustain the first point; and Colonel Serrano took the other (commanded by Major Ontiveros) by his left to cover the opening of Palliser. The enemy advanced boldly to the edge of the position; but the reserves immediately deployed, and advanced to the charge with so much spirit (supported by the troops of the first line) that the enemy was overthrown and put into the greatest confusion; nor could he again form until he had returned to his position on the summit of the hill of Doncel.

'Colonel Casans of the 2nd Regiment of Murcia, to whom, as already mentioned, I had trusted the command of the left, was attacked by upwards of 800 men in strong skirmishing parties, supported by a column of grenadiers and chasseurs, and a numerous reserve. But this officer ordered his grenadiers and cazadores to advance and support the Majorca Regiment, which was warmly attacked; and with that of Murcia, in the post of Olla Redonda, the cazadores of the 5th Grenadiers, and the 1st of Guadalaxara kept up a steady fire; which the enemy notwithstanding disregarded, [being] resolved to break the line. But Colonel Casans having brought out his reserves, and given the command of his right to Major Bascon, of his left to Lieutenant-Colonel M. Sas, and of his centre to Major Guerra, they kept up the fire till half-past four in the afternoon; when, annoyed by the obstinacy of the enemy, Colonel Casans ordered the before mentioned troops, with four companies of the cazadores of Majorca, to charge with the bayonet; which they did immediately with such a countenance that the French dared not await them, but fled shamefully, and with too much expedition to allow our men, who were much fatigued, to make many prisoners.

'I can assure your Excellency that the force with which the enemy attacked [us] was greatly superior to mine; and that, after a most obstinate conflict of three hours and a half, he was repulsed at the same time on the whole line, leaving the field covered with his dead.

'I subsequently received your Excellency's orders to move my line forward, in proportion as the other troops of the army should advance. As soon as I perceived the general movement, I left Colonel Casteras with the battalion of Burgos in the position, and advanced with the

5th Grenadiers and the 1st of Cordova, covering my front with two companies of Majorca as skirmishers.

'I marched in this order to the summit of Doncel, following the first line of the English troops, on which my right leaned.* At the same time I sent by my left, by the Montaña del Aquila, Colonel Casans with the regiments of Murcia and Majorca, strengthened by his Britannic Majesty's 1st Italian battalion, with the view of flanking the enemy's right: which they accomplished by descending into the plain, and taking the direction of Monte de los Zerres. The skirmishers were charged at the foot of that hill by a detachment of the enemy's cavalry, which they succeeded in repulsing with loss, when the whole column halted, on the approach of night, and returned to its position, by your Excellency's orders.

'To your Excellency I particularly recommend, in the strongest terms, Colonel Serrano, Chief of my Staff, to whose exertions, valour, and knowledge, is owing much of the success of this day. I also particularly recommend Lieutenant-Colonel Catanelli, who was in the whole of the action and gave much assistance. The second adjutant of the General Staff, and the assistants, Don Joseph Serrano and Don Samuel Alvares, Colonel Gelabert, quartermaster-general, Captain Montenegro, of the engineers, and my aide-de-camp, Don Antonio Ruti, and the Baron de Halberg, completely fulfilled their duties and carried my orders with the greatest dispatch and precision.

'The spirit and correctness of the officers of my division have been so distinguished, that I must in justice call your Excellency's attention to the conduct of Colonels Casans, Romero, Campbell, Casteras, and Lieutenant-Colonel Ochoa, and all the other commanders and officers. In one word, both men and officers have completely done their duty; and having been all equally engaged, they are equally

* It is meant that he *dressed* his line by that of the English in its advance.

entitled to the gratitude of their country; particularly the memory of those brave men, Lieutenant-Colonel Sudrez of the 5th Grenadiers, Lieutenant-Colonel Pizarro of [the regiment of] Burgos, and Lieutenant-Colonel Puerto of the Majorca, who fell in the action. Major Bascon received a contusion. Lieutenant Morales of the Cordova, Lieutenant Castañeda of the Guadalaxara, and the sub-lieutenant of the Majorca, Serrano, were wounded; with 66 rank and file killed, and 163 wounded; which with the 29 men that the battalion [there engaged] lost on the 12th on the pass of Biar, make a total of 258 men.

'I have, &c.,
'SAMFORD WHITTINGHAM.'

It is proved by two dispatches of Lord Wellington, dated 5th May and 9th August, 1813, that the Spanish division of General Roche was at Castalla very weak in the field, nearly all the men being at the depôt. Moreover, that division being on the right, was not actively engaged. The state and conduct of the Majorca division appear to have been achievements *with Spanish troops* quite unrivalled in the Peninsula.

The following extracts from Sir John Murray's dispatch of the battle of Castalla to the Marquis of Wellington, refer to General Whittingham and his division :—

'The position of the allied army was extensive. The left was posted on a strong range of hills, occupied by Major-General Whittingham's division of Spanish troops, and the advance of the allied army under Colonel Adam.

'The skill, judgment, and gallantry displayed by Major-General Whittingham and his division of the Spanish army, rivals, though it cannot surpass, the conduct of Colonel Adam and the advance.'

That the British General-in-Chief, should thus acknowledge that Spaniards had rivalled Britons in the battle was assuredly a sufficient proof that the labours of the zealous organizer in Majorca had not been thrown away. General Murray also forwarded and endorsed the recommendations made by General Whittingham of his gallant subordinates.*

On the 9th May, 1813, the great hero deigned to indite a paper of 'Observations on General Whittingham's memorandum of the 24th April, 1812, in regard to the draft of supplies from the country'†; and though he declared it to be 'impracticable to execute what is proposed,' he yet discussed it with respect and condemned the project solely on the ground of the inferiority to the French on certain points both of English and Spanish troops. Such measures experience indeed proved, owing to Lord Wellington's marvellous successes, to be unnecessary. But it might have been otherwise, but for the invasion of Russia; and if Napoleon, abandoning that mad project, had reinforced his Peninsular army by 100,000 more soldiers. In that case forced requisitions, or an abandonment of Spain would have been the only alternatives to keep the army from starving. The retreat after Talavera was mainly caused by the absence of such requisitions, and by the indolence and ill-will of the Spanish authorities, who scrupled not themselves to take what was wanted for their own troops, though they took no trouble to supply the British.

After the praise given to the Majorca division by Sir John Murray on so many occasions, it will surprise no one that the Spaniards were rendered almost wild with enthusiasm by the accounts of the prowess of their countrymen against the detested invaders. In the 'Redactor General' (a Spanish journal) of April 1813, there is a long and

---

* Though *thrice* honourably mentioned in General Orders, and again in the dispatch, no one would suppose from Napier's accounts of the Eastern Campaign, that either Whittingham or his Spanish division had done anything particular. *The Duke* knew better.

† Vol. x. p. 366.

glowing article on the Te Deums and rejoicings on account of the victory of Castalla, in the usual inflated style of warm southern imaginations. The translation of one of its paragraphs is sufficient on the present occasion:—

'General Whittingham, that chief so zealous in inspiring all warlike virtues into his beloved soldiers, must be superabundantly satisfied and recompensed in seeing his labours in the organizing of these never-sufficiently-to-be-praised Spaniards thus crowned with success.'

The following incident of the battle of Castalla is taken from the 'Recollections':—

'I was directed to march upon Castalla with the whole of the force under my command, except two battalions which were to remain at Alcoy. On my arrival at Castalla, I occupied a range of heights on the left of the town. The British left and my right were contiguous. Suchet had advanced from Valencia with about 12,000 men; and had attacked some posts of General Elio, and taken a thousand prisoners. Our advanced guard under Brigadier Adam was driven through the pass of Biar upon our main body at Castalla. But the retreat was a beautiful field-day, by alternate battalions. The volleys were admirable, and the successive passage of several ravines conducted with perfect order and steadiness. From the heights occupied by my troops it was one of the most delightful panoramas that I ever beheld!

'About ten o'clock on the next morning, I received orders from Sir John Murray, through Lieutenant-Colonel Catanelli (an Italian officer on the staff of Lord William Bentinck) to take ground to my left till I should reach the head of a ravine in that direction, then to bring my left shoulder forwards, descending the valley, and form perpendicularly to the right of Suchet's line.

'In the meantime Sir John was to advance with his whole force from Castalla, and attack Suchet in front. I told Catanelli that I should of course obey but that I did not believe in the correctness of his communication; and Sir John Murray afterwards assured me that he had never given any order to Catanelli. Luckily, foreseeing that the heights which I occupied would probably be attacked as soon as my movement to the left should be perceived, I left all the advanced posts and their supports standing; and passing by their rear in columns of companies left in front, I had hardly begun to descend the valley in single file, when a report was brought to me that the French were advancing to the attack of the heights of Castalla, and that the outposts were already warmly engaged. I instantly countermarched, and formed columns of companies at double quick, as the troops successively cleared the defile; and I re-occupied my former position just in time to repel the final attack of the French.* Our loss did not exceed 300 men; the French suffered severely, not having fewer than 3,000 men *hors de combat*.

'Our advantage was not followed up, and Suchet was permitted to retire without further molestation, through the pass of Biar, by which he had advanced.'

* This account of the mistake of Catanelli is confirmed by Southey. Indeed he probably received the particulars from General Whittingham, or found them at the Horse-Guards, in the letters of that officer.

CHAPTER X.

1813—continued.

INCREASE OF FRENCH AND DECREASE OF ENGLISH FORCE—REPUTATION OF THE MAJORCA DIVISION—DEATH OF HONOURABLE COLONEL CADOGAN—LORD WILLIAM BENTINCK SUPERSEDES SIR JOHN MURRAY—GENERAL WHITTINGHAM COVERS THE RETREAT FROM TARRAGONA—EFFECTED WITHOUT LOSS—WHITTINGHAM EXCEPTIONALLY FAVOURED BY LORD WELLINGTON—AN ORDER MORE FLATTERING THAN AGREEABLE—CAVALRY UNSHOD FOR WANT OF MONEY—A GERMAN AIDE-DE-CAMP—OFFICIAL JEALOUSIES AND PERSECUTIONS—GENERAL WHITTINGHAM'S RESIGNATION OF COMMAND—HIS REASONS FOR RESIGNING—ACCOUNT OF PASSING THE EBRO—A DRUNKEN COMMANDER—THE FRENCH MURDER COLONEL O'REILLY—RETALIATION BY THE SPANIARDS—GREAT EVILS REQUIRE STRONG REMEDIES—MAGAZINES FILLED IN A WEEK—LORD WELLINGTON FEELS THE UTMOST CONCERN AT GENERAL WHITTINGHAM'S RESIGNATION—WITHHOLDS HIS PAPERS TILL HE SHALL HEAR AGAIN—GIVES HIM A LARGE COMMAND OF CAVALRY—THE GLORY AND DUTY OF OBEYING WELLINGTON—STATE OF SPANISH CAVALRY—HAZARDOUS ALTERNATIVE—A FRATERNAL *ÉPANCHEMENT DE CŒUR*—TRAINING OF SPANISH CAVALRY—COLONEL TORRENS'S LETTER TO MR. DAVIS—ROUTINE CARRIED TOO FAR—LORD WELLINGTON RESIGNS THE COMMAND OF THE SPANISH ARMY—IMPROVEMENT OF SPANISH CAVALRY—A DISAPPOINTING PEACE.

General Whittingham to his Brother-in-law.

'ALCOY, 13*th May*, 1813.

'SUCHET's force has been reinforced since the action [of Castalla] by the junction of the division that he had in Aragon (about 5,000 men), and by the arrival of about 2,000 conscripts. Ours had been lessened by 3,000 men lost by General Elio at Gerla and Biar, and by the detachment of three regiments sent to Sicily. We received yesterday the news that General Hill had entered Toledo, and that the Duke del Parque was at Almaraz.

'The Spaniards are not in a state to act alone even a subordinate part; and one of two things must result from sending Sir John Murray's army away. Either the army acts alone, entirely composed of Spanish troops, and under the command of the Duke del Parque, in which case it will be entirely destroyed in the first action in which it may be engaged; or Lord Wellington will be obliged to detach General Hill with his *corps d'armée* to take the supreme command here; and by so doing weaken considerably the effect of his great mass [of troops]; had he been able to keep them concentrated in one sole line of operation.

'As to this unfortunate country I see it in a more deplorable point of view every day. Nine months have nearly passed away since the battle of Salamanca, two-thirds of Spain have been free during that period; and yet the only increase to our army is about 12,000 men under O'Donnel, and the troops are neither better paid nor better fed than when Spain was reduced to Cadiz.

'My little division has established a certain reputation* in the country, which is highly advantageous to the *esprit de corps* that I have always endeavoured to keep up. But as I have no means of recruiting my losses, a few months of active campaign will lead us fairly and softly to a natural death. I live in hopes, however, that in consequence of the battle of Castalla, I may receive some augmentations to my force.'——

The death of his dear friend the Honourable Henry Cadogan at Vittoria on the 21st June, 1813, must have been a grievous blow to the subject of this Memoir and deserves a passing allusion. Cadogan had been gazetted on the 4th June to the rank of Colonel, but he died before his promotion was known in the Peninsula.† Lord Wel-

---

* More than he was then aware of, since its commander had gained (as will be seen hereafter) the high esteem of the able Marshal Suchet, Duke of Albufera.

† Had Colonel Cadogan survived, he would have succeeded to the earldom of Cadogan in 1832, instead of his younger brother George.

lington on the 22nd of June, in his dispatch to Earl Bathurst, writes, 'I am concerned to have to report that Lieutenant-Colonel the Hon. H. Cadogan has died of a wound which he received. In him His Majesty has lost an officer of great merit and tried gallantry, who had already acquired the respect and regard of the whole profession, and of whom it might have been expected that, if he had lived, he would have rendered the most important services to his country.'

On the 24th, Lord Wellington writes to his brother Sir Henry Wellesley, 'I know how much you will feel for the loss of poor Cadogan, which has distressed me exceedingly. He was so anxious respecting what was going on, that after he was wounded and knew that he was dying, he had himself carried to a place whence he could see all the operations.'

Thus heroically died the beloved and loving friend of Samford Whittingham.

On the 28th of May, Sir John Murray's army embarked for Catalonia, and sailed on the 31st; disembarked on the 3rd June, and immediately invested Tarragona. The abandonment of that enterprise, owing to the advance, with a large force, of Marshal Suchet to the relief of the town, was effected in such haste as to cause a considerable loss of guns and military stores, and also eventually to bring before a court-martial the British Commander of the Forces. On the 17th June, Lord William Bentinck relieved Sir John Murray of his command, and then was renewed the acquaintance between that distinguished nobleman and General Whittingham, which quickly ripened into mutual esteem, and ended in durable friendship. We resume the 'Recollections':—

'At the siege of Tarragona, my division of infantry occupied the left of the investment. Suchet had advanced to the relief with 10,000 men, but without artillery. I submitted to the consideration of Sir John Murray that

[General] Copons, and the Spanish corps under his command, should be left before Tarragona, and that he [himself] should move upon Suchet with all his force. My opinion was not approved; and a few days afterwards the siege was ordered to be raised, and with such precipitation that several guns were abandoned, and our honour unnecessarily compromized. Before our re-embarkation for Alicante Lord William Bentinck had arrived, and taken the command of the army. His Lordship forthwith advanced a second time upon Tarragona, but by land. Suchet, determined to save the place if possible, brought up all the disposable force under his command, to the amount of 30,000 men.

'Lord William's army consisted of the divisions of Sarsfield and Whittingham, about 6,000 men each, and of the force under the Duke del Parque of 12,000 men. The three Generals were directed to meet at Lord William's head-quarters, and a council of war was held on the expediency of risking a general action with Suchet. It was determined in the negative; and a general retreat being ordered, I was left to cover it with my division.

'The country which we then occupied was intersected by stone walls enclosing fields of a moderate size, and every road formed a small defile. Between my advanced post and the enemy there was a deep but very accessible ravine, at the head of which stood a village occupied by my troops. In rear of the village there was a large open space; and beyond that a long wall of about four feet high, pierced through its centre by the common road. Besides the infantry, I had with me two eight-pounders, horse artillery, and nearly 2,000 cavalry. Having ascertained the proximate approach of the enemy, I sent the artillery and cavalry to the rear, excepting only fifty hussars, which, with two companies of grenadiers, I pushed across the ravine, as a check upon the too rapid advance of the French. I then lined the wall on the farther side of the common with Campbell's light infantry, and sent a staff-officer with all the battalions of the line, to form them on either side of the road at convenient distances successively, in order the better to secure our retreat.

'I had scarcely made all these arrangements, when the troops on the farther side of the ravine were driven in at double quick; and they had just commenced filing to the rear through the opening in the wall, when the French hussars came through the village at a gallop—formed to the front—and charged the troops entering the defile.

'It was now my turn. The whole battalion of light infantry, which had been concealed behind the wall, stood up; and commenced, from that rest,* a most destructive fire, which brought down a great number, and sent the remainder to the right-about as speedily as their horses' legs could carry them. A General of division should always be *the first to advance and the last to retreat.* That is invariably his post. I consequently retired with Campbell's battalion, and gradually and successively sent on the different battalions, as they came up in their echelons to more distant points in our rear.

'The pursuit was warmly followed up till nightfall; when having crossed a ravine at ——,† we ascended the height on the opposite side, and took up our position for the night. In the village we found five thousand rations of bread, which had been prepared for the French. I ordered them to be distributed to our men, in spite of the reclamations of the civil authorities. I then proceeded to open communications through the walls in my rear for the passage of the troops, on their retreat in the morning; and having detached on our right a subaltern and twenty hussars, to ascertain the security of that flank, I threw myself down on a bundle of straw, and in a moment was

---

* Rest for their muskets on the wall; ensuring steadiness of aim.

† The name was left in blank, having slipped from the memory of the writer.

fast asleep; for I do not recollect ever, in my whole life, to have been half so tired. At one o'clock a.m., my servant awoke me to say that a dish of stewed partridge was ready; and I certainly did eat, as most starved people are wont to do—like a hunter.*

'I waited the next morning till near daylight, in the hope that my hussar-patrol would make its appearance. But I was disappointed; for it turned out that the young officer had disobeyed my orders not to dismount, much less to enter any house, and had in consequence been surprised and taken prisoner with the whole of his party. Our further retreat to Lord William's head-quarters was effected without loss. The distance was ten miles, and we marched it in two hours and a half.'——

Lord Wellington did not approve of the Spanish system of divisional inspectors, but as Commander-in-Chief of the Spanish armies he did not venture to abolish them generally:—

The Marquis of Wellington to Lieutenant-General Lord William Bentinck.†

(Extract.)

'IRURITA, 8*th July*, 1813.

'You will have seen that by the Constitution, all military regulation is in the hands of the Cortes, and they have a board of officers now sitting to consider of a military constitution for the army, which it is intended to republicanize. Any proposal for an alteration, therefore, is laid aside till the new military constitution shall be fixed. One of the defects in the constitution of the Spanish army, as now existing, is in the office and power of the

---

* The critical reader must remember that these *Recollections* (as explained in the *Preface*) were written for a beloved niece, and were never intended for publication.

† Vol. x. page 516, edition of 1838, of *Wellington Dispatches*.

inspectors of cavalry and infantry, in whose hands is the nomination of all officers to commission, and for promotion.

'*This cannot be altered. Whittingham, contrary to all rule, is both Commander and Inspector of his own division. I have not the power to make the same arrangement in favour of anybody else.*'*

'I have no objection to your allowing the Duque del Parque cavalry to act under the command of Whittingham for the moment; but I beg you not to make any alteration in the existing organization of any of the Spanish armies. If you do, you will bring me into difficulties.'——

With Lord William Bentinck, as with every commander he successively served under, confidence in General Whittingham seems to have been the invariable rule: but indeed it appears to have been equally so in the case of civilians, whether statesmen or diplomatists, with whom he came in contact; always excepting that brief episode with the Governor of Gibraltar, where he had not the opportunity by personal intercourse of gaining the esteem of that over-punctilious functionary.

The formation of the rival division of General Roche appears to have been, comparatively speaking, a failure; as on the 9th August, 1813, we find Lord Wellington writing to Lord William Bentinck: 'I shall not allow any pay in future for a division under General Roche, as he has no such division serving in the field.' This clearly proves (and it is therefore quoted) the immense difficulty of the task which General Whittingham succeeded in accomplishing at Majorca.

---

* The Editor ventures to place in italics a sentence so honourable to the subject of this Memoir. Not only the confidence of the illustrious Chief is here displayed, but the great popularity of General Whittingham in Spain is strikingly manifested.

To his Brother-in-law.

'TORRENTE, 11*th July*, 1813.

' At the request of Lord William Bentinck, of the Duke del Parque, and of General Elio, I have taken the command of the cavalry of the 2nd and 3rd army, which, added to that of my division, makes about 2,500 horse. I have accepted this command because I have been ordered to do so; but I have declared to them all that I cannot be answerable for the consequences. If I had them for some months, they might be formed into good soldiers. But at present there is no time for instruction; and in the present condition of the Spanish cavalry, there is not a single regiment in a state to fight the French, with the most distant chance of success.

' In the year which has elapsed since the battle of Salamanca, the Spanish army has not been increased by 20,000 men; nor do I see the least hope of a change of system. Lord Wellington has been doing wonders; but England, as I have repeated again and again, can never save Spain if Spain will do nothing for herself.

' In short, my dear Davis, I am tired of a scene where my mind is continually harassed, and where it is not in my power to do the least good; and I entreat you to obtain an order for me to return home, and get my accounts with Government passed. They are long and voluminous, and, if not settled during my life, they will probably be the cause of infinite vexation and loss to my family.

' No man has considered the Spanish Revolution with greater impartiality than myself. When we were reduced to Cadiz and the Balearic Islands, my spirits were high, and I trusted that a day of reaction would arrive which would place the Spaniards in the situation of the French in the year '94. That day has arrived. Lord Wellington's memorable battle of Salamanca put the

Spaniards in possession of the best part of their country, and gave them the means of forming great and powerful armies!

'Have they taken advantage of these circumstances? Have they done anything for their own salvation? Their whole time has been occupied in the forming of a cursed Constitution, and their army has been forgotten and neglected! We have not, I again repeat, increased our army 20,000 men in the last year, nor is there in my opinion any hopes of amendment.

'About four months ago General Freyre, with 3,500 cavalry, was sent to Seville by order of Lord Wellington, to clothe, arm, equip, and instruct the corps. I saw a letter from General Freyre, about a fortnight since, in which he states that he had received nothing; and that he was not able to exercise his cavalry *for want of money to pay for the horses' shoes*!

'You must be satisfied that a year's reflection is sufficient. That time has elapsed since I first wrote to you on the subject. Get me recalled, and allow me to pass some years at least of happiness with you and yours.'——

In a letter marked *private*, and dated Torrente, 17th July, 1813, he gives to his brother-in-law a detail of the advice he had given to Sir John Murray at the camp of Tarragona, which, as it is embodied in Southey's history, need not be here detailed.

To Colonel Torrens, Military Secretary.

'TORRENTE, 17*th July*, 1813.

'My dear Friend,—I beg leave to recommend to your attentions and civilities, my aide-de-camp, Baron Halberg, who passes through London on his way to Germany. He is a gentleman I much esteem as an officer, and a friend; and as he has been with me for two years, he can give you a good account of the state of the troops which I have the honour to command.

'I remain, my dear Friend,
'Yours most truly,
'SAMFORD WHITTINGHAM.'

Although General Whittingham was exceedingly popular with the Spaniards with whom he came in contact, or rather, perhaps, on that very account, high-placed Spanish officials were often very jealous of the Englishman, who by his zeal and energy appeared to put to shame their own lack of such qualities. These officials gratified their malice by all kinds of slights and insults, and amongst the worst of them were the Ministers of War and Finance. At last matters were carried to such a length, that patience was exhausted. On the 5th August, 1813, General Whittingham sent in his resignation to the Regency; and on the day following he sent it also to Lord Wellington, who was not only the Commander-in-Chief of the Spanish army, but to whom the Ambassador, Sir Henry Wellesley, had yielded the chief control over the British military agents.

Thus, in the course of a year, the two brothers had successively received letters of resignation from the same subordinate. Sir Henry Wellesley had condescended to request the withdrawal of the resignation in 1812. The Majorca division and its commander had since greatly distinguished themselves; but Lord Wellington was different from, and sterner than, his brother. Would he condescend in a similar manner? General Whittingham, at all events, expected no such result:—

Major-General Whittingham to the Marquis of Wellington.

'CAMP BEFORE TARRAGONA, *6th August*, 1813.

My Lord,—I have the honour to enclose translations of various official letters which have passed relative to the subsistence of the troops under my command. I have endeavoured to the best of my power to act up to your Lordship's instructions considering that if a smaller sum than had at first appeared necessary, should be found sufficient, the difference ought necessarily to result in diminishing the sum appropriated by the British Government; inasmuch as your Lordship's order is positive that no part of the money destined for the division of Majorca should be employed in the purchase of provisions. The Duke del Parque, and General Elio, both perfectly agreed with me in the interpretation of your Lordship's instructions; but the official communication which I have just received upon this subject from the Minister of Finance is couched in such terms that I cannot in justice to my own feelings avoid sending in my resignation, which I have directed to General Wimpffen, to be forwarded, with your Lordship's permission, to the Spanish Government.

'I cannot take my leave of this country without availing myself of the opportunity of returning my most grateful thanks to your Lordship for the many favours which I have received at your hands. The obligations, indeed, which I am under to your Lordship, to Marquis Wellesley, and to Sir Henry, will never be effaced from my memory; and nothing will afford me through life so much satisfaction, as to have an opportunity in my limited sphere, of proving the sentiments of respect and gratitude which animate my mind towards everything bearing the name of Wellesley.

'If your Lordship will be pleased to grant me permission, I wish to return immediately to England, and I should take it as a particular favour if Captain Foley might be permitted to accompany me; as I am extremely desirous of getting my account with the British Government settled as soon as possible.

'I have the honour to be, with the highest respect,
  'Your Lordship's most obedient humble servant,
            'SAMFORD WHITTINGHAM.'

On the 22nd August, he gives to his brother-in-law the reasons in detail which had induced him to resign. The Ministers had begun to stop indirectly his acknowledged right to promote the officers of his division; in one case going so far as to separate the regiment of Burgos, which he had formed, from his command. They took in fact every opportunity of slighting him, and letting it be understood that his favour was no recommendation in their eyes. Carrying insult to the extreme limits of falsehood, the Intendant of the 2nd army—eager, no doubt, to please the Ministers—told some of General Whittingham's officers, 'that the division of Majorca was more prejudicial than useful to the nation, and the Minister of Finance ventures to tell me that I am ignorant of the duties of a Spanish General.' The letter continues as follows:—

'The measure, my dear Davis, is at last *full*. I have borne with patience insults and persecutions, because I conceived that my efforts would do good, in our great and glorious cause. In the present case, the opposite impression is strong upon my mind. I am satisfied that, not having it in my power to forward the interests of the war—inasmuch as I am become the innocent cause of ruining the career of all who serve under my orders—it is my duty not to hold a command which could only serve to flatter my vanity at the expense of interests that I have always held dearer than my own. I have, as Buonaparte says of his politics, a morality of my own; and I can never for a moment consent that for my personal advantage, the interests of those whom I am bound to protect and cherish should suffer the least detriment.

'On the point of quitting the military career, I have had the satisfaction of executing two operations well.

'When Lord William retired from before Tarragona, on the approach of Soult, my corps which was the most advanced, was attacked by a French column of 5,000 infantry, and 300 cavalry. I had with me 1,300 infantry, and 40 dragoons. This little force retired with admirable order upwards of ten miles—checked and repulsed the enemy whenever he pressed upon us, and about seven in the evening effected a junction with the remainder of the division, which by my orders occupied a commanding position in Biar. At one in the morning we again began our retreat, and joined the main body of the army at Cambrils. Our retreat was from the Coll de St. Christina to Brassin-Valls—Reus, and Cambrils—a distance of thirty-three miles.

'On the 17th, Lord William Bentinck ordered me to leave the division of infantry of my command at Coll de Balaguer; and with the whole of the Spanish cavalry to continue my retreat to the Ebro, and to cross the river as quickly as possible. The whole of the baggage of the 3rd army, and one division of 2,000 men under the command of the Duke del Parque had taken the same route the evening before.

'At ten at night I arrived on the banks of the Ebro, and found the only means of passage to be a raft, capable of carrying over four carts; and one small boat. Tortosa was distant two leagues; its garrison 6,500 men; and reinforcements immediately expected from Suchet.

'The division of infantry of the Duke's army took up a position on our right. The baggage of the Duke's army began to pass, and by dint of the greatest efforts, I collected by the morning eight small boats; each boat held two men with their saddles, &c.; and two horses swam the river, *each man leading his horse.** With these miserable means, I passed over in the day and night of the 18th [August] the whole of the cavalry and artillery, excepting six pieces and two squadrons. On the morning of the 19th, the French attacked General Berenger

* This was a slight error, corrected in his *Recollections*, as will be seen hereafter.

(who commanded the covering division) with six pieces of cannon, 4,000 infantry, and ninety dragoons. Things looked very ill; when the rapid advance of three of my guns on the right, and three on the left, and their truly well-directed fire, checked the progress of the enemy, and induced him to order a retreat. A battalion of grenadiers, sent by the Duke from the other side of the river, ably supported by the guns on the left, and the arrival of the head of the Duke's staff, remedied the errors and follies of the General commanding,—*who, I am grieved to say, was literally as drunk as a beast.*

'My artillery had never been in fire before; but they did wonders. [The French] General Robert's aide-de-camp dined with me yesterday, and informed me that they thought the whole of our cavalry and artillery had crossed the river; and that General Robert determined upon retreating as soon as he found out his mistake. We had two other guns, which could not be used for want of men and horses, these being on the other side of the river. I drew them up, however, in the plain, and formed on their right an immense squadron of all the servants and mounted followers of the army; who made a great show, and served to impose not a little.

'We have lost about 400 men in killed and wounded, and the French about double that number. Suchet has blown up the works of Tarragona, and our troops have entered the town.

'I hope to be with you in the month October: and I trust in God that we shall pass many happy days together in the renewal of those first and beloved impressions which in good minds are never to be effaced.'——

In his 'Recollections,' Sir Samford has given a very graphic account of his passage of the Ebro, which, though more picturesque, differs from the letter written at the period in only one very trifling fact, and, strange to say, in that, the 'Recollections' appear the more accurate and probable. Perhaps the letter written on active service was hurried. What was written in 1840, is as follows:—

'On arriving at the Ebro we found ourselves without boats to effect our passage. We tried to swim the horses over without dismounting the men. But invariably as soon as the horse felt a little tired he dropped his hind quarters, and his rider floated out of the saddle. I linked a division of horses together, but they had not half crossed the river, when they began to fight, and they were all drowned. I finally adopted the plan of putting two men in a small boat, *one to row and one to lead the horses.*'

That portion of the 'Recollections' on this subject which only repeats what has been already given in quotations from the letter of 22nd August is omitted, but what comes next is here subjoined, beginning after the repulse of the garrison of Tortosa:—

'Having failed in their surprise, the French continued their retreat closely followed by our troops. Like old and experienced soldiers, they took advantage of every obstacle to impede our advance, and to cover their retreat. In this affair I lost a dear and much esteemed friend, O'Reilly. He was nephew to the famous Count O'Reilly, and as gallant a soldier as ever drew sword. We had studied together at High Wycombe: and on his joining me in Spain, I made him colonel of a regiment of grenadiers;—for all power of promotion, of organization, of distribution, and of employment of the troops under my command had been placed by the Spanish Government, with the approbation of the Duke of Wellington, exclusively in my hands.

'In following up the French too eagerly, at the head of a single detachment of cavalry, his (O'Reilly's) horse was shot under him, and he fell. His cavalry fled, and the French soldiers who had fired from behind a wall, leaped over and murdered him in cold blood. I was not two hundred yards from the spot when he fell; but in a moment he was stripped, and on his bleeding body were discovered no less than seven bayonet wounds, one of which was quite through the throat. Severely, however, did the enemy pay for this act of barbarity. Several hundreds of their wounded men remained on the field of battle, every one of whom fell a sacrifice to the manes of O'Reilly, for our infuriated soldiers gave no quarter after his death.'——

The exact time when the following circumstance occurred, the Editor has not been able to discover. The account is taken from the 'Recollections,' and is worthy of being recorded:—

'My instructions during my stay in Aragon were to take care of the condition of the horses, and to form the largest possible depôt of grain, and of the means of transport for our future advance into Catalonia. I had no other means of feeding my troops but by requisitions, which, however, the Commissary-General alone was allowed to make, countersigned by me. But the distribution of the quantity to be furnished by each town was made by the municipality of the principal town in the district, upon the returns furnished by the Chief Commissary, which returns were countersigned by me. All arbitrary proceedings were thus checked; and the receipts of the Commissary were invariably received by the Spanish Government in payment of taxes and dues of all kinds. I adopted the same system in Aragon; but the result had not been satisfactory, and the horses were starving for want of food. Had this abomination been suffered to continue for a fortnight longer, so far from being in every respect ready for the field, my 3,000 cavalry and 36 pieces of horse-artillery (the whole of my force in Aragon) would have been totally inefficient, and good for nothing. Sancho has an apt saying for such desperate cases, *A males graves remedios fuertes;* (great evils require strong remedies.) So I directed my favourite Ruti to take fifty hussars, and to collect and bring to my quarters every

Alcalde (mayor) who had failed to obey my orders. He brought thirteen! "Gentlemen," said I to them, "it grieves me more than I have words to express, to be forced, by your want of patriotism, to have recourse to measures of severity, at all times repugnant to my feelings, but peculiarly so in a war entered into in defence of your religion, your country, and your King! Coolly and deliberately you appear to have made up your minds to aid and assist the French, by every indirect means in your power; and as I cannot tolerate so pernicious a system, I am desirous that you should experience personally how very disagreeable it is to be reduced in point of diet to the lowest possible expression; and how little can be expected of men or animals so treated.

'"Ruti," I continued, "escort these gentlemen to the Castle. Let each be lodged in a separate cell, and be furnished *daily* with a loaf of bread and a pitcher of water. Furnish them also with pen, ink, and paper for their correspondence; and let them know, that no change will take place in their position till all my requisitions have been attended to."

'In less than a week my magazines were full, and I never had any further cause of complaint.'——

We now return to the correspondence of the period, at an interesting moment to General Whittingham.

On the 9th August, 1812, he had sent in his resignation to the English Ambassador of his Spanish command; but had withdrawn it at the request of that amiable and distinguished functionary, under whom he was serving as a military agent. Since then the division had established an honourable reputation. Yet on the 5th August, 1813, he once more resigned his Spanish command in disgust at the treatment he had received from Spanish Ministers. On that day he sent his resignation to the Regency; and the day following to Lord Wellington.

On the 28th and 31st August, and on the 4th September small parties of the Majorca division greatly distinguished themselves in skirmishes; the details of which are carefully preserved in Reports numbered 1, 2, and 3. There is only space to record that on the 28th August, Captain Francisco Fernandez, of the regiment of Light Dragoons of Olivencia, by repeated and successful charges against a superior body of French horse and foot, covered himself with glory and put the enemy to flight.

The following letter signed by the illustrious Commander-in Chief of the allied armies, after being carefully written by one of his Staff, (evidently meant to be secret and confidential, though not so marked) instead of as usually in a clerk's hand, speaks for itself:—

The Marquis of Wellington to Major-General Whittingham.*

'LESACA, 20th *September*, 1813.†

'Sir,—I have received your letter of the 6th August, by the Chief of the Staff of the division of troops under your command, who now returns with this answer.

'I feel the utmost concern that you should think it necessary to retire from the Spanish service in consequence of the use of an expression in the correspondence between two ministers, which would never have reached you if the arrangement made with me by the Spanish Gov^t. had been adhered to—that all reports and applications from the army to the Gov^t. and their answer, should pass through my hands.

'I must also observe, that you have mistaken my in-

---

* The Editor does not know why Colonel Gurwood left blanks in this letter, which was so flattering a testimony to the value of General Whittingham's services.

† In the punctuation of this letter, *Gurwood* is followed; but the rest of it accurately copies the original now lying before the Editor, which differs from the letters given by Gurwood—1st, in the order of dating; 2nd, in the number of the word 'arrangement'; 3rd, in abbreviations of the word 'Government.'

tentions in my letter of the 8th of January, 1813. I stated that the funds placed in your hands by His Majesty's Ambassador, were not to be employed in provisions, hospitals, or means of transport, but in the pay of the General and other officers and soldiers present with the division.

'What I meant by ordering that the money should not be employed in provisions, was that it should not be employed in the purchase of bread, to which every Spanish soldier has a right, besides his daily full pay, which article was to be found by the Spanish Gov^t.; but I understood then, as I now understand, that when a Spanish soldier receives his full pay, he is not entitled to what is called *étape*, or any other support from Gov^t., excepting bread; and I could not, therefore, mean that the money should not be laid out to supply the soldier with food necessary for him besides bread, according to the Ordenanzas of the Spanish Gov^t.

'I think this is sufficiently clear in my letter of the 8th January; but if that letter should leave any doubt on that subject, the enclosed extract of a letter to General Sir John Murray, which I have reason to believe was communicated to you, and to General Roche, will have shown in positive words what my opinions were.

'The practice upon this subject has, I believe, differed from the regulation, and this may have fallen into disuse; and at all events, it may be difficult to subsist the soldier upon his pay. But that is a matter for representation and further regulation, but not for your resignation.

'Under these circumstances, I have thought it best to withhold your papers till I shall hear further from you in answer to this letter.

'I am afraid that it is not in my power to prevail on the Gov^t. to promote Colonel Serrano.

'In regard to the other objects referred to in your letter of the 22nd August, as it is possible that you may alter your determination of retiring from the Spanish service in consequence of this letter, it is not necessary that I should consider them at present.

'I have the honour to be, Sir,

'Your most obedient servant,

'WELLINGTON.

' M.-General Whittingham,
   '&c., &c., &c.'

As for the mistake referred to in this letter, (a mistake equally made by General Elio, and General the Duke del Parque,) that was a circumstance of comparative indifference to General Whittingham. That Lord Wellington felt *the utmost concern* at his leaving the Spanish service, was inducement enough to make him brave any amount of mortifications which continuance in that service might entail.

On the 9th August Lord Wellington informed Sir John Murray that the English Government had determined, on Admiral Hallowel's letter, to bring him to a court-martial. Later in the year, in a letter dated Reus, 25th November, 1813, General Whittingham writes to Colonel Torrens the military secretary at the Horse-Guards: 'I hope Sir John Murray will not call on me as an evidence. It was my opinion and still is—and Sir John knew it all the time,—that we ought to have marched on the 9th against Decaen,—have driven him across the Llobregat, blown up the bridge, and returned instantly to meet Suchet, who could not have been at Montoblanco before the 16th. It is, and was my opinion, that Sir John might on a small scale have equalled the glory of Buonaparte at Mantua. The evening before we broke up, Sir John came to my camp, and told me that he had determined to march against Decaen, and that I should move at daylight with three of my battalions. I have hitherto not mentioned my opinions, or what passed between Sir John and me to anyone. He is unfortunate, and God forbid that I should appear against him in the light of a public accuser.'

To his Brother-in-law.

'CALANDA, *7th October,* 1813.*

'I have received so kind a letter from Lord Wellington, in which his Lordship is pleased to say that he feels the utmost concern at my idea of leaving the Spanish service, that I have determined to remain and take my chance to the end of the war. His Lordship has appointed me to a very large command of cavalry; not less than 5,000 horse.

'I have with me, at this place, fifteen squadrons. Our daily exercises have already rendered them very dexterous, and I do think that another month will make them everything I could wish. This is the first time you have heard me speak with enthusiasm of the Spanish cavalry. I cannot, however, help feeling a considerable degree of pleasure at the idea of succeeding in the regeneration of the Spanish cavalry, when everybody else has failed! 5,000 horse, with fifteen pieces of horse artillery, is certainly a fine command; and if I can make the rest of the cavalry as good as that which I have now with me, I do not doubt that the exit will be as favourable as we could wish.

'If you see General Donkin in town, I pray you be attentive to him. He is a real friend of mine, and a good officer and worthy man. In my opinion, he has been very unfairly coupled with Sir John Murray, in the unfortunate affair of Tarragona!

'I should be obliged to you if you would order from Whippy a hussar saddle complete, such as he has always made for me, and a hussar bridle; the bit of which to be large and heavy like those used by the soldiers of the 1st regiment of German hussars.

'I am grieved most deeply to be again deprived of the pleasure of seeing you and yours this winter. But I am

---

* In this letter he announces the birth of his eldest (surviving) son.

sure that you will agree with me, that when such a man as Lord Wellington condescends to express a wish, it must be the glory, as well as the duty, of any soldier to obey [him].

'Yours ever,
'SAMFORD WHITTINGHAM.'

General Whittingham was not present at the action, in the pass of Ordel, in which Lord William Bentinck's advance guard under Colonel Adam (who had so distinguished himself at Castalla) was attacked and forced to retire with the loss of four pieces of artillery. In his dispatch to Field-Marshal the Marquis of Wellington dated Tarragona, 15th September, 1813, Lord William states: 'I had not numbers equal to those which the French could bring against me; I had been obliged to leave the division of General Whittingham at Reus and Vals, from the want of provisions and means of transport.' General Whittingham must have been greatly mortified at his enforced absence on this occasion, though he must have derived some consolation from learning that such of the Spanish troops as were present at that unfortunate affair, equally, with the English, distinguished themselves by their steadiness and gallantry.

To his Brother-in-law.

'CALANDA, 10*th October*, 1813.

'The state of politics in this country is woeful. The Government are doing everything in their power to incommode Lord Wellington. But great changes are soon expected.

'The Spanish cavalry has done nothing during the war. It is in a state of complete disorganization: immoveable from want of discipline and instruction; sunk and depressed from misery and want; accustomed to defeat, and almost deprived of the hope of success! Under these circumstances, you will readily conceive that I have not a moment to lose in commencing a system of organization, and I may say of regeneration; which must either, on the trial of the effects produced, lead them and me to immortal glory, or plunge us one and all into the abyss of disgrace and dishonour!

'I have been for the last month at work with twelve squadrons. Their daily progress has exceeded my warmest expectations, and I trust in God and our good cause that " every man will do his duty."

'If, in speaking to you in the confidence of the truest friendship, any expression should escape me which may look like self-praise, do not attribute it to vanity. I certainly believe and hope that it could not proceed from so poor a source.

'The great advantage that I have hitherto had in the different commands which I have held in the Spanish service, has arisen from the study I have always made it to cultivate the greatest harmony and good-will amongst the corps, officers and soldiers, of the troops under my orders. I have laid it down as a system—to behave kindly to all, —to cultivate by every means in my power the happiness and comfort of officers and men; to forgive and forget the errors and wanderings of youth and inexperience, and to punish with a severity even beyond the law everything which could throw the slightest blemish upon that honour and exaltation of sentiment, without which no soldier can deserve the name.*

'The result, my dear Davis, has been the heartfelt satisfaction of being idolized both by soldiers and officers; and of seeing officers and soldiers of these different armies, all now united under my command, living together as one family, and without a single instance having occurred of the slightest dispute or disagreement.

* This sentiment has long been carefully fostered in the *Prussian* army, and greatly contributes to its excellence.

'On this basis I build my principal hopes of success. The *morale* of the Spanish cavalry has been destroyed by neglect, and I hope to raise it by being their friend and protector; by participating in all their hardships and sufferings, by providing, by every means in my power, for their wants and necessities, and above all by showing them on the day of battle, that example, without which all the tactics in the world are of no avail.'

If the reader will recollect that the writer was a British Lieutenant-Colonel of only little more than two years' standing, he will not be surprised that the being entrusted by Lord Wellington and the Spanish Government with the prospective command of 5,000 cavalry, should have raised his hopes of being serviceable to his country and its allies, to the highest pitch of enthusiasm. Had the Peninsular war been prolonged for a couple of years, the example of the Majorca division might have been repeated on a larger scale, by the cavalry of Spain, under the orders of an Englishman who had gained the confidence of the Duke of Wellington and of the Spanish nation.

To his Brother-in-law.

'REUS,* 18*th November*, 1813.

'I have this moment received your affectionate letter of the 2nd October, and am grieved beyond measure that my silence should have occasioned so much uneasiness to you. It was occasioned by my waiting for Lord Wellington's decision upon my resignation. With his lordship's flattering answer you are already acquainted. I have for the last two months been hard at work with the cavalry. The twelve squadrons, which I have sent to Saragossa, manœuvre well at a gallop, and charge in a very fine

---

* Here he had been left, as already explained, by Lord William Bentinck; and was thus saved from sharing a repulse: which, however, it is by no means improbable his division might have changed into a victory, as it was by superior numbers that the French gained their advantage.

style. In Calanda I have as many more to form; and the whole is shortly to be increased to 5,000—if any attention can be paid to rumours; my future destiny is still, however, undecided. One report says that I am to command all the cavalry of the right; another, that I am to command a separate *corps d'armée* in upper Aragon; a third, that Copons goes to the Ministry of War, and that I am to command in chief the army of Catalonia.'

Colonel Torrens to R. H. Davis, Esq. M.P.
(Extract.)
' HORSE-GUARDS, 19*th November*, 1813.

'I now return the interesting papers which you enclosed me in your letter of the 31st ultimo; and I assure you that in those which so strongly mark the military energy and talents of my friend Whittingham, I have derived a satisfaction equally decided with the disgust and indignation naturally excited by a perusal of his correspondence with the Spanish Government. It is no wonder that such treatment and base insinuation should induce him to give in his resignation; though, at the same time, one could not help regretting that he should have given way to the evident aim which they had in view. Now that danger is removed from the immediate door of the Spanish nation, their little jealousies will lead them to disgust, and dismiss if they can, every foreign officer. But I rejoice to find that Lord Wellington's interference has induced Whittingham to disappoint them for this time. The command which his Lordship has given W. is most desirable and flattering; and I have no doubt but that he will derive great credit from it. I have also had a letter from him, acquainting me with this change in his destination.'

Major-General Whittingham to his Brother-in-law.
' REUS, 25*th November*, 1813.

' Lord Wellington has proposed that I shall have the command of about 6,000 cavalry. Nine regiments are already under my orders. I am ordered to reorganize them completely. I have already sent four regiments to Saragossa in a very good state of manœuvre. Having now this very large command of cavalry, I have been obliged to mount myself with a couple of good English hunters; and, I am sorry to say, they have cost me so much money that I fear that my affairs will be a little deranged by it. They have each cost me 550 dollars.

'Torrens, in a *private letter* of the 21st October, concludes his truly kind and affectionate epistle by saying: "Should you quit the Spanish service, you *must* be placed at the head of a regiment of cavalry: I have already mentioned this to the Duke,* who has received it most graciously." What a magnificent thing this would be for me!'——

This was a bitter subject to him afterwards. Though his only real English regimental service had been in the cavalry, yet, unfortunately, his promotions successively to Major and Lieutenant-Colonel had been to infantry half-pay. At the period in question he might have been transferred to the cavalry. But in later years, when a general officer, he could obtain only the honorary colonelcy of an infantry regiment, on the plea that he had not served in the cavalry as a field officer! That was carrying routine rather far in the case of a man who had always served in the cavalry, English or Allied; and to whom Lord Wellington had, towards the close of the Peninsular War, entrusted 6,000 Spanish horse for complete organization!

On the 23rd October, 1813, Lord Wellington writes to Sir Henry Wellesley: 'The Cortes have acted in respect of the resignation as they have on every other

---

* Of York—the Commander-in-Chief.

subject.* The delay is a matter of indifference to me; and things may go on as they are, as long as they choose to delay. In the meantime the Minister of War has written me a most impertinent letter, of which I shall take no notice.' Lord Wellington adds: 'I would recommend you, if you find the new Cortes act upon the same democratical system as the last, to quit them, and travel about to amuse yourself.'

Lord Wellington had little reason to be pleased with the democratic government of the Cortes, which continued most of the abuses of Old Spain, without the responsibility or regularity of the monarchical rule.

It cannot, therefore, be surprising, that General Whittingham shared the feelings of his chief; and that, though (unlike the latter) his antecedents were not likely to make him otherwise than liberal minded, he was not pleased with the very republican form of government now established in Spain; for which that country was then, *as it is now*, quite unfit, for want of sufficient education and civilization. It is necessary to take these facts into consideration, in judging of the future proceedings of General Whittingham in Spain; and also to bear in mind that, as a foreigner in command of troops, he deemed it his duty to take no part whatever in any political intrigues or changes of government; unless, at the request of the English Ambassador, when his services were deemed necessary.

To his Brother-in-law.

'SARAGOSSA, 28th *December*, 1813.

'As a proof how much more easy it is to feel the extent of the sacrifices which one may be called on to make, than to carry that sentiment into execution, Lord Wellington himself—in spite of his admirable system

* Lord Wellington had, in disgust, sent in his resignation of the command of the Spanish army.

of forbearance—sent in his formal resignation of the supreme command of the Spanish armies, not long since; and in the discussion in the Cortes, whether it should be [accepted] or not, the point was only carried in his favour by a majority of four votes!

'He is, however, thank God! again firmly seated; and I hope and trust, that when all the members of the Cortes have taken their seats, we shall see a new Regency, and a new Ministry of War—without which, believe me, things cannot go on long. The cavalry under my command is composed of nine regiments. The division of Majorca is under my command as before. The artillery fifteen pieces, horse.

'The Inspector-General of Cavalry wrote to me the other day, to say that I might consider myself as possessing all his powers; and that I had nothing to do but to propose whatever arrangements might appear to me good, in the certainty that they would be approved of by him. The Inspector [General] wished to have placed all the cavalry in the kingdom under my orders; and he did me the honour to assure Lord Wellington that the only cavalry worthy of the name would be that which I should form!

'May I hope that these flattering circumstances will aid and assist my anxious desire to be placed at the head of a British regiment of cavalry?* Several officers of no great interest have lately been put at the head of cavalry regiments at home. M——, of the 13th, has got the Inniskilling Dragoons.

'You would be delighted to see how extremely well eighteen of my squadrons manœuvre. I am fearful to say all I think of them. But I doubt whether I have seen anything better in any country. I cannot tell you what Lord Wellington means to do with my cavalry. I hope to God he will attach it to his army. It is really good. I am capitally mounted, though half ruined with

* As Lieutenant-Colonel commanding.

the expense. I have now seven nags fit for the field. The harmony and union which reign in all the corps of cavalry under my command is the admiration of all! I shall write to Lord Wellington to request that he will allow me to send an officer to England for the clothing.

'Torrens has already made me an effective Lieutenant-Colonel from the 30th May, 1811.*

'I have been elected a member of the Royal Academy of Arts and Sciences of San Luis, established in this town; and the flattering distinctions that I have received here are beyond description. My route to and from the Sunday parades appears more like a Roman triumph than anything else; and the whole population of Saragossa appear to vie one with another in doing me honour! Yet in the midst of all the brilliancy of parade and distinction, my heart beats to return to the scenes of love and affection which await me in your beloved society; and the happiness I enjoy is only the anticipation of the blessings which await me at home!'——

Alas! for the enthusiastic pride and hopes of the warrior. At length he had obtained a rank and position, and a command sufficiently large to give him sanguine hopes of being able to serve his country (through its allies) on a larger scale and in a more effectual manner than ever. But peace was rapidly approaching, and with it was to disappear the last chance of the re-establishing in the field the lost character of the Spanish cavalry. 'Tis not in mortals to command complete success; but it is at least something to have deserved it, not only by the testimony of his own conscience, but by the approval of that great and fortunate man who, besides securing his own renown, had acquired authority to stamp deserving merit with the seal of his invaluable and durable recognition.

* An effective infantry Lieutenant-Colonelcy, being a matter of rejoicing to a General commanding 6,000 horse, forms here an amusing incident.

CHAPTER XI.

1814.

SPANISH PROMOTIONS—A PRAYER NOT HEARD—LORD WELLINGTON'S FEARS REGARDING SPAIN—RECEPTION OF FERDINAND VII. AT SARAGOSSA—A TRIUMPHANT ENTRY—CONSTITUTION UNPOPULAR IN SPAIN—THE KING REQUESTS GEN. W. TO ACCOMPANY HIM TO VALENCIA—THE ROYAL PRESENT—ARRESTS—'THE MAJESTY THAT DOTH HEDGE A KING'—THE KING AND DON CARLOS'S FLATTERING REQUEST—*THE DUKE'S* TESTIMONY TO THE MERITS AND SERVICES OF GENERAL WHITTINGHAM—HIS CONVERSATION WITH THE DUKE—UNPOPULARITY OF KING FERDINAND IN ENGLAND—APPOINTED AIDE-DE-CAMP TO THE PRINCE REGENT—PROMOTION TO LIEUT.-GENERAL IN SPAIN—SIR JOHN MURRAY'S COURT-MARTIAL—SIR HENRY WELLESLEY RECOMMENDS GENERAL WHITTINGHAM TO VISCOUNT CASTLEREAGH—THE EARL OF FIFE'S LETTER—MARSHAL SUCHET'S OPINION OF WHITTINGHAM—INQUISITION ESTABLISHED IN SPAIN—SPANISH FINANCES—SIR JOHN MURRAY'S TRIAL—UNLUCKY 'BUTS'—GENERAL MINA'S REBELLION—RECOLLECTIONS OF KING FERDINAND—TRIUMPHAL ROYAL ROUTE—THE KING AND THE CONSTITUTION—ROYAL THANKS—GENERAL WHITTINGHAM COMMANDED TO CONTINUE WITH HIS MAJESTY—GENERAL ZAYAS SOUNDS GENERAL WHITTINGHAM—HIS OPINION NOT APPROVED—ARRESTS—MARCH ON MADRID—CAVALRY FIELD-DAY—LIEUTENANT-GENERALSHIP CONFERRED BY THE KING—MINISTRY OF WAR OFFERED—DECLINED AFTER REFERENCE—TAKES LEAVE OF THE KING AND DON ANTONIO.

To his Brother-in-law.

'ALUMNIA, 12*th February*, 1814.

'CONVINCED that peace must soon take place, I am doubly anxious to secure at home such a situation as may enable me to live amongst my best and dearest friends, with the respectability which I conceive necessary, after the command which I have held in this country.

'In my campaigns in this country I have the singular satisfaction to be able to state that all my [Spanish] commissions have been gained in the field of battle; and have been granted to me as a reward of service, without the slightest intervention on the part of any person. In [the case of] Baylen, I was made effective colonel of cavalry. In Mora and Consuegra,* brigadier. In Talavera, Mariscal de Campo. Still, however, I long to return to the service of my own country; and I would not hesitate a moment between being a British Colonel, or a Lieutenant-General in any other service. If, however, circumstances should render this impossible, I must, I fear, give up those hopes which have ever been most cherished by my heart; and continue my services here.

'I confess to you that I have not the best opinion of the future state of things in this country. I enclose a gazette containing the peace treated of by Buonaparte and Ferdinand the Seventh; and the decree of the Cortes in consequence. We expect the King to return here soon. It is not easy to imagine what Buonaparte's motives can be for sending him. I fear much that disputes will occur between the King and the Cortes, which may lead to a civil war; or at least to differences, which the Corsican may know too well how to avail himself of. All will depend upon the class of men in whom the King may place his confidence, God grant that he may choose well!†

'I enclose also another gazette of a review of my fourteen squadrons of cavalry, and of one of artillery given by me to the authorities of Saragossa.'

To the Same.

'SARAGOSSA, 20th March, 1814.

'Nothing can be more grievous than the uncertainty and delay of our correspondence! I [only] yesterday received your letter of the 31st January!

---

* No accounts of the combat of *Consuegra* have reached the Editor's hands. It was one of Alburquerque's successful actions.

† This prayer was not heard.

'I enclose the state papers which have been published here relative to the mission of the Duke of San Carlos.*

'In this country I have no idea of remaining. The republican party is every day gaining ground; and civil war must ultimately decide the contest.

'Lord Wellington is finally arranging the form and number of the Spanish armies. This will determine when and how, and where I am to be employed. In the mean time my cavalry continues to improve and is very fit for any service.'†——

Lord Wellington writing to his brother the Ambassador on the 22nd March, 1814, says: 'I am very much afraid that the real mischief is only now beginning in Spain. I was always certain that the conduct of the people of Madrid towards the Cortes would, after a short time, be the same as that of the people of Cadiz. No popular assembly can exist if it opens its galleries under any other system than that in use in England, unless the press is restrained. I heard at Tarbes the other day that the King had passed Toulouse on his return to Spain. Again on the 27th March, Lord Wellington writes: 'You will have heard that King Ferdinand passed Toulouse on the 18th on his way to Spain.'

On the 30th April from Toulouse Lord Wellington writes to his brother: 'I shall be very anxious to hear of the King's decision and conduct in regard to the constitution.'

Major-General Whittingham to his Brother-in-law.

'MADRID, 21st *May*, 1814.

'I enclose copies of all the official papers which have passed relative to my march here; and I shall now at-

---

* Friend of, and Minister to, Ferdinand VII.

† By a Return of 1st April, 1814, in Spanish, General Whittingham's force at Saragossa consisted of nine regiments of infantry, eleven regiments of cavalry, and 18 pieces of horse-artillery: a large command for a British Lieut.-Colonel.—Vide *Appendix* B.

tempt to give you some idea of what took place from the time of my going to meet the King in upper Aragon.

'On the 12th of March, we received advice at Saragossa, that the King had determined upon taking that route, instead of going direct to Valencia; and that he would be at Seville on the following day. I immediately pushed on about 300 dragoons; with orders to station themselves by troops on the route, and to advance as far as possible; and myself taking post* set off immediately in the same direction. I met the King at ——†, where my cavalry relieved that of the first army.

'As soon as I approached the King's carriage, His Majesty said to me ' *Como va? Tiempo ha que tenemos mucha gana de conocerte.*' ‡ From that day, I received the most marked attention from His Majesty, and the Prince, Don Carlos. The King's entrance into Saragossa, and, in short, into all the towns of Aragon, was such a triumph, as it is impossible to express, and not easy to conceive, except by those who witnessed those happy scenes. But if the marks of joy and exultation were strong beyond measure at the King's return, the expressions of dislike and detestation of the Constitution were not less general and strong: and His Majesty, from his entrance into Aragon till his arrival at Madrid, never heard any language that could induce him for a moment to believe that the Constitution had merited the approbation of his subjects. Nor is this to be wondered at. In the fury of their republican zeal, the rulers of the Cortes had attacked, openly and in the most violent manner, the nobility, the clergy, and the army; and consequently had made the whole of these respectable classes their

---

* Travelling post by relays of horses was then the mode of quick travelling in Spain.

† At the moment of writing, he appears to have forgotten the name of the place (perhaps a small village) where he met the King.

‡ 'How do you do? For a long time we have much desired to know you.'

enemies. They had also, in the plenitude of their financial ignorance, done away with all the old duties, and revenues of Spain; and established, in stead, what they called '*la contribucion unica y directa*'; a tax exactly similar to our income tax. You will recollect with what reluctance this tax was admitted in England, although it was only to meet a small part of our expenditure, and although England from her commerce, interior and exterior, has so large a circulating medium, that disbursements must be to her, compared with Spain, of little burthen! You will easily, therefore, conceive the effect of such a tax on the Spanish peasantry,* and to an extent sufficient to meet the whole expenditure of government.

'The mind of the Spanish nation was in a state of ferment; and the presence of the King produced an immediate explosion.

'Had the King found the nation in general attached to the new Constitution, he would undoubtedly have sworn to it. But never was a national opinion more decidedly, or more openly pronounced. Not a shadow of doubt could remain upon the King's mind.

'The King staid four days at Saragossa; reviewed my cavalry; and was pleased to say everything that was kind and flattering. I accompanied him, with relays of troops, as far as the frontier of Aragon, where I met my Commander-in-Chief, General Elio. On my approaching the King to take leave, he said '*No te vayas. Tengo mucho gusto en que me accompañes. Ven conmigo á Valencia.*' †

'At Valencia, I remained two days, and on taking

---

* It appears that in Spain, no income, however small, escaped the tax in question—a law that would never be tolerated in England.

† His brother-in-law being a good Spanish scholar, the original alone is in the letter. His Majesty said, ' Don't go. I have much pleasure in your accompanying me. Come with me to Valencia.'

leave, the King made me a present of a beautiful mosaic snuff-box, which he desired me to keep in remembrance of him.*

'The remainder of the details of my march you will be perfectly acquainted with by the enclosed official correspondence. Many of the leading people were arrested the night before the King arrived at Madrid, by the Captain-General Eguia, and there is no longer a shadow of doubt, from the republican papers that have been seized, and the secret correspondence with France, that had the King sworn to the Constitution, he would have gone to the scaffold in less than six months.'——

From this letter, a great deal in praise of King Ferdinand has been here omitted, as General Whittingham at a later period reluctantly discovered that the amiable and plausible but fickle and weak-minded prince was very far from being the promising Sovereign he had mistaken him for in the first excitement of His Majesty's return to his loving and enthusiastic subjects, for such were at that time the great masses of the Spanish nation. Shakspeare confesses that there is 'a Majesty that doth hedge a King,' but a King smiling, flattering, grateful, plausible, affable, is surrounded by a double hedge of Majesty. No wonder that for a time the Englishman in his service should have imbibed a personal partiality for a Sovereign, who on his part displayed so flattering an appreciation of his foreign General.†

---

* This box Sir Samford, some nine or ten years later, gave to his beloved and respected friend, the Hon. Sir Edward Paget. This not very valuable gift was all Sir Samford ever received from King Ferdinand.

† If General Whittingham erred in his opinion of King Ferdinand, and of his popularity at this time in Spain, he erred in good company. In a letter dated 'Madrid, 25th May, 1814,' and addressed to Sir Charles Stuart, the Duke of Wellington writes, 'you will have heard of the extraordinary occurrences here, though not probably with surprise. *Nothing can be more popular than the King and his measures, as far as they have gone to the overthrow of the Constitution.* The imprisonment of the *Liberales* is thought by some, I believe with justice, unnecessary, and it is certainly highly impolitic;

To his Brother-in-law.

'MADRID, 23rd *May*, 1814.

'The King of Spain continues to distinguish me by every possible mark of attention. I expect daily the commission of Lieutenant-General.

'The King and the Infante Don Carlos, are anxious that I should remain in their service: but they know not of what materials my heart is composed, and that I prefer the love of my best and dearest friends to all the glory in the world!'——

Lieutenant-Colonel Whittingham, for he now usually reverts to his British rank, determined to return to England; but before leaving he desired to obtain from the great Duke, '*never prodigal of praise,*' some more decided opinion as to the merits of his services in Spain than was to be gathered from the many strong but indirect proofs of confidence which had been hitherto vouchsafed to him.

The result was the following letter, and, considering the character of the illustrious writer, a more comprehensive testimonial can scarcely be imagined, than the words now placed in italics :—

The Duke of Wellington to His Royal Highness the Duke of York.

'MADRID, 4th *June*, 1814.

'Sir,—Colonel Whittingham (Mariscal de Campo,* in the service of Spain) having informed me that it would

---

but it is liked by the people at large.' In the same letter the Duke writes, '*I entertain a very favourable opinion of the King, from what I have seen of him, but not of his Ministers.*'—*Wellington Dispatches,* vol. xii. p. 27.

* Had this letter been delayed a little longer, instead of 'Mariscal de Campo' (that is Major-General), the Spanish rank would have been Lieutenant-General, that is the highest; for Captain-General was (then at least if not now) rather an appointment than a rank, and for it all Lieutenant-Generals were eligible.

be necessary for him to return to England in a short time, and having expressed a desire that I should lay before your Royal Highness my sense of his services and merits, I beg leave to inform your Royal Highness, *that he has served most zealously and gallantly from the commencement of the war in the Peninsula; and that I have had every reason to be satisfied with his conduct in every situation in which he has been placed.*

'I have the honour to be, &c.

'WELLINGTON.'

'His Royal Highness the Duke of York.'

His Grace probably styled Lieutenant-Colonel Whittingham, *Colonel* by courtesy, but he may have known that on that very day, the 'London Gazette' was publishing his promotion.

To his Brother-in-law.

'MADRID, 4th June, 1814.

'I have had a long and very satisfactory conversation with the Duke of Wellington. He is decidedly of opinion that I should by no means think of giving up the British service, although he believes that there will be no objection to my continuing in this part for the moment. He has promised to speak to the Duke [of York] upon the subject of my commission being dated in the year [180]9, which he seems to think may be done with perfect propriety. He also gave me a letter of recommendation to H.R.H. the Duke, "although" as he kindly said "that will not prevent my speaking to H.R.H. as I shall see him before you."

'Castaños has given me a letter to General Gordon, reminding him of the King's [George III.] promise, and begging him to submit my case to H.M.'s consideration. I hope also to obtain from the King of Spain a strong letter of recommendation to the Prince Regent.'——

Meantime, the conduct of the King of Spain had made him very unpopular in England, and that unpopularity was destined later to extend to General Whittingham, as if he could have in any way interfered in the political government of Spain, or had the least authority for so doing.

The Duke of Wellington wrote from London, (20th July, 1814), to Sir Henry Wellesley. 'It is not easy to describe the unpopularity attached to the King's name, from the occurrences at his return to Madrid. The newspapers afford some specimens of it: but at a late dinner at Guildhall, I recommended to the Lord Mayor to drink the King of Spain's health, and he told me that he was become so unpopular in the city, he was afraid that, if the toast were not positively refused, it would at least be received with so much disgust as to render it very disagreeable to me and to every well wisher to the Spanish Government.'

To his Brother-in-law.

'MADRID, *8th June*, 1814.

'I march this evening to Alcala, where I have directed sixteen squadrons of cavalry, and one of horse-artillery, to assemble. They are to manœuvre under my direction, fifteen or twenty days previously to their being seen by His Majesty. This will occasion a small delay in my return home.'

To the Same.

'MADRID, *1st July*, 1814.

'I have seen by the Gazette [of the 4th June] that I have had the high and distinguished honour to be appointed aide-de-camp to his Royal Highness the Prince of Wales! It would be indeed difficult to express my feelings on this occasion.

'The King of Spain has promoted me to the rank of Lieutenant-General;* and [H.M.] assured me the other day, in a manner truly affecting from its kindness, that nothing could grieve him more profoundly than my quitting his service; an event which he hoped and trusted would never take place.'

To the Same.

'MADRID, 14th *July*, 1814.

'My dear Davis,—This night I begin my march for Bourdeaux, through Saragossa.

'I had scarcely taken the pen in my hand, when I received an official summons to attend Sir John Murray's court-martial at Tarragona. This will create a considerable delay. Mrs. W. will remain at Saragossa; and I shall proceed on to Catalonia. I have written to you fully, under cover to Torrens, a few days since. I send this to Bilboa.

'Yours ever most truly,
'SAMFORD WHITTINGHAM.'

Before leaving Madrid, the English Ambassador added his testimony to the services of General Whittingham, entering into more details than his illustrious brother had done:—

Sir Henry Wellesley to Viscount Castlereagh.

'MADRID, 22nd *July*, 1814.

'My Lord,—Lieutenant-General Whittingham being about to embark for England, I have taken the liberty of giving him this letter of introduction to your Lordship.

'The services of General Whittingham, from the period of the breaking out of the general war against France, have obtained for him the approbation of his Royal Highness the Prince Regent, as well as that of the

* This commission as Lieut.-General was dated 16th June, 1814.

Spanish Government. He was with General Castaños, as a military agent at the battle of Baylen; and, in the following campaign, was severely wounded at the battle of Talavera, while leading a Spanish corps into action.

'During the period of his residence at Cadiz, he was employed in the formation of a corps of cavalry: and he afterwards formed the division, which, under his orders, behaved with the greatest gallantry at the battle of Castalla; where it repulsed the attack of nearly the whole of Suchet's corps, and where General Whittingham was again wounded.*

'I have before informed your Lordship that General Whittingham had the good fortune to receive the King at Saragossa, at the head of a division of cavalry, of which he undertook the formation, at the desire of the Duke of Wellington. This division has since been reviewed at Madrid by the King, and was so highly approved by His Majesty, that immediately after the review he conferred upon General Whittingham the rank of Lieutenant-General.

'I have thought it my duty to mention these circumstances, so honourable to an officer whose conduct during his employment in Spain has entitled him to general respect and esteem.

'I have, &c.,
'H. WELLESLEY.'

The following letter, as being also a testimonial to General † Whittingham's services, equally flattering, is here inserted a little out of its place, to complete the estimate of his military services at this period:—

---

* It was at Concentayna (an action that took place a little before that of Castalla) that General Whittingham was the second time wounded in the face. The Editor can find no record of his having been hit at Castalla.

† Whilst he was still in Spain, in spite of the peace, English as well as Spaniards still called him General; but on the part of the English this was now only by courtesy.

The Earl of Fife to General Whittingham.

'PARIS, 31*st December*, 1814.

' My dear Whittingham,—As you know my friendship for you, and everyone who served in Spain is aware of the great regard and high opinion I always entertained of you, it will not be surprising when I inform you how much pleasure I had in hearing your praises from the *highest authority*, concerning your conduct in the last two campaigns.

' I was particularly anxious to know from the French officers who had served in that part of Spain where you were latterly employed, their opinion of your merits and exertions; and, believe me, yourself, or your warmest friends, could not have wished more favourable answers.

' The Duke of Albufera, Marshal Suchet, spoke to me a long time about you, and told me that he was surprised at the perfection you had brought your division to, and that they were in as high a military state as any of his own troops, and, he believed, as any other soldiers in Europe; that he had had frequent occasion to admire your conduct in the field; and his opinion of you was that of a most meritorious officer.

' I was witness to a great part of your exertions in the cause, and was aware what difficulties on all sides you had to encounter. Nothing can be more satisfactory than the result; and I most heartily congratulate you, on your having so steadily persevered in a contest which has gained you a reputation even among your former enemies, of an excellent officer. With every good wish, believe me, my dear Whittingham,

'Your very sincere friend,

' FIFE.' *

---

* See *Preface*, for Lord Fife's letter to the Editor, (in confirmation of the above testimony,) in 1845.

Such a letter, written by one of the bravest of Englishmen, who courted danger as a volunteer, almost for its own sake, is valuable in itself; but as conveying also the more important approval of one of Napoleon's cleverest Marshals, it must ever be treasured by the descendants of General Whittingham, as an invaluable testimony to his merits and exertions; second only to the comprehensive certificate of the Duke of Wellington.

*To Major-General Sir Henry Torrens.**

(Extract.)

'SARAGOSSA, 2nd *August*, 1814.

'My dear Torrens,—Your letter of the 12th [ultimo] I received here on the 21st July; and am most particularly obliged for the leave you have obtained of His Royal Highness the Prince Regent, and His Royal Highness the Commander-in-Chief, [for me] to continue my services in this country.

'I had come thus far on my route to Tarragona, to attend the court-martial of Sir John Murray; but on my arrival at this town, I received intimation that it would not take place at Tarragona, but was transferred to London.

'Previous to the return of my division of Cavalry to Aragon, we had a field-day before the King, [at Madrid] who was pleased to express his highest satisfaction. Immediately after the review His Majesty said to me, "In proof of how much I esteem you, and how highly penetrated I am with [a sense of] your merit, you will receive to-morrow the commission of Lieutenant-General."

'When I waited upon His Majesty to inform him of the honour His Royal Highness the Prince Regent had

---

* All extracts from letters, where the writers are not named, are from the letters of General Whittingham.

been pleased to confer upon me, and to ask leave to return to England for eight or twelve months, His Majesty expressed much satisfaction at my appointment. At the same time he did me the honour to say, "I hope that you do not mean to quit my service. Be assured it would be a matter of great grief to me that you should do so."

'Many things have taken place since the arrival of His Majesty at Madrid which will, I fear, produce much discontent; and most particularly the re-establishment of the Inquisition! The army at least has received this [measure] with decided disapprobation.

'The question of the Inquisition was long and warmly disputed. The Duke of San Carlos; Macanar, Minister of *Gracia* and *Justicia*; Lardizaval, Minister of [the] Indies; Escoiquez, the priest who accompanied the King to France; were decidedly against it: and His Majesty had said that he would take no determination till the reunion of the Cortes, when he would submit the question to their decision. But the weight of influence of the Infante Don Antonio; of Ostalara confessor to the Infante Don Carlos; of the Minister of War, Eguia; of the Marquis of Palacio; and the representations in favour of its re-establishment, of very many towns; at length prevailed, and the King was induced to reauthorize a tribunal of secret despotism, and to legalize tyranny of the worst class.

'The greatest, or at least the most pressing evil, however, which affects this country is the deranged state of the finances.

'Under these circumstances, His Majesty ascended the throne; and although orders were given to do away [with] the income tax, and to re-establish the old duties, yet a very considerable time must elapse before any beneficial consequences can be expected.'*———

---

* These details having been mentioned in a previous letter, are not repeated in this extract.

As in his letter to his brother-in-law, so in his letter to Sir Henry Torrens, his personal attachment and partiality to King Ferdinand, is very conspicuous. That plausible and personally popular monarch, by his gracious smiles and by his really friendly appreciation of the Englishman who had served him so well, had thrown a temporary veil over his real character and vices; which after all were those of a weak and timid, rather than of a depraved and wicked nature.

To Sir Henry Torrens.
(Extract.)

'SARAGOSSA, 30*th September*, 1814.

'My dear Torrens,—I was on the point of beginning my journey to England to appear as a witness on the trial of Sir John Murray, when I received a letter from Sir John, dated Barcelona, stating that he was still in hopes, in consequence of his representations, that the trial would take place in Catalonia; and requesting that I would await at Saragossa the final determination of H.R.H. the Regent. I have now received a letter from him saying that he has received the final answer, and that the trial is to take place in London, to which place he returns by land to France.'

'As Sir John travels through France with his own horses and carriage, I hope to be in England as soon as he can. At all events, the difference cannot be great.

'Could I have avoided quitting Spain at this moment, I have been given to understand, I should have been appointed Inspector-General of Cavalry. But these unlucky *buts* must at times happen to all men.

'General Mina, on receiving the order of the Government to deliver up the command of his troops to the Captain-General of Aragon, Palafox, has refused to obey, and is at present in open rebellion. He has, however, few followers: most of his battalions have come over to the Captain-General. He still, however, keeps the field between this and Pampeluna. In the present instance, it would not be possible for me to take that route to England. I trust, however, that a few days will put an end to his wild enterprise.'——

The following account of Ferdinand the Seventh's return to his kingdom is taken from the often quoted 'Recollections,' and is confirmed by the letters written at the period in question.

'Upon the King's return to Spain, I advanced to the frontier of Aragon to meet him, distributing a sufficient force of Cavalry to form His Majesty's escort on the road, and to furnish his guard at night.

'The charge of the King's person, as well as of his brother Don Carlos, and of his uncle Don Antonio, was made over to me on the frontier of Aragon, by General Copons, then commanding in Catalonia. My reception by His Majesty and the Royal family was infinitely gracious and most flattering. Our marches were twenty or thirty miles a day. The coach or rather landau in which H.M. travelled was English built. The roads were tolerably good, and the royal party suffered little or no fatigue. I rode always at the side of the carriage, and we generally arrived at our resting-place between three and four in the afternoon, having started at about half-past nine. I always dined with the King during the march, and the whole route was one continued scene of triumph. I never saw such a wild expression of joy as the Spanish people universally gave way to on the return of their King from his infamous captivity. His Majesty, during the journey, was constantly occupied in studying the Constitution which he was required to swear to.

'As I rode close to the side of his carriage, he often entered into conversation with me. One day he said,

"Santiago, you will hardly imagine what book I am reading. It is the new Spanish Constitution, formed and published by the Cortes during my absence. I find much that is good in it, but also many things quite inadmissible. Notwithstanding, if the refusal of my sanction is to cost one drop of Spanish blood, I will swear to it to-morrow." *

'Such were then the sentiments of Ferdinand. His Majesty remained three days at Saragossa, and did me the honour to inspect the two thousand cavalry and sixteen pieces of artillery, at my head-quarters. I commanded the field-day. We manœuvred in two lines: and I did everything in my power to give it the appearance of a real action. The King was quite enchanted, and thanked me most warmly for all the services that I had rendered him during his absence.

'On arriving at the frontier of Aragon, I dismounted, and requested His Majesty's orders, previously to making over the charge of his royal person to General Elio, who commanded in Valencia. "I desire," said His Majesty to me, "that you accompany me to Valencia. I am much pleased with you, and you must come on with me."

'At Valencia, the plot began to thicken, [General] Elio was a violent ultra-royalist; and was too well supported by a host of fanatical priests and grandees; and hence the first false impressions were made on the King's mind.

'General Zayas was sent to sound me: for the General commanding so large a body of cavalry and horse-artillery was too important a person to be neglected at such a crisis. "If," said I to Zayas, "you are sent by order of His Majesty to obtain my real opinion upon the present state of affairs, I shall be happy to submit them frankly and fully, for I conceive the measures now to be

---

* Lo juraré mañana.—In the '*Recollections*' all the royal speeches and his own answers are given in the original Spanish, followed by the English translations.

adopted of infinite importance to the well-being of His Majesty and of the Spanish Nation.

'"In my opinion, there is much that is good in the new Constitution; but as there is also much which requires to be modified, it is not in His Majesty's power to swear to it in its present form; especially, on account of the article which requires His Majesty to swear that no change, alteration, or modification shall take place for eight years.

'"Still, however, it must be kept in mind, that the Cortes have rendered the royal cause good service; and that they deserve the gratitude of the King and of the Spanish Nation. On his arrival at Madrid, I humbly conceive, His Majesty should in person thank the Cortes for all their good services, and express his intention to invoke the ancient Cortes of Spain, for their opinion and advice; and having thus announced his royal will, that His Majesty should forthwith dissolve the present Cortes."

'It would seem that my opinions were not approved of; for, the next day, I received orders to return to Saragossa, with the escort which I had furnished for the King's guard, and there to await further orders.

'In the meantime, orders were despatched to General Eguia, at Madrid, to arrest a number of the leading members of the liberal party; and the charge of the King's person was made over to General Elio.

'A few days after my arrival at Saragossa, I received orders to march upon Madrid with the cavalry and horse-artillery under my orders. On my arrival at Guadalaxara, I was directed to halt until further orders; and I did not enter the capital till the morning of the King's entrance; and then only to line the streets in parade order. The arrests had all taken place several days before.

'Nothing can give a true picture of the enthusiastic

joy manifested by the people of Madrid, on seeing their beloved sovereign once again amongst them. A young and handsome *manola* came close to the head of my charger, and shouted with a most audible voice, " May'st thou be blessed, Ferdinand of my soul; Thou shalt be an absolute King, and thou shalt always do whatever may be thy royal pleasure; and if it be thy will to tread us under thy royal feet, thy will and pleasure shall be our only law ! "

'This anecdote brings to my mind a circumstance, which occurred during my march from Saragossa to the frontier of Aragon, to meet the King. I had received my billet in the house of a most respectable yeoman, and after supper, he stated his utter incapacity to comprehend the meaning of the doubts and difficulties which seemed to be generally felt. " Whilst the master was absent," said he, " I understand very well that his head servants* must act in his name; but now that the master has returned home, what have the servants to do but to obey his orders ? "

'As soon as the King had entered the palace [at Madrid], the troops were dismissed; and I retired to my lodgings. A few days afterwards, I had the honour of giving His Majesty a field-day of the cavalry and horse-artillery, which so highly pleased him that he made me a Lieutenant-General on the field.†

'My favour at court was every day increasing; and I had it in my power to be of service to Sir Henry Wellesley, as he has been pleased to state in his letter to Lord Castlereagh. But Tatischeff, the Russian Minister, was too cunning for the straightforward dealing of English diplomatists; and he obtained from Ferdinand

---

* ' Los criados de confianza.'

† From the correspondence of the period it would appear that King Ferdinand only took that graceful occasion to announce the reward already intended for his services.

the *Toison d'or*, which had been refused to Sir Henry Wellesley.

'At this time I spent almost every evening, from eight till ten, in the King's private apartment. The Queen often joined us; and conversation was as free and as general as could have been the case in the house of any private gentleman. His Majesty never took offence at anything that I said. "I cannot comprehend," said I to him one evening, "the interest which your Majesty takes in the affairs of Russia! Your respective countries are placed in the opposite extremes of Europe; and they have not, nor ever can have, any community of interests. On the other hand, England offers to your Majesty her most advantageous friendship, which you appear to despise." "What an excellent Englishman thou art, Santiago!" said the King; "would to God all my subjects were as good Spaniards!"

'Some time afterwards,* His Majesty proposed to make me his Minister of War. I submitted the proposal to Sir Henry Wellesley; and he referred it to Lord Castlereagh, who declared its acceptance to be incompatible with the duties of a British officer; and particularly with those of an aide-de-camp of the King of England.

'Shortly after this, I announced to the King my intention of returning to England. His Majesty and the Infante Don Antonio were full of expressions of grief at my departure; and the King was pleased to say, "Santiago, tell me what you wish, and on condition that you do not leave me, there is nothing in my power that I will not do to please you."† But the day of confidence was passed; and I could not make up my mind

---

* This may mean any time between 1815 and 1819 that he passed in Madrid.

† "Santiago, dime lo que deseas, y con tal que no te vayas y te quedes en mi servicio, no hay cosa en mi poder que no haré por complacerte."

to give up friends and country, on so unstable a base as the caprice of a weak mind. I pledged myself, however, to return to Spain, should His Majesty call for my services.'——

They were destined to meet again; but the history of that reunion must be deferred for a time, and form part of the following Chapter.

CHAPTER XII.

1815—1819.

SIR JOHN MURRAY'S TRIAL—SENTENCE OF ADMONISHMENT NOT CARRIED OUT—AN ABSURD PARLIAMENTARY CALUMNY—A DUEL PREVENTED BY THE SPEAKER—QUARREL ADJUSTED—COLONEL CAMPBELL'S LETTER FROM MADRID—HIS DESCRIPTION OF THE ANGLO-SPANISH OFFICERS—GENERAL WHITTINGHAM'S APPOINTMENT IN THE SPANISH ARMY—FAILED TO OBTAIN EMPLOY WITH BRITISH TROOPS—WANT OF RANK IN THE BRITISH ARMY—THE SECRET DISPATCH—ARISTOCRATIC NATURE OF WELLINGTON—COMMISSIONERSHIP WITH AUSTRIAN ARMY DECLINED—THE SPANISH OFFER PREFERRED—GEORGE IV.'S AIDE-DE-CAMPSHIP NO SINECURE—DUKE OF YORK'S LETTER TO SIR HENRY WELLESLEY—DISAPPOINTING PEACE—GRAND CROSS OF SAN FERNANDO—STATE OF FINANCES IN SPAIN—GENERAL WHITTINGHAM'S MEMOIR TO THE KING ON THE SLAVE TRADE—WHY UNEMPLOYED AT MADRID—ROYAL FAVOUR—RUSSIAN INFLUENCE—MR. B. FRERE'S ENGAGEMENT—AN EXPENSIVE HONOUR FOR LADY WHITTINGHAM DECLINED—LEGITIMATELY EXERCISED INFLUENCE—EXPLANATION OF HIS CONDUCT TO LORD CASTLEREAGH—DECLINES ALL REWARDS—THE ONLY FAVOUR ASKED OF THE KING—GOVERNMENT DECLINED—SERVICES UNREWARDED—STARVATION IN THE MIDST OF HONOURS—MR. VAUGHAN'S RECOMMENDATION OF THE GENERAL—HIS DIPLOMATIC SERVICES TO MR. VAUGHAN—DIPLOMATIC SERVICES TO SIR HENRY WELLESLEY—COMMERCIAL SERVICES TO HIS BROTHER-IN-LAW—INTRODUCES HIS NEPHEW TO THE BEST SOCIETY—MARRIAGE OF MR. B. FRERE BY PROXY—SIR H. WELLESLEY'S LETTER TO THE DUKE OF YORK—THE ROYAL REPLY—PLENTY OF *PRAISE*, NO *REWARDS*—TROUBLES IN SPAIN—DEFENCE OF THE KING A POINT OF HONOUR—DECLINE OF ENGLISH AND RISE OF RUSSIAN INFLUENCE—SECRET NEGOCIATIONS BY THE RUSSIAN MINISTER—DEATH OF MRS. B. FRERE—GENERAL WHITTINGHAM LEAVES MADRID—HIS SUCCESS AGAINST THE SLAVE TRADE—CHAMOIS-HUNTING IN THE PYRENEES—OFFERED THE GOVERNMENT OF DOMINICA—BIDS FAREWELL TO THE KING OF SPAIN—AN ATTENTIVE ROYAL HOST—OPINION APPLAUDED BUT NOT FOLLOWED—THE AMBASSADOR'S FINAL TESTIMONY—NOTHING ASK, NOTHING HAVE—GENERAL WHITTINGHAM'S LETTER TO MR. MURDOCH—FRUITLESS MISSION OF THE COUNT DE CORRES—LORD CASTLEREAGH'S TESTIMONY OF MR. DAVIS—BARON HUGEL'S DESCRIPTION OF THE WEST INDIES.

At the commencement of 1815, Colonel Whittingham for the second time in his life had to perform the disagreeable duty of giving evidence on the court-martial of a Commander under whom he had served. But in the case of Sir John Murray, Baronet, his task was light compared to what it had been on the trial of General Whitelocke in 1808.

Lieut.-General Sir John Murray was tried by a court-martial that sat in London from the 16th January to the 7th February. He was tried (for his conduct in June 1813) on three charges; the first implying imprudence in his plans; and the second, disobedience of orders. But of both these charges he was fully and honourably acquitted. The third and last charge was for his hasty embarkation after raising the siege of Tarragona, although no enemy was near; whereby he unnecessarily lost guns and stores. He was found guilty of 'an error of judgment'* in regard to these losses, as specified in a part of the last charge; and he was sentenced to be admonished. But the Prince Regent thought it needless to admonish for an error of judgment, and the result was a virtual acquittal.

Soon after this trial, General Whittingham, (for so he was styled on this occasion) became the object of a parliamentary calumny, which might be termed atrocious, had it not been too ridiculous to merit so strong a denunciation; and he sent to his friend, Sir Henry Torrens, a Bristol newspaper, giving an account of an exciting scene in the House of Commons, in fuller details than were inserted in the London press.

It is needless to reproduce the details of this calumny. It is sufficient to say that Mr. Whitbread in fact argued as if General Whittingham † were responsible for all the

---

* His errors in judgment were numerous, but Lord Wellington acknowledged his abilities, and he was otherwise a worthy man.

† As his services for the greater part of the war had been per-

pecuniary assistance which *the English Ambassador, and the English Commander-in-Chief had, with the consent of the English Government, given to their Spanish allies!* But not satisfied with this absurdity, he was not ashamed, in the hope of shaking a ministry, to accuse an English officer of distinction of having received more than 50,000*l.* as a bribe to place Ferdinand VII. on a despotic throne; the fact being that the accused officer had lately returned to England a far poorer man than when he had left it; having spent a considerable part of his private patrimony on his commissions and in the public service! But the waves of party spirit then ran mountains high; and even the great Duke himself did not escape their fury; as he has recorded in his immortal 'Dispatches.'

Mr. Hart Davis, member for Bristol, the affectionate brother-in-law of the calumniated General, a man of high character, naturally retorted with spirit on the privileged calumniator, and a duel appeared imminent. The affair is thus recorded by the Bristol journal. [After Mr. Whitbread's motion had been made and rejected.] 'The House had proceeded to the order of the day, when the gentlemen above named retired. The *speaker* felt it to be his duty on the instant, to call the attention of the House to the conduct of two of its members, and to require that the individuals to whom he referred should be immediately called back, to give the House their assurances that no further proceedings should take place in consequence of what had fallen from them in the course of debate.' [The members were brought back, and the gallery was cleared]. 'Strangers were not again admitted, but we understand the Hon. Gentlemen readily gave the assurances required, and the business was in a few minutes satisfactorily adjusted.' The Bristol paper which had warmly taken the part ' of our gallant townsman, General Whittingham,' ends its article by stating:

formed in the rank of General it was natural he should be so called in Parliament.

'General Whittingham is at this time at the house of Mr. Davis at Clifton;' one of the brief and rare visits, that he paid to his native country.

Whilst he was thus calumniated in England, in Spain on the contrary—let it be said in justice to the Spaniards—his merits were still appreciated.

The following letter was written by an excellent officer and brave man, who was also a most estimable gentleman in private life :—

Colonel Patrick Campbell to General Whittingham.*
(Extract.)

'MADRID, 25*th March,* 1815.

'Whatever failings or vices I may have, ingratitude is not amongst them : and truly ungrateful should I be, were I to forget one to whom I owe so very much, and who has shown me so many acts of friendship. Most heartily do I rejoice at the very handsome reception you have received from the Prince Regent. I would to God that you were here again. A.† at present is the only countryman of ours *at this moment* in the peninsula, who has any reputation. B. and C. are only spoken of in derision. D. is never mentioned at all. You, however, are always mentioned both with respect for talents, and instruction, and [with] enthusiasm for your gallantry. An army of 8,000 men is ordered to be formed on the frontier, in consequence of the escape of Buonaparte. Who is to command is yet a secret. Castaños has offered his services; and some say he is to command. Others say, the Infante Don Carlos is to go there: but the present deranged state of the finances will not bear that additional expense.

'My business of Brigadier is not yet decided. Sir

---

* He was then Major in the British, and Colonel in the Spanish, service.
† A. B. C. D. These letters are used to conceal real names.

Henry [Wellesley] however, has done whatever he could; and in consequence Ceballos wrote to Eguia. But he is such an enemy to everything English, that he tries all he can to delay it. I have got the supernumerary cross of Charles III. I do not think old Herasti will ever go to Barcelona. I would you were here, as that is the best Government in Spain; and, as you know, if one is not on the spot nothing is obtained. I wish much you would speak to Sir Henry Torrens for the rank of Lieut.-Colonel [for me]. You were my Commander-in-Chief; and consequently, the only one who can recommend me. It is the step of the greatest importance to me. How does Mrs. Whittingham like England? What an infamous, shameful, and lying attack Whitbread has made! I saw it here in the English papers. He talks of 52,000*l.* as given to you for your own purposes; and you above all men; *who, it may be said, never even saw the public money, much less handled it.** I wish you could tell me, how we serving here are to be considered, particularly *Don Patricio Campbell,* as I am much interested about him, Castaños and Zayas are well, Giron is in Seville, Serrano is in Badajos.'——

Colonel Patrick Campbell was in Spain usually styled 'Don Patricio Campbell' to which he playfully alludes. As Lieutenant-Colonel of the Light Infantry Regiment of the Majorca division, as well as on the Staff of General Whittingham, he had always distinguished himself greatly by zeal, intelligence and courage, and, as usual with all who served under the General, was devotedly and permanently attached to his Chief.

Meantime the escape of the great Napoleon had again aroused to arms the greater part of Europe; and reopened prospects of fresh distinction to all soldiers:—

---

* General Whittingham had had the responsibility, had negotiated the bills, and conducted the correspondence; but until Paymaster Foley was appointed, Colonel Campbell performed the actual payments required.

To Major-General Sir Henry Torrens.

'LONDON, 28*th May*, 1815.

'Sir,—I have the honour to inform you, that I received by last mail my appointment of Lieutenant-General employed in the army of Catalonia under the orders of General Castaños. I have therefore to request you will be pleased to submit this appointment to the consideration of H.R.H. the Commander-in-Chief; and at the same time that you will express my hope that H.R.H. will condescend to allow me to proceed to Spain immediately.

'*Having failed in my solicitations for employment in Flanders*,* I am anxious to join the army in Catalonia with as little delay as possible; and as my appointment there has taken place, I cannot, I conceive, use too much expedition in getting to my post. I have the honour to be, Sir,

'Your most obedient servant,
'SAMFORD WHITTINGHAM.'

This letter establishes the fact, that he had previously desired rather to serve under Wellington as a Colonel, than with the Spaniards as a Lieutenant-General. Had his request been granted, he would doubtless have justified himself to the King of Spain, under the sound plea that there was no danger to be immediately apprehended in Spain from Napoleon, as was well-known to be the case.

The word solicitations being in the plural, there rests a strong suspicion in the Editor's mind, that Colonel Whittingham, not only applied direct to the Duke of Wellington, but did so also through His Royal Highness

---

* Till perusing the words now placed in Italics, the Editor was wholly unaware of the fact of such applications. No doubt their refusal had been too sore a subject to mention, in spite of the flattering terms in which they had been couched.

the Duke of Kent. In short the Editor has some reason to believe that the letter of the Duke of Wellington dated 'Bruxelles, 14th April, 1815,' and addressed to Her Majesty's illustrious father, refers to Colonel Whittingham. Colonel Gurwood having unfortunately left this name in blank, and none of the original applications having reached the Editor's hands, the matter must remain for the present doubtful. To desire eagerly to serve under the Duke of Wellington was sufficiently praiseworthy to have justified Gurwood in printing the name of the rejected applicant, especially as the rejection was coupled with the flattering words; 'he knows that if I could have gratified him I would have done so, without the aid of your Royal Highness's powerful influence.'*

There can be no question, however, that besides merit, some high aristocratic connection was required at that moment, to obtain a place on the Staff, then ambitioned by hundreds of meritorious officers. It was no disgrace to fail in such an application, but rather a high honour when accompanied by an observation, which so plainly and strongly implied that no want of merit occasioned the writer's non-compliance with the request. If a list were made of all those who served on the great Duke's staff throughout his life, it would be found that birth or rank had ever the strongest claims on his favour; and that the kind of liberality which was so frequently displayed by kings and royal dukes, was never one of the traits of the essentially aristocratic as well as illustrious Duke of Wellington.

It appears, however, that though to serve under the Duke, Sir Samford would have retired from the Spanish service, this was before his services had been called for by the Spanish King. For he declined (subsequently)

* Vol. xii. of *Wellington Dispatches*, page 308, edition 1838.

the offer of the post of British Commissioner to the Austrian army, when offered to him by Lord Castlereagh.

Now that he was once more going to serve in Spain, he became again a General even at the Horse-Guards. He had also been made C.B. and knighted.*

To Lieutenant-General Sir Samford Whittingham.

'Horse-Guards, 2nd June, 1815.

'Sir,—I have not failed to lay before the Commander-in-Chief your letter of the 28th ultimo, communicating to me, for His Royal Highness's information that you had received your appointment of Lieutenant-General employed in the army under General Castaños; and requesting permission to proceed to Spain to join the same in Catalonia.

'I have His Royal Highness's commands to acquaint you that as circumstances do not admit of your talents and experience being rendered available to the services of the British army itself, in a manner adequate to your claims and pretensions, he can have no objection to your being employed in the general cause, by assuming the duties in the Spanish army to which you have been called in so flattering a manner by His Catholic Majesty. I am therefore charged by the Commander-in-Chief to apprize you, that you have the Prince Regent's leave of absence to proceed to Spain without delay; and likewise His Royal Highness's *special* permission to absent yourself for the same purpose from your situation in the household. I have the honour to be, Sir,

'Your most faithful and obedient humble servant,

'H. Torrens.'

'Lieutenant-General Sir Samford Whittingham.'

The reference at the close of this letter, to the duties of aide-de-camp to the Prince Regent, gives occasion to state

---

* At that time no one could be made K.C.B. under the rank of Major-General; but distinguished officers, who had earned the C.B. were sometimes knighted.

that in this capacity Colonel Whittingham appears to have been very successful. It is to be regretted that he did not write of George IV., similar recollections to those he has left of Ferdinand VII. The English monarch, there is reason to believe, treated him with scarcely less kindness than did the Spanish sovereign :—and he used when on duty, to be called into the royal private apartment, to be consulted as to the equipment and clothing of the cavalry. At the levées also, owing to their rarity, and consequent crowding, the post of Royal aide-de-camp would appear to have been no sinecure at that period; and physical strength was quite as needful a qualification as courtly manners and bearing. At the royal drawing-rooms especially the crush was tremendous. There also the King alone receiving the ladies, it sometimes happened when some bashful young persons were to receive *the royal lip salute*, that they required to be almost forcibly propelled up to the dreaded spot.

We revert to the 'Recollections' :—

'Not long after my return to England, Napoleon re-seated himself on the throne of France; and a general war was the consequence. I received a letter from [Count] Montenegro, written by order of the King of Spain, desiring me to return immediately to take the command of the cavalry, under General Castaños,* who had been appointed Commander-in-Chief. I accepted the offer, and was preparing for my departure, when Lord Castlereagh sent for me to inform me, that he purposed sending me as British commissioner, with rank and pay of Brigadier-General, and 1000*l.* per annum extra allowance, to the head-quarters of the Austrian army, about to advance upon Lyons.

'I stated to him the position in which I stood to the King of Spain, should His Majesty call for my services.

* His old patron and friend had been created Duke of Baylen, in honour of the first victory gained over the French in the Peninsular war.

His Lordship gave it as his opinion, that under all the circumstances, he thought I was bound in honour to return to Spain.'——

General Whittingham took with him on his return to Spain, for which he embarked from Falmouth, with part of his family on the 30th June, the following letter, for the English Ambassador:—

The Duke of York to Sir Henry Wellesley.

'HORSE-GUARDS, 14*th June*, 1815.

'Sir,— Colonel Sir Samford Whittingham having been called to a command in the Spanish army according to his rank of Lieutenant-General in the service of His Catholic Majesty, I have to acquaint you that the Prince Regent has been graciously pleased to approve his acceptance of the same: and I cannot permit this deserving and distinguished officer to take his departure from this country without making him the bearer of my desire that you will be pleased in your diplomatic as well as in your private character, to show him all the countenance and attention which a British officer in a foreign army may frequently require from a person in your high position.

'It may be necessary to add, that a sense of Sir Samford Whittingham's merits would have made me desirous of affording him employment in the British army now in the field; and it has only been in the impracticability of making an arrangement suitable to his pretensions, that I have been induced to facilitate the permission he has received to serve in the Spanish army.*

'I have, &c.
'FREDERICK.
'Commander-in-Chief.'

---

* Being only Colonel in the English army, he was not eligible to a high command with the troops of his own country, by the then inexorable laws

His return to the Peninsula is thus described in his 'Recollections:' 'On my arrival in Spain I found the war at an end; for the battle of Waterloo had taken place, and I had not only lost the opportunity of being present at that memorable action, but I had also deprived myself of the advantage of forming part of the army of occupation commanded by the Duke of Wellington, whose field-days at the head of the principal armies of Europe formed the best school for grand military operations.'

He here alludes to his rejection of Lord Castlereagh's offers, which, however, was under the circumstances unavoidable.

To Sir Henry Torrens.

(Extract.)

'Madrid, *8th August*, 1815.

'Ill health and bad spirits have made me delay writing to you till I am almost ashamed to take up the pen. It appears to me very doubtful whether I shall go to Catalonia or not. The minister of war, Ballasteros, has recommended me to wait for General Castanos's answer.

'It has been determined* that the division of Majorca, which I had the honour to command during the late war, and which consisted of eight battalions of infantry, two regiments of cavalry, and two troops of horse-artillery, formed a separate *corps d'armée*, and that the cross which I received as General of Division, should have been the grand cross of [a commander of] a *corps d'armée*. In consequence I have received the grand cross, and kissed the King's hand upon this new honour.† Now,

---

of routine, though he had for so many years commanded in the field as a general officer to the full satisfaction of the Duke of Wellington.

* That is, decided by the Spanish Government.

† The *London Gazette* of the 28th November, 1815, sanctions the wearing of this order 'with which His Catholic Majesty has been pleased to honour him, as a signal testimony of His Catholic Majesty's approbation of the distinguished services rendered by that officer on the field of battle, during the Peninsular war.'

in the true spirit of chivalry, I pray you to lay the grand cross at the feet of Lady Torrens, and to assure her that all my knightly services are at her command.

'I assure you, we often talk of our trip to Cheltenham; and look back with delight upon the gaiety and constant good humour of our quartetto! Alas! what a contrast did our journey from Coruña to Madrid form. Galicia, naturally poor and wretched and now desolate by the late war, is miserable beyond expression. Nor is it possible that anyone could form an idea of want and woe equal to what you meet with from Coruña to Madrid.

'The state of the finances is so very shocking that I can only convey to you an idea of it by saying that many, very many, meritorious officers would ere this have perished from absolute want had they not received their daily food, and even a room to sleep in, from the charity of the convents! How long this can last, God only knows. In any other country in Europe it could not have subsisted so long; but even here the discontent, particularly of the army, is great, and sooner or later evil must arise.

'This is a sad picture, my dear Torrens, and would to God it were not so very true; still resources might be found; but the good and amiable Ferdinand is surrounded by men of little, miserable minds, incapable of doing good, but very well disposed to do evil.'——

To his brother-in-law, he had written, on the 7th August, a long letter to the same effect, adding that he received no Spanish pay as Lieutenant-General owing to the state of the finances.

The great affability of the King, and his flattering partiality for Sir Samford Whittingham, inclined the latter, for some time, to regard his weaknesses with indulgence, and to throw the blame of his conduct upon his Ministers. Indeed Ferdinand does not appear to have been a man of bad natural disposition, and he was certainly very amiable in private life. But his narrow and bigoted education and his want of discernment, incapacitated him from being a good ruler, and his reign was mainly tolerated on account of his personal popularity amongst the mass of his subjects, especially the lower orders. This feeling the King appears to have cultivated in a manner resembling that of our Charles II.; *minus*, however, the immorality, for His Majesty was a very good husband. Sir Samford used to relate how Ferdinand, when handing his beautiful Queen Christina into the royal carriage, would turn round smilingly on the loyal crowd, and observe familiarly to them, '*Is she not a fine woman?*' or some similar remark.

By desire of the King of Spain, General Whittingham wrote a long Spanish paper on the reasons that should induce his Majesty to abolish the Slave Trade. This request was the result of a conversation with his Majesty, for Sir Samford now felt it his duty to use what influence he had with the King, in favour of civilization and good government, reluctant though he was as a thorough soldier to embark in matters which savoured of political intrigues. But ample proofs exist of the noble and patriotic manner in which he exercised his influence with the Spanish King, and especially in the letters of His Britannic Majesty's representatives at Madrid.

Meantime, as the war was over and his active services were no longer required for the safety of the country, the jealousy regarding the employment of an Englishman, (who as such could not but be too partial to liberty in royal eyes,) in a high military command, coupled with the intrigues of courtiers in Spain and the calumnies propagated at home, all combined to deter General Whittingham from either seeking for, or obtaining, a high command. If, indeed, he would have consented to abandon his own service, (in which, for want of military rank, he could expect for many years only a very subordinate position) there is every reason to believe that a fine career was before him; but to this idea he never could resign himself, though sometimes tempted to it by natural ambition of distinction, and by the laudable desire of commanding armies for which he felt himself fully capable.

His voluminous correspondence from 1815 to 1820 shows but too clearly how his active mind revolted from the compulsory idleness, in a military point of view, to which he was at this period condemned by uncontrollable circumstances, however useful he frequently was to the embassy at Madrid. Brief extracts of his correspondence are all that can be laid before the reader.

The following relates to his claims for a small pension from the British Government, afterwards granted to him on the same terms as other officers similarly situated. He had now no salary except his half-pay as a British Lieutenant-Colonel, and was involved in difficulties.

To his Brother-in-law.

'Madrid, 15*th September*, 1815.

' I was, as you know, employed by Mr. Pitt on a secret mission to Portugal. My expenses were, as you also know, very great; but notwithstanding Mr. Pitt's generous offers of remuneration upon my return to England, I declined receiving any reimbursement of my expenses, and felt happy at being able to render what was then thought a good service, without the possibility of having my motives misinterpreted.

'In the Spanish service, I never received any pay as Colonel, Brigadier, or Major-General, till I was appointed to the command of the cavalry in the Island of Leon, and the scale of my expenses in consequence unavoidably increased.

'Would to God I could follow the same system at present! but the diminution of my private fortune by unavoidable expenses, and the increase of my family, have placed me in a situation, in a pecuniary point of view, very different from that I have heretofore enjoyed.'——

General Whittingham endeavoured to counteract by his influence with the King the overbearing influence of the Russian Ambassador and the Holy-Alliance principles which the latter warmly advocated. In a letter of the 24th November, he writes to his brother-in-law: 'I have been able to render some good service of late.* The King continues his decided partiality towards me; I have frequent interviews and conversations with him. I have had many opportunities of studying Mr. Vaughan lately;† I do not think our affairs could be in better hands.'

But King Ferdinand could not forgive the evident sympathy of England with his revolted colonies, and threw himself the more readily into the arms of Russia.

To detail all the circumstances that occurred between King Ferdinand and General Whittingham during the time, (nearly four years,) that the latter resided in Madrid, would swell this work far beyond its intended limits, and being of a diplomatic and commercial rather than military nature, forms no necessary part of a military memoir. But it will be requisite to establish hereafter on incontrovertible testimony the fact, that even in matters of diplomacy, in which he had no official business, he did good and recognized though unrewarded service to his own country.

To his Brother-in-law.

'MADRID, 8*th December*, 1815.

'Mr. Barthelemy Frere, brother to John Hookham Frere, went to Constantinople, as Secretary of Embassy to Mr. Liston. Mr. Liston is now at home, and B. Frere

---

* He means *to the British Embassy.*

† This was the Minister, Mr. Charles Vaughan, acting as such in the absence of the Ambassador.

will of course have remained there as Minister Plenipotentiary, in the same manner as Vaughan has remained here, as Minister Plenipotentiary in consequence of the absence of Sir Henry [Wellesley]. Mr. B. Frere is going to be married immediately.'*

The year 1816 was a gloomy one in Madrid; the King from his despotic and Russian proclivities becoming odious to all men of liberal opinions in Spain, and the recovery of the Spanish American colonies being already nearly hopeless. Sir Samford Whittingham was now thankful that he held no responsible post in Spain, and in spite of his low rank in the English army desired, more and more, employment under the English Government; turning his thoughts meantime to a residence in the south of France. For he writes to Mr. Davis, (in January 1816) alluding to his poverty,† '*it is impossible for me to live in England.*'

To the Same.

'MADRID, *6th March*, 1816.

'The state of things does not mend, though a momentary tranquillity reigns. An attempt has been made to assassinate the King.' [After a long description of the wretched state of Spain, financial, military and political, he adds :]— 'I have been appointed to form the chapter of the military order of San Fernando, with the Duke del Parque, Palafox, Zayas, Blake, Giron, O'Donnel, Venegas, and La Pena.

'Magdalena‡ has had the offer of being appointed one of the ladies of honour to the Queen. But this I have declined on account of the expense of diamonds necessary,

---

* To Donna Barbara Creus, sister-in-law to the General.

† It is not superfluous to record such a fact in this Memoir, when it is borne in mind that others similarly situated had undoubtedly enriched themselves, and that he had been calumniated. Many people are slow to believe that when a man *can*, he *will not* enrich himself.

‡ Lady Whittingham.

and which amounts to about 4,000 dollars. In short honours and distinctions are crowded upon me, but honours and distinctions will not pay bills, and the higher a man rises in society the more he stands in need of an increase of pecuniary means. This has induced me to turn my thoughts to a high command in America; and the more particularly as the delay in the English brevets gives me no chance of getting out to India as a Major-General, till old age will have rendered the voyage unadvisable.'——

On the 7th April, 1816, he defends himself to the same correspondent from a charge that had reached Lord Castlereagh of his meddling with the general politics of Europe; a charge that appears to have resulted solely from his private letters not having always been sufficiently kept secret by his correspondents. On all these matters it is useless to dilate, for Marquis Wellesley, Mr. Hookham Frere, Sir Henry Wellesley, and Mr. Charles Vaughan, were the four ambassadors or ministers from 1808 to 1819, and on their final judgments of him may safely rest the verdict regarding Sir Samford Whittingham's diplomatic conduct. His exceptional position in Spain had made the successive representatives of Majesty thankfully use his services when occasion offered, especially latterly, in his conversations with the King. But the only political memorandum (besides a letter on the Slave Trade) that he ever gave the King was at the desire of the latter, and given with the *private* consent of the Minister, Mr. Vaughan; and was only calculated to make Spain prefer the alliance of England to that of Russia, which would have redounded to the eventual benefit both of England and of Spain. In the same letter he further requests Mr. Davis to make Lord Castlereagh acquainted with the following circumstances regarding King Ferdinand's return to Spain :—

'It was the conviction of my mind, and of General Zayas, and of all those I intimately knew, during the march from Saragossa to Valencia, that the King meant to swear to the Constitution under such modifications as might appear necessary; and His Majesty's proclamation from Valencia is a convincing proof that we had a right to form that opinion.

'I did not accompany the King on his march to Madrid. He was escorted by General Elio and his infantry, by the high road from Valencia to Madrid. My orders were to march from Saragossa to Guadalaxara; and there wait for further orders.'

The letter then describes the King's triumphant entry into Madrid, which has been already described in this work;* and continues: 'Soon after his arrival at Madrid, His Majesty sent me a message through the Duke of San Carlos,† desiring I would ask for any favour I might desire. I begged the Duke to assure His Majesty that I considered myself amply rewarded for my services during the war, by the rank of Major-General that had been conferred on me after the battle of Talavera, and I did not desire any other recompense. Had I done otherwise, my conduct in obeying the order to advance with the cavalry from Saragossa to Guadalaxara might have been interpreted into a vile speculation for my own personal advantage, rather than as proceeding from that high sense of duty and obedience to superiors which should form the basis of every military character.

'The only favour I ever asked of the King was the pardon of two artillery soldiers of my division who were under sentence of death for desertion, not to the enemy, but to their home! This was granted.

'The cross of San Fernando was gained by me in the

---

* See page 245.

† By the fuller detailed letter at page 283, it would appear that it was the Duke's son, the Count de Corres, who actually delivered this message.

field of battle, according to the established rules of the order ;* and my claim legitimated by a public examination in the face of all the troops concerned. It was therefore no favour of the King.

'The rank of Lieutenant-General was conferred upon me by the King without any application on my part, for my general services during the war. But the same rank was also conferred by His Majesty upon upwards of thirty Major-Generals, all under me in the list.

'I was finally offered one of the best governments in Spain, which I declined from the motives before alleged, *for I have always been of opinion that it is not sufficient to be satisfied entirely with the motives of our conduct. It is necessary that there should be no possibility of doubt as to the purity of the motives by which we are actuated.*'†

Thus did his rash English calumniators not only deprive him of the legitimate rewards of his services after the Peninsular war, but also force him into a spirit of self assertion foreign to the natural modesty of his nature, which led him to trust to his superiors for the record of his merits and services. Nor was it a vain trust. For rarely has an officer, not sprung from the aristocracy, enjoyed such numerous and striking acknowledgments of his merits and services, as fell to the lot of General Whittingham before the close of his career.

Meantime he no longer even desired a military command in Spain, because no person was paid in Spain his nominal salary, so that the only effect of such appointment would be to increase his already too great expenses. On the 7th October, 1816, he writes: 'In my situation, with the high rank I hold in this country, it is morally impossible for me to reduce my expenses more than I

---

* By the votes of officers and men under his command.

† Such sentiments do not facilitate the attainment of wealth and success, but they are the characteristics of a nobility of nature which forms the truest aristocracy.

have done. *Once only in the year and a half I have been here, have I asked a friend to dine with me.'*

Only those who have known Sir Samford Whittingham's habits of profuse though refined hospitality, can feel the true force of these words.

The letter thus continues: 'Thus you see, my dear Davis, that I am exposed to starvation in the midst of honours and distinctions, and I see no road to salvation except through the East Indies. Barbara [Creus] is now with us, and I am only waiting for the pope's licence to celebrate her marriage [by proxy] with Mr. B. Frere, British Minister at Constantinople. I have Mr. Frere's full powers to effect the marriage.'

In November 1816, an unfounded report of the probable retirement of the Governor of Trinidad, induced General Whittingham to apply through H. M.'s minister, Mr. Vaughan, for the supposed vacancy. There seemed no disinclination on the part of the British Government to serve him, had the opportunity really occurred, if the Editor can judge by the brief notes written by Lords Liverpool, Castlereagh, and Bathurst, now in his possession. The letter, however, of Mr. Vaughan alone is here recorded, placing in *italics* the parts relating to the General's (not then sufficiently appreciated in England) diplomatic services :—

The Right Hon. Charles Vaughan to Viscount Castlereagh.

'MADRID, 23rd *November*, 1816.

' My Lord,—I have received the enclosed from Lieut.-General Sir Samford Whittingham, *and grateful for the services I have ever found him anxious to render me, as His Majesty's Minister at this Court,* I think it my duty to recommend his present application, to be employed in the island of Trinidad, to the most favourable attention of your Lordship.

'In support of General Whittingham's application, I can venture to testify to his accurate knowledge of the language, the customs, and the laws of Spain; and his conduct in this country has obtained for him the confidence of His Catholic Majesty, and the respect and esteem of all classes of Spaniards.

'I have no occasion to refer to the distinguished military services of the General, as they have long since been acknowledged by His Majesty's Government. But I feel it my duty to recommend him to your Lordship, *in acknowledgment for the services which he has rendered to me as His Majesty's Minister, through the confidential intercourse he enjoyed with the King of Spain, and which has enabled me to communicate to this Court opinions by which I have thought it of consequence that the Spanish Government should be influenced.**

'On these grounds I trust that your Lordship will pardon the liberty I have taken, in recommending General Whittingham for the employment he solicits.

'I am, &c., &c.,
'Charles Vaughan.'

On the 14th January, 1817, Sir Samford writes: 'Nothing can exceed the King's attention to me, nor the confidence he shows me. But as I have before said, I am fully of opinion that in order to ask for any high employment here, I must leave the service of my own country—a step I can never make up my mind to take. So that I am exactly in the situation of the man who seated himself between two stools, and thus came to the ground.'

In the same letter Sir Samford writes: 'I have lately

---

* On the 12th Decr. 1816 Mr. Davis writes, from London, to Mrs. Harford: 'Your uncle has been the happy instrument of settling the question of the Slave Trade. This is a secret, and I learnt it by accident, not from himself. Mr. Vaughan states that it is wholly owing to your uncle's personal influence with the King.'—Mr. Davis gives the details and adds: 'These terms are beyond the expectation of our Ministers here.'

had it in my power to be of some service to Sir Henry Wellesley, and he seems disposed to do anything in his power to serve me.' He adds his intention, if he fails to obtain employment from the British Government, to retire to 'some small town in France, where I shall always be able to live perfectly well on my small income. I think, however, it is best giving things a fair chance to wait at this Court eight or ten months longer, particularly as I am in hopes that Sir Henry will not find my services altogether useless.'

On the 3rd February, 1817, was born his third surviving son, to whom Don Antonio the King's uncle stood godfather. Sir Samford's influence was not only great with the King and the Royal Family, but extended to many of the first Spanish nobility, such as the Dukes of Frias, Infantado, Osuna, &c. With some of these he arranged wool-importing business for his brother's mercantile house in Bristol. Thus he writes on the 27th February, 1817: 'I am also endeavouring to persuade the Duke of Infantado, to send you his pile [of wool] for the future. He does not seem very well satisfied with his correspondents in Bristol, but unfortunately he has taken it into his head that by sending [his wool] for some time to London he shall obtain better prices.'

'It has appeared to me that you would not disapprove of my introducing —— into the best society of this town, inasmuch as that by no means militates against his attention to business. I have therefore taken him to the Russian Minister's, to the Duchess of Osuna, to the Duchess of Frias; and on Sunday next I shall take him to Pizarro's, the Minister for Foreign Affairs. To Sir Henry's Saturday evening parties he also goes with me.'

In a letter dated 'Madrid, 18th March, 1817,' he writes:— '——. begins his riding lessons this evening. The Duke of Alagon, commander of the King's Body-Guard, has ordered the director of his *manège* to pay him every attention, and to employ every means in his power to make him a complete horseman. ——* goes on in every respect most charmingly. Miss Creus was married some days ago, by proxy, to Mr. Barthelemy Frere.'

Sir Samford now (no Colonial government being forthcoming) resolved again to ask the Duke of York for employment, in spite of the difficulties about his want of rank; and having conversed with Sir Henry Wellesley (who had returned to his post) on the subject, he was enabled to transmit to the Duke of York, through his brother-in-law, the following satisfactory letter:—

Sir Henry Wellesley to the Duke of York.

'MADRID, 3rd April, 1817.

'Sir,—Understanding it to be the wish of Sir Samford Whittingham to obtain active employment in His Majesty's service, and your Royal Highness having been pleased in a letter to me, under date the 14th June, 1815, to express your approbation of his general conduct, I venture to take the liberty of recommending him to the notice of your Royal Highness, as an officer who was not only eminently distinguished during the war in Spain, but to whom *I feel under great obligations for the assistance which, since his return to Madrid, he has afforded to this Embassy in its intricate negociations with the Spanish Government.*

'I have, &c., &c.,

'HENRY WELLESLEY.'

The Duke of York to R. H. Davis, Esq. M.P.

HORSE-GUARDS, 28th April, 1817.

'Sir,—I have to acknowledge the receipt of your letter of the 26th instant, with its enclosure, and to assure you

---

* When Mr. ——, at the termination of his lessons sought to pay for them, he was informed that all had been done *gratis*, for the love of his uncle, General Whittingham.

that I have had great pleasure in receiving from Sir Henry Wellesley, so favourable a testimony of Sir Samford Whittingham's zeal, ability, and assiduous attention to every duty assigned to him, though nothing was wanting to add to the opinion I had previously entertained of that officer's distinguished conduct.

'I have, &c., &c.,
'FREDERICK.'

But nothing came of the application at this time. On both sides of the water *plenty of praise* from high quarters, *but no rewards.* Praise is good, but it cannot feed a family, and has a satirical aspect when attended with no practical result. It is however, certain that '*the Soldier's Friend*' was hampered by the difficulty of finding a Colonel's post suitable to such a deserving officer, and he might also naturally think that the nature of his latter services might give him a claim for *civil* employment pending his want of British military rank.

Troubles began now to arise in Spain. There was also a danger of General Whittingham being ordered to South America, to reconquer the revolted colonies, which command he must have declined to accept, as incompatible with the then policy of England. He therefore prepared to quit Spain; but signs of a civil war then began to appear, and his high feeling of honour, and regard for the King, made him inclined to remain in order to protect His Majesty. Sir Henry Wellesley, however, recommended his withdrawal, at least for a few months, and he obeyed.

On the 24th May, whilst staying with his family at Aranjuez on a visit to the Duke and Duchess of Frias at their beautiful family seat, he requests his brother-in-law to consult Lord Castlereagh's wishes, as to his leaving or remaining in Madrid, in one of the sentences of which his chivalrous nature asserts itself, scorning to escape a disagreeable duty, by the excuse of ingratitude in the highest quarter. Speaking of the danger of taking high command in civil war he writes : 'Personally this does not occupy me one moment. I only wish it to be clearly understood, *that I cannot wear the King of Spain's uniform, and abandon him in case of need.*' *

To his Brother-in-law.

Private. 'MADRID, 8th June, 1817.

'Since the return of the King, the English interest at this Court has been gradually declining, and strange to say, the Russian influence as gradually increasing. This has depended principally upon the personal character of the King, but has been considerably forwarded by the intriguing abilities of the Russian Minister Tatischeff. The King from his infancy has been taught to suspect and dislike the English, and these feelings have been not a little fomented by the repeated obstacles thrown before him and his Government by the British papers, and in the British Parliament. The Emperor [of Russia] on the contrary has been constantly occupied in flattering his vanity, and gaining his good will by numberless presents both to him and to the Queen. At the present moment, Tatischeff reigns despotically at this Court, and his influence appears to be almost irresistible. Some time since, Tatischeff began a treaty with his Government, by which Russia was to interpose all her power in favour of Spain against Portugal, and Spain was to cede to Russia, in consequence, the island of Minorca. This treaty was not at that time approved of by the Emperor, and the whole fell to the ground. However, the subject has again been taken in hand, and the intrigues to gain possession of Minorca, have again been renewed.'——

* He could not say 'draw the King's pay,' because *he drew none.*

The above is a brief fragment of a long letter:—It proves that the Emperor Alexander, was less of an intriguer than his Minister, and more upright in his intentions. At least, this is the impression it now leaves on the mind of the Editor.*

In the summer of 1817, sickness seized the General and all his family, and finally ' Mrs. B. Frere was taken ill of a nervous fever early in July. Water was thrown out upon the brain, and in the short period of four days, she was no more. Three months previous to this dreadful calamity, she was married by proxy in the very room in which she died. Sorrow and grief have borne us to the ground.'

The above is an extract from a letter to Mr. Davis, dated 'Madrid, 12th July, 1817,' and containing the sad end of the virgin wife of one of the best and most amiable of men, who is said to have received at Constantinople, the news of her death by the very ship in which he expected her to arrive. To complete the sad romance, the widower remained single for the remainder of his, by no means, short life.

The same letter says: ' I have seen Sir Henry, and he is of opinion that I should do well to absent myself, for some time at least, from Spain. I have therefore determined to go to Toulouse, and there wait events. I hope to be able to set off in the course of next month.'

The General and his family left Madrid in August. Here his public life ceased for the time, so that it is not necessary (with a few exceptions) to quote his letters for the remainder of 1817, or the whole of 1818. He first went to Toulouse. In September he was at Bagnières de Bigorre. In November again at Toulouse, where he remained till, at all events, the third week in February 1818. For on the 17th of that month, he wrote to Mr.

---

* It proves also that Russian intrigue is an institution too fixed to be much shaken by any moderation or weakness in the ruler of the day.

Davis :—' I received some time back, a letter from [Count] Montenegro, whose situation at Court you must recollect, enclosing the King's manifesto on the abolition of the Slave Trade. I copy the words of the letter, because I am forced to speak of myself* and because I know you will be pleased to see the effects of *my* influence so decidedly acknowledged. *Dirijo á Vm. el Real Decreto aboliendo el comercio de negros, creyendo darle con esto una satisfaccion por lo mucho que ha contribuido al logro de un negocio tan importante.*† Sir Samford continues :—

' I had upon the subject of the Slave Trade, repeated and long conversations with the King. At his desire, I gave him a memorial upon the subject, which merited his acknowledged approbation, and which he gave to his Minister for Foreign Affairs, desiring him to read it with the greatest attention. I read the memorial to the King myself.'

In the summer of 1818, General Whittingham and his family, to avoid the great heat, again visited *Bagnières de Bigorre* in the Hautes Pyrénées. Commencing with the 4th July, he received a three months' visit from his eldest nephew, Hart Davis, junior, who had been compelled by delicate health to abandon a very promising parliamentary career, and who had lately married the truly beautiful and accomplished daughter of Major-General and Lady Eleanor Dundas. Mr. Hart Davis had a genius for sketching, especially figures, and many romantic sketches of Pyrenees' scenes and peasantry were collected on this occasion in his scrap-book.

In a letter addressed to Mr. Barthelemy Frere, and dated, ' *Chez Monsieur Jalon, Cabinet littéraire, Bagnières de Bigorre,* 6*th August,* 1818,' Sir Samford writes : ' Hart

---

* In consequence of the calumnies to which he had been exposed.

† ' I enclose you the Royal Decree abolishing the traffic in negroes believing that I shall thereby do you a pleasure, *on account of your having greatly contributed to the settlement of so important a business.*'

Davis and I are just returned from a chasse de chamois, amongst the highest and most inaccessible cliffs of the Pyrenees. We were out four days. The fatigue was excessive, but Davis bore it very well. We expect Richard [Vaughan] Davis on his return from Spain. Could you not make an effort to join us?' It does not appear, however, that his old friend and brother-in-law, Mr. B. Frere, joined him on that occasion. After the departure of his guests, the General returned to Toulouse.

Early in 1819, the sudden and unexpected law for the enforcement of cash payments caused the failure of many mercantile houses, and the ruin of many families. Mr. Hart Davis was a great loser on this occasion, and in the crash Sir Samford also lost, it appears, all his capital. With an increasing family it became more imperative for him to obtain active employment of some kind or other. But a portion of 1819 was passed between Toulouse and the Pyrenees and Bordeaux, in enforced inactivity. At last in July 1819 he received the offer of the Lieutenant-Government of Dominica, an unimportant post, not very remunerative, and subordinate to the Governor-in-Chief at Barbadoes. It was, however, more lucrative then than at the present period, and he accepted it, without ceasing to hope for more profitable employment in the East Indies. But though he received the appointment in July, in anticipation, he was not ordered out immediately. Probably the time of the preceding Governor wanted six months before expiring. Meanwhile he thought it his duty before embarking for Dominica to take leave of the King of Spain:—

To his Brother-in-law.

'MADRID, 18*th July*, 1819.

'I am this moment returned from the baths of Sacedon where I was obliged to follow His Majesty. He received me with the greatest kindness, approved highly of my acceptance of the government of Dominica, and assured me that he should preserve my name in the list of the Generals of his army. I dined with His Majesty during the two days of my stay at the baths; and on my taking leave his behaviour was affectionate in the extreme.

'Pray tell me if you think it would be possible to obtain from the Duke of York, the local rank of Brigadier-General for me in Dominica. I have been now ten years a General; and it is an unpleasant feeling to change the name for Colonel if it can be avoided.* It is indeed woeful to see that the expense of my commission [as Governor] will amount to nearly 600*l*.'———

In this letter to his brother-in-law, Sir Samford Whittingham gave only the above very brief account of his farewell to King Ferdinand. Fortunately in the 'Recollections,' which have been so often quoted, there is a fuller account of his last intercourse with that Prince, which will now be laid before the reader:—

'In 1819 I accepted the government of Dominica, in the West Indies. But previous to my departure I thought it my duty to go to Madrid to take leave of the King of Spain. Troubles had again surrounded him, and the army of Andalusia was in a state of insurrection. His Majesty was at the baths of Sacedon, and desired my immediate attendance.

'The order of the day was as follows:—At daybreak His Majesty walked to the baths. At eleven he held a little Court of the persons present at Sacedon. At one, all the officers of a certain rank dined with His Majesty, at a round table calculated to hold sixteen; His Majesty doing the honours as host, and paying the greatest atten-

---

* A natural regret for the man whom the Duke of Wellington had addressed as a General so many years previously.

tion to all his guests. Soon after dinner a plate of the finest Havannah cigars was presented to the King, who selected one, and sent it to some one of his guests, with whose taste for smoking he was acquainted. His Majesty then lighted his own cigar and soon after retired to his apartment. The Duke of Alagon, Captain of the *Gardes du Corps*, then took His Majesty's seat, and the whole party began to light their cigars. Excellent coffee was introduced, and we sat smoking and talking till five p.m., when His Majesty commenced his evening walk, accompanied by all his little Court.

'At the first levée after my arrival, as soon as the strangers were dismissed, the King said to the Duke of Alagon, " Leave us, I desire to speak in private with Santiago."* It is the etiquette of the Spanish Court, that the Captain of the *Gardes du Corps* should never quit the King's person; and great was the surprise of the Duke at so novel an order.

'As soon as we were alone, His Majesty opened the conversation in the most flattering and confidential manner, by saying: " Santiago, you well know the confidence with which you have inspired me, and how very highly I esteem you. Tell me, therefore, frankly and openly, your opinion upon the state of Europe in general, and upon the revolutionary movements which threaten on all sides; and particularly tell me what you think of this country." " Sir," I replied, " your Majesty well knows my devoted attachment to your Royal person, and how sincerely I desire and hope for the happiness and prosperity of your Majesty and of Spain. I feel, therefore, no hesitation in answering your question frankly, fully convinced that the purity of my intentions will not be doubted. The minds of your Majesty's subjects are gene-

---

* 'Dejanos, deseo hablar á solas con Santiago.' It was, and probably still is, the fashion in Spain for friends to address each other by their Christian names.

rally unsettled. Novelty and change are the order of the day: if your Majesty takes the initiative, and makes a few concessions in harmony with the times, I am of opinion that they will be received gratefully, and produce the best effects. If, on the contrary, the people should take the initiative, nothing short of anarchy and destruction will satisfy them, and the worst consequences may be feared."

'The King applauded my opinion, and apparently coincided with it; but he had not strength of mind to act in consequence. The next day I took my final leave and never saw him more.'——

The following was the final testimony of the English Ambassador under whom General Whittingham had served so long as a British Military Agent in the war in the Peninsula:—

Sir Henry Wellesley,* to Viscount Castlereagh.

'MADRID, 1st *August*, 1819.

'My Lord,—Sir Samford Whittingham having retired from the service of His Catholic Majesty, I cannot suffer this occasion to pass over of repeating the sense which I entertain of his distinguished services during the war in the Peninsula, as well as of his uniform desire to promote, by all the means in his power, the views of the British Government in this country, which has *been manifested upon many important occasions* since the restoration of peace.

'I hope, therefore, that your Lordship will allow me to avail myself of this opportunity (probably the last I shall have) of recommending Sir Samford Whittingham to the protection of the Prince Regent's Government.

---

* In 1828 Sir Henry was raised to the peerage as Baron Cowley. His son—the well-known Ambassador at Paris for many years—has been raised to an Earldom.

'He leaves this country with the testimony of all ranks in his favour, *but without any other reward from this Government for the valuable services rendered by him to the Spanish cause, than that of being allowed to retain his rank in the Spanish army.*

'I have, &c.,

'Henry Wellesley.'

The words placed by the Editor in italics though strictly true, imply a greater charge of ingratitude against the King of Spain, than the facts really substantiate. As Sir Samford was not prepared to give up the service of his own country, the King knew that there were marked limits to the extent of his devotion to His Majesty, which, with his natural dislike of England and Englishmen, was calculated to check his liberality. Moreover, the King had peculiar notions in the matter of rewards. Some one having asked His Majesty, why a certain distinguished officer had never been recompensed, he simply replied, (as if conclusive) that 'He never asked for anything!'[*] His Majesty could have pleaded the same excuse on this occasion in justification for neglecting to reward General Whittingham, for assuredly the latter never did ask for any reward from His Catholic Majesty. But the fact is that the King had made an exception in the Englishman's favour; and, as we have seen[†] had not waited to be asked in his case. This will be again proved by the following letter, which is here inserted *out of its place*, in order to finish at once with the Peninsular portion of this Memoir:—

---

[*] The Editor frequently heard Sir Samford Whittingham narrate this trait of Ferdinand VII.

[†] At page 266.

Sir Samford Whittingham to Thomas Murdoch, Esq.

'DOMINIQUE, 23rd September, 1820.

'My dear Friend,—I am glad you have touched upon the Spanish question. I have been so deeply involved in that affair, and so often and so unjustly attacked, under the false supposition that I had been the principal actor in the destruction of the liberties of the Spanish people, that I feel particularly anxious to put you in possession of everything which occurred on the King's return to Spain.

'His Majesty after leaving Barcelona chose the route of Aragon. I commanded at that time all the cavalry and artillery in that kingdom. I met the King on the frontier, and accompanied him by his express order to Valencia. During the King's stay at Saragossa his mind was certainly by no means prepared for the plan of action he was subsequently induced to adopt. For, speaking to me of the Constitution, he said, "There are many parts of this work I do not approve; but if any opposition on my part were likely to cause the shedding of one drop of Spanish blood, I would swear to it immediately."

'At Valencia I was asked my opinion as to whether the King should swear to the Constitution or not. I answered then, as I should do now, for my sentiments have not changed: "The Constitution, as it now stands, is too democratic to be in unison and harmony with the habits and ideas of the Spanish people, or with the laws and customs of the Spanish monarchy.* It must be modified in many parts to give well-founded hopes of its duration. Yet one article of the Constitution forbids the

---

* This letter, written in 1820, is of course likely to be more accurate than the *Recollections*, written entirely from memory in 1840; but there is no material discrepancy between the two documents. The later accounts written for his nieces were briefer than the more business-like letter of explanation to Mr. Murdoch.

slightest alteration during the space of eight years. The King, therefore, must either deprive himself of the possibility of amelioration, or be guilty of wilful and predetermined perjury. It is therefore my opinion that the King, under existing circumstances, cannot swear to the Constitution as formed by the Cortes. But it is also my opinion that the members of the Cortes have deserved well of the King and of the country; that His Majesty unaccompanied by a single soldier should dissolve the Cortes in person; should thank them for the good services they have rendered to the state, and should express the pleasure he anticipated in seeing them re-elected by their constituents as members of the Cortes he was about to summon."

'The day following, I was directed to return to Saragossa. Three days afterwards I received an official order from General Elio, in the King's name, to march with all the cavalry and artillery under my command to Guadalaxara, nine leagues from Madrid. On the road I was met by an officer from the Regency, who desired to know by what authority I entered Castile. I sent a copy of the order to the Regency; and on my arrival at Guadalaxara, I received orders from Elio, in the King's name, to wait the pleasure of His Majesty. On the day of the King's entrance into the capital, the cavalry under my command marched in, to line the streets. But so far were they from being necessary, that the people had gone out three leagues to meet the King; had taken the horses out of his carriage, and were bringing him in triumph into the city, when we arrived at the gates of Madrid.

'As to the arrests of the members of the Cortes, they had taken place the night before by order of Eguia, when not one soldier of mine was within thirty miles of the capital.

'This is a plain statement of facts; and I confess I

am not aware that I could in anywise vary my conduct had I again to act in a similar situation.

'A few days after His Majesty arrived in Madrid, he sent to me the Count de Corres, nephew to the Duke of San Carlos,* "to desire me to point out any favour I wished to have granted, as his Majesty was desirous of giving me some proof of his esteem.' I requested the Count de Corres to state to his Majesty, "my gratitude for his kindness; but at the same time, to assure His Majesty that I felt amply rewarded by the military promotion I had obtained during the war, and that I desired nothing further." One word from me at that time would have obtained me a title, and a military *encomienda*.† But I felt that my position was delicate; and I preferred without hesitation, as I trust in God I always shall, poverty to dishonour. Had I accepted a reward from Ferdinand, it might have been said that I had been bribed; and I have always considered, that it is not sufficient to be satisfied in your own conscience that you have acted rightly; it is necessary to deprive even your enemies of every plausible pretext for attacking your reputation.

'Believe me, &c.
'SAMFORD WHITTINGHAM.'

From Madrid, Sir Samford returned early in August, 1819, to Bagnières de Bigorre; whence he removed in October to Bordeaux.

In November, he took his two eldest children *via* Paris to London, to his brother-in-law's, and saw them soon after established at a school in Hammersmith, at which were staying the two sons of his dear friend Sir Henry Torrens. He passed less than two months in England on this occasion.

* The Duke was then the King's principal Minister.
† Either the product of a certain amount of land, or a claim on the rent.

Whilst still there, he wrote a letter to Mr. Davis dated 14th December, 1819, in which he informed him that he had 'had a long conversation with Lord Castlereagh the other day' on the subject of his (Mr. Davis) losses, by the great commercial crisis of that period. The Minister assured Sir Samford that notwithstanding these losses his brother-in-law 'never stood so high in the opinion of Government.' His Lordship added:—' He has borne his unmerited misfortunes with a strength of mind which does him infinite honour; and the value of his character was never so well known as since his late trial. His Royal Highness the Regent said the other day, "There is not a man in the House of Commons, without one single exception, for whom I have a higher esteem than for Hart Davis."' *

It may be easily imagined what pleasure it gave Sir Samford Whittingham to communicate Lord Castlereagh's observations to his oldest and best friend and connection, in whose losses his own fortune had likewise disappeared. He had now to take leave of Mr. Davis and his old friends, to proceed to the West Indies.

Before sailing, the account of which will be given in the following chapter, Sir Samford received a farewell letter from his old friend Baron Hugel, which contained the following not very encouraging passage:

'*Comment, mon ami, vous allez donc vous ensevelir dans un pays sans souvenirs et sans espérances? Un pays de sucre, de café et d'esclaves? Un pays où tout le monde végète dans le vice et dans l'ignorance? Que le bon Dieu vous bénisse, et vous tienne dans sa sainte garde!*' †

---

* Lest the reader should suppose this to be a mere party opinion, it may be well here to state that the liberal Lord William Bentinck, in one of his letters to Sir Samford Whittingham, written in 1831, states, 'I have always had a great respect for Mr. Hart Davis.'

† 'What, my friend, you are going to bury yourself in a country without recollections, and without hopes? A land of sugar, of coffee, and of slaves? A land in which all the world vegetates in vice and ignorance? May God bless you, and shield you with his holy protection!'

CHAPTER XIII.

1820—1822.

GENERAL WHITTINGHAM'S ARRIVAL IN DOMINICA—RESTORES ORDER AND CONCORD—ANXIOUS TO OBTAIN EMPLOYMENT IN INDIA—HIS SYSTEM OF GOVERNMENT—FAVOURS THE SLAVE POPULATION—TESTIMONIALS BOTH FROM THE ISLANDERS AND THE PROPRIETORS RESIDENT IN ENGLAND—BOON TO THE WHITE SOLDIERS BY SIR SAMFORD'S RECOMMENDATION—WILBERFORCE'S LETTER TO THE BISHOP OF CALCUTTA—HIS AUTOGRAPH LETTER TO SIR SAMFORD—GEORGE IV. AND THE DUKE OF YORK'S LETTERS OF INTRODUCTION—SIR HENRY TORRENS'S PROPHETICAL LETTER—A MOST DELIGHTFUL PERSONAGE—A POPULAR MARQUIS—UNCLE TOBY AND CORPORAL TRIM—A GOVERNOR-GENERAL'S SMILES AND FROWNS—VISIT TO LORD HASTINGS AT BARRACKPORE—HIS LORDSHIP'S FLATTERING CONFIDENCE—HOW LORD HASTINGS SILENCED AVA'S KING—ARRIVAL OF SIR EDWARD PAGET, THE NEW COMMANDER-IN-CHIEF—LORD HASTINGS'S GREAT ERROR.

ON the evening of the 1st January, 1820, Sir Samford Whittingham arrived at Dover, 'after spending a delightful day at Maidstone with Sir John Brown.'* On the 3rd he recrossed the Straits, and returned to Bordeaux *viâ* Paris, as he had come. Sickness in his family detained him many weeks; † so that the embarkation did not take place till near the end of February; and Dominica was reached on the 28th of March.

By May, he was obliged to send home one of his children from sickness, and the remainder of his family were laid up with fever. But he had the satisfaction of speedily restoring order and concord in Dominica, which had been in a discontented state before his arrival.

---
* Letter to his brother-in-law.
† During this detention, the sad news must have reached him of the premature death of his earliest illustrious patron, the good and kind-hearted Duke of Kent, who expired on the 23rd January, 1820.

In a letter, dated 'Roseau, 24th August, 1820,' he writes:—'We are going on perfectly well here, and I hope shall continue so to do. I make it a point to employ all possible forbearance and moderation in all my transactions with the [local] Colonial Government, and I love to hope that my efforts will be crowned with success.' On 2nd October, he records the destructive effects of a gale, and sends a memorial on the subject to His Majesty. In a later letter he writes, 'Exercise is generally considered as contributive to health in this country. For myself I never took harder exercise even in Europe. The other day I walked upwards of twelve miles in a broiling sun; and found myself all the better for it.' This was pretty well in a tropical mountainous Island. But Dominica with its small garrison had no attractions for a zealous soldier, whose thoughts were entirely turned to India. As early as May 1821, he had hopes of an Indian appointment; and was anxious to get Earl Bathurst's leave to quit his government as soon as he should be nominated to the new post. At this time Lady Whittingham's health compelled her to return to Europe with the two younger children. From his country seat, '*Babillard*' on the 20th May, 1821, he writes to his brother with no love for his solitary life in the little sugar Island, in which there was little to interest him: 'Were I not provided with books it would be difficult to prevent my spirits from sinking under it. I go to town [Roseau] Tuesdays and Thursdays. I start at five in the morning, and leave Roseau at five in the evening.' He amused himself by writing home instructions for the education of his children, the eldest of whom was less than eight years old.

In the same letter he records his simple system of colonial government. It is perhaps not unworthy of record; as it is certain that there seldom was a more popular government than his brief one of Dominica:—

'I have not hitherto occupied your attention about the affairs of this government; because I have not thought it of sufficient importance. My own system has been simple and unvaried. I have never courted any man. I have never favoured any particular party. I have constantly inculcated, both by precept and example, that in all our acts and deeds the good of the Colony should be our only object; and that a spirit of harmony reigning without interruption in all the councils of this Colonial Legislature would be the best and surest mode of re-establishing our reputation at home! I have lived retired from society except on particular occasions; and I have endeavoured, as much as in me lay, both by my public and private conduct, to justify my principles by my example. I am happy to be able to add, that success has crowned my endeavours, and that the inhabitants of Dominica are satisfied with their Governor.'

He here omits, however, one of the well known causes of his popularity throughout his life, his hospitable dinners, which, in spite of his own temperate habits, he took care should be most excellent of their kind. His friend Mr. Murdoch, the great wine merchant, selected his sherry and madeira. His French friend Count Turenne, who had been in the household of Napoleon, ordered for him his champagne and claret direct from France, and ensured him the best vintages. Especially was this the case in India, but the system was commenced in Dominica.

In the letter before quoted, he writes: 'I hope to be able to forward to Lord Bathurst by this packet an act of this Colonial Legislature, containing many useful regulations in favour of the slave population. The 35th clause, which establishes the admission of the evidence of people of colour in criminal cases, a privilege they did not before enjoy, I consider as most just and highly expedient.' A long discussion on the state of the Island concludes the letter.

On the 5th of October, 1821, he describes his joy at receiving the news of his appointment as Quartermaster-General of the royal army in India, and adds: 'In consequence of the letters by this packet, I have called the Council and Assembly together for Monday next, when I shall address to them my farewell speech. I shall, however, of course, not give up the reins of government till I quit the Island. The sale of my few moveables will begin immediately: I fear their produce will be trifling. My outfit was expensive, but consisted almost exclusively of eatables and drinkables, and has therefore vanished without leaving a trace. You will not hear from me by letter after this packet: for as I go home in the next, I should only be the bearer of my own dispatches.'

The popularity of Sir Samford Whittingham in Dominica (in spite of his short stay and his haste to depart) was proved by something more lasting than words, more convincing than addresses, though these were not wanting. The inhabitants of the Island presented him with the Grand Cross of San Fernando, beautifully set in diamonds, in testimony of his important services, whilst he administered the government of that Island. And the proprietors of estates resident in England also made him a present of a dress sword, as a testimony of their approbation of his conduct. His Majesty George IV. was moreover graciously pleased, on his return to England, to make him a Knight Commander of the Hanoverian Guelphic Order.

But even in Dominica with its small garrison, so different from the force he had commanded in 1813, he did not forget the interests of his soldiers; for, as full Colonel, he had commanded the troops as a consequence of being Governor. The following letter was written to Sir Samford Whittingham (some months after his return to England) by the Secretary at the Colonial Office:—

'DOWNING STREET, *Friday*, 18*th January*, 1822.

'Sir,—Perhaps it will be superfluous for me to inform you that your proposition with respect to the attachment of ten black men,* &c. &c. will be immediately recommended by Lord Bathurst to the consideration of His Royal Highness the Commander-in-Chief; and that your other valuable suggestions have been attended to. But as you were so obliging as to write to me at my desire upon these points, I have thought it right to apprize you myself of the effect of your letter. I have the honour to remain,

'Your most obedient humble servant,
'R. WILMOT.'

'Sir Samford Whittingham, &c.'

In this letter was one to Mr. Wilmot from Sir Herbert Taylor, conveying the intention of H.R.H. the Duke of York to apply in future the practice suggested, 'in the proportion of ten men for each company of the European regiments serving at any time in the West Indies.' What a boon this was to the non-commissioned officers and privates serving in that trying climate, even civilians will be able to comprehend.

Previously to this correspondence, the health of Lady Whittingham not permitting her to proceed to India, the General had taken her and the younger children to Paris, and leaving the elder at their school in England, to spend their holidays with their uncle Mr. Hart Davis, he started on his first long Indian exile, rendered necessary by his increase of family and the partial expenditure and partial loss of his private fortune.

It was and is usual to take introductions on going to India; and certainly, Colonel Sir Samford Whittingham carried out with him, testimonies of which any man might well have been proud.

* To each company of infantry.

The following letter was dictated, all but the postscript, by the celebrated William Wilberforce, a great friend of Mr. Harford of Blaise Castle, Sir Samford's nephew by marriage :—

To the Lord Bishop of Calcutta.*

'NEAR LONDON, 22nd April, 1822.
(Extract.)

'My dear Lord,—I at once esteem it an honour and feel it a pleasure to have devolved on me the welcome office of introducing to your Lordship Sir Samford Whittingham, who is going out to India to fill the important station of Quartermaster-General. Notwithstanding your having been so long removed into another hemisphere, and your attention solicited by such a variety of new and interesting objects, I can scarcely doubt that you have kept in view what has been going forward in the Western world, sufficiently to render it almost unnecessary for me to state to you how high and important a place General Whittingham has occupied both on the Continent (in Spain), and since as a Governor of one of our West Indian Islands. But I have still greater pleasure in telling you that he is, I trust, under the influence of religious principles, which render him very favourable to those high objects, which though less brilliant in the eyes of men of the world, are justly considered to be of a higher order, and more important to the best interests of our fellow-creatures.'——

The rest of the long dictated letter relates to missionary work in India. The signature and postscript are alone written by the great philanthropist himself. The postscript says :—'A complaint in my eyes, which has become habitual, compels me to write by the hand of another.'

* The Bishop (Dr. Middleton) died a few months after the arrival at Calcutta of Sir Samford Whittingham.

This no doubt applied only to long letters; for, five days later, he writes to Sir Samford the following entirely in his own hand, which however apparently must have been a great exertion to him, being somewhat difficult to decipher:—

'45 BROMPTON Row, *27th April,* 1822.
(Extract.)

'My dear Sir,—My friend Mr. Harford gratified me some time ago by telling me that you would allow me to have the honour and pleasure (for I can truly say it is both the one and the other in my judgment and feelings) of introducing the Bishop of Calcutta to your acquaintance. Allow me, therefore, to request of you to be the bearer of the inclosed letter. I hope to have the pleasure of wishing you a good voyage in person: but as you may make up your letters, &c. before your departure, I had better send it now. The Bishop, I scarcely need assure you, is a man of learning and talents, and of piety too, I trust; though there was at one time, not quite that feeling expressed towards some of the best of men in India, I mean regular clergymen, too, that was to be desired. I hope the liberal grant of 5,000*l.* to the Bishop's College, and at his disposal, will have done away all jealousy, and have shown his Lordship the wish our society really feels to testify their respect for his station and character, and their desire of aiding his endeavours for the public good. Of course all this I take the liberty of throwing out confidentially,* and remain, with every good wish for your health and happiness, my dear Sir S.

'Your faithful servant,
'W. WILBERFORCE.'

'General Sir S. Whittingham, &c.'

* After forty-five years, it is to be hoped that these doubts about the Bishop's likings for certain missionaries may be published without indiscretion.

Lieut.-General Sir H. Clinton whom Sir Samford had served under for a short time in 1813, and Sir Herbert Taylor, Military Secretary, whose acquaintance he had recently made, and Lieut.-General Sir John Murray, who had so often praised him in General Orders, all wrote flattering letters introducing him to the Commander-in-Chief in India, the Hon. Sir Edward Paget, that brother of the Marquis of Anglesey, who both from his public and private character might be truly called the pearl of the Pagets.

From limited space only three more introductions are inserted in this work. These are of no common kind:—

H.M. King George IV. to Sir Edward Paget.

'CARLTON HOUSE, 27th *April*, 1822.

'My dear Sir Edward,—This will be delivered to you by my aide-de-camp, Sir Samford Whittingham,* a very smart, excellent, and distinguished officer; but this must be as well known to you as to myself. I do desire, therefore, that you will take every opportunity of shewing him kindness and advancing his interests: this will be truly felt by

'Your sincere friend,
'GEORGE R.'

'To His Excellency Lieut.-General
'The Hon. Sir Edward Paget, &c., India.'

The next is official from H.R.H. the Duke of York; and gives Sir Edward his local rank of (full) General:—

'HORSE-GUARDS, 3rd *May*, 1822.

'Sir,—Colonel Sir Samford Whittingham being about to embark for India, to take upon himself the duties of Quartermaster-General of the Force under your com-

---

* Was it the gentlemanly repugnance to call a man *Colonel* who had so long served as a *General*, that made His Majesty omit the military rank altogether?

mand, I cannot suffer him to proceed without recommending him to you as an officer highly deserving of your confidence.

'I am, Sir, yours,
'FREDERICK,
'Commander-in-Chief.'

'General the Hon. Sir Edward Paget, G.C.B.'

The following letter is, on several accounts, especially worthy of record:—

From Sir Henry Torrens, Adjutant-General.*

'HORSE-GUARDS, 4th *May*, 1822.

'My dear Paget,—I am desirous of presenting to you the bearer, Sir Samford Whittingham, in a manner quite different from the common run of introductions; for as an officer and a gentleman, I think you will find him a peculiar acquisition to your Staff. He joins to a practical knowledge of his profession every scientific acquirement which is necessary to render him a useful and distinguished Staff officer; and I only regret that the Constitution and usages in India are so little calculated to enable you to benefit by Whittingham's talents,† in the duties of his appointment, should you happen to have any service in the field.

'Depend upon it, however, that you will always find him capable of fulfilling your expectations, in any situation in which the exigencies of the service may require you or enable you to place him. You perhaps know that Sir Samford was employed with the Spanish army from the earliest period of the revolt of that nation against the

---

* So appointed 25th March, 1820.

† Sir Henry Torrens alludes to the jealous provisions against the influence of King's *versus* Company's officers. The Quartermaster-General, for instance, of all the King's forces in India was, in each Presidency, a less influential officer than the Quartermaster-Generals of the three local armies. With the abolition of the Company, all have become Royal officers.

power of France; and that he held a very considerable command until the period when he conducted King Ferdinand to Madrid. His devotion to the Spanish cause has led him into expenses in the public service of that country which he has never recovered, and which has so materially impaired a private fortune once considerable, that he is forced to proceed to India as the only probable means left him of benefiting a numerous family, which he leaves in Europe.* Exclusive of this inducement, I must add in justice to Whittingham's military zeal, that he has long wished to serve in the East, where the extensive scale of operations affords an ample field to a soldier's laudable ambition. It is difficult now to say whether any operations may occur in India for a length of time. *If they do, depend upon it you will never find him fail you:* and whether they do or not I feel confident that you will lend your friendly hand towards the aid of his interests in any manner in which you can benefit the King's Quartermaster-General.

'I sincerely join, my dear Paget, in the desire felt by all your friends in this country to hear from you, and in the hope of good accounts, I remain ever,

Yours most sincerely,
' H. TORRENS.'

'General Sir Edward Paget, G.C.B.'

The words of Sir Henry Torrens which the Editor has placed in italics, were (as the reader will see in due time) realized to the letter in the organization of the Indian army, and in the preparations for the campaign in Burmah, and for the siege of Bhurtpore.

---

* Sir Samford, it seems, had not imparted to Sir Henry Torrens the cause of his other losses of fortune.

Sir Samford Whittingham to his Brother-in-law.

'MADRAS, 30th September, 1822.

'Our passage was long and tedious, but tranquil and easy. General Sir Alexander Campbell' [Commander-in-Chief at Madras], 'sent one of his aides-de-camp on board the "*Lady Raffles*," with a very kind note requesting me to occupy a room in his house. I had not seen him since the battle of Talavera, where we were both wounded. The 24th, I landed early in the morning, and breakfasted with him. His attentions to me have been unceasing. Lord Hastings will sail from Calcutta towards the end of December. A vessel in the service of the Company has already sailed from Bombay, with orders to touch at Ceylon and bring Sir Edward Paget and family to Calcutta. He will probably arrive in the course of November.

'*2nd September.*—To-morrow we sail for Calcutta.'

How Sir Samford had been appreciated at Madras is recorded in a letter written some months later in London by Mr. Bartle Frere, dated only 'Friday night,' and without address, but evidently written to Mr. Hart Davis :—

'On returning home to-night, I find a letter from my friend to whom I recommended Whittingham, at Madras, by which I have the pleasure of informing you of his safe arrival there. It is dated October the 4th. I suppose he must have been there some days, for my correspondent says : " he is a most delightful personage, much liked by all who have had an opportunity of cultivating his acquaintance." In another passage he says, "your friend is still detained here, and will not proceed on his voyage yet for a few days. He resides with Sir A. Campbell, so that we meet almost daily, and so pleasant do we all find him that we not only regret the shortness of his stay among us, but wish that he were finally fixed at Madras, instead of Calcutta." I am surprised that we have nothing from Whittingham.'

It appears by one of his letters that the latter arrived at Calcutta on the 2nd November, 1822. The following was written by Sir Samford after making acquaintance with the Marquis of Hastings, then Governor-General and also Commander-in-Chief :—

To his Brother-in-law.

'CALCUTTA, 25th November, 1822.

'I have not yet been enabled to procure a house, but I am in hopes of succeeding within a day or two. Commodore Hayes has very kindly given me a lodging in his house, without which assistance I really know not what I should have done; for Sir Thomas Macmahon[*] has no spare room, and the hotels are not frequented by gentlemen. I have spent a week in Barrackpore with Lord Hastings. I never knew a more delightful man.'——

He sent his brother-in-law some extracts from his journal since his arrival in Calcutta, a very few of which, and these curtailed, follow here.

'*Calcutta, 2nd November,* 1822.—Nothing can exceed the magnificent view which the entrance into Calcutta presents.' [Here, there is a long description, needless to quote, of oft-described beauties.] 'The climate is now as delightful as the scenery is enchanting, the thermometer ranging from 65° to 75°. Land of magnificent recollections, I hail thee! Thy history of the past, thy present greatness, thy future changes—are all equally interesting; and nothing which relates to India can be considered with indifference.

'At half-past two I landed at Calcutta, and Commodore Hayes insisted upon my occupying rooms in his house. I never in any part of the world experienced such

---

[*] Then Adjutant-General of the royal army in India.

hospitality from anyone as from the Commodore and his family.*

'*7th November.*—I called this morning on Marquis Hastings at Government House. He received me very kindly, spoke with much interest on the subject of the late war, and finally took credit to himself for the present prosperous state of India. The 16th Lancers are just arrived, and we compared the advantages and disadvantages of the sabre and the lance. To elucidate the discussion, the Marquis ordered two of the native lances to be produced. They are made of bamboo, very elastic and very light. The Marquis took one lance, I took another; we pointed our weapons, and advanced to the charge. *My Uncle Toby and Corporal Trim* could not have done it better.

'At seven in the evening I returned to dinner. Lady Hastings made her appearance at half-past eight.' [A very graphic but not equally flattering description of her Ladyship is here omitted.] 'The Marquis himself is the model of a perfect English gentleman, and had Lady Hastings† not accompanied him to India, he would have been the most popular Governor-General that ever yet presided over the affairs of that Government.

'Lord Hastings dines in the French style, the gentlemen accompany the ladies to the drawing-room. This is to me on every account delightful, and particularly so in the present case, as it furnishes ample opportunity for long and interesting conversations with his Lordship.'

Sir Samford then describes at large the details given by his Lordship of his successful administration of the

---

* Nothing strikes an Englishman on first arriving in India more than the boundless hospitality of his countrymen.

† A haughtiness of manner (that may have been unintentional) was apparently the chief cause of this lady's unpopularity in India. She is said, however, to have also habitually kept her guests waiting dinner for hours.

finances of India, in spite of the great expenses of a three years' war.

The journal then proceeds,—'His Lordship related many amusing anecdotes of Scindiah, Ameer Khan, and Holkar. His system of espionage was so well organized during the war, that he always received with the least possible loss of time, copies of the information sent to the enemy. This generally consisted of observations made on him personally, and the deductions were very curious. His Lordship's smiles and frowns, seriousness and gaiety, nay, the very pace he rode in his morning's exercise, were, according to these deep observers, all the result of political causes. And not a single action of his life, however trivial, could they allow to take place, without attributing it to some great and mighty hidden cause.'

Next comes the visit to Lord Hastings, at Barrackpore. The Marquis had been more than nine years in his high position, having been appointed on the 12th March, 1813:—

From the Marquis of Hastings.

[CALCUTTA], '9th November, 1822.

'My dear Sir,—Next Friday morning, we shall return to Barrackpore, to pass a week, possibly our last, at that pleasant place. As you may like to see it, and your company there would be gratifying to Lady Hastings and myself, I cannot omit trying to tempt you thither. It will be a novelty to you to be lodged in a bungalow, but I trust you would find it no uncomfortable accommodation.

'I have the honour to be, my dear Sir,
'Your very obedient servant,
'HASTINGS.'

'Sir S. F. Whittingham, &c.'

Extracts of Journal continued.

'*Barrackpore, 16th November*, 1822.—I left the hospitable mansion of Commodore Hayes, at six this morning, and arrived at this beautiful mansion of the Governor-General, at half past seven, distance sixteen miles.'* [After describing the luxurious comforts provided for him and the kind attentions shown him by the Marquis, and also detailing the habits of the household at Barrackpore; he describes his 'first elephantine excursion']: 'Captain Doyle called for me at five o'clock. The howdah or castle contains two persons with ease. The elephant lies down, a ladder is placed against his side, which you ascend, to take your lofty seat. The animal is commonly twelve feet high. I like his motion, and prefer this mode of conveyance to any other. A thousand recollections of the grandeur of the House of Timour, of war and battle, and the rise and fall of mighty empires, are conjured up by being mounted on this noble animal.

'17*th Nov.*—Lord Hastings took me with him this morning at five o'clock, on his favourite elephant, through the cantonment of four battalions of native infantry, situated on the open ground beyond the park. His conversation is always interesting and instructive, and his goodness and kindness to me are flattering in the extreme.

'18*th Nov.*—The house in which I am lodged, is not properly a bungalow (which is in fact a thatched cottage), but a square building composed of four habitations, with a large dining-room in the centre. Mr. Adam, who will hold the Government *ad interim*, after the departure of Lord Hastings, occupies one suite of rooms, Major Taylor, the director of the college of writers, another, the third is vacant, and I occupy the fourth. The Marquis

---

* All mere local descriptions are omitted. This journal alone would make a good sized pamphlet!

is kind and attentive to me beyond measure, and I find in the familiar intercourse with which he is pleased to honour me, the greatest source of enjoyment. I certainly never experienced so much confidence from any great man in so short an acquaintance, as from Lord Hastings.

'19th Nov.—This morning after breakfast, Lord Hastings* desired me to accompany him to his study, where he was pleased to submit to my perusal the following interesting documents.'—[Briefly, they were five important political correspondences, on the principal transactions of Lord Hastings, political, diplomatic, and financial affairs, including matters concerning the King of Oude, the Peishwa, and the Rajah of Bhurtpore. Of these documents, one was :—] 'A letter from the Resident at Oude, giving an account of his having communicated to the King the intended departure of Lord Hastings. The King of Oude was so affected at the news, that for some time, he could not speak. At length, a flood of tears came to his relief, and he burst forth into the most bitter lamentations.' [The Rajah of Bhurtpore had very practically proved the influence over him of the Governor-General. Sir Samford remarks :—] 'When we reflect upon this Rajah's triumph over our forces under Lord Lake, and upon his extreme vanity and arrogance since that period, this change of sentiment and manner does great credit to the able negotiations of Lord Hastings.'

[When he penned these words, Sir Samford little imagined that he himself was destined to contribute greatly to the final downfall of this haughty Rajah.]

'After finishing the perusal of these documents, his Lordship related the following anecdotes of the King of Ava and of Scindiah.

'Whilst the Marquis was engaged in the war against

---

* Lord Hastings being Commander-in-Chief as well as Governor-General, the Quartermaster-General was under his immediate orders. But officially the latter had nothing to do with civil affairs.

Central India, he received an embassy from the King of Ava, ordering him to restore immediately to the empire of the Burmese, their natural frontiers, by delivering up, to the officers he should appoint, Dacca and all its corresponding territories. The Governor-General sent back the King of Ava's letter upon the pretended supposition that it was a forgery quite unknown to the King, and evidently invented by some enemy to the peace and tranquillity which so happily reigned between the two empires. Nothing more was heard of the pretensions of the King of Ava.'

The anecdote regarding Scindiah, (too long for insertion here) proved how Lord Hastings had won his gratitude and effective services by boldly reposing confidence in him at a critical moment.

The following is the only other note of his Lordship's to Sir Samford, besides the one already quoted, that has reached the Editor's hands:—

[CALCUTTA] '25th November, 1822.

'My dear Sir,—If you have no other engagement for Wednesday or Thursday, let me beg of you to favour us with your company to dinner on either of these days which may best suit you. Many thanks for the Archduke Charles's narrative. Though I have only been able to give a hasty glance at it, I have had a lesson from it. With decent self-sufficiency, I had flattered myself that I had conceived and digested novel principles respecting mountain warfare, and I have found all my notions, superiorily detailed in the observations on the inroad into the Tyrol.—

'I have the honour to be, my dear Sir,
'Your very obedient servant,
'HASTINGS.'

'Sir S. F. Whittingham, &c.'

Sir Samford Whittingham to his Brother-in-law.

'CALCUTTA, *9th December,* 1822.

'To-day the address has been presented to Lord Hastings, and he made his reply. Sir Edward Paget is arrived in the river.* On the 28th Lord Hastings sails in the "*Glasgow*," Captain Doyle, for the Mediterranean. It is strongly rumoured here that Mr. Canning will not come out, that Lord Wellesley will be appointed Governor-General, and Lord Hastings go to Ireland in his room. This arrangement, if there were any truth in it, would please the people of this country amazingly: for Lord Wellesley is more popular amongst all ranks and all classes than I can possibly express.

'To-morrow I commence the Persian language; at which I shall work as though recommencing life.'——

The account of the first meeting of Sir Samford Whittingham with Sir Edward Paget, the man who was to become to him a more than second Cadogan, has not reached the Editor's hands. The appearance and manners of the new Commander-in-Chief, even before there was time to appreciate his inestimable mental and moral qualities, were calculated to win all hearts, and to command universal respect. Though both the Chief and his Quartermaster-General had fought and bled in the Peninsula, they had never yet met as acquaintances. But they were soon destined to become both officially and privately the best and truest of friends, thus realizing in a wonderful degree the sanguine anticipations of Sir Henry Torrens's remarkable letter of introduction.

Sir Samford Whittingham's first opinions in favour of the Marquis of Hastings were afterwards considerably modified, on discovering the wretchedly inefficient state in which that nobleman had left the army of Bengal,

* From Ceylon, where he had been Governor.

which he had sacrificed entirely to his otherwise laudable schemes of economy. In India, especially, to be ready for war is indispensable to the permanent security of peace; and the expenses of the Burmese war, and of the Bhurtpore campaign were of course greatly increased by the Marquis's neglect of this maxim. Though he saved money himself, he became a main cause of the expenditure of his successors, who were compelled in haste to supply what he had failed at leisure to provide—a well organized military force.

In this respect Sir Edward Paget had a great and arduous task to perform, and he performed it well, with the assistance of that Staff-officer whom he most esteemed and on whom he most relied; and to whom, with a generosity as magnanimous as it is rare, he gave to the utmost of his power, his full share of the honour and credit due to their united and indefatigable exertions; as will be seen in the next and following chapters.

CHAPTER XIV.

1823—1825.

DEATH OF THE MARQUIS OF LONDONDERRY— DEATH OF BISHOP MIDDLETON—SIR EDWARD PAGET'S FLATTERING PROPOSAL—INDIA SHOULD BE RULED BY A VICEROY—THE KING OF OUDE — A HANDSOME COMMANDER-IN-CHIEF—REORGANIZATION OF BENGAL ARMY INDISPENSABLE—WRETCHED STATE OF MILITARY MEANS—ARDUOUS OFFICIAL LABOURS—ENCOURAGEMENT TO SMOKERS—SIR EDWARD PAGET'S SOLE SOURCE OF COMFORT—THE MUTINY AT BARRACKPORE—SIR SAMFORD'S REPORT OF THE MUTINY—HIS SUBSEQUENT DEFENCE OF SIR EDWARD PAGET—DEATH OF SIR ALEXANDER CAMPBELL—THE *ALTER EGO* OF THE COMMANDER-IN-CHIEF—SIR HERBERT TAYLOR'S LETTER TO SIR SAMFORD—ILLNESS OF SIR EDWARD PAGET—ADVICE FOLLOWED FORTY YEARS LATER—LORD COMBERMERE'S ARRIVAL—FIRST IMPRESSIONS OF HIS LORDSHIP—CHARACTER OF SIR EDWARD PAGET—PARTING EXCHANGE OF PRESENTS—THE HOOKAH AND THE 'ADMIRAL'—LORD COMBERMERE'S ADVANCE TO BESIEGE BHURTPORE—EFFICIENT PREPARATIONS OWING TO SIR EDWARD PAGET—LORD COMBERMERE'S TEMPORARY COLDNESS TO SIR SAMFORD WHITTINGHAM.

Sir Samford Whittingham to his Brother-in-law.

'CALCUTTA, 12*th January*, 1823.

'WE yesterday received the melancholy intelligence that Lord Londonderry * had put a period to his existence. Gracious God! when such a man as this finds life too great a burden to be borne, who amongst us can place confidence in himself? Who can say, "fountain of thy waters I will never drink"? No doubt his mind must have been partially deranged, but this is a poor consolation; for madness has so many shades that its boundaries are scarcely to be defined, nor can its approaches be easily guarded against.

* Better known as Viscount Castlereagh.

'Lady Harriet Paget will sail for England this month. The General will begin the journey to the interior early in July.'

On the 19th January, 1823, Sir Samford Whittingham writes, 'Lady Harriet Paget sails the latter end of this month. She is without exception one of the most amiable women I ever knew. I cultivate Sir Edward's friendship, and am every day more delighted with him.'

To the Same.

'CALCUTTA, 8*th February*, 1823.

'The season is very fine, and yet we have lost many men of mark within the last six months; the Bishop,* the Archdeacon, the Chief Justice, the Surveyor-General Mr. Good, one of the principal judges, Dr. Jameson, brother-in-law to Torrens, and many others!

'I continue my water and vegetable diet. I do not even eat fish. Sir Edward is not yet returned from accompanying Lady Harriet down the river. He is expected to-day. She has taken charge of a letter for you. You will find her to be everything that is amiable and good and kind. We expect to begin our journey at the end of June. Our expedition will last full two years. We are all anxiety to know if Mr. Canning comes out, and if not who replaces him.'——

The following letter gives the earliest indications of Sir Edward Paget's desire to profit by the zeal and ability of the Quartermaster-General of the King's army, in India; qualities the more valuable from the (at that period) generally notorious inefficiency of the wonted channels of the General Staff, the Company's officers, for carrying on the business of the Commander-in-Chief:—

* Dr. Middleton, to whom Mr. Wilberforce introduced Sir Samford.

Sir Samford Whittingham to the Hon. Sir Edward Paget.

'CHOWRINGHEE, 16*th February*, 1823.

'My dear General,—Lieutenant Colonel Marley* has mentioned to me your truly kind intentions of employing my very weak means, but most excellent good will. I shall be delighted to be made useful in any way you may think proper; and to merit your approbation will be ever my highest ambition. I have taken the liberty of enclosing a sketch of the information I ought to have been able to lay before you on your arrival, if I had been really the Quartermaster-General of the Indian army. Would you have the condescension to point out to me anything I have omitted, or to suggest any other arrangement that may appear to you better? It is true I am now but a cypher, but should the chance of war ever render me effective under your command, I should be most anxious to be enabled to anticipate your general ideas, as well as to implicitly obey your commands.

'I fear this crazy machine of mine will again deprive me of the honour of dining with you. Nicholson talks of bleeding and medicining again to-morrow; but no bodily illness that leaves my reason free will ever prevent my employing myself in the execution of your orders.

'I have the honour to be, with the most profound respect, 'My dear General,
'Your most devoted servant,
'SAMFORD WHITTINGHAM.'

'General the Hon. Sir Edward Paget,
'Commander-in-Chief, G.C.B., &c. &c.'

* Colonel Marley was the Military Secretary of Sir Edward Paget, and head of his Personal Staff.

On the 19th February, he mentions to Mr. Davis the intention of Sir Edward Paget to employ him 'in drawing up a general state of India at present, particularly as to the military department. He has let me know that he does not mean to take the merit of the *exposé* himself, but to send it to the Duke of York as mine. And he has been pleased to add that he knows nobody more capable of executing a plan of such high importance.'

On the 24th March, 1823, he writes: 'We have received the accounts of the nomination of Lord Amherst as Governor-General.' On the 4th April he tells his brother-in-law 'I am on the point of setting off with the Commander-in-Chief, on a visit to the Governor-General.' He adds a sentence worthy of record, as regards its bearing on a stormy future, then approaching: 'Sir Edward and Mr. Adam' [the temporary Governor-General] 'are perfect models of what rulers should be. God grant the new Governor may harmonize with all their feelings, and fully co-operate with all their measures. A hundred millions of souls, and an army of 250,000 men are weighty concerns to be arranged by such men as the East India Directors. If this were a Vice-Royalty under the King's government, it would be the brightest jewel in the crown; the most powerful Colony that ever existed in the world.'

For the long and many letters describing his tour with his Chief in Bengal, from July to December, there is not space even for extracts. He was all this time (besides keeping up a voluminous correspondence with Mr. Davis) making himself, practically as well as theoretically, thoroughly acquainted with the great Indian Empire in all its bearings; and his pleasant intercourse with his Chief was daily ripening into the warmest personal friendship, as well as mutual official esteem. Though Quartermaster-General, Sir Edward insisted on his living with him on the tour like one of his personal staff; thus adding to his comfort and lessening his expenses.* They visited Patna, Gazeepoor, Cawnpore, Futtyghur, and Agra.

His letters to his brother contain graphic pictures of an Indian Commander-in-Chief's tour through the provinces. Two sentences must suffice to give an idea of accounts which would fill a volume:—

'2nd Nov[ember, 1823.]—Unless I were to copy one of the stories of the Arabian Nights' Entertainment, it would be very difficult for me to convey even a tolerably just idea of the fête of last night given by the King of Oude to Sir Edward Paget.'

After describing the almost incredible splendours of the entertainment, the profusion of jewels and precious metals, and all the forms and ceremonies and magnificent presents, he thus winds up his account:—'I have never before witnessed so enchanting a scene. No description in Lalla-Rookh exceeds the reality of what we saw, and only such a pen as Moore's could paint the delightful illusion of this fairy fête! The King did the honours of the reception with dignified ease, and his benign and good countenance well became the costly diamonds and lovely pearls with which his head and neck and arms and hands were ornamented. His dress was a shawl pelisse of inestimable value, and his whole appearance truly magnificent.

'Sir Edward Paget's noble and handsome countenance, the emblem of every manly virtue, did honour to the distinction he was receiving, and completely filled up the picture, by a living demonstration that there is no real greatness but that which has virtue for its basis. I have never, in the course of my long wanderings, met with any man approaching so near to perfection as a soldier, a gentleman, and a Christian.'

---

* The Commander-in-Chief at that time had more than £16,000 a year.

In the beginning of 1824 Sir Edward Paget, now on his tour, was encamped at Meerut. In a long letter to his usual correspondent, dated Meerut, 20th February, Sir Samford relates how he had offered his services to Sir Edward for an expected Burmese Campaign, no enviable command, considering the terrible climate. 'He replied, "*Where I go, you shall go, and you never shall be separated from me.*" Few things in this life have ever given me more pleasure. It is and has been ever my utmost ambition to merit the esteem and confidence of this model of everything that is great and good.'

On the 20th March Sir Samford returned to Calcutta. There he and his Chief were busy making preparation for the Burmese war. Whilst at Calcutta Sir Samford received a letter dated 'Fyzabad, May 1824,' from his young friend Mr. (now Lord) William Godolphin Osborne* (who had at one time been his guest), giving a long account of a very successful, exciting, and dangerous tiger hunt. His friendship for Mr. Osborne lasted for life, as did their occasional correspondence.

If our Indian empire can now be considered safe, it is because many of the reforms considered indispensable by Sir Edward Paget and Sir Samford Whittingham have been introduced since the faulty old system came to an end with the great Indian Mutiny.

On the 17th May, 1824, he reports the commencement of the Burmese War, and also adds the following sentence, ominous of that coming mutiny, which, if Sir Edward had met it with the coaxing and rose-water system by which the articles of war were then constantly diluted for the benefit of the natives, might have anticipated in its horrors its successor of thirty-three years later. 'The new regulations have curtailed the allowances of this

---

* In 1832 he became *Honourable*, on his father being created Lord Godolphin; and in 1859 he obtained the title of *Lord*, on the succession of his brother to the Dukedom of Leeds.

[the Bengal] army, to such an extent that the highest discontent prevails throughout. If they are carried into effect, you will, I fear, hear of very serious consequences.' On the 20th he gives his brother-in-law some details of the progress of the Burmese War, and of the excitement and even anxiety in India.

On the 10th May he had written: 'You will be pleased to hear, *entre nous*, that Sir Edward Paget has been pleased to honour me with his complete and unreserved confidence. He calls for me every morning at daylight in his open carriage, and we ride alone till the sun obliges us to retire.'

To his Brother-in-law.

'CALCUTTA, 10*th June*, 1824.'

'I wrote to you yesterday, enclosing a letter to Sir Herbert Taylor, giving some account of our late proceedings. But it is impossible to convey a just idea of the state to which we are reduced as to military preparation, without entering into details too minute for the contents of a letter. Suffice it to say that we have not a single twelve-pound shot in the arsenal, and that we are 700 gun carriages short of our present wants!

'Sir Edward has given up the organization of the flotilla to Commodore Hayes and myself. By the end of this month we shall, I trust, have thirty gunboats and twelve armed brigs completely equipped, manned and armed, and soon after complete our number of gunboats to a hundred.'——

On the 30th June he writes: 'The work of this month has been great, and we are fast recovering from the state of weakness we were in when I last wrote;' and he proceeds to enumerate the details.

He had still hopes that Sir Edward Paget was about to take the field in person in Burmah, and longed for active service as a field for military distinction. On the 1st August he writes: 'The season has been uncommonly sickly. Not five people out of one hundred have escaped fever: but the mortality has been trifling in comparison to the number who have been ill. The three great smokers of Calcutta, viz., Sir Edward Paget, Laruletta,* and myself, have escaped, probably owing to the abundance and the goodness of our cigars. I long for the campaign to open; I shall then have something to write about.'

The Burmese War was eventually satisfactorily concluded by Sir Archibald Campbell, without the personal intervention of the Commander-in-Chief.

To his Brother-in-law.

'CALCUTTA, 20*th September,* 1824.

' Sir Edward Paget has been pleased to say that I was the only person in India from whom he had derived comfort and support, and to whom he could unbosom himself freely, openly, and without reserve. He has been pleased to honour me with his friendship and fullest confidence; and I feel more proud than I can express at having obtained the esteem of this best model of what a man should be!

'The longer I stay in India, the more I am convinced of the correct truth of all my former statements to you. *The country hangs upon a thread.* The slightest reverse would set the whole in a flame; and *you have not the smallest hold upon any class of men in all your vast Indian dominions, except that which immediately derives from the opinion, or rather the conviction, that your bayonets and sabres are superior to theirs.*† The Indian army

---

* A well-known merchant of Calcutta.

† It is evident that the *great* Indian mutiny, had he survived to hear of it, would not have surprised Sir Samford Whittingham.

must become, and that speedily, a King's army, the number of officers must be greatly increased, and the broken spirit of both officers and men regenerated.'——

The month of October continued to give the Quartermaster-General abundance of work in preparing the expedition to Ava of the Commander-in-Chief, with a force of irresistible strength, should the prolonged resistance of the Burmese require it.

November, 1824, opened in a melancholy manner, with the Mutiny of Barrackpore. There is no space here for the discussion of that vexed question. The infatuated adherents of the Indian coaxing system, whose eyes even the great crisis of 1857 has failed to open, and who would still employ rose-water to put down open rebellions, are impervious to the arguments of reason and experience; and especially to the imperative necessities of military discipline. In affairs of government, civilians, though subjects, may and must be listened to and reasoned with; but soldiers must be silent and obey, or the army becomes a mere rabble, more dangerous to its friends than to its enemies, as was proved in 1857. Whether a Government be despotic, constitutional or republican, does not affect this rule.

As the dear friend of Sir Edward Paget, and as an officer who ever considered obedience as the chief duty of a soldier, it is needless to say that Sir Samford Whittingham sympathized fully with his Chief, who not without great reluctance, and even anguish of mind, trod out the dangerous mutiny of Barrackpore in the most decisive manner.

It appears that Sir Samford was employed to send in a brief report of this mutiny and of its suppression, for the information of the Governor-General's secretary; at least so the Editor interprets the following copy (written in

Sir Samford's hand), of the original, which he wrote on the occasion; and which copy bears no address to show to whom it was written :—

(Private and Confidential.)

'BARRACKPORE, *5th November*, 1824.

' Dear Sir,—The Commander-in-Chief, being extremely occupied at the present moment, has requested me to communicate for your information the following detail of a daring mutiny which broke out amongst the Sepoy battalions at this station on the 1st instant.

' The 26th, 47th, and 62nd Regiments of Bengal Native Infantry were under orders for foreign service, and were to march to Chittagong from this cantonment successively, with an interval of two days between the time of their respective departures.

' On the 1st of this month, it was officially reported to His Excellency that the 47th Native Infantry had refused to march, and that they were in a state of open mutiny.

' The Commander-in-Chief proceeded immediately to Barrackpore in the hopes that his presence might produce some effect upon the mutineers. But they continued firm in their determination, and it became necessary to have recourse to coercive measures to bring them to reason.

' Before twelve at night, the Royals,* H.M.'s 47th Regiment, the Governor-General's body-guard, and a battery of field artillery, had arrived, and were assembled in the park at Barrackpore.

' At daybreak two battalions N.I.; H.M.'s 47th, and the body-guard with its gallopers,† were formed on the

* H.M.'s First Regiment of the line is called the 'Royals.'

† *Galloper guns*, as they were called, were formerly attached to all regiments of cavalry in India.

left of the cantonment. The Royals, and the battery of field artillery drew up in the rear of the huts of the mutineers.

'During the night 160 men of the 62nd [Native Infantry] went over to the mutineers, together with twenty-four men of the 26th [N.I.]; both taking their colours with them.

'The mutineers formed on the parade of the 47th N.I., in front of their own lines.

'The Commander-in-Chief, who was with the troops on the left, had formed the hope that the imposing attitude of so large a force would have been sufficient to overawe the mutineers, without having recourse to extreme measures. But, being disappointed in that expectation, he sent the Adjutant-General and Quartermaster-General of the [Bengal] army, accompanied by his Persian interpreter, and the Colonel of the 47th N.I. to intimate to the mutineers, that, unless they laid down their arms, and surrendered at discretion, they would be immediately attacked. The Adjutant-General* ordered them to ground their arms. They refused to obey, and expressed their resolution to resist force by force.

'At the signal of two guns fired from the left, the battery in the rear of the mutineers opened, and the Royals advanced up the road which led to their right flank. At the same time, the whole line on the left advanced.

'In less than five minutes the mutineers were broken, and the dispersion was so complete that not two men were to be found together. They threw away their arms, stripped themselves of their military insignia, and fled in

---

* It was afterwards discovered that the Adjutant-General of the Bengal army (a Colonel) had received a petition from the mutineers before he came on parade, and had put it into his pocket, instead of giving it at once to the Commander-in-Chief. It contained a list of their grievances, and *might*, if listened to, have averted the destruction of the mutineers.

all directions. A considerable number were killed, and more taken prisoners. Of these latter, numbers are constantly [being brought] in.

'A court-martial was immediately assembled. Forty of the prisoners were tried and condemned. Six were executed yesterday morning. The punishment of the other thirty-four the Commander-in-Chief has been pleased to commute into exile and hard labour for life in chains.

'The court-martial is still sitting, and will continue so to do till all the prisoners shall have been tried.

'These misguided men appear to have had no real grounds of complaint to palliate their misconduct. They had stated that the means of transport for their effects were not sufficient; and ten bullocks per company were assigned [to them]. They had been told, they said, that they were to be embarked: but the Commander-in-Chief assured them he had never thought of such a thing; and that no Bengal sepoy should ever be embarked, under his command, except as a volunteer.

'It is to be apprehended that much blame attaches to the Native officers of the battalion; and it is feared that a dislike to the war against the Burmese had also its influence upon the sepoy.

'The Commander-in-Chief is still at Barrackpore, where he will probably remain till the 26th and 62nd [N.I. regiments] have broken ground for their destination.

'I have the honour to be, dear Sir,

'Your most obedient servant,

'SAMFORD WHITTINGHAM.'

About nine years later, the falsehoods of an anonymous calumniator in the 'Meerut Observer,' were refuted in the following letter, which is here given in order to finish at once with the affair of the mutiny.

From the 'Meerut Observer,' of Thursday, 18th April, 1833:—

To the Editor of the 'Meerutt* Observer.'

'Sir,—On the first report which Sir Edward Paget received of the mutiny at Barrackpore, he proceeded thither without a moment's delay. On his arrival he found the mutineers in open insurrection. Every effort was made, during that evening and the ensuing night, to induce the misguided men to return to their duty, but in vain. During the night, the colours of two other regiments, with detachments from each, joined the mutineers. At daybreak the next morning they were under arms, and the force at the disposal of Sir Edward Paget was drawn up within full view. Sir Edward then made another attempt to convince them of their error. The General commanding the division, the Adjutant, and Quartermaster-Generals of the army, the Persian interpreter, and the Commanding Officer of the regiment were sent in a body to the mutineers, and directed to state to them that, "if they would lay down their arms and submit their claims to the justice of the Commander-in-Chief, they should be immediately investigated and attended to, and their past conduct forgiven and forgotten; but that it was impossible for the Commander-in-Chief to treat with armed soldiers." The deputation returned with the report that the men would listen to nothing; and it was then only that Sir Edward ordered the signal gun to be fired, and the line to advance.

'The very instant the line of the mutineers broke, Sir Edward ordered the firing to cease, and directed the *Quartermaster-General of the King's troops* to proceed at speed to Colonel Armstrong, commanding the Royals, with orders that all pursuit should be stopped. The Colonel, and the *Quartermaster-General of the King's troops* rode forward *to the front* of the Light Company of the 47th and Royals, and made every exertion in their

---

* Meerut, it appears, was formerly spelt Meerutt by the press of India.

power to stop the firing, in which they succeeded in a very short time, and brought the Light Company back.*

'The anonymous writer in your paper of yesterday, in what he says of an officer of high rank in His Majesty's service, *sniping* the sepoys, &c., is guilty of an infamous falsehood, and only screens himself from the punishment he deserves, by concealing his name.

'The name of the author of this answer to the vile attack upon the character of Sir Edward Paget, contained in the 'Meerutt Observer' of the 11th April, is lodged with the Editor, and will be given on application.

'MEERUT, 12th April, 1833.'

This refutation was written by Sir Samford when in command at Meerut. It remained without an answer, and proves—what no one who knew Sir Edward Paget, and Sir Samford Whittingham doubted—that there was no desire on their parts to use more severity than was absolutely necessary for the occasion. By riding in front of the angry British soldiers who were firing at the mutineers, Sir Samford proved the sincerity of his exertions, at the evident risk of his life, as did Colonel Armstrong, the commanding officer of those soldiers.

Two more extracts from his letters to Mr. Davis will fill all the space that can be spared for the year 1824:—

'*Calcutta*, 12*th December.*—I am very anxious to know whether Lord William Bentinck comes out to this country as Governor-General or not? It would certainly be a pleasant thing to meet my old commander; and I love to hope that he would have no objection to having me again under his orders.

'24*th December*, 1824.—We have received Sir Archibald Campbell's dispatches, with the account of a complete victory gained by him over the Burmese. The

---

* Probably, picked men of the two regiments had on this occasion been formed into one Light Company.

victory was rapid and decisive: 5,000 men were left on the field; 240 pieces of cannon fell into our hands; and the whole army of the enemy dispersed and fled.

'Sir Alexander Campbell, the Commander-in-Chief at Madras, is dead. His loss will be greatly felt. He was a most able man, and a most honourable soldier; and his zeal to meet Sir Edward's wishes, in everything concerned with this war, had been conspicuous throughout. When I saw him two years ago at Madras, he was healthy and strong, and really a wonderful man for his time of life, upwards of seventy. But the last rains and heats had tried the strongest constitutions, and sent many a wanderer to his long home.'

Seventeen years later, the writer of the above words, a greater wanderer still, was to close his career at the same place and in the same command!

The truly voluminous correspondence of Sir Samford Whittingham was for the first four months of 1825 full of the Burmese war, in which he had hoped at one time to have taken an active part. But Sir Edward Paget, as we have seen, could not spare the man who had become the real though not nominal Chief of his Staff, as well as his confidant, counsellor, and general secretary. Colonel Patrick Paget, Sir Edward's surviving military son, was as much astonished as the Editor of this work, on searching the contents of a large and heavy box of papers left by Sir Edward (containing apparently the whole of his correspondence either in original or in copies) to find that one third at least of the writings were either letters or memoranda written by Sir Samford Whittingham, or at least, in his handwriting. When the Adjutant-General of Bengal and the Adjutant-General of the King's army charged each other, pen in hand, with a considerable amount of faults on both sides, the task of preparing the letter of the Chief blaming both, was evidently given to the Quartermaster-General of the King's troops. The copy of the letter found has the appearance of being the first draft of the intended dispatch, and it is all in Sir Samford's handwriting, and was afterwards marked as copy. If thus fully consulted in so delicate a matter, it may easily be conceived how he was entrusted with the ordinary special correspondence of an able commander, who disliked writing (though he could write so well) and was moreover unable, from the loss of his arm, to write much. In fact Sir Samford became, without exaggeration his right hand, his *alter ego*, and that aid which most chiefs seek almost equally from their principal staff officers was here sought and found in all important matters from one alone.

Sir Herbert Taylor to Sir S. Whittingham.*

'HORSE-GUARDS, 3rd *April*, 1825.

' My dear Sir Samford,—I wished to have thanked you for your obliging and interesting letter of the 18th July, at the same time that I wrote to Sir Edward Paget, whose letter dated in August reached me a few days after your's. But I was so hurried at the time, and have been since, by the additional business produced by the augmentations, &c., that I have been unable to keep up my general correspondence so regularly as at other times.

' I showed your letter to the Commander-in-Chief, and he received great pleasure from the satisfactory report it contained of the change produced in our military situation and prospects by the ability, zeal, and intelligence of your excellent Commander-in-Chief. . . . The general impression, is that you will not proceed much beyond the frontier on the eastern side; and that the operations against the Burmese will be confined to those of Sir Archibald Campbell's force, and possibly to an attack upon Arracan. I sincerely hope that these may

---

* Then Military Secretary to the Duke of York.

suffice to bring to a speedy termination this unsatisfactory and unprofitable war; so destructive to our best men, from the effects of climate and the deficiency of wholesome food. I know not what the feeling may be in India; but here the war is most unpopular, and all are grumbling.

* * * * * * *

'Our friend Torrens is in better health than he had been some time ago, though still not well and very thin.

'Believe me to be ever, my dear Sir Samford,

'Most sincerely yours,

'H. TAYLOR.'

On the 20th June Sir Samford records the illness of Sir Edward Paget, and that, though less severe, of Lord Amherst. On the 22nd June he writes:—' Sir Edward Paget's health still continues, I am sorry to say, in a very alarming state. But pray keep this to yourself, lest it should get to the ear of Lady Harriet. I am most anxious to get him on board ship as quickly as possible.'

'*24th June.*—In a few days I am going on the river with Sir Edward Paget. I hope it may prove beneficial to his health. I am very anxious about him: for I think I never saw a man so completely shaken by climate.

'Sir Edward will not delay his departure a single unnecessary day after the arrival of Lord Combermere. Lord Combermere will not find India a bed of roses. To suffer as Sir Edward has done, however, he must possess the same exquisite sensibility, and the same extreme, anxious desire to do his duty.'

In a letter dated Calcutta, 31st July 1825, consisting of thirteen pages of foolscap paper, Sir Samford gives Mr. Davis a summary of all the improvements introduced, and of the benefits conferred by Sir Edward Paget during his command, of which only a few sentences can be here quoted:—

'I do not, however, by any means assert that the Bengal army is what it should be. The moral of the army is deeply affected, and a general spirit of insubordination pervades the whole. The want of a sufficient number of European officers with the battalions is universally felt; and the dependence of the sepoy upon his commanding officer has been destroyed, by making, during the whole of the late administration, the head-quarters of the Commander-in-Chief, the *only* source of either reward or punishment.

'The mistaken lenity of Lord Hastings's administration has engendered a spirit of reasoning, and a fervour of writing throughout the whole mass; and this spirit is too much fomented by the system of promotion by seniority, whilst it gives the officers mistaken notions of their own independence, shuts the door to the exertions of genius, and makes a good constitution and a long life the only objects of ambition.

'I do not mean to say that these and other evils have been remedied. They are of too serious a nature to be cured by anything short of making the Indian army a King's army, and the Indian Government a King's government. But I do assert, and I am borne out by the facts, that the present Commander-in-Chief, supported by the Government, has done more for the tranquillity and security of India during this year of his administration, than has ever been done with the same means in the same given space of time. And I am bold to say that no man could, under existing circumstances, have effected more important changes in our military state, and in that of the country at large than he has done.'

It required the Indian mutiny of 1857 to convince our statesmen of the necessity of those reforms and alterations which, thirty-two years previously, Sir Edward Paget and Sir Samford Whittingham had deemed indispensable to the security and good government of our Indian empire.

On the 1st of August, 1825, Sir Samford expresses his indignation to Mr. Davis at the news from England of the abuse then directed at the conduct of Sir Edward Paget, whose plain speaking and writing had deeply offended the great Company in Leadenhall Street, whilst the nation was disgusted with the Governor-General on account of the Burmese war. Sir Samford's letter in defence of his friend resembles a small pamphlet.* Even up to this date he writes: 'Lord Amherst and the Commander-in-Chief have ever been upon the best and most friendly terms;' and he mentions the unanimity of the Council of India as quite extraordinary.

On the 14th September, after long details of the progress of the Burmese war, he writes : '*The Rajah of Bhurtpore*, the Rajah of Alwar, and the Ranee of Jeypore have all disputes with this Government, which I think will only be decided by the sword. The sooner we begin the better.'

'*Calcutta*, 7*th October*, 1825.—On the 3rd of this month we received the long-expected brevet, having come out it appears on the 27th May, the day you had mentioned in your letters of the 12th and 13th May.† The same day arrived Lord Combermere, our new Commander-in-Chief.

'Yesterday Sir Edward Paget sent in his resignation, and to-day Lord Combermere will be sworn into his new command.'

'23*rd October*.—I have written the inclosed to our dear friend' [Sir William Knighton], 'on the subject of his nephew, Mr. Seymour.‡ I assure you I shall be

---

* This letter Mr. Davis sent to Lord Liverpool, as will be seen hereafter.

† This brevet made Sir Samford at last a general officer in the British service.

‡ Captain James Seymour, 38th Regiment, son to the late and brother to the present Admiral Sir Michael Seymour. Sir Samford had promised to

delighted to have this opportunity of manifesting to a person I so much esteem my grateful feelings for all his kindness. I do not enter more into this subject, from having fully done so in the inclosed letter.

'What I have seen of Lord Combermere I like much. He is open and plain in his communications, and has exerted himself in my favour as far as in him lay. I have no doubt we shall soon become well acquainted.*

. . . .

'Sir Edward Paget has amongst his other most excellent qualities, that of being an able, a first-rate negotiator. Of all men I have seen, he is the best qualified to gain an ascendancy over others. His manners are reserved, mild, and unassuming; and he never increases opposition by offending self-love. His temper is naturally violent, but he has learnt to correct it, without in the least diminishing that firmness of mind which never abandons him for a moment. His judgment is as clear as it is solid, and he is a beautifully perspicuous military writer. When he came down to Calcutta from the Upper Provinces, at the breaking out of the Burmese War, his influence in Council was absolutely null; and he was so hard pressed as to be obliged to ask whether he or Colonel Casement commanded the army. The opinions of every little civilian, nay even of Captains in the army, were put in opposition to his; and the Commander-in-Chief was to all intents and purposes a nonentity.

'For many months past, the whole Council have been with him; and whatever he has proposed has been willingly and cheerfully acceded to.

---

make him his aide-de-camp whenever he should obtain a command as a General.

* Notwithstanding this happy commencement, directly after the departure of Sir Edward Paget, some persons who had long been jealous of Sir Samford's influence, succeeded *for a brief period*, in prejudicing against him the new Commander-in-Chief.

'Sir Edward Paget possesses the singular advantage which public men always derive from rectitude of intention. In his mind there are no *arrières pensées*. His object is always what it appears to be; and the measures he employs, simple, clear, and honest. He is, in every sense of the expression, an English gentleman.'

Before Sir Edward left India, he presented Sir Samford with a beautiful roan-coloured Cape horse, called 'the Admiral,' of great value; and also with a huge and magnificent silver hookah, with two gold mouthpieces, and other presents. And Sir Samford gave to Sir Edward the beautiful mosaic box which he had received from the King of Spain.

His best friend was now about to leave him, having taken his passage in the '*Madras*,' to sail for England, leaving Lord Combermere to reap the fruit of his predecessor's labours.*

'*Calcutta*, *8th November*, 1825.—I accompanied Sir Edward Paget to Diamond Harbour, where I had post-horses waiting for me, and returned to Calcutta, on the 3rd. The "*Madras*" got to sea on the 5th. God send her a speedy and prosperous passage. On the 11th I shall leave this for Agra, *Dâk*, which is our mode of posting. You travel in a palanquin, and are carried by four men, who are relieved at short stages. I shall reach Agra in about ten days. My horses went off on the 5th. My heavy baggage goes by water. Lord Combermere leaves this on the 19th. Every day from the 11th to the end of this month will be filled up by different officers of the Staff proceeding Dâk to the same destination. The army will be assembled on the 1st December. Eighteen bat-

---

* It is said that all the preparations for taking Bhurtpore having been made before Lord Combermere's arrival, Sir Edward was recommended, as senior officer, not to resign till after the fall of the fortress! But he deemed it his duty to resign at once, and did so.

talions, forty squadrons, a hundred and ten pieces of heavy artillery, two regiments of horse-artillery, besides an ample field train.'

He himself, till a vacancy on the Staff of Generals took place, retained, by leave from the Horse-Guards, his post as Quartermaster-General of the Royal army; but Bengal custom gave the Quartermaster-General of the local army the general authority, though a very junior officer; and therefore it was with a heavy heart, having no scope for his abilities, that he hastened to swell the Staff of the new Commander-in-Chief. He had the more time to note and describe the siege, and send home the accounts of a conquest, to the mighty preparations for which, as will be proved hereafter, he had himself greatly contributed, by his ceaseless labours, whilst under the command of Sir Edward Paget. The whole of the siege is described in his journal-like letters, from the beginning of December 1825 to the 6th February 1826; but we will conclude this chapter with part of another letter to his great and faithful friend:—

Sir Samford Whittingham to the Hon. Sir Edward Paget.

(Extract.)*

'AGRA, 24*th November*, 1825.

'My dear General,—I left Calcutta on the 11th, at four p.m., and arrived here yesterday morning at eight a.m., nothing fatigued with the journey, thanks to your *tonjon*, which is certainly a great relief from the recumbent position of the palanquin.

'It is calculated that we shall commence our advance

---

* The original letter of successive dates fills twelve sheets of foolscap! The military news and opinions it contains, regarding the siege of Bhurtpore, would too much lengthen this work by its insertion.

about the 15th December. Our battery train is superb; 144 pieces of heavy ordnance. They are advancing at present upon one road, and the length of the column extends to fourteen miles!

'To your unparalleled efforts in the good cause we are indebted for all the noble means we possess of bringing this contest to a speedy and happy issue. I only lament that another should pluck those laurels which so justly and truly belong to you. . . . .

'*1st December.*—Lord Combermere arrived this morning at five. Hostilities recommenced with the Burmese on the 10th of November. The two crores of rupees were insisted upon, and refused. Lord Combermere has entered his protest against continuing a war so fraught with difficulties and sacrifices of every kind upon any such ground. It is remarkable that both Commanders-in-Chief should have exactly coincided in their views of the Burmese War. A few days will, I hope, set us down before Bhurtpore.' [After narrating that Sir Charles Metcalfe, acting Governor-General, was coming to Muttra immediately, he adds:] 'Lord Combermere proceeds thither to-morrow.'——

The long letter, from which the above is extracted, also acquainted Sir Edward Paget with an incident which implied great coldness on the part of Lord Combermere to Sir Samford Whittingham; the result of prejudices instilled into him by those officers who were jealous, (and naturally so) of the great confidence which Sir Edward had always displayed in Sir Samford, and of the latter's consequent power and influence. Lord Combermere could not then know how *spontaneously* Sir Edward Paget had acted, in making the King's Quartermaster-General his principal Staff officer; and that it in no way resulted from any ambitious strivings on the part of the subordinate. His Lordship indeed, probably, only desired to make Sir Samford understand, that his exceptional position was at an end, and that in future he must restrict himself to the duties of the King's Quartermaster-General. At all events that coldness was destined, ere long, to be exchanged for a friendly confidence, both in private and public matters; as will hereafter be proved to the satisfaction of the reader.

CHAPTER XV.

1826.

SIR SAMFORD RECEIVES A CONTUSION AT THE SIEGE OF BHURTPORE—HIS NARROW ESCAPE—EXTRAORDINARY VALOUR OF LIEUT. CAINE—DEFENCE OF SIR EDWARD PAGET—AN INVALUABLE INTELLECT—A SATISFACTORY LETTER—A MEERUT SCANDAL—A MEERUT DUEL—COOLNESS UNDER FIRE CONSIDERED CRIMINAL—EFFECTS OF A MASTERLY LETTER—SLOW POSTS CAUSED LUDICROUS RESULTS—ILL HEALTH OF THE DUKE OF YORK—SIR HERBERT TAYLOR'S EULOGISTIC LETTER—DEFECTIVE MILITARY ORGANIZATION IN INDIA—INCREASE OF EUROPEAN FORCE NECESSARY FROM THE INSUBORDINATION OF NATIVE SOLDIERS—SIR EDWARD PAGET'S GENEROUS LETTER TO EARL BATHURST—HOW THE MEANS WERE *CREATED* FOR TAKING BHURTPORE.

RESTRICTED space will not permit much quotation from the long journal-like letters which, with accurate plans, Sir Samford Whittingham transmitted to his brother-in-law and Sir Herbert Taylor, respecting the siege of Bhurtpore. Indeed the task would be superfluous, in consequence of the publication of Lord Combermere's Memoirs. A few extracts will suffice:—

'13*th January*, 1826.—In going to the batteries this morning, a spent ball from a matchlock struck the calf of my leg; and obliged me to come home in a *doolee*.* I should not have mentioned this trifling circumstance, but as it has made me very lame, it will probably confine me to my tent for a day or two, and thus

---

* A *fragment* of a Calcutta newspaper of 1826, concludes a paragraph about Bhurtpore thus: 'A letter of the 15th, we are sorry to observe, states that Sir Samford Whittingham had been wounded in the leg by a matchlock ball, but the wound was not of a serious nature.'

prevent my being present at what may take place for that time.

'I must, however, mention a providential escape I had on my return. A little to the right of the old mortar battery, the doolee, in which four men were carrying me, was stopped for a moment, by a Major Hunter, of the Bengal Infantry, a friend of mine, to enquire how I was. A servant who followed him stopped just before my doolee, and whilst Hunter was speaking to me, a cannon ball took off the servant's head, exactly where the doolee would have been had not Hunter arrested my progress a moment before.

'*15th January.*—My leg is better but still very painful, particularly when I attempt to move. It shall not, however, prevent my doing my duty to-morrow to the best of my ability.'

On the 18th January, he records the final springing of the great mine, and the assault and capture of Bhurtpore. One of the officers who most distinguished himself at this siege, Lieutenant Caine of the 14th regiment, was afterwards selected by Sir Samford Whittingham for his own aide-de-camp. Already distinguished in previous Indian wars, he on this occasion eclipsed his former feats of valour. Leaping across a ditch, where his British soldiers were unable at once to follow, he found himself opposed single-handed to three of the enemy. Of these he destroyed two with his double-barrelled pistol, then closing with the third, and finding that his sword could make no impression on his armour, he hurled him by main force over the rampart into the ditch! Lieutenant Caine was also the first officer up at the taking of the Khumbeer Gate, which was carried by him with about thirty men of the 14th.*

---

* Vide *Appendix* C for Sir Samford Whittingham's official letter to Lord Combermere, on the services of Lieutenant Caine.

To his Brother-in-law.

'HEAD QUARTERS, CAMP BEFORE BHURTPORE,
'6th February, 1826.

'Yesterday evening the young Rajah was installed in due form; and this morning the principal bastions and curtains of the fortress were blown up. It would perhaps have been more civil to have sprung the mines first, and have installed His Highness afterwards.

'I am daily persecuted with an access of fever, which all Dr. Burke's skill cannot get rid of; and which he attributes to too much exertion before the leg was well. Change of air will be the best remedy, and at the close of the campaign, I mean to go to the hills. Don't be uneasy on my account. I shall be quite well again very shortly.'——

In a letter dated Meerut, 28th March, 1826, and addressed to Lieutenant-General Sir Herbert Taylor, Adjutant-General at the Horse-Guards, he enters into a long and eloquent defence of Sir Edward Paget, against the accusations of Lord Amherst, on which it is here needless to enter further than to say that it was considered equally clear and convincing by those to whom it was addressed.

In the course of the spring Sir Samford must have received a letter from Sir Edward Paget, dated St. Helena, 15th January, 1826, full of the most affectionate expressions of regard.

The following two letters probably reached India in the course of June. The second, forwarded to him by his brother-in-law, referred to Sir Samford's defence of the Bengal Government:—

Sir William Knighton to Sir Samford Whittingham.

'LONDON, 19*th January*, 1826.*

'My dear Friend,—This will be put into your hands by Captain James Seymour, the second son of Sir Michael Seymour, and I can safely recommend him to you, not only for his own worth, but for the affection you bear towards me. The King takes a great interest in Sir Michael Seymour's family, who is the Captain of His Majesty's own yacht. I mention all this to you, to show that this young gentleman is not pressed upon you as an aide-de-camp, without proportionate feelings and motives!

'I have read all your different accounts, military and otherwise. Nothing can be more admirable, or more like your own invaluable intellect. That the Almighty may prosper you is the sincere prayer of

'Your affectionate and sincere friend,
'W. KNIGHTON.'

The Earl of Liverpool to Mr. R. H. Davis.

'FIFE HOUSE, 1*st February*, 1826.

'My dear Sir,—I return you, with many thanks, Sir Samford Whittingham's letter. I should not have kept it so long, but I thought it so satisfactory in all respects that I was anxious to communicate it to the Duke of Wellington, Mr. Canning, and Mr. Wynne.

'Believe me to be very sincerely yours,
'LIVERPOOL.'

Lord Liverpool doubtless alludes to the voluminous letter Sir Samford wrote to Mr. Davis on the 1st August, 1825.

---

* This letter was written two or three months before Sir William could have received the promise mentioned in last chapter.

In the course of this summer, Mr. William Osborne was again staying as a guest with Sir Samford Whittingham at Meerut. He was at that time a Lieutenant in the 10th Hussars; and it would appear that his regiment must then have been stationed somewhere in Bengal. Young as he was, he and Sir Samford were already friends, and in spite of the wildness of his youthful spirits, his cleverness and amiability made him very generally a favourite everywhere. The General was a man so little given to gossip and small talk, that the Editor cannot resist inserting the following letter on a youthful *escapade*, which gives a graphic specimen of scenes of frequent occurrence, formerly at least, in Indian society:—

Sir Samford Whittingham to the Honourable Sir Edward Paget.

'MEERUT, 26*th June*, 1826.

'My very dear General,—Meerut has been full of histories and scandals for the last week. Captain E. chose to take offence at a trifling circumstance which took place at Mrs. M'Combe's, and serious consequences have ensued. After dining as usual at 4 p.m., we took our ride on the course. On our returning to M'Combe's* to pass the evening, we remained smoking our cigars on the platform before the door; and the ladies, Mrs. M'Combe, Mrs. P——, Mrs. C——, and Mrs. E—— went into Mrs. M'Combe's verandah dressing-room to arrange their hair. Osborne and Finucane† passed by on horseback. The mat-curtain blew up a little on one side; and they certainly did commit the heinous sin of looking upon the fair ladies arranging their hair, but separated from them by an exterior railing, and certainly without the least idea of giving offence. For they came running into the party

---

* Brigadier, commanding the station.
† Finucane was a Captain of the 14th Regiment.

—which the ladies immediately joined—and said laughing: "You must take care in future to fasten the curtains of your dressing-rooms, and not put temptation into the way of the curious." All the ladies laughed—called them impudent fellows;—and I declare I had not the slightest conception that any offence had been given.

'On our entering the drawing-room, however, Captain E—— spoke to his wife in the roughest and rudest manner—told Osborne that he had not behaved like a gentleman—and led Mrs. E—— out of the room. Osborne called him out the next morning; and E——, by the advice of his friends, made to Osborne and to Mrs. M'Combe, a most ample apology. But, in the meantime Osborne had had the imprudence to write a letter to Mrs. E——, to say that he thought E——'s conduct so constantly unkind and improper with regard to her, that he would strongly recommend her insisting upon a separate maintenance, and returning to her father's house. This foolish letter took away all our vantage ground, and placed us in a totally false position. E—— called Osborne out. Baron Osten was second to Osborne, and Captain Luard to E——. They tossed up for the first fire. Osborne won it, and fired in the air. E—— in very gross language, which left no alternative, insisted upon going on. They fired together; Osborne fired wide of the mark. He had determined on no account to hit E——. E——'s ball struck a round cigar-case in Osborne's pocket, and, glancing off, passed obliquely through the side. The seconds interposed, and the affair ended. The bone has not been touched. He is doing well, and has promised me to leave Meerut for Calcutta, as soon as he is fit to make the journey. All the ladies in the place have made a point of visiting Mrs. E——; and peace having been generally signed, we remain in *statu quo ante bellum*. "What great events from trifling causes spring!"

'*16th July.*—Osborne left us last night on his way down to Calcutta. Nobody could have behaved better than he has done since the affair between him and E——. But an illiberal spirit of persecution has been raised against him; and the most ridiculous and malicious reports have been spread abroad to do him injury. One of the attacks against him is founded on the hardness of the boy's heart; who had so little of the fear of death before his eyes, as to continue quietly smoking his cigar whilst he was receiving E——'s fire!

'Lord Combermere has had an attack of fever, and Colonel Finch, Kelly, Dawkins, Stapleton, and Mundy have all been ill a second time. In short, Calcutta seems like one great hospital.

'Ever, &c., &c.,
'Samford Whittingham.'

Returning to his correspondence with Mr. Davis:—

'*Meerut*, 24*th August.*—Day after day rolls on without any arrivals from England. I cannot describe to you the anxiety with which I wait for the arrival of the post. You will have heard, ere this letter reaches you, of the death of Captain Amherst! A fever of a few days carried him off. He was universally beloved. His friends are inconsolable. Lord Amherst is, however, on his passage up the Ganges; and Lord Combermere installed as Vice-President and Deputy Governor-General.'

In this last letter, and in a later one of the 7th September, he is anxiously expecting the arrival of Captain Seymour, who was to be his aide-de-camp, as soon as he obtained a General's command, on a vacancy occurring. Captain Seymour had arrived at Calcutta, but was destined never to meet Sir Samford Whittingham.

Sir Edward Paget was now Governor of the Royal

Military College at Sandhurst, and the following letter must have reached Sir Samford near the close of the year :—

Sir Edward Paget to Sir Samford Whittingham.
(Extract.)
'SANDHURST, 16*th June*, 1826.

'You will, I am sure, be thoroughly happy to hear that the reception I have met with in this country has been, as *you foretold*, most flattering and gratifying. A few months before I arrived in England, there had been a tremendous hubbub about the mutiny at Barrackpore; and I verily believe that nothing but the firmness of the Duke of Wellington, who took up the cudgels most manfully, would have kept the Cabinet straight. But happily the intrigue was defeated; and I have not the least doubt, that the masterly letter which you wrote to Hart Davis in defence of the measures of the Bengal Government, and which he sent to Lord Liverpool, who communicated it to several leading members of the Cabinet, had a powerful influence upon that decision. Infinite pains had been taken to make it appear that Lord Amherst and I were *two*;* but I have completely set this question at rest by taking every opportunity of defending him and his measures.'

[The slow posts in those days often gave rise to strange and ludicrous results. Here we find Sir Edward fighting for a friend, who was now attacking him with all his strength and interest! But we must give another extract from this monster letter of sixteen pages. This part is written by Lady Harriet Paget, who often relieved her one-armed husband with the pen.] 'I most heartily and sincerely rejoice, without one particle of envy—

---

* The Governor-General had abandoned a supposed fallen cause meantime; a fact, the possibility of which Sir Edward seems never to have imagined for a moment.

which *you* will give me credit for—at the glorious termination of the siege and assault of Bhurtpore; and have but one drawback to my satisfaction, by knowing that you have received a hurt in the enterprize, by understanding from you that the deportment of my successor towards yourself is most ungracious, and by observing how careful he has been, in his official report of the capture of Bhurtpore, not to make too much mention of you. These things are most galling and distressing to me.'

[It is needless to quote more of this disagreeable matter. Lord Combermere had a great respect and regard for Sir Edward Paget; and his coldness to the friend of the latter was not destined to be of long continuance. In this letter, also, Sir Edward describes his having made the acquaintance of Mr. Davis and his family, and adds:] 'The return of Hart Davis for Bristol, in spite of his teeth, is a most unprecedented instance of attachment and respect, and I long for the opportunity of congratulating him.'

[Mr. Davis had retired from the contest from motives of economy, but was re-elected at the expense of his constituents. The letter continues:] 'You will grieve to hear that the health of the Duke of York has sadly declined during the last twelvemonth. Still, if he can be prevailed upon to take more care of himself, much may be done. The King gets fonder daily of retirement; and it is a rare thing to get a sight of him. I have seen him but once, about a month ago; and though much increased in bulk, he seemed to be enjoying good health.'

From Sir Herbert Taylor, Military Secretary.

'HORSE-GUARDS, 1*st August*, 1826.

'My dear Sir Samford,—Extraordinary pressure of business has obliged me to delay, much longer than I had wished or intended, thanking you for your letters of the 8th and 23rd December, and 8th and 16th January, containing a detailed and most interesting journal of the proceedings and operations of Lord Combermere's army preparatory to, and during, the siege of Bhurtpore; and accompanied by sketches of the ground and positions of the troops and works. My acknowledgment has, indeed, been in part delayed by the communication of these valuable documents to our friend Sir Edward Paget and others, to whom I felt that I might afford the benefit and satisfaction of the perusal, after submitting them to the Commander-in-Chief.

'H.R.H. [the Duke of York] orders me to assure you of the interest with which he has read these clear and able statements of the important operations which they describe; and how sensible he is of the trouble you have taken in making them, amidst the hurry and pressure of your avocations, and the share you took in the active duties arising from the services in which you were engaged. . . . I sent the plans to Sir Edward Paget and Mr. Hart Davis, as you desired; and the former caused some beautiful copies to be made of them at the College.

'I heartily rejoice that you escaped so well, and that the contusion you received on the 13th from a spent ball did not prevent your being one of the actors in the glorious and brilliant scene of the 18th; to have been excluded from which would have been truly mortifying. Although we have to lament the loss of some valuable officers and men, and however serious we must consider the loss of such men, it must be admitted that this important conquest has been achieved at a much less price than might have been expected, from the nature of the works and the strength and character of its garrison. And this advantage is due not only to the vigour and ability of the operations, but, as you justly observe, also to the foresight and previous arrangements of Sir Edward Paget.*

'Your letter of the 27th January, which reached me shortly after the former, fully confirms your anticipations of the result of the blow struck at Bhurtpore; and I trust that its impression will be lasting; at least, that it will prevent any combination of the native princes, and discourage all attempt to disturb our *imperfect* administration of India. I say imperfect, with reference to many measures of the Company; and more especially its military system, so palpably defective, yet so obstinately persisted in. Yet they cannot plead ignorance: for means are taken to apprize them of all that reaches us on this subject; and Sir Edward Paget has candidly stated to the Chair,† the opinions which you know him to hold. Of the defective organization of the commissariat, and of the hospital department, you have stated ample proof.

'The courts-martial on deserters to the enemy have evinced the spirit and feeling of the Company's officers. The inefficiency of their regimental system and arrangements is placed beyond doubt by every return; and the consequences of this evil are apparent in the comparative inferiority of the native troops, and their misconduct on various occasions, especially in the Burmese war. Nevertheless all this is suffered to continue; all is sacrificed to the anxiety to procure patronage. And the security of that overgrown empire is risked from an obstinate adherence to errors and prejudices.

'It is obvious that the present extent of the Company's territory, the increase of its native military force, and above all the spirit of insubordination which has been manifested by portions of it, require an amalgamation of European forces. Nevertheless this is strenuously resisted.

* It will shortly be seen what Sir Edward himself thought on this matter.
† Chairman of the Directors of the East India Company.

And the opposition of the Court of Directors is encouraged by some of its officers of distinguished reputation, and acknowledged talent and experience: who must, therefore, be supposed to suffer selfish views and prejudices to overpower their better judgment. . . . .

'I am happy to acquaint you that the Duke of York's health is essentially improved, and I trust that with proper care H.R.H. will soon recover from every effect of his serious indisposition; great weakness and want of appetite being now the chief evils. Torrens has had the gout, and been generally out of health, though improved of late; but he is grown miserably thin. I am very hard worked, but neither sick nor sorry; and my business goes on satisfactorily. I hope you approve of our recent arrangements for giving rewards to old officers, and efficiency to corps by the promotion and removal of brevet officers. This, and the sale of half-pay, has renovated our ranks.—Believe me to be, with the best wishes for your welfare and success, my dear Sir Samford,

'Most truly and faithfully yours,
'H. TAYLOR.'

'Major-General Sir Samford Whittingham, K.C.B.'

The following letter proves that Sir Edward Paget was a friend in deeds as well as in words. His generosity is obvious, and needs no comment:—

From Sir Edward Paget to Mr. Davis.
(Extract.)
'SANDWELL, BIRMINGHAM, 12th September, 1826.

'My dear Sir,—Your letter of the 6th instant, addressed to Sandhurst, reached me at Lord Bagot's, at Blithfield, the day before yesterday; and I instantly wrote to Lord Bathurst a letter, of which what follows is an extract. "Having heard that the two Major-Generals, Reynell and Nichols, have been recommended by Lord Combermere for the honourable distinction of Knights Commanders of the Bath, I should feel myself guilty of a very great neglect of duty and friendship, if I omitted to entreat your Lordship to give a favourable consideration to the claims of Major-General Sir Samford Whittingham for admission to the same honour.

'" Of his services generally, your Lordship is no doubt to the full as well aware as I am, and that they have obtained for him diverse badges of distinction. But I may be permitted to observe with reference to the fall of Bhurtpore (at the siege of which he assisted, and also got a hard knock) that neither your Lordship nor Lord Combermere are probably aware, *how mainly the success of that enterprize was due to the indefatigable zeal and industry of Sir Samford Whittingham in preparing—I may safely say, in creating the means by which it was obtained.*" *

'I grieve that I did not get your letter some days sooner, though if my feeble voice can have any influence in this question, I trust it will be heard in time to have its effect, as Lord Bathurst (if in London) will have got my letter this morning.'——

---

* In his noble generosity Sir Edward forgets that it was *he himself* who set to work and encouraged and directed that indefatigable King's officer in his labours.

CHAPTER XVI.

1827—1828.

TWO LETTERS OF SAME DATE TEN THOUSAND MILES APART—SIR EDWARD PAGET'S CONGRATULATIONS—DEATH OF THE DUKE OF YORK—CAPTAIN SEYMOUR'S DEATH—COPY OF SIR EDWARD'S LETTER TO LORD BATHURST REACHES INDIA—AIDE-DE-CAMP SELECTED FOR HIS MERIT—LORD COMBERMERE THE GUEST OF SIR SAMFORD—THE TALK OF THE GARRISON—THE KING OF OUDE—LORD COMBERMERE'S FRIENDLINESS—THE REACTION OF A GENEROUS MIND—LORD WILLIAM BENTINCK'S APPOINTMENT—SIR EDWARD'S PRESENT OF GENUINE HAVANNAHS—THANKS OF THE HOUSE OF COMMONS—SIR EDWARD'S GENEROUS DISCLAIMER OF THANKS—WILLOUGHBY COTTON'S AFFECTIONATE LETTER—A MODEL OF WHAT A MAN OUGHT TO BE—WILLOUGHBY COTTON'S OPINION OF SIR EDWARD PAGET—THE PRINCIPAL PROMOTER OF THE PASSAGE OF THE DOURO—LORD COMBERMERE'S KIND LETTER—LORD WILLIAM BENTINCK'S ARRIVAL—HIS REQUEST—SIR HERBERT TAYLOR'S OPINION OF SIR E. PAGET—THE CONFIDANT OF THREE SUCCESSIVE KINGS—LORD COMBERMERE'S PROOF OF CONFIDENCE—SIR EDWARD'S AFFECTION—SIR SAMFORD'S GREATEST AMBITION.

WHILST the pleasure-bearing letter which closed the last Chapter was on its tedious voyage, unwonted gloom and despondency oppressed its future recipient, accustomed as he had so long been to the favour and confidence of his superior officers.

On the 4th January, 1827, the Quartermaster-General of the King's army in India was inditing letters full of grief at the reports which were circulated, that he alone of the Major-Generals at the siege of Bhurtpore, had not been recommended for the Commandership of the 'Bath' and was considered to have been then only a Colonel on the Staff, having received no command as yet as Major-General. In the first supposition, however, he was in error, for Lord Combermere had made no recommendations for any particular honour for anyone. But it was true that the Commander-in-Chief considered the Quartermaster-General as on the footing of the other staff officers who held similar positions, though with inferior army rank.

That Sir Samford Whittingham instead of being restricted, according to custom, as a King's Staff Officer to very limited duties, had been the right-hand man, the friend and counsellor of the late Chief, was of course no claim on the new Commander; and, moreover, the latter in the first instance was probably not aware of the facts, which the just and excellent Sir Edward had impressed on Lord Bathurst on the 12th September, 1826.

There can be no doubt now, that Lord Combermere only followed the then usual rule and custom of India, to subordinate the King's Staff's influence to that of Bengal, in spite of the generally superior army rank of the former. And though highly offensive to the King's army, there were not wanting excellent reasons for the practice, if the matter be impartially considered. King's officers newly arrived as strangers from England, and belonging to a then comparatively uneducated army, could not vie in knowledge and experience with the local army; at least as a general rule, in spite of the patent defects of the Bengal military system. And, moreover, the exceptional claims of Sir Samford Whittingham on Sir Edward Paget, were not transferable to a new Chief under the circumstances. But enough of the temporary cloud of discontent alluded to; since it passed away as rapidly as a twelvemonth's post (for it took nearly a year to be answered from England in India) would permit.

On that same 4th January, 1827, at the Royal Military College in England, another letter was being written, as follows:—

From Sir Edward Paget.

'SANDHURST, 4*th January*, 1827.

' My dear Whittingham,—I am roused from my lethargy by reading in the Gazette this morning the name of my dear, good, but neglected friend amongst the batch of K.C.B.'s. I congratulate you on this distinction with all my heart and soul; and wish you all health, happiness, and length of life to enjoy it and all other honours that may fall to your lot. . . . . In the midst of these discordances I find *my friends* of the India House have been voting you all chests, and cotton bags of thanks, for your performances at Bhurtpore, and only introducing my name for the purpose of vilifying it, as the author of the wanton massacre at Barrackpore. This brings me, my dear but neglected friend, to thank you, though late, for the curious and interesting account of Lord A.'s generous proceedings on the occasion of the panic, with which he was seized at first hearing of his recall. . . .

'*January* 6*th*.—Alas! my dear Whittingham, the account has reached me to-day of the death of the poor Duke' [of York], 'who after several fainting fits in the course of the day, breathed his last at nine o'clock last night. Every man, whose esteem is worth possessing, must deeply lament his loss—to me it is irreparable. During the long period of two-and-thirty years I never received from him aught but acts of kindness, condescension and consideration. Father and steady patron of this College, his demise will in all probability rouse its enemies and the sticklers for economy to new acts of hostility. But I will not anticipate evils; but still hope I may have your two dear lads under my eye. I saw them about three weeks ago, and nothing could appear in a more prosperous condition. Who is to succeed the poor Duke as Commander-in-Chief, nobody appears to know. Some talk of the Duke of Cambridge; some of the Duke of

Wellington; others of a Military Board, heaven defend us from this last! . . . God bless you, my very dear Whittingham, and with the warmest regards of my good wife, believe me ever most affectionately yours,

'EDWARD PAGET.'

We must now return to India.

Sir Samford Whittingham to his Brother-in-law.

'MEERUT, 10*th January*, 1827.

'My dear Davis,—The intelligence of the loss of poor Captain Seymour [38th Regiment] reached me this morning; and it would be in vain for me to attempt to describe my feelings! Sent to this country under my especial care, I have ever considered him as a son; and it would have been my pride and glory to have proved myself a second father to him! Assure my dear and beloved friend Sir William [Knighton] how deeply I sympathize in his affliction.'——

In this month, Colonel Willoughby Cotton was the guest of Sir Samford Whittingham; for in a letter dated the 20th, he thanks him for his hospitality. Colonel Cotton was on the Staff of Lord Combermere, and also aide-de-camp to the King. He died in 1860, as Sir Willoughby Cotton, G.C.B.

On the 31st January he writes from Kirkondah, twenty-four miles from Meerut: 'I left this morning on my march to Cawnpore, where I expect to find the order for my taking the command of that division. Lord Carnworth goes home in the "*Prince Regent*," General Pine is appointed to command the Presidency division in his place, and I am to command at Cawnpore.' On his march to the latter he writes on the 12th February, 'I have received the kindest, the most affectionate letter from Sir Edward Paget! His letter is dated 27th July;

yet others have arrived in India dated the middle of September.'

Long after he was gazetted as Commander of the Bath, he was lamenting that he had not been thought worthy of his promotion. The telegraph has put an end to similar trials at the present day.

On the 20th February, his brother-in-law's letter of the 6th and 12th September, 1826, reached him, and rejoiced his heart with the intelligence that there was every reason to hope that he would not be left unrewarded. Later letters of the 14th and 17th September reached him, and on the 3rd April, 1827, he writes, 'Sir Edward Paget's letter to Lord Bathurst, is the most honourable testimony of service I could possibly have received. My mind,' Sir Samford adds, 'is now quite at ease, and my position in India all I could wish.'

It may be here stated, that on being appointed to the Cawnpore command, Sir Samford Whittingham selected as his aide-de-camp the gallant lieutenant who had so distinguished himself at the siege of Bhurtpore, William Caine, a man without interest and with nothing but his merit to recommend him. The letter continues: 'the four battalions of infantry I have with me at Cawnpore are encamped about five miles off. Every morning I rise at half-past three and do not return till nine : the whole of that time, deducting the space for going and coming, being employed in drilling and manœuvring the troops! I am thus every morning on horseback for five hours; and Sunday is my only day of rest.'

The details of Lord Combermere's stay in Cawnpore are not recorded in any letters which have reached the Editor. But two survivors, one a general officer of the Indian army and the other then aide-de-camp to Sir Samford, well remember the circumstances of that visit.

His Lordship arrived on the 29th November, 1827, and left the station on the 6th December. During his week's stay, he and all his Staff were the guests of Sir Samford Whittingham. Moreover all the superior officers, and such others as Lord Combermere desired to see, were invited on each day to dinner. Those of the Staff and their servants for whom there was not room in the house pitched their tents in the General's own ground. The expense of such a visitation may be imagined. '*It was the talk of the garrison.*' *

Sir Samford accompanied Lord Combermere to Lucknow. In a letter from that city dated 11th December, 1827, he writes: 'We arrived here this morning amidst the crash and jostling of 150 elephants, all pushing forwards at the same time, to enter a narrow street of about two miles long, which leads to the palace of His Majesty the King of Oude. About half my howdah was carried away. One elephant was pushed over a bridge; and divers were the mishaps which occurred. But I am happy to say, no serious evil resulted from the scramble. We breakfasted with His Majesty of Oude; and tiffed † with the Resident, with whom we are also to dine.'

To his Brother-in-law.

'CAWNPORE, 27*th December*, 1827.

'Many happy returns of the season to you and yours, and to all the dear circle. The important news of the death of Mr. Canning, and of the appointment of the Duke of Wellington to be Commander-in-Chief at home and of that of Lord Combermere to be Viceroy of Ireland ‡ has just reached us. Lord C. will I believe return immediately to Calcutta to embark for England. His behaviour to me, since his stay with me at Cawnpore, has become uniformly that of a sincere and affectionate friend. It is the reaction of a generous mind, which

---

* The words of an eye-witness. Sir Samford, however, *invited* his Lordship, who preferred a good house to his own tent.

† Luncheon is called tiffin in the East.

‡ This report was wholly unfounded.

feels it had been imposed on and deceived. The *canaille* at Calcutta had made him believe that I was a very dangerous monster, from whom it behoved him to keep quite clear. Now that he knows me well, he has seen that I had not merited the honour done me by my kind good friends in the city of Calcutta. And like an honest man, he endeavours to repay by unlimited confidence the injury done me by the false impression that had been made on his mind. I rejoice at this, for I am really glad to be honoured with Lord Combermere's good opinion . . . .

'Nothing could have given me more sincere pleasure than the appointment of Lord William Bentinck.* I love and admire my old commander and am quite happy at the idea of again serving under his orders.'——

In the meantime at home, in the spring of 1827, Sir Edward Paget had been rancorously attacked in parliament by the ardent partisans of what may be called the Indian mutiny-coaxing system; but he was victoriously defended, though the supporters of the system were powerful enough to postpone for years the necessary reforms, which would involve a painful loss of patronage and power to themselves. Sir Samford rejoiced, as may be supposed, in Sir Edward's triumphs at home.

In a letter of Sir Edward's dated, 'Sandhurst, 17th July, 1827,' after apologizing for his laziness with his pen, he continues, 'Instead of looking back, however, I will look forward; and I trust I may do it with confidence. For, as I am to have your brave boy here [as a college cadet] in the course of next month, I am greatly mistaken if he don't give an activity to my pen, the want of which you have sound reason to complain of.

'You have long known the fate of Hume's motion on

---

* As Governor-General. During the last two years of his stay in India his Lordship was also Commander-in-Chief—a veritable King of India.

the Barrackpore question; and before this, must be in possession of the wonderful events which have produced a change of administration, &c. One of the appointments arising out of the recent changes, is that of Lord William Bentinck to India. I have had one long talk with him, and I think the probability is that I shall have more, and I promise you, my dear friend, that you will not escape the severity of my criticisms. He is in the expectation of starting some time in the month of September.

'The last letter I received from you grieved me to the soul. A moment's consideration, however, soon set me at ease, as it satisfied me that very shortly indeed after it was written you must have become acquainted with the fact that your merits and services were better known and appreciated at home, than they were by *your friends* in India. If you want any proof of this you may read the enclosed.*

'I am off for Cowes, to pass a day or two with my brother, who has escaped from the Ordnance Board, to enjoy a few weeks' sailing. I hear and believe that he is destined to succeed Lord Wellesley in Ireland. Lady Harriet, with some of the children, is also on the move, to pass a week with her mother at Blackheath. These are holiday times at Sandhurst, which we are turning to account. In truth, I may say that the whole is holiday time to *us*. For we like our situation here exceedingly, have a delightful house, garden, and grounds. And I have just enough to do, to be interested without being oppressed; and daily chant the Te Deum, at having escaped from W——, S——, C——, S——, and Co.; and from the pestilential vapours of Chowringhee with a *mens sana in corpore sano*.

'Hoping, my dear Whittingham, that you still find health and comfort in a cigar, I this day dispatch a cargo of real and genuine Havannahs to Hart Davis, with a

* The enclosure has disappeared.

request that he will take the best means of forwarding them to you. I have also sent in the same box, Sir Walter Scott's "Life of Napoleon," which struck me as a book you would like to read. I will beg of him to let you know by what ship the box is sent.

'God bless you, my dear and excellent friend! And believe me, in spite of my idleness and neglect, your sincerely attached and affectionate friend,

'EDWARD PAGET.'

[P. S.] 'Lady Harriet charges me with the best wishes and affectionate regards to you.'

In a letter signed, 'Combermere,' dated 'Head-quarters Calcutta, 15th October, 1827,' and addressed to Major-General Sir S. F. Whittingham, K.C.B., the thanks of the House of Commons were conveyed to the latter, his Lordship writes, 'for the meritorious and gallant manner in which you performed the duties which were assigned to you in the late operations against Bhurtpore.' Though quite official, it ends somewhat unusually with *very sincerely*, your obedient servant.

The following proves the nobleness of Sir Edward Paget's mind:—

To Sir Samford Whittingham.

(Extract.)

'SANDHURST, 10*th December*, 1827.

'I assure you, my dear good friend, you greatly overvalue the step I took in representing to Lord Bathurst your just claim to the Bath, as I am quite certain that you would have got it, at the very time you did, though I had been altogether silent upon the subject. It is the will and not the deed, therefore, that you must lay to my account.' *

---

* He had done his best with Lord Bathurst and the President of the Board of Control, to get the Bath for Commodore Hayes; and had failed.

'God bless you, my very dear and excellent friend. Take care of yourself, and don't think that you can despise the rays of the sun with impunity . . . . and believe me ever

'Most affectionately yours,
'EDWARD PAGET.'

The year 1828 opened more cheerfully to Sir Samford Whittingham than had its predecessor. The system of brief extracts from the fraternal correspondence will be continued, omitting (except on rare occasions) the politics of India, that have lost their interest:—

'CAWNPORE, 6th *January*, 1828.

'How many things call for our present gratitude to the Great Disposer of all things! My position in this country could not be happier or more comfortable. Peace and harmony reign throughout the whole of my command; and I have every reason to believe that the commander of the Cawnpore district is not less popular than was the governor of Dominica! Lord Combermere writes to me in really affectionate terms, and my old friend and commander, Lord William Bentinck, is on the point of arriving. My health was never better, and my mind is quite at ease.'——

General Whittingham had invited Colonel Willoughby Cotton, then on the Staff of his relative, Lord Combermere, to accompany him on a tour of inspection who, however, could not obtain his Lordship's leave, but sent an excuse full of the most flattering affection, from which a brief portion is here extracted (dated January 23rd, 1828):—' Nothing on earth could have given me so much pleasure as to have accompanied you. I never flatter, but truth must be spoken, and I have the highest opinion of your head and heart. Your ideas are all those of the

---

It was not then usual to give the K.C.B. to anyone under the rank of Rear-Admiral or Major-General.

high-bred gentlemanly officer, and depend upon it all you want is opportunity; whenever that offers the result is certain.' Colonel Cotton alluded to the opportunity of a large command in war. The letter ends thus: 'There is a report the Duke of Wellington has appointed me, immediately on re-entering office, Quartermaster-General, *vice* yourself. I have reason to think this is true. God bless you, and believe me always with the truest sincerity, your faithful and affectionate friend,

'WILLOUGHBY COTTON.'

Sir Samford Whittingham to Sir Edward Paget.

(Extract.)

'CAWNPORE, *6th February*, 1828.

'My dear General,—Many, very many thanks for your kind letter of the 17th July; and for the very acceptable present of Havannah cigars, and the "Life of Napoleon."

'No one knows better than I do, how little letter-writing is a hobby-horse with you. But as long as I continue to hold the same place in your affections, I shall be happy and contented though I should not hear from you above once a year. I shall write to you as often as anything occurs worthy of your attention. I cannot tell you how happy I am at the idea that C. and —— will be formed into manhood under your guidance and direction.* My old opinion is in nowise changed; and I look upon it as the greatest blessing that could have befallen me and them, that they should have such a model of what a man ought to be before their eyes! Davis will have told you all about Lord Combermere's visit to Cawnpore. . . .

'Nothing that I can recollect in the whole course of my

---

* That is a general superintendence. The Governor of the College interfered but little in the petty details, which were under the charge of subordinate officers beginning with a Lieut.-Governor.

life has given me such heartfelt pleasure as the assurance of the complete happiness you and Lady Harriet enjoy at Sandhurst.

'I have long ceased to exist for myself, but I have great and serious duties to perform, and there is in the very performance of your duty a source of real and permanent enjoyment. Besides I enjoy perfect health; and when I look around and compare my lot with that of others, I bless God and am thankful.

'Adieu, dear and beloved friend. To feel that I have a right to call you by that endearing name is the delight and solace of my exile, and gilds the thought of my return to my native land. Once more adieu.

'Ever your most devoted and attached,

'SAMFORD WHITTINGHAM.'

On the 5th April, 1828, Colonel W. Cotton wrote to Sir Samford, amongst other things: 'When you write to Sir Edward Paget pray offer him my best, warmest, and most humble remembrances. I like him and esteem him as one of our best officers. . . . .

'The whole arrangements were formed for the siege of Bhurtpore by Sir Edward. The execution fell into Lord C——'s hands, which if done by Sir Edward would have given him the peerage, and 60,000*l.* His unfortunate capture lost it [the peerage] to him with Lord Wellington's army. He deserved it for the passage of the Douro; at which I was present and can safely aver that it was owing to the admirable celerity with which he seized the vantage ground on crossing, that the Duke gained the victory that day.'

When years later the 'Wellington Dispatches' were published, they amply confirmed the above opinions of the late Sir Willoughby Cotton. At page 329 of the fourth volume of that immortal work, Sir Edward is done full justice. Here there is room but for one sentence.

After reporting his brother's wound to the Hon. Berkeley Paget, Sir Arthur Wellesley continues: 'I cannot express to you how much I regret the loss of his assistance, or how much the joy of the whole army on account of this success has been damped by the misfortune of him who has been *the principal promoter of it*. I hope, however, that he will soon recover.'

The enthusiastic affection, and esteem felt by Colonel Willoughby Cotton for Sir Samford Whittingham is proved by many letters in the Editor's possession.

They are all very similar in tone to one dated 'Camp, December 9th' (probably in 1828) which thus begins, 'Many thanks for yours, this day received by me. It contains as all your letters do, most valuable opinions, couched in most forcible and gentlemanly terms.'

On the 24th of June Lord Combermere writes to Sir Samford: 'What changes have taken place at home! The Duke will be everything; and I hope he will recollect his old and steady friends. Hill is named as Commander of the Forces. But our friend Paget (who is senior to Hill) is much more fit for the situation.'

In his private notes,* his Lordship never signed his name in full. This one ends: 'yours my dear Whittingham, most truly, C.'

Viscount Combermere to Sir Samford Whittingham.

(Extract.)

'SIMLA, 30*th June*, 1828.

'My dear Whittingham,—I rejoice to hear that you are so much better. I did not like to tell you, before you had recovered, that Lord C——h was trying hard through C——t (no friend of yours) to get the Government to put him on the Staff of Bengal. I think it rather cool of Lord C. requesting me to send you to

---

* In one of these notes Lord Combermere candidly tells Sir Samford that he has no reason ' to complain of Dame Fortune ' and mentions his obtaining 'this command' as one of the best specimens of his good luck.

Madras, and to remove Pine in order to make room for him at Barrackpore. I shall protest against it. I had a letter from Torrens. He says I should have been Commander-in-Chief had I been in England.'

From the Same to the Same.
(Extract.)

'SIMLA, 18th July.

' It is too late now for me to think of going home this year. I have sent my resignation home, and have requested that my successor may be at Calcutta by the end of October [18]29; and I am bound to remain till relieved.

' I fancy by Paget not having been appointed Commander-in-Chief, that he was told it would be only temporary or perhaps it was offered, and he refused to take it upon the terms on which Hill holds the situation. Any General Officer would have been glad to take the College for him, with an understanding that Paget was to return to it upon his giving up the command of the army. But you will no doubt hear from Sir Edward, or from Mr. Davis by the " *Undaunted*." '———

Lord William Bentinck landed at Calcutta on the 4th July, 1828. Soon afterwards Sir Samford sent him a congratulatory letter, and expressed the sincere pleasure he felt ' at being again placed under his command.'—His Lordship replied as follows :—

Lord William Bentinck to Sir Samford Whittingham.

'CALCUTTA, 19th July, 1828.

'My dear General,—I assure you that it gives me very great pleasure to come again in contact with you. I never entertained other than the most sincere esteem and respect for you; and I am confident that I shall find nothing in your Indian history, which will not increase my former good opinion.

'I have to ask of you the favour of naming to me two or three officers of my own regiment,* from the Captains and subalterns; from whom I may select an A. D. C. Among others, I should be glad to know your opinion of Captain M——e. I need not describe to you the character required; but as Lady William is with me, it is very important to have a gentleman in every sense of the word, who will not be disagreeable to us as an inmate; and who will be civil and respectful to all who have access to the house. I naturally should have asked this question of [Brigadier] General Sleigh,† for whom I have always entertained feelings of respect. But I learn with regret that there have been great dissensions in the Corps; and I should rather like to have an opinion entirely impartial. As I do not mean to be a prisoner at Calcutta, and am of opinion that I can best judge of the state of things by personal inspection and information on the spot, I trust at no great distance of time, to have the pleasure of seeing you. In the meantime believe me, my dear Sir,

'Ever most sincerely yours,
'W. BENTINCK.'

'Major-General Sir Samford‡ Whittingham, K.C.B.'

Of the reply to the above letter the Editor has no copy.

From the Same to the Same.
(Extract.)

'CALCUTTA, 18*th August*, 1828.

'My dear Sir,—I feel much obliged by the kind and friendly manner in which you have so fully and satisfactorily entered into the question I took the liberty of

* The 11th Light Dragoons, now Hussars.
† Though a local Brigadier-General, Sleigh was the Commanding Officer of the 11th Dragoons.
‡ Curiously enough in the original letter Lord William has written Sandford instead of Samford, exactly as George IV. did in the letter of introduction to Sir Edward Paget.

putting to you. I have offered the situation to Captain Mansell. The favourable opinion expressed by you has been fully confirmed by the reports of others.'——

The Editor has omitted to allude in its proper place to a letter from Sir Herbert Taylor to Sir Samford Whittingham, which must have reached India in the spring of 1828, being dated 23rd October, 1827. It consists of no less than fifteen pages of old-fashioned letter paper. In it he says: 'Thank God, I am released from a drudgery which nothing but a feeling of attachment to the Duke of York, and to the King in the first instance, and a sense of duty in the next, could have enabled me to get through. I have resigned my office to a most trustworthy and amiable man,* and I trust that he will not be embarrassed by any of my proceedings when I held it.' In this interesting letter Sir Herbert attributes to 'the zealous and disinterested exertions of Sir Edward Paget,' the success of the Burmese campaign. He also gives him credit *'for the preparations which ensured success in the attack on Bhurtpore,'* adding, 'I have always regretted that our friend did not stay and reap the benefits of these exertions.'

Sir Herbert also expresses his approval of Sir Samford's plans of Indian reforms. The whole voluminous letter shows how this able and trusted confidant of (eventually) three successive Kings of England respected and esteemed the subject of this Memoir, as well as his noble friend Sir Edward Paget.

Viscount Combermere to Sir Samford Whittingham.
(Private.)
'SIMLA, 17th *August,* 1828.

'My dear Whittingham,—Davis's next letters will be most interesting. We must have April ships in soon.

* Lord Fitzroy Somerset, afterwards Lord Raglan.

C——t could not carry his friend Lord C——h through. Lord William Bentinck, I am glad to find, does not consider the Colonel his oracle, as Lord —— did. Several things that had been refused by Colonel C——t in Lord ——'s and Bailey's administration were brought before Lord William by my desire for consideration, and all have been granted. . . . .

'I am going to send you a Regiment (44th) in November, which will require a deal of *surveillance*. Colonel S——n is a very gallant officer; but his officers are either bad or he does not know how to manage them. However you will find all this out, and I trust you will make this corps what it ought to be. You had better not mention my intention respecting this change of quarters, except (confidentially) to Colonel Frith.*

'In haste, my dear Whittingham, most truly yours,
'C.'

Enough has been shown of Lord Combermere's letters to prove how friendship and confidence had replaced the coldness which had been at first infused into his mind, by jealousies, which after all were only too natural, under the circumstances, which had formerly thrown into the hands of a King's Officer the influential Staff duties usually performed by two or three Company's officers. In the opinion of a surviving General, a man of sound sense and ability, who then served the Company in a subaltern capacity, (and whose judgment therefore cannot be biased in favour of the King's officer) the state of the Head Quarter Staff had perfectly justified Sir Edward Paget in departing from the then usual practice. But it was not to be expected that those who actually lost power and influence would be contented, and it was certain that

* Lord Combermere no doubt feared that the General from whose command the regiment was moved to be put in order might take offence. There is reason to believe that the commanding officer of the regiment was chiefly to blame, if not entirely so.

their discontent would be generally sympathized with by the Company's officers. But though the jealousy and hostility was natural, the affair was not the less creditable to the zeal and talents of the King's officer. The good sense by which Lord Combermere rescued himself from the influence of a powerful clique, and admitted Sir Samford Whittingham to his confidence, and, even friendship, is perceptible in his later correspondence, where he is ready to combat for the interests of the very man whom at the outset he had treated with a coldness approaching to discourtesy.

Far away in England, his late Chief still retained his ardent affection for Sir Samford Whittingham :—

Sir Edward Paget to Mr. Hart Davis.
(Extract.)

'SANDHURST, 25th *November*, 1828.

'My dear Davis,—A thousand thanks for your most kind letter. It grieved me to the soul to hear that my most dear, most excellent, but alas! neglected friend, has had so serious an illness at Cawnpore. God grant that he may be entirely recovered, and that your next letter may bring you the grateful tidings. Pray, pray, let me hear from you when they arrive. I know not the individual out of my own family, whose loss would so deeply wound me. Would that the time were arrived, at which he could withdraw himself from that infernal land of cholera. His life is of infinitely more value to his family and friends, than lacs of rupees, and I hope you will join me in telling him so.'

Sir Samford Whittingham to his Brother-in-law.
'CAWNPORE, 5th *December*, 1828.

'The Duke of Wellington, in my humble opinion, possesses more of sterling British good sense, and real sound judgment than any man I have ever yet known.

Sir George Murray you will find a most able man of business, and the new Secretary-at-War,* with whom I was at High Wycombe, possesses very superior abilities. I have received a letter from Finucane, as late as the 18th June, in which he says that you were again quite well. How nobly your friends at Bristol constantly behave! Tell our old friend, Mr. Bush, that I have got his son attached to a regiment at Cawnpore, and that I will do everything in my power to serve and take care of him. In January, I shall meet Lord Combermere at Keitah— take leave of him—inspect the troops at Bundelkund and return to my camp of instruction at Cawnpore, on the 1st February. Brigade and field days will occupy that month, and the greater part of March. Four battalions of infantry, eight squadrons of cavalry, and twelve pieces of artillery, will be the manœuvring force. I will send you one of my field-days, to show my good friend Torrens.† To many people, all this would be tiresome. I confess I delight in what I contemplate as merely necessary preparation for some great and glorious day. "My fortune's on my saddle-bow", and my greatest ambition an honourable grave on the field of battle.'

* Sir Henry (afterwards Viscount) Hardinge.
† Sir Henry Torrens had been dead some months when Sir Samford wrote these words.

CHAPTER XVII.

1829—1830.

ON ROUTE TO MEET LORD COMBERMERE—TAKES FINAL LEAVE OF LORD COMBERMERE—LETTER OF SOUTHEY TO MR. HART DAVIS—GREAT UNPOPULARITY OF LORD WILLIAM BENTINCK—CAPTAIN CAINE A.D.C. AND THE TIGERS—DELIGHTFUL CLIMATE OF MEERUT—UNIVERSAL HARMONY AT CAWNPORE STATION—LORD COMBERMERE'S LETTER—MUSSOURIE HILLS—INDIA NOT A GOOD SCHOOL FOR YOUNG SOLDIERS—A HOME ON THE HILLS—LORD HASTINGS VERSUS LORD AMHERST AS A FINANCIER—ACCOUNTS MYSTERIOUSLY WITHHELD—SIR HENRY HARDINGE'S CORRESPONDENCE WITH SIR SAMFORD—EXPECTED VISITS FROM LORD WILLIAM BENTINCK AND LORD DALHOUSIE—ANXIETY FOR A PROLONGED COMMAND.

'*Calpee:* 3rd *January*, 1829, 50 *miles from Cawnpore.*—I am thus far on my route to Keitah, to meet Lord Combermere, and have been passing some days with Mr. Saunders, one of the civil servants of the Company, and commercial resident for them here.' [He speaks most highly of this gentleman's skill, zeal, and management; and enters copiously into cotton details, unsuited for this Memoir; then after repeating and dwelling on his unalterable belief on the subject of the transfer of authority in India, he ends with]—'So strong, indeed, is this the conviction of my mind, that I know of nothing in public life that would give me more pleasure than to hear that India, civil and military, was placed at the disposition of His Majesty.'

'*Banda:* 29*th January.*—This morning I took my final leave of Lord Combermere, who has been kind and attentive to me beyond expression. He proceeds through Cawnpore, &c. to Calcutta; and I am on my return to Cawnpore, where I expect to arrive on the 3rd February. On that day I inspect the artillery. Yesterday's letters and papers brought us the melancholy news of the death of our old and much esteemed friend, Torrens! I do not know any event that has more completely affected me. To Sir Herbert Taylor, who succeeds him,* I have written a few lines, enclosed in this letter. I rode eighteen miles to breakfast this morning, without the slightest fatigue. Indeed, I never recollect to have been in better health. Lord William Bentinck is travelling dâk about Bengal, but his movements are so completely kept to himself, that we have no certainty as to his real intention. I wish he may come to Cawnpore, I shall be delighted to see him. Lord Combermere goes home about the middle of next November.'

About the middle of 1829 Sir Samford Whittingham must have received from his brother-in-law the following note, written by Robert Southey:—

Mr. Southey to Mr. Hart Davis.†

'KESWICK, 15th *January*, 1829.

'Sir,—I have this day been favoured with your obliging note, and the papers from Sir Samuel F. Whittingham. In the course of the present year, I hope to produce the facts contained in these papers in a manner which will satisfy Sir Samuel, by representing the true case. Indeed he had put me in possession of them before he left England; and they had enabled me sometimes to render him that justice in private which I shall with great pleasure render him in public. I never write with more pleasure than when rendering due honour to the living or the dead.

---

* Sir H. Taylor was appointed Adjutant-General on the 25th August 1828.

† This note of Southey's came into the Editor's possession only after he had finished writing this work as far as Chapter XX. It amply confirms directly the conclusion which he had already arrived at indirectly.

'Many years have passed since I have been connected with Bristol in any other way than by a family burial-place in Ashton churchyard. But I love my native city dearly, am proud to be noticed as a Bristolian by you its worthy representative, and shall continue to labour while I can, in the hope and belief that I may leave a name which may be held there in good remembrance. I have the honour to remain, Sir,

'Your obliged and obedient servant,
'ROBERT SOUTHEY.'

But in addition to the information that Southey obtained direct from General Whittingham, he must certainly have obtained, as explained in the preface, the most important of the letters which the latter addressed to the successive Military Secretaries at the Horse-Guards.

A long letter (to Mr. Davis of the 17th June) narrates the reduction in the pay and allowances of the military officers made by Lord William Bentinck, and its effects, and adds: 'The Governor-General is unpopular to a degree beyond belief, and I am really afraid he will receive open marks of disrespect in his journey through the Upper Provinces.'

'*Cawnpore*, 18*th July*, 1829.—My aide-de-camp, Captain Caine, H.M.'s 41st Regiment, has been out on a shooting party lately; and, with two companions, killed forty-three tigers, and twelve young ones. He begs you to accept of two skins, truly the largest and finest I ever saw; and which I send to you by Cornet Hindman, of H.M.'s 11th Light Dragoons. He has promised to take great care of them, and to deliver them to you. He is a gentlemanly young man, who will, I think, rather please you. In order that you may have some idea of Caine, I forward you a copy of the statement I gave Lord Combermere of his conduct at the storming of Bhurtpore, where he had acted as Brigade-Major to Brigadier-

General M'Combe. Such very extraordinary gallantry should be made as public as possible, and I know that you will peruse the statement with interest and pleasure. I spoke to Lord Combermere in his favour, and his Lordship gave him very shortly afterwards a Company in the 41st, which has, to my great delight, been confirmed by Lord Hill.'*

'CAWNPORE, 25th December, 1829.

[Alluding to past gifts he writes to Sir Edward Paget]— 'The *hookah* is the admiration of everyone who has seen it. The little *Admiral* is still the darling pet. The hats, the tonjon, the iron chest, all are mementos of the man whom of all others I have most esteemed and loved.'

The following is to his Brother-in-law :—

'CAWNPORE, 1st January, 1830.

'The compliments of the season to all the dear circle! Will you send these compliments, which truly come from the heart, to our dear friend,† and all his amiable family; and also to my much loved friends Sir Edward and Lady Harriet Paget. I enclose a Calcutta paper containing an account of our mode of carrying on the war at Cawnpore.‡ I am proud of the *universal* harmony which now prevails at a station famous in former days for a very opposite spirit. I enclose also Lord Combermere's last letter to me, written in a tone of friendship, which delights me, and will I am sure highly gratify you. Lord Combermere is one of the best soldiers I have known, and a man of great sense and judgment; I sincerely love him.'——

The re-action caused by the change in Lord Combermere's treatment of him, filled his warm and affectionate heart with gratitude; and it is to be regretted that this

---

* Vide *Appendix* C. Surely the *Victoria Cross* might be back-dated and given to such veterans as Colonel Caine.
† Sir William Knighton.
‡ This paper is not forthcoming.

letter of his Lordship has been lost or mislaid. But it was already quite evident from previous letters, that both Chief and subordinate understood and appreciated one another, and were on very friendly terms.

In the beginning of 1830, Sir Samford was anticipating official visits from Lord William Bentinck, the Governor-General, and from the new Commander-in-Chief, the Earl of Dalhousie. In the letter mentioning the above facts, occur the following natural lamentations :—' Nothing is to me so grievous in India as the slowness of our correspondence. From the date of my writing to you, my beloved brother, till the receipt of your letter in answer, seldom less than a year elapses; and it is impossible to get rid of the idea that a thousand things may have happened between the date of your letters and their reception by me.' *

Voluminous letters about the education and prospects of his children abound this year. He has also hopes of effecting a pleasant change of military command.

'10*th March*, 1830.—Lord Dalhousie has promised that I shall succeed Sir Jasper Nicholls at Meerut. Sir Jasper resigns in January 1831. He would stay longer, but a large family of daughters requires his presence in England. I am very glad of this change; the climate of Meerut is better than that of Cawnpore, and it is so near the hills, that a change of air if necessary can be procured in twenty-four hours.'——

He was taken ill this spring, and removed for change of air to the Hills :—

To his Brother-in-law.

'MUSSOURIE *in the* HIMALAYAN MOUNTAINS; *six miles above* DHOON DEYRA, 140 *miles from* MEERUT, 9*th May*, 1830.

'You will I know be greatly rejoiced to hear that my health is already perfectly restored by this most delightful

* He lived himself just long enough to witness great modification of this evil, by the establishment of the overland postage to India.

climate, I never breathed so pure an air. The thermometer ranges from 62° to 65°. I sleep under a double blanket, and we seldom pass a day without lighting a fire; yet this is the hottest season of the year. On the 1st of November, I shall return to Meerut, where I assume the command.

'Lord Dalhousie is better, and keeps to his resolution of sailing up the Ganges for these upper provinces in July next. I shall see him at Meerut instead of Cawnpore; and I shall have hard work in November and December, to get the troops in as good order as I had them in at Cawnpore. Lord William writes to me in the same kind and friendly style he has ever done. I expect he will be at Meerut in January.'

To the Same.

'MUSSOURIE *near* LANDOUR, 22*nd May*, 1830.

'In regard to —— I would not upon any account that he should come out to India, which I look upon as the worst school into which a young military man can be thrown. Habits of idleness, dissipation, and great expense are almost invariably acquired; and but seldom corrected by that spirit of subordination and strict military discipline which is so forcibly inculcated in our regiments in Europe. I am sorry B——s* is placed in the ——th. It is a particularly good fighting regiment; but I am afraid so admirable a young man as you describe B——s to be, will find but little congenial to his feelings amongst the officers of that corps. I am particularly anxious that ——, when he has passed his examination at Sandhurst, should obtain a commission in the Rifle Brigade, and if no opportunity should offer of his obtaining it gratis, I would purchase him his first commission rather than see him enter any other corps. Pray talk this matter over with Sir Edward Paget; and tell him at the same time, how

---

* Now Major-General, lately commanding the Cork district in Ireland.

much I feel gratified and honoured by his choosing me godfather to his little boy.

'When I came to these heavenly mountains, I purposed residing with my old and good friends Mr. and Mrs. Grant. But the sudden death of Mrs. Grant changed all my projects, and threw me upon the wide world with the least preparation for such an unexpected change. Dr. and Mrs. Daunt of H. M.'s 44th, who are here for their health, kindly took compassion upon me; and I am now living with them (and with Dr. and Mrs. Magrath, who form part of the family), with more real comfort than I have enjoyed since my arrival in India. It is delightful to meet with such estimable friends, in this far distant land, and close to the snowy range.'——

The following extract from a letter to Mr. Davis is a proof of the activity of the writer's mind, who even when on leave in the hills *could* not be idle :—

'MUSSOURIE, 28*th May*, 1830.

'When Lord Hastings left India, the surplus revenue exceeded 800,000*l*. per annum. The deficit is now 1,400,000*l*. per annum. This evil must be remedied; but not by such trifling means as cutting 15,000*l*. per annum from the army. In my opinion the great evil arises from the unproductive territory of the Presidency of Bombay. All territory not productive costs enormous expense, which must be paid by the Presidency of Bengal. Such territory should be divided between and given to petty rajahs, under a trifling rent, which however small, would be so much clear gain, whilst all expense on our part would cease. The enclosed queries I drew up and sent to a high civil servant to be answered. I extract a part of his letter to me in answer, and if you think it worth your attention, pray call for such records of the House of Commons as may bear upon them; you will thus acquire much more positive information than it is in my power to send you. My friend says: "Without books and papers I cannot answer distinctly these questions. In either the second or third report of the committee of the House of Commons previous to the last charter, there are numerous accounts from which the matter might be collected. In the 'Asiatic Journal,' some of the late accounts annually laid before Parliament were printed. I have not with me any of the Accountant-General's annual estimates and reports on accounts, which are the foundation of all the accounts of India. *For the last three years, these accounts have been withheld from us."*

'It is only therefore in the records of the House of Commons that full and authentic information can be acquired.

'Sincerely yours,

'SAMFORD WHITTINGHAM.'

This year he carried on a most friendly demi-official correspondence with the Secretary-at-War, Sir Henry (afterwards Viscount) Hardinge, on the subject of soldiers' pensions, and quartering troops on the hills.

On the 2nd of August, he writes to his brother-in-law:—

'I am glad to see Lord Clare's appointment to the government of Bombay, inasmuch as it will insure Lord William's coming up the country, which might have been prevented had Sir Charles Metcalfe been appointed as was here reported. Sir Charles is a member of council, and an old and experienced Civil servant; and Lord William might not have felt it expedient to have left the council without him. I hope to have many a long conversation with Lord William on the interesting subjects of those hills. I shall quit them [the hills] with deep regret, and return to them with infinite pleasure. They have perfectly restored my health; and they have afforded me an existence of quiet and tranquil happiness, such as I have never experienced since I left home.'

'*20th August.*—My exchange with Sir Jasper is in orders to take place on the 1st November.'

'*Meerut, 6th November.*—Here I am again on the plains, in perfect health and vigour; full of business and preparations for our great men—Lord William first; and then Lord Dalhousie. I shall give them first a review of a brigade of infantry; then of four regiments of cavalry, and thirty pieces of horse artillery; and then of the whole together: each day commanded by S. W. Be assured, my dearest brother, they shall not see the like in India. Imagine to yourself with what delight I shall ride my favourite hobby.'

'*Meerut, 15th November.*—I am occupied from morn till eve, and delighted with my new situation. My health is perfect.'

'*Meerut, 1st December.*'—[In this letter he explains his anxious desire to have his command, which would be completed on the 26th January, 1833, prolonged to the 26th January, 1836, giving various reasons: his desire to see his civil and military sons, soon about to embark on their careers, around him, and his belief that the expected demise of Runjeet Singh, would at last give him that active command in the field at the head of British troops which was now the great object of his zeal and labours. He continues]—' To be called away from the field just at the moment of commencing operations would absolutely break my heart. I entreat you therefore, dearest brother, to use every influence in your [power] to obtain this boon for me, and be assured of my eternal gratitude.* The late brevet has doubled my chance of a high command, should the troops take the field, and made me a thousand times more anxious to remain at my present post. The Duke of Wellington would perhaps listen to the supplication of an officer who has had the honour of serving under him.'

---

* The influence of Mr. Davis, the Conservative Member of Bristol, soon about to vanish under the crash of the great Reform Bill, was at this time very considerable with the Ministers.

Well would it be if parliamentary interest were never exerted in a worse cause than in endeavouring to give to a brave, zealous and skilful officer an opportunity of actively serving his country! Providence alone can furnish the desired opportunity; but the hope may always exist and thus keep active and able minds, so long as life and strength are granted, from stagnation and fatal despair.

CHAPTER XVIII.

1831.

VISITS OF THE EARL OF DALHOUSIE, AND OF LORD WILLIAM BENTINCK—THE DUKE OF WELLINGTON'S REPEATED OBSERVATION TO MR. HART DAVIS REGARDING GENERAL WHITTINGHAM—WHOLLY ADOPTED AND REJOICED IN BY LORD WILLIAM BENTINCK—THE DUKE'S DECLARATION AGAINST REFORM—THE DUKE'S LOSS OF OFFICE INJURIOUS TO SIR SAMFORD—THE RIVAL CHAMPAGNES—A CANDID NOBLE SPORTSMAN—LIEUTENANT (NOW SIR HENRY) DURAND—ONE OF THE DUKE'S LAST OFFICIAL ACTS—LORD WILLIAM BENTINCK'S OPINION OF DANIEL O'CONNELL—HIS CONFIDENCE IN HIS COUNTRYMEN—A CHARACTERISTIC LETTER BY 'THE DUKE'—LORD HILL'S OPINION OF SIR SAMFORD.

How Lord Combermere would have been recalled, had he not resigned, has been explained in his Memoirs, by Lady Combermere and Captain Knollys. He opposed himself to those retrenchments in military expenditure, to which Lord William Bentinck was pledged, and which the then peaceful aspect of affairs facilitated.

We continue the extracts from the fraternal correspondence.

'*Meerut, 29th January*, 1831.—Your dear letter of the 28th July, with extracts from the newspapers, relative to your election at Bristol reached me yesterday, and gave me greater pleasure than I have words to express. It is most delightful to see the constant, and warm, and firm attachment of your friends at Bristol; because that feeling arises from the fullest conviction of your merits, and not from the feasting system, which so greatly captivates John Bull. By doing your duty ably, punctually and graciously, you have conciliated all the *amours propres* in your favour, and you have admirably preserved your own dignity, without neglecting the humblest of your constituents.'

'*Meerut*, 10*th February*.—What a magnificent triumph you have obtained my dearest brother!* As far as honour can confer happiness, we have abundant reason to be satisfied. It would not be reasonable to expect all the good things of life together. Lord Dalhousie will be here on the 20th, remain here 21st and 22nd, and leave on the 23rd. Lord William will arrive on the 24th, and go from hence to Hurdwar, whither I shall accompany him as well as to the hills of Landour. I hope to show both their Lordships first-rate specimens of cavalry and artillery. My infantry is broken up for the season by the departure of the 31st Regiment for Kurnaul. But next cold weather I hope to give them some line movements.'

The letters recording Lord Dalhousie's visit are not extant, but there is no doubt that all passed off satisfactorily. Sir Samford accompanied Lord William Bentinck to the Mussourie hills; and whilst there he received the following convincing proof that his constant exile had not obliterated him or his services from the memory of the greatest of Englishmen :—

Richard Hart Davis, M.P. to Sir Samford Whittingham.
(Extract.)
'[38] † CONDUIT STREET [HANOVER SQUARE],
'28*th September*, 1830.

'I delayed writing for a day or two expecting to have a communication from the Duke of Wellington respecting your regiment. This has taken place; and what will delight you above the hopes of having the regiment soon, is the observation which the Duke made "*that we had not such another officer in the army*," as yourself, "and that

---

* Mr. Davis, unable to bear the expenses of an election, had again been returned in 1830 at the expense of his constituents.

† Then a handsome private house; now a tailor's shop.

you ought to have a Regiment, and that you should have one quickly." . . . . . .

'I forgot to say that the Duke of Wellington twice repeated "*that we had not such another officer in the army*" as yourself.'——

Mr. Davis's letter having reached Sir Samford whilst he was in the camp of the Governor-General, he at once sent it on to Lord William, evincing thereby much confidence in the generosity of the latter, considering the great military seniority of his Lordship, under whose command-in-chief he had served in the Peninsula.

The following was the truly magnanimous as well as kind reply of that distinguished nobleman:—

Lord William Bentinck to Sir Samford Whittingham.

'Camp, 20*th March*, 1831.

'My dear Sir Sam. F. (*sic*)—It would be paying you a poor compliment to apply the same comparison in reference to this Presidency, as the greatest of all authorities, in a manner so exceedingly gratifying, has made in your favour in respect to the army at large. In fact no other officer has had the same large means and varied opportunities of improving his own military talents, and of employing them for the benefit of his country. *I wholly adopt the Duke's sentiments, rejoicing and proud of them as an old friend, and delighted moreover in having the benefit of those services in a country where they are so much wanted. May they long be continued in India.** . . . . .

'Ever, my dear Sir Samford,
'Most sincerely yours,
'W. Bentinck.'

This flattering letter emboldened Sir Samford to request his Lordship's kind aid with Lord Ellenborough,

---

* Thus the *liberal* Lord William, emulated the generosity of the *conservative* Sir Edward Paget's striking letter to Lord Bathurst (see page 340).

then President of the Board of Control, to procure the prolongation of his command in India. Lord William replied as follows:—

'CAMP, 23rd March, 1831.

'My dear Sir S. Ford,—When you have such a friend in the Chief,* any interference on the part of myself or of Lord Ellenborough, were he ever so well disposed to give effect to my wishes, seems useless; but the letter, as you desire, shall be sent to Lord E., and dispatched by this day's *dâk*. I hope it may be of more use than I expect.

'Ever sincerely yours,
'W. BENTINCK.'

Lord William appears to have continued his tour soon after the above, whilst Sir Samford returned to Meerut. He now uses the word 'Samford' instead of 'S. Ford' in his next letter to Sir S. Whittingham:—

From Lord William Bentinck.
(Extract.)

'CAMP RINJOAR, 6th April, 1831.

'My dear Sir Samford,—I have to thank you for your letters of the 31st, and 2nd April. . . . . . .

'I have received from Lord Clare a file of "Galignani," from the beginning of November to the 11th December. These I have sent to Lord Dalhousie. The only three English papers I received are herewith transmitted. I have no copy of the King's speech at the meeting of Parliament: but I see by the papers that it contained a strong declaration against Reform, which had made *the Duke* extremely unpopular. There seems to be little doubt, that had the King gone to the Lord Mayor's dinner—the intention having been abandoned only the day before—there would have followed great tumults. I have a letter from Lord Clare, dated Bombay, 20th March, in which he says: 'You will have been as much surprised

---
* The Duke of Wellington.

as I was to hear of the change in the English administration. Before I left London on the 8th September, it was known that the elections had gone against the Duke's friends; and as it was believed he intended to meet Parliament without any accession of strength to his Government, so the stability of it was very generally doubted.'

'The D. of Northumberland has resigned the *Blues* and is succeeded by Lord Hill. I should think the D[uke of Wellington] will return to his command of the army. He and Lord Grey were always well together, and as I have heard, nothing but the late King's positive refusal prevented the D. from taking him into his cabinet. In the Duke's case I would not take the command. It would be a false position. A rival having the ear of his Sovereign would be suspected, let his honour and integrity be ever so undoubted.

'Sir Edward Paget, and Sir Willoughby Gordon are variously stated as Master-General of the Ordnance; the former is the most likely, Lord Anglesea* (*sic*) having accepted the Lord-Lieutenancy of Ireland.

'Sincerely yours,
'W. BENTINCK.'

The removal of the Duke of Wellington from power, as he did not revert to Commander-in-Chief, was a great blow to Sir Samford Whittingham, pledged as his Grace was to give him an early regiment.

The following anecdote being familiar to the Editor of this work, and again lately confirmed by two surviving witnesses, exemplifies the excellence of Sir Samford Whittingham's dinners, especially the wines. In this he had formed a great contrast to one exalted official who on his tours of inspection was mainly indebted to the guns of his Staff and of Captain Caine for eking out his scantily supplied table. But this observation by no means applies

---

* The 'Peerages' have *Anglesey*, not Anglesea.

to Lord and Lady William Bentinck, who always gave excellent dinners. It was about this period that Lord William invited Sir Samford to dinner expressly that he might taste some superior champagne, which had been sent as a present to Lord William by his good friend Louis Philippe, King of the French. Now the General had long obtained all his French wines direct from France, where they were selected by his old friend Count Turenne, formerly employed in the household of the great Napoleon. When his Lordship asked Sir Samford's opinion of the citizen King's wine, he replied, that he would give him better if his Lordship would honour him with his company to dinner.

Soon after this, Lady William Bentinck gave a station ball at Meerut, and borrowed for the purpose the officers of the artillery's mess-house. At the same time, that she might have leisure to superintend the preparations, her Ladyship desired to escape the trouble of having to provide the same evening the dinner of her Lord and his Staff, and she therefore requested Sir Samford to take this opportunity of settling the disputed champagne question. There had been much previous joking, and Lord and Lady Bentinck were both certain that it was impossible to surpass the wines of French royalty.

The dinner took place accordingly. Amongst the guests were Doctor and Mrs. Magrath, the latter of whom is now a widow, residing in London. To the good-humoured discomfiture of the Governor-General, even his own Staff awarded the palm to Sir Samford's wine, nor did his Lordship himself impeach the verdict. His Staff had not always been so candid. On one occasion when they were attending Lord William out tiger shooting, an enraged tiger sprang on his Lordship's elephant, when the unerring gun of Captain Caine (who was of the party) came to the rescue and disabled the animal. His Lordship, who had been cool and calm to an exemplary degree, now gave the finishing shot. The moment the beast fell, the officers of the Staff shouted out 'The Lord done it, the Lord done it!'* But Lord William quickly replied: 'No! Captain Caine, luckily for me, killed him, and I by no means liked the unpleasant predicament in which I was placed.'

In a letter to Lord William Bentinck, dated Mussourie, 25th July, 1831, Sir Samford encloses a plan of the chain of heights upon which *Thannah Toongra* is situated, drawn by Lieutenant Durand of the Bengal Engineers. Before entering into the details, Sir Samford calls his Lordship's attention to the very able manner in which Lieutenant Durand had executed the plan of the ground.

This able officer thus specially brought to the notice of the Governor-General, is now the well-known Sir Henry Durand, who blew up the gates of Ghuznee in 1839, and whom, as a member of the Supreme Council in India, Sir John Lawrence, the present Viceroy of India, invested at Simla on the Queen's birthday in 1867, with the Knight-Commandership of the Star of India, accompanied by an eloquent panegyric on his past services.

To explain the next letter, the reader must know that Sir Samford's eldest son had, by the deaths of certain gentlemen, lost two successive nominations to Bengal writerships, which was a grievous disappointment to his father, after the special and expensive education which he had received to fit him for the appointment. One of the great Duke's last official acts was to give to Sir Samford's son, through Mr. Davis, the only appointment of the kind left in his gift, but which unfortunately was a Madras instead of a Bengal writership; so that the father could no longer cherish the hope which had long cheered him, of ushering his son into civil official life under his own

---

* When Governor-Generals, or minor Indian Governors were noblemen, their Staff, usually spoke of them as '*The Lord.*' It certainly was done at Madras less than 30 years ago, as the Editor can testify.

eye, and with the immediate and powerful protection of the good and great Lord William Bentinck:—

From Lord William Bentinck.
(Extract.)

'SIMLA, 18*th April*, 1831.

' My dear Sir S. Ford,—Thanks for yours of the 28th. I am glad of your success in the writership; and I hope you may have the same good luck as to the Staff. The artillery report is very satisfactory; and not less so that of *Thanna Toongra*. Two days' march will bring it within convenient distance of the plains. The state of England itself is represented by all letters as very perilous. O'Connell seems determined to produce an insurrection in Ireland, of which I trust he may be the first victim.* I have before seen a union of protestants and catholics, as is the case at present. But it was then, as it will be now, of short duration; and the old feud and animosities [will] prevail over those which O'Connell may endeavour to arouse against the English connection. Catholic, a patriot and a man and religion, was a much more popular banner than the repeal of the Union can ever be.'

From the Same.
(Extract.)

'SIMLA, 26*th September*, 1831.

'My dear Sir S. F.—I thank you for the interesting extract from H. Davis's letter. The transaction is in its results more honourable to him than a successful election. It shows the force and the power of the prevailing feeling. The Government henceforth will be directed by a Republican influence, little under the constraint of that which has hitherto mainly directed the councils of the country; namely the aristocracy and clergy. I think we could not have gone on without great changes, to which these latter

---

* It is curious to see how frightened even some Liberal Whigs were then, of the democratic spirit they had helped to raise.

interests would never have consented. Whether those that *will* be brought about by the former, may not greatly outstep the just limits of our wants, is another question, which time alone can solve. My confidence has always been in the united sense and courage of the country, and, as the experience of near forty years' actual intercourse with mankind has led me to the conclusion that there is now infinitely more knowledge and morality, than in my younger days, so I cling with confidence to a rather favourite maxim with me, *Nil desperandum*. I believe that all we see going on in England and Europe will combine to the eminent good of the human race. To those who have the most wisdom and firmness, these benefits will the earlier come. To the rest, who, for no fault of their own, but from bad government, have been sunk under all the evils of ignorance, superstition, and immorality, they, like the Republics of S. America, will have to go through all kinds of suffering, before they reach the goal. This is a cruel dispensation of providence in appearance, but so it is in fact, and probably or rather certainly for the very best reasons, could our limited faculties dive into these great mysteries.

'I send herewith a book, in which your first introduction upon the military stage of the Peninsula is flatteringly mentioned. It is probable that you will not have seen it.* . . . .

'Yours sincerely,
'W. BENTINCK.'

The following letter is truly characteristic of its writer :—

The Duke of Wellington to Mr. Davis.

'LONDON, 15th *August*, 1831.

'My dear Sir,—I return the enclosed letter. I know that there is a positive rule at the Horse-Guards that a

---

* The Editor will be greatly obliged to any person who can inform him of the title of this book, apparently published in 1831.

general officer shall not be employed on the Staff more than six years. I have carried this rule into execution, and so has my successor. I can have no objection to his departure from it; but I am convinced that you will see that I cannot with propriety make myself the solicitor for such a departure. I hope that you will excuse me, and will not ask me to take a course so inconsistent with what is the line of my duty.

'Believe me, yours most sincerely,
'WELLINGTON.'

'R. Hart Davis, Esq.,
    'Conduit Street.'

On the 21st December of same year, Lord Hill wrote officially to the same effect to Lord Ellenborough, who transmitted the decision to Lord William Bentinck. In his letter Lord Hill who had never met General Whittingham in Spain, nor had ever been in communication with him there, yet, writes: 'I entertain a very high opinion of Sir S. Whittingham, and believe him to be fully entitled to the encomiums passed upon him by Lord William Bentinck.'

CHAPTER XIX.

1832.

MUSSOURIE—CHIEFS AT SIMLA, WITH THEIR RESPECTIVE STAFFS—SIR EDWARD BARNES—BAD HANDWRITING NO PROOF OF GREATNESS—LORD WILLIAM ON THE ROYAL DISCRETION—SIR EDWARD BARNES—THE COMMANDER-IN-CHIEF'S DEATH WARRANT—THE DUKE'S DICTUM ON THE DISAGREEMENT OF INDIAN CHIEFS—LADY WILLIAM BENTINCK—INJUSTICE OF NAPIER'S EARLIEST VOLUMES—THE NON-PUBLICATION OF THE 'WELLINGTON DISPATCHES' AN INSUFFICIENT EXCUSE—THE BARROSA INJUSTICE—COLONEL CAINE'S RECOLLECTIONS—SIR SAMFORD WRITES TO SIR EDWARD PAGET FOR REDRESS AND SATISFACTION.

THE extracts from private letters to his brother-in-law must, from the limited space left, be henceforth fewer and briefer than hitherto :—

'*Mussourie, 4th May*, 1832.—I have been up on these delightful hills nearly a fortnight. We are now nearly in the hottest season of the year, and the thermometer ranges in the house from 66° to 68°! Lord and Lady William Bentinck, Sir Edward and Lady Barnes,* and their respective Staffs, are all at Simla, enjoying the climate as much as I do. How much I wish the consent of the directors may be obtained to the building of barracks for one King's Regiment at Thannah Toongra and at Dumoultrie.'

'*Mussourie, 22nd June.*—I send you a plan of the house, garden, and fields at Meerut. The house is one of the best built houses in India, and the garden produces, in the greatest abundance, strawberries, peaches, grapes,

---

* Sir Edward Barnes succeeded Lord Dalhousie as Commander-in-Chief (See *Appendix* E.)

apples, pears, and all sorts of vegetables. The oat-field produces oats for twelve horses. The whole extent of the ground is about twenty acres. Lord Dalhousie was particularly pleased with the beauty and comfort of the house and all its appurtenances.'

'*Mussourie, 7th July.*—Education and experience will form any man to all the duties of our noble profession, with one solitary exception. The Commander-in-Chief must be formed by nature. Such men as our immortal Duke are born, like poets, and not made. Everything short of that highest pinnacle of glory is to be acquired by a strong and determined resolution to neglect nothing connected with our duty; and that duty we shall never neglect, if we constantly keep in mind that the lives of thousands may become the sacrifice of either ignorance or indifference on our part! . . . . . .

'Because some of the greatest men have had the misfortune to write very ill, many silly dandies have had the weakness to try to imitate them. They might as well fancy they were imitating the greatness of Alexander by getting drunk.'*

'*Mussourie, 20th September.*—What I most desire is always to be employed somewhere. Once laid upon the shelf, and a man is lost. My health is so perfect in this delightful climate, that I walk from five to six miles every morning, and ride from ten to twelve every evening. Business and general reading employ the rest of the day. I always dress by candle-light, and am generally out of the house soon after five [a.m.] My occupation at Meerut, during the cold season, will be incessant. Ten squadrons of cavalry, and twelve pieces of horse-artillery, will enable me to give Sir Edward Barnes some good reviews. And by the time he returns from Lucknow I shall have four battalions of infantry ready for him, which will

* This general remark was appended to some strong criticisms upon the penmanship of one of his sons.

enable me to give him some field-days of the three arms together.'

From a letter from Lord William, dated 'Simla, 21st October, 1832,' his Lordship expected to meet Sir Samford at Delhi, soon, and probably did so; but no letters of the period are at hand.

Lord William Bentinck to Sir S. Whittingham.
(Extract.)
'GWALIOR, 10*th December*, 1832.

'I have letters to-day of an old date (June) from England. They speak, like their predecessors, gloomily of affairs present and in prospect; and of the loss of respect which our institutions have suffered. One tells us that we must expect to find England *Americanized* by our return. The King is said to dislike very much his Whig ministers, as I supposed. I never saw this so directly stated before. It cannot be otherwise. I fear he has neither discretion nor *silence* to get well through the difficulties with which he is beset, and much imprudence may compromize the very throne itself. I hope you have succeeded with your cavalry plan.

'Ever sincerely yours,
'W. BENTINCK.'

[P.S.] 'Since I saw you, your Chief's new order about King's commissions has appeared. Unless he has great luck, and great protection, that order may prove his death warrant.'

This postscript reminds the Editor of an appropriate anecdote, which Sir Samford Whittingham often narrated. A certain Commander-in-Chief, very fortunate, but not of the very highest mental calibre, propounded to the Duke of Wellington this important question, before sailing for his new command: 'Supposing that the Governor-General and I should not agree, what would happen?' To which his Grace quietly and deliberately replied: 'If the Commander-in-Chief and the Governor-General were to disagree, *one* of the two would go to the wall. I leave you to decide *which* of the two that would be!'

The General is said to have retired quite dumbfounded.

Lady William Bentinck, one of the best and most amiable of ladies, also occasionally corresponded with Sir Samford Whittingham, who from his almost Quixote-like pure and chivalrous feelings, manner, and conduct towards all the fair sex, was naturally rewarded by universal popularity in that quarter. But limited space forbids entering into such matters.

We come now to the greatest trial of Sir Samford Whittingham's long and arduous career. Although he had been far from being what could be called one of Fortune's favourites, and had had to work his way against great difficulties to the distinction which he had acquired, yet that distinction in 1831 had been very great and very gratifying to his feelings. That the great Duke had not forgotten his merits, more than confirming by words what he had, sixteen years earlier, declared in writing; and that Lord William Bentinck, his former Commander, and present ruler of India, should in writing have confirmed and adopted the great Duke's opinion, were priceless honours calculated to turn the head of their recipient. Perhaps, therefore, it was as a lesson of humility, that Providence within a twelvemonth of vouchsafing the honours, delivered on the General's head its severest blow, or at least permitted its infliction.

Of all the readers of 'Napier's History,' probably not one sat down to peruse it for the first time with greater interest and pleasure than the subject of this Memoir. Certainly, very few were as capable, by natural and acquired military talent, and by ardent military zeal, to appreciate and relish its great merits. The volumes of that work came out one by one, and already when the two first were out, it was evident how little justice General Whittingham could expect from that brilliant but prejudiced writer.

True it is that ignorance might partly account for the injustice. The greater part of the 'Duke's Dispatches' were still sealed to the public, and their use was refused to Colonel Napier, unfortunately, probably, for the cause of truth and impartial justice. But this was only a partial excuse. The dispatches of victory had been published in the 'Gazettes,' and these at least might have been quoted as the best authority for history. The first man of the age had given in his 'Talavera Dispatch' an honourable place to Brigadier-General Whittingham, mentioning both his wound and the fact of its being received whilst leading two battalions of Spaniards into action. Not the slightest allusion to either of these facts did 'Napier's History' make! Such was the justice of the man, whose third volume, (the first edition of which came out in 1831), with his account of the battle of Barrosa, must have been seen by Sir Samford Whittingham at Meerut in the early part of 1832. Captain (now Colonel) Caine remembers the extreme indignation with which the General came to his aide-de-camp's room to point out what he *then* considered to be a vile calumny. And though he afterwards modified his opinion, his first judgment was not far wrong, if a fact true in itself may be so unfairly stated as to leave a calumnious impression on the reader, which was certainly applicable to Napier's description.

But the absent are always in the wrong. And General Whittingham was not only absent, but separated from all those documents the study of which proves him free of blame, and confirms the Duke of Wellington's repeatedly expressed opinions of his merits and services.

CHAPTER XX.

1833—1835.

AN INAUSPICIOUS DAY—SIR FREDERICK ADAM, GOVERNOR OF MADRAS—
'LES ABSENTS ONT TOUJOURS TORT'—A RECKLESS RIDER—A GENERAL
CALLS OUT AN ENSIGN—AN UNEXPECTED BROAD FRONT—CRUEL ONLY
TO BE KIND—LORD WILLIAM BENTINCK'S COMMENTS ON THE DUEL—THE
GOVERNOR-GENERAL APPOINTED COMMANDER-IN-CHIEF—APPLICATION
FOR THE MILITARY SECRETARYSHIP—SIR SAMFORD'S VALUE TO LORD
WILLIAM—A VERY HARD CASE—COLONEL NAPIER'S STATEMENT TOO
FAVOURABLY JUDGED BY ITS VICTIM—SIR SAMFORD UNJUST TO HIMSELF
—AN OFFICIAL LETTER ON BROKEN PROMISES—FIRST MEETING SINCE
CHILDHOOD OF FATHER AND SON—THE NILGHERRY HILLS—SIR EDWARD
PAGET AND THE 'UNITED SERVICE JOURNAL'—LORD WILLIAM'S CONFIDENCE IN GENERAL WHITTINGHAM—BABINGTON MACAULAY, MEMBER
OF COUNCIL—SIR SAMFORD'S ADMIRATION FOR THE PRUSSIAN MILITARY
SYSTEM—REQUESTS SIR EDWARD TO BE HIS SECOND IN A DUEL WITH
COLONEL NAPIER—SAILS FOR ENGLAND IN THE 'CURAÇOA.'

Lord William Bentinck to Sir Samford Whittingham.

(Extract.)

'CALCUTTA, 21st *March*, 1833.

'I HEAR that our Commander-in-Chief returns to Simla on the 1st of April, (an inauspicious day) but I doubt whether his preceding discussion can be so soon brought to a close. I am happy to say that so far our councils have passed off with great harmony: and all that has happened would never have occurred, had we started all together in council, where he would better have understood the business of the Government, and the absence of all disposition on our parts to trench upon his just authority. His ignorance of all these matters, and his unwillingness to be informed by those about him here led him into much present annoyance, and possibly to very unpleasant future consequences.'

Sir Samford wrote this year a 'Memoir on the Competency of the Bengal Army,' which bears the date of 'Meerut, 22nd February, 1833.' Its more appropriate title would have been: '*The Present Military and Political State of Bengal and its Future Prospects.*' There is no space to touch on this pamphlet, which embraced Europe as well as Asia in its discussions.

In a letter dated 'Calcutta, 7th April, 1833,' after an able commentary on European politics, Lord William writes: 'I am still confident as when I last wrote, that there will be no war. Your Chief is still here, and will remain till further intelligence arrives. This place and its gaieties suit him better than the monotony of Simla. He has been fighting all his battles with the council o'er again, but with of course the same success. I suppose you are by this time snug in your cool cottage at Mussourie. With best wishes ever sincerely yours,

'W. BENTINCK.'

We revert to the correspondence with Mr. Davis:—

'*Meerut, 8th March.*—C—— appears to apply as we could wish to his studies at Madras, and Sir Frederick Adam * has been very kind to him. I have been very busy of late preparing the field-day for the Commander-in-Chief on his return to Calcutta. I have to show him three battalions, ten squadrons, and twenty-four guns; and I think he will be pleased. I cannot tell you how anxiously I am looking out for ——'s name in the Gazette. I expect to be relieved on the 29th July. Should this be the case, I shall go down to Calcutta and stay a little time with Lord William, then proceed to Madras to see C——, and home!'

'*Meerut, 15th March.*—I have written to you to-day with my best thanks and fullest approbation of every-

---

* Sir Frederick was then Governor of Madras, after having been Lord High Commissioner of the Ionian Islands.

thing you have done about Colonel Napier;* but my mind is so troubled at the idea of ——'s being sent to the West Indies, that I have no rest and send you these few lines by another conveyance, to request you will immediately wait on Lord Hill and beg and entreat he will exchange him into a regiment at home. I have not in the last thirty years spent one year at home. My children do not know me. I have been ten years in the East Indies and two in the West. . . . . . I should not have courage to bear up against such a disappointment.'

'*Meerut, 2nd April.*—I yesterday received your letter of the 20th October. Colonel Napier's answer is conclusive, and the matter must now rest till my return.

'What I complain of in Colonel Napier's statement is, not the fact of the non-co-operation of the Spanish cavalry, which depended upon the repeated orders of the Spanish Commander-in-Chief, but of the sneering manner in which he has been pleased to introduce my name, and which leaves me no choice but to convince him on the field of honour that my conduct did not proceed from any want of resolution.'

The 'Wellington Dispatches,' yet unpublished, and the absence of all his papers, and the lapse of some twenty-two years, made him overlook more tangible injustices than a mere sneer, namely great misrepresentation of his rank, position, and command on that day, and of his employment (as *General* of the advanced guard) in protecting the right flank, which he had reported in writing to La Peña, and, more succinctly, verbally to Graham. *Les Absents ont toujours tort* applied too truly to the case. That very year came out in London, the second edition of that third volume, which the permanent edition now

---

* Mr. Davis had written that Napier's account of Barrosa was 'an unfounded calumny' in General Whittingham's opinion, for which he would demand satisfaction as soon as he returned to England.

used entirely follows; and the injustice is thus perpetuated for ever!'

In a letter from Lord William, dated Calcutta, 15th June, 1833, addressed to Sir Samford (then on the Mussourie hills) and marked 'private' and full of local politics and of his difference with Sir Edward Barnes, occurs this friendly passage: 'Pray let me know when you expect to be in Calcutta. We shall be most happy to receive you whenever you come.'

At the Mussourie hills on the evening of the 26th June, 1833, Sir Samford Whittingham was taking his evening ride, with a party of ladies and gentlemen, amongst the former of whom was the wife of Doctor Magrath. At a narrow and dangerous part of the road, a European without hat, jacket, or cravat, came riding at a furious pace. Most of the persons who saw him considered him drunk. He nearly ran against some of them, and frightened several ladies. The General was riding with four or five of the party at the time, when the European in question rode up against him and nearly knocked his pony over the precipice. Sir Samford, feeling indignant at this outrage, and conceiving the offender to be some low European, in a hasty moment, struck him with his whip. The person rode on without taking any notice, and the General sent an officer after him to see who he was. He was discovered to be Ensign H———, 26th N.I., then on leave at Mussourie.

This officer, it appears, on learning who had struck him, revenged himself by sending round next day an abusive circular against the 'person on horse-back' who had assaulted him, justifying his outrageous language under the pretence of having been unable to discover the aggressor.

The General sent his aide-de-camp, Captain Caine, to call out the Ensign, and the meeting was arranged for the next morning. That evening Sir Samford had a dinner-party, at which he was as gay and agreeable as usual, as if nothing serious had occurred. Mrs. Magrath was one of the party, and had no suspicion whatever of any impending evil. She knew indeed of the circular; for a Colonel of infantry, almost with tears in his eyes (so affected was he by the insult to his Chief), had acquainted her with the circumstance; but she doubtless never supposed that a General Officer would fight a duel with an Ensign. Her younger brother, a youth who was awaiting his commission in the army, through the interest of the General, had, however, his suspicions, and following the duellists unperceived on the morning of the 28th June witnessed the result of the meeting, and hastened to his astonished sister not long afterwards, with the joyful exclamation, 'The General is safe!'

Ensign H—— fired at Sir Samford without effect; who in return fired in the air; he who it has been said could snuff a candle with a pistol ball, and to whose skill as a shot the late gallant Lord Fife has borne his spontaneous testimony.* The General then told the Ensign, that having now met him as a gentleman, he had no hesitation in saying that when he (Ensign H.) rode up against him, he (the General) could not have supposed him to be an officer. In fact he had taken him for some low drunken European, and under that impression, added to the irritating attendant circumstances, had struck him. The General added that private satisfaction having been afforded, they resumed their relative positions, and he ordered Ensign H—— to go to his room and consider himself in arrest. The young gentleman then expressed great contrition for his offence. He said he did not know the General at the time and that he 'felt highly honoured by the handsome manner in which Sir Samford had behaved to him.'

In this duel, the General who was very stout in person,

* Vide *Preface.*

astonished his second by unexpectedly presenting his full and broad front to his youthful antagonist. Colonel Caine writes (on the 16th July, 1867, to the Editor): 'The opponents were placed by me with their right sides facing each other, and on giving the signal to fire I was astonished to see Sir Samford coolly change position by offering his entire front to his adversary. Before I could interpose, Mr. H—— fired in the direction of the General, and the latter discharged his pistol in the air.'

The General observing that his aide-de-camp did not look pleased at the affair ending with an arrest, kindly explained to that officer 'that by thus taking the matter into his own hands, the three Lieutenant-Colonels who had been desirous to try Mr. H—— by court-martial, would now be disarmed.' So that the aide-de-camp was (to quote his own words) 'fully satisfied that the General's reasoning was sound and kind.'

Ensign H—— afterwards sent to Captain Caine a written apology to Sir Samford, and a request for lenient consideration, accompanied by another apology to the ladies and gentlemen concerned. On Captain Caine delivering the two apologies to the General, he, in consideration of Mr. H——'s youth and inexperience, and his being the son of General Sir M. H——, governor of —— Castle, pardoned and released him from arrest.*

It appears that on the 17th August Sir Samford sent Lord William Bentinck an account of this affair of honour that never reached its destination; so that he had to write again. The following was the reply of his Lordship:—

'CALCUTTA, 28*th September*, 1833.

'My dear Sir S. Ford,—I am sorry to say that I have not received your letter of the 17th August; and as being

* This account (*so far as relates to the contending parties*) is abbreviated from one of the formal copies of the full proceedings made out by Captain Caine on the 1st July, 1833. The greater part of Colonel Caine's recent letter only contains the same statements which he signed in 1833.

upon a question in which your own person and honour, all, in short, upon which a friend ought to feel the most anxious and concerned, I do indeed lament that I did not sooner express the feelings I entertain. But in this case particularly, and with all such cases, all's well that ends well. It appears to me that the first sally apart, which it might be almost too fastidious to find fault with, no friend of yours could have wished a different decision upon any of the incidents which occurred in this transaction. It was a disagreeable predicament; but as long as the opinion of the world holds its present sway, and toleration, in these matters, I think you could not have acted otherwise than you did.

'I have said to you nothing of the honour, which, according to report, has been thrust upon me; because, except where some necessity might compel me to act otherwise, delicacy required me to be silent. I have had no letter from London till to-day later than the 14th May. This day, by the "*Anna Maria*," I received an official letter from the Adjutant-General informing me of the King's having appointed me to command his forces in India. . . . This is a feather in my cap; it is a mark of confidence which, as I must soon make my bow to the public, I am well pleased to receive. But there may be much trouble, and no advantage to myself, that I at present foresee. I say there *may be* much trouble, for if I take only as much as two of my three predecessors—perhaps I may say of the third also—save and except the time spent in altercation, the office would be very much of a sinecure. I cannot do as much as I could wish, or I ought; but what remains of zeal, health, and strength, I shall not fail to put into the work. But my career is too near its end to enable me to deal efficaciously with some evils, the nature of which you know better than I do. This event makes me regret more than ever your departure from India. But why expend lamentation upon an evil, which it has been attempted in vain to remedy. I have no conception how Sir Edward [Barnes] will like this order. I have been in the predicament,* and I know therefore how unpleasant it is. I sent him by express the earliest intelligence of the fact, which I had first received from Sir F. Adam. I think he will take kindly my having done so; though it is not quite a certain matter of calculation what he will say or do, even on points where the greater number generally coincide. But I hope he may. For though his impracticability has been an annoyance, yet his fine qualities interest and please. He, no doubt, will think himself the worst used man in the world. It would give me sincere pleasure [to find] that he was going to the Cape. But I doubt the truth of the report. That appointment must have been filled up before the causes leading to Sir E.'s recall could have been known.

'Ever sincerely yours,
'W. BENTINCK.'

Before this letter was written, viz., on the 20th September, Sir Samford had written from Mussourie to congratulate the new Commander-in-Chief, and to ask to be his Military Secretary, being anxious for his children's sake to prolong his stay in India. But Lord William had already offered the post to his old friend General Sleigh, the late Lieut.-Colonel of the cavalry regiment of which his Lordship was Colonel.

From Lord William Bentinck.

(Extract.)

'CALCUTTA, 19th October, 1833.

'My dear Sir S. Ford,—[After explaining why Brigadier-General Sleigh had been offered the Secretaryship, Lord W. writes:] 'You certainly occurred to me. But

* His Lordship in his younger days had been recalled from the government of Madras.

I did not imagine that the appointment, curtailed as it is likely to be, would be acceptable to you.' [He then promises it if Sleigh should refuse it, and adds:] 'Your acceptance of it will be very agreeable both to myself and Lady William. Our long acquaintance—our mutual friendship—your experience and knowledge of the Indian army—are all circumstances combining to make me contemplate the event with great satisfaction.'

Lord William, in a letter dated 'Barrackpoor, 23rd October, 1833,' reminds Sir Samford that all ostensible business in India passed through the Company's, not the King's, staff officers; and that merely as military secretary, he could not be of much use to Lord William. His Lordship continues: 'Your value to me will arise from your filling a very different character, *that of friend and counsellor; whose capability to give the most useful assistance is derived from great knowledge of India and of her armies, coupled with great practical experience in the art of war and the formation of armies. This estimate is formed upon no conjecture, but upon my long personal acquaintance with you; to say nothing of the valuable papers, upon all subjects, which you have had the goodness to give me from time to time.*'

We see that the cold and calm *Dutchman** (the great civil and military ruler of India) could almost rival Sir Edward Paget in esteem for Sir Samford Whittingham; and hard it certainly was that the man thus highly honoured and esteemed by so many successive chiefs and rulers, was driven eagerly to desire once more to risk a life so valuable to his children and so useful to his country, to vindicate his honour and that good name which by word and pen Wellington himself had established—or at least had *endeavoured* to establish!

General Sleigh accepted the Military Secretaryship;

---

* So he was called in allusion both to his ancestors, and to his own imperturbability.

but owing to the sickness of Mrs. Sleigh, at first delayed his journey to Lord William, and Sir Samford therefore acted in his stead, and thus became one of the Governor-General's family for nearly all the rest of his stay in India.

His private correspondence this year with his brother-in-law is chiefly taken up with domestic matters. But in one letter of 30th November he repeats more at large his intentions of calling out Colonel Napier,—without returning his fire, however,—and only to convince him of his courage.

General Sleigh took up his appointment as Military Secretary, and Sir Samford prepared to sail to Madras, on his way to England, as he had now no employment in India. To his brother-in-law he writes:

'*Calcutta, 4th January,* 1834.—I thought I should have long since sailed for Madras, but Lord William has detained me on business; and as I shall accompany him to that presidency, and may be detained there some months, I fear the time of our meeting is more distant than we had both hoped. My only consolation is that it will give me time to become acquainted with dear C———, in whose fate I take the deepest and most lively interest. In his correspondence with me he is amiable beyond expression. All that he appears to me to want is more confidence in himself. I am living at Government House, and I am treated more like a brother than a guest.'

General Sleigh preferring to remain at Calcutta, Sir Samford accompanied Lord William Bentinck, as acting Military Secretary.

'*Calcutta, 9th January,* 1834.—I go with Lord William to Madras, and shall carry home his dispatches. We shall leave this immediately after the arrival of Sir Edward Barnes, who is expected in a few days.' *

---

* Though recalled, Sir Edward Barnes was allowed to await his successor.

AN OFFICIAL LETTER ON BROKEN PROMISES.

The following official letter testifies that the word *neglected*, which Sir Edward Paget was so fond of applying to his 'dear and excellent friend' was becoming more applicable than ever, as far as regarded the Home authorities:—

To His Excellency General the Right Honourable Lord William Bentinck, G.C.B. &c.

'CALCUTTA, 10th *January*, 1834.

' My Lord,—The friendship with which for upwards of twenty-five years you have been pleased to honour me, leads me to hope you will have the goodness to submit the following statement to the favourable consideration of Lord Hill.

'The whole of my military career has been in the cavalry. I have never done a day's duty with any corps of infantry. I began in the Life Guards, and held a troop in the 13th Light Dragoons on the breaking out of the Spanish war. In Spain, I had under my command twelve regiments of cavalry; and the 'Book of Tactics for Brigade Exercises,' which I arranged and published at my own expense, for the use of the Spanish cavalry under my orders, was adopted for the whole of that arm in Spain.

'During the eleven years of my service in India, my time and attention have been directed particularly to that branch of the army, and during the last cold season ten squadrons were assembled at Meerut, by your Lordship's direction, for the purpose of Brigade exercise under my command. I was promised a regiment by the late Duke of York, by his late Majesty George the Fourth, and by the Duke of Wellington.

'The chances of life* have prevented the realization of these promises. But if your Lordship should be pleased to recommend me to the Commander-in-Chief for the first regiment of cavalry that may become vacant I love to

---

* The deaths of the two first, and the removal from office of the third.

hope [that] my claims might be taken into favourable consideration.

> 'I have the honour to be,
> 'My Lord,
> 'Your obedient servant,
> 'SAMFORD WHITTINGHAM.'

'*Madras, 6th February*, 1834.—My dearest Brother, I arrived here yesterday morning, after a tedious voyage from Calcutta, which I left on the 17th of last month. I found my dearest C. in rather better health than I expected, and am now lodged in the comfortable mansion of Colonel Monteith, who is so complete a soldier that I am quite delighted with him. Mrs. Monteith, who is a worthy daughter of her admirable parents,[*] received me as the friend of her early days. She is looking quite well and very happy, and as fond of India as I am, which is saying a great deal. I knew her instantly. But of C—— I had not the smallest recollection; when he came into the room, I said, "are you C?" and when he said "yes," I could scarcely believe him! . . . . I know of no career in any part of the world to be compared to the civil service of India.'

'*Bangalore, 11th March.*—A severe indisposition of Lord William renders it advisable to look out for a change of air; and we are in consequence all going with him up to the Nilgherry Hills. I am with him as his acting Military Secretary, and cannot of course leave him till he returns to Calcutta. . . .

'C—— is here *by order*, and employed in the office of the Governor-General's Private Secretary.

'It was truly kind in Lord William to propose this himself.'

In a letter dated 'Bangalore, 12th March, 1834,' Sir Samford sends Lord William a rough copy of his inten-

---

[*] Mr and Mrs. Murdoch, of Portland Place, very old friends of Sir Samford Whittingham.

tions regarding the writing of an 'Exposé of the State of Indian Affairs.'

The scene now changes to England :—

Sir Edward Paget to Mr. Davis.
(Extract.)
'ROYAL MILITARY COLLEGE, 18*th March*, 1834.

'My dear Davis,—The observations on Cavalry Movements, mentioned in Whittingham's letter, I have sent to the Editor of the 'United Service Journal.' You see all the doctors have not yet done much for my feeble arm.'*

The following letter was enclosed in Sir Edward's note :—

Major Shadwell Clerke to Major Procter.
'ATHENÆUM, 20*th March*, 1834.

'My dear Procter,—I have just received and, though late in the month, shall make a point of inserting in the next (April) Number of the Journal, the striking suggestions of Sir S. Whittingham on Cavalry Tactics.

'Assure Sir Edward, with my best compliments, that I receive this communication with much satisfaction both on account of the medium through which it is offered, the recommendation of Sir Edward being in any case conclusive with me, and also as giving earnest of further contributions from the same eminent and competent quarter. Perhaps Sir Edward would do me the favour to state my hopes on this point to his experienced correspondent, whom I should feel pride in numbering amongst the *Paladins* of the U. S. Journal. . . .

'In haste, but ever truly yours,
'T. H. SHADWELL CLERKE.' †

---

* His left, the only one he had, which it appears had been ailing; and which fact was visible in his hand-writing.

† Major T. H. Shadwell Clerke, K.H., had lost a leg in the Peninsular war. The *monthly* he edited is now styled 'United Service *Magazine*.' Thirty years ago it had a great circulation in the army.

At the commencement of 1834, Sir Edward Paget sent to Lord Fitzroy Somerset, General Whittingham's last Memoir on India. On the 11th January it was returned with thanks, and with the observation: 'Our friend Whittingham's views are very extensive.' We return to India, and the fraternal correspondence.

'*Bangalore, 17th March*, 1834.—Lord William left us on the 15th for the Nilgherry Hills. Colonel Casement and his party follow to-morrow. C—— is with us, and attached to the office of the Governor-General's Private Secretary. I am with Lord W. as his "Acting Military Secretary," as Sleigh, Torrens, Lumley, &c., have remained with their respective offices at Calcutta. My employment is ample, but I like everything connected with Lord William, and never think I have too much to do. Since our arrival here his Lordship has been dangerously ill; but he is now quite recovered, and only wants change of air. Lord William is most anxious to render C—— every service in his power; and I could not be kinder to him than is Sir Frederick Adam. Lord William and Sir Frederick really take as much interest in C—— as I do.'

In a letter dated 'Outacamund, 13th April, 1834,' he gives the Governor-General his opinion on 'the late short campaign with the Rajah of Courg,' and on its results and their general importance, observations much in the style of those which Lord William had before so flatteringly appreciated.

On the 29th April he thanks his Lordship for transmitting for his perusal two interesting minutes of the 26th March, 1831, and of the 27th January, 1834. It was a case of contention between the Governor-General and the Court of Directors, who objected to certain necessary new roads on the score of expense. Sir Samford as usual takes the opportunity of criticizing the Company's system, in which he had the full sympathy of his noble and able correspondent.

'*Outacamund, 9th May*, 1834.—I do not recollect at any period of my life to have been more busily and constantly employed than at present. But I am so sincerely attached to our excellent Chief, that I go through the work with pleasure.

'*Outacamund, 14th July.*—I cannot tell you in what month I shall embark for England. I leave my movements entirely to the decision of Lord William, to whom I every day feel a stronger attachment, and whose kindness to me is unbounded.

'His Lordship's health, and that of all the party have found infinite benefit from our residence in this cool climate, where the thermometer at no part of the summer has exceeded 65° in a room with a fire. The Supreme Council of India has commenced its sittings in these remote mountains. Mr. [Babington] Macaulay has arrived and taken his seat. He lives with his Lordship, and is assuredly one of the best informed men I ever met with. Your old friend, Sir Frederick Adam, is also up here, and a temporary member of the Council. It is to me a source of great delight and comfort, having C. with me under the same roof. His room adjoins to mine, and he forms one of his Lordship's family.'

Soon after this, a vacancy occurring amongst the Generals of Madras, General Sleigh received the appointment, and the acting Military Secretary was, on his return to Calcutta, to obtain the permanent appointment during the rest of Lord William's stay. Hitherto he had done all the duties gratis, receiving 'no pay from any one.'

Sir Samford Whittingham to Sir Edward Paget.
(Extract.)
'BANGALORE, *5th October*, 1834.

'I send you rather a long Memoir in three parts, the result of twelve years' meditation on a most interesting subject.* I know you will read it for my sake, and I beg you will make what use of it you please. You will see that it is quite of a confidential nature. I have given a copy of the Memoir to Lord William, who has been pleased to call it excellent, and to say that every word contained in it is true. To you and to him, as the two best friends I have in the world, I have submitted it, but to no other person. . . . .

'It is now settled that I am to remain with Lord William as his Military Secretary till he quits India. He is now on his way down from Outacamund, on the Nilgherry Hills, and I expect he will arrive to-morrow. I came here yesterday. We shall soon proceed to Madras, and we hope to be in Calcutta in the course of the month of November. His Lordship's health is quite restored by his *séjour* on the hills.'——

Reverting to the fraternal correspondence :—

'*Calcutta, 16th November,* 1834.—I accompanied Lord William Bentinck to this place from Madras, and landed on the 12th instant. I have derived no other benefit from acting as Military Secretary than that of making myself useful to a man I so highly respect and admire. But it was not in his Lordship's power to give me pecuniary remuneration of any kind.'

'*Calcutta, 24th November.*—General Sleigh will be put in orders in a few days to succeed Sir J. Barns at Poonah, Bombay; and I shall then be put in orders as Military Secretary, and will commence the first pay I shall have drawn since the 1st of last August twelvemonth. I certainly never was more honoured and distinguished than under my present Chief; but my case is somewhat like that of Gil Blas with the Duke of Lerma, '*y la hambre corre parejos con la gala.*'† If they don't give me a

---

* The Editor is uncertain in regard to the subject of this Memoir. (See *Appendix* F.)

† 'And hunger runs in couples with display.'

regiment on my return home, I know not what to do; for it is late in life to look out for another trade!'

'*Barrackpore, 30th November.*—C—— was to join his station at Cuddalore on the 1st January next. His health was good, and he appears now to prefer the Madras Presidency to this. Nothing can exceed Sir Frederick Adam's kindness to him. Sir Frederick is now here on a visit to Lord William.'

'*Barrackpore, 2nd February*, 1835.—As I am most anxious that —— should pass at least a year at Potsdam,* I purpose taking him there within a month of my arrival in England, if I can obtain Lord Hill's leave to do so. Will you procure, from Mr. Frere, the necessary information as to the best mode of settling at Potsdam under the care of some old Prussian officer, who is in the habit of taking a limited number of pupils? I consider this finish to his education as of great importance to ——.

'From this date I receive pay. Before not a rupee. I had the honour and labour, but not the profit. I was a hardy volunteer in the ranks of his Lordship, whom I have known for twenty-seven years. I was employed by him in the year 1808, in his negotiations with the Spanish Government at Aranjuez. I served under his orders on the eastern coast of Spain, and now in India. By the enclosed letter and statement, which both his Lordship and Sir Frederick Adam have seen and approved, you will perceive that I ask my good friend Sir Edward Paget, to arrange a meeting between me and Colonel Napier. It is a military business altogether, and I feel satisfied Sir Edward will not refuse my request.† Pray send the letter and statement to him *immediately*, and tell him that I will, with his permission, go direct to his home from the place of my landing in England, and from

* In numberless letters he had repeated this determination, so high was his opinion of the Prussian military system. He did not, however, go to Berlin himself.

† In this he was mistaken; nor can anyone blame Sir Edward Paget.

thence to the meeting, wherever it may be appointed to take place.

'I return to England in the "*Curaçoa*," with Lord William Bentinck. We shall sail at the latest by the middle of March, and only touch at the Cape, so that, it is thought, we shall be at home very early in July.'

To judge fairly on points of honour thirty or forty years ago, the reader must remember facts then considered natural, which if they occurred now would excite mingled ridicule and indignation. A few years before Sir Samford returned to England, the Duke of Wellington had, *when Premier of England*, challenged and fought with the Earl of Winchelsea, on account of a hasty and not very insulting remark on the part of the latter peer. And Sir Robert Peel had frequently displayed his eager readiness to resort to the arbitration of a pistol-shot. In this case both Lord William Bentinck and Sir Frederick Adam had approved of the determination taken by Sir Samford Whittingham—a fact which should be remembered in forming an opinion on the matter:—

Sir Samford Whittingham to Sir Edward Paget.

'CALCUTTA, 7th *February,* 1835.

'My dear General,—I avail myself of the friendship with which you have so long honoured me, to request you will have the goodness to arrange a meeting between me and Colonel Napier, and accompany me to the ground.

'The enclosed statement, which I will thank you to deliver to the Colonel, after the meeting shall have taken place, will explain the cause of this appeal, and the object I have in view.

'It is not my intention to return the Colonel's fire, and if I fall I request that no proceedings may take place against Colonel Napier. The affair is exclusively my own seeking, and neither blame nor responsibility should attach to him.

This circumstance* could alone justify my application to you in your position as a father and a husband. I feel confident you will not refuse an old friend the only favour he ever asked at your hands. I am anxious the meeting should take place with the least possible delay.

'Ever, my dear General, most sincerely yours,
'SAMFORD WHITTINGHAM.'

'General The Hon. Sir Edward Paget, G.C.B.,
'&c. &c. &c.'

The '*Curaçoa*' must have sailed in February, probably soon after the above letter was written, for it arrived in England in the early part of July, and a voyage was rarely less than five months at that period.

He thus returned to England, after an absence in India of nearly thirteen years, passed in continuous hard labour —mental and bodily—in the service of his King and country, under the orders of six successive Commanders-in-chief, all of whom he had served to his own credit, and to their complete satisfaction. His popularity with his subordinates, in spite of his great professional strictness, was a matter of general notoriety; and, as the late Lord Cowley said of him at his departure from Spain, it might have been said in regard to India: 'He leaves this country with the testimony of all ranks in his favour.' The completion of Lord Cowley's remarks as to the absence of rewards for his 'valuable services' would equally have applied to his long services in India.

---

* Not returning his adversary's fire; and thus lessening the responsibility of his second.

CHAPTER XXI.

1835—1836.

MR. DAVIS'S LETTER TO SIR E. PAGET—SIR EDWARD DECLINES TO TAKE PART IN A DUEL—SIR RUFANE DONKIN'S DECISIVE CONDUCT APPROVED BY SIR EDWARD PAGET—A DOUBLE BREACH OF FAITH—A QUESTION LEFT TO THE JUDGMENT OF THE READER—INTERVIEWS WITH 'THE DUKE' AND LORD GLENELG—MEN OF NO PARTY APT TO BE NEGLECTED—THE COMPILER OF THE IMMORTAL 'DISPATCHES' CONSULTS SIR SAMFORD—LORD AUCKLAND'S INVITATION—HIS LORDSHIP'S NOTES TO SIR SAMFORD—THE HON. ADMIRAL FLEEMING — LORD ELPHINSTONE — LORD WILLIAM BENTINCK'S DINNER TO LORD AUCKLAND — LORD GEORGE BENTINCK—ROYAL PRESENTATION — THE KING'S QUESTIONS — WILLIAM IV.'S FLATTERING FINALE—SIR H. TAYLOR'S LETTER ON THE DEATH OF SIR WILLIAM KNIGHTON — THE DUKE OF WELLINGTON ON THE SAME SUBJECT — SIR SAMFORD WHITTINGHAM'S REPLY TO HIS GRACE — SIR EDWARD PAGET'S FAREWELL — LORD WILLIAM BENTINCK'S FAREWELL — HIS LORDSHIP'S PHILOSOPHY — CORRESPONDENCE BETWEEN SIR SAMFORD AND LORD PALMERSTON—PORTSMOUTH HOSPITALITIES—EMBARKATION.

Mr. Davis to the Hon. Sir Edward Paget.

[Fenton House] 'HAMPSTEAD HEATH, *8th July,* 1835.

'MY DEAR SIR EDWARD,—The enclosed papers from dear Whittingham reached me this day. I forward them without a moment's delay, as we may now expect his arrival from day to day. Whittingham has mentioned this affair to Lord William Bentinck and to Sir Frederick Adam. They both approve of the mode our friend has taken to vindicate his military character. If you accept the office, the time and place must be determined by your own convenience. Make use of me in any way in which I can be made serviceable. I shall feel deeply until this painful affair is at an end, and I pray God that the result may be favourable.

'Ever, my dear Sir Edward,
'Your affectionate friend,
'R. Hart Davis.'

Sir Edward Paget to Mr. Davis.

'Cowes Castle, 9th *July*, 1835.

'My dear Davis,—I have this morning received your letter, and the inclosures from Whittingham, which caused me the greatest uneasiness. To refuse anything to him or to you, who have been to me such warm and zealous friends, is one of the severest trials I have had in my life. But I have no help for it. My position (which my circumstances will not permit me to abandon) imperatively forbids me to take part in this affair. Whittingham, in his letter to me, most kindly considers my situation as 'a father and a husband;' but he quite overlooks (which I imagine is also your case) the public position in which I stand at the head of the Royal Military College. In fact, I am reduced to the necessity of divulging to you that this consideration compelled me advisedly to decline a similar proposal made to me by Lord C—— S—— some years ago. And I will tell you further, that foreseeing the possibility of the present case arising, I could not satisfy myself without confidentially consulting Sir George Murray on the subject—an old and tried friend and before me Governor of the establishment—who gave it as his fixed and deliberate opinion, that it was impossible for me (consistently with my tenure of the appointment) to engage in such an affair.

'Thus, my dear Davis, you have the fact; which I will not clog with reasonings, which, I have no doubt, will occur both to Whittingham and yourself, the moment the subject is proposed to you. Under these circumstances, I have nothing for it but to return to you the written statement which accompanied Whittingham's letter to me, and to intreat you, when you return it to him, to place this letter in his hands at the same time. Heaven protect him!

'Ever, my dear Davis, yours affectionately,
'E. P.'

Sir Edward Paget to Mr. Davis.

'R. M. COLLEGE, 14th July, 1835.

'My dear Davis,—I have received this morning the duplicate of the letter and statement, which you sent to me on the 8th instant. It has the Portsmouth postmark upon it, and is dated "Calcutta, 7th February." I see in the papers the arrival of the "*Curaçoa*" on Sunday at Portsmouth; but am left in doubt whether the letter came by that ship, or whether Whittingham himself is a passenger in her. This would add perplexity to my sorrow and vexation of spirit, if I did not feel certain that you will be the first to see him on his arrival, and will show him at once how I am circumstanced with respect to the matter he writes to me upon. Pray put me out of doubt on the question of his arrival, by return of post. The kind and considerate letter which I received from you on Sunday has afforded me the only moment of comfort I have had since your letter of the 8th instant reached me at Cowes. Your son will have told you before this reaches you that your nephew has passed his examination, and is placed in the same company with Dundas.

'Ever affectionately yours,
'EDWARD PAGET.'

The reader is aware that Sir Samford did arrive in the '*Curaçoa.*' On learning at Mr. Davis's house, that Sir Edward could not be his second, he appears to have immediately applied to Sir Rufane Donkin, his old Peninsular friend, to whom he had formerly afforded a friendly countenance and support, when virulently attacked by a brave but impatient British admiral, about the Tarragona affair. Sir Rufane took the matter into his own hands, settled it his own way and having obtained the sanction of Mr. Davis—who was naturally inclined (if possible, with honour), for a peaceful solution—he, in a manner, ignored the wishes of his principal altogether.

On the 24th July, Mr. Davis wrote to inform Sir Edward Paget that 'this day the affair between Sir S. W. and Colonel N. has been arranged to the mutual satisfaction of each party.' But this was rather a sanguine view of the matter in regard to his brother-in-law, as the following letter will establish:—

Sir Samford Whittingham to Sir Edward Paget.

(Extract.)

[38] 'CONDUIT STREET, 28th July, 1835.

'My dear General,—I will not apologize for not answering your letter with greater punctuality, because it has not depended upon myself.

'When I placed my statement in the hands of Sir Rufane Donkin, and requested him to arrange a meeting with Colonel Napier, he gave me his opinion without hesitation—that it was too absurd to be thought of, and that he must be allowed to come to an explanation with the Colonel (his particular friend) on the subject. . . . .

'A long correspondence ensued, and the result is that Hart Davis has withdrawn his accusation of unfounded calumny; and that Colonel Napier will state my explanation of the peculiar circumstances under which I was placed at Barrosa, in the third edition of his work on the Peninsular War, now about to appear.

'I have yielded a reluctant consent to this arrangement, because I conceived, and do still conceive, that after what had passed, the explanation would have been more proper, and certainly more in harmony with my feelings, after I should have received the Colonel's fire.

'Once again let me thank you, from the very bottom of my soul, for the deep interest you have taken in my welfare. Your friendship and esteem are the glory and honour and comfort of my life. I know of no earthly advantage against which I would exchange them.

'Most devotedly and affectionately attached,

'SAMFORD WHITTINGHAM.'

Sir Edward Paget to Sir Samford Whittingham.

'R. M. C., 29th *July,* 1835.

'Accept, my dear good friend, my most sincere and cordial thanks for the gratifying letter received from you this morning. In spite of your personal feelings, you must allow me to say that I cannot admire sufficiently the judicious and off-hand course pursued by Sir Rufane Donkin on this occasion. Neither was it possible for Hart Davis to do otherwise under the circumstances of the case than he has done. I will not attempt with pen and ink to talk over this long and interesting history with you; but let me hope that the day is at hand, when I may have the happiness of seeing you under this roof with our dear and excellent friend Hart Davis. Arrange your own time with him, but let it be before the 10th August, as I have engagements after that day for a fortnight, over which I have no control. Lady Harriet most cordially joins in my petition to you both, and I rather fancy there is up at College a certain little A 17* who will not be sorry for such an arrangement.

'E. P.'

---

* Richard Hart Whittingham, youngest son of Sir Samford, was then a college cadet. He did not survive his father two years, but as Adjutant of the 71st Highland Light Infantry, he had already obtained the affection and esteem of his Commanding Officer, Lieut.-Colonel (now General) the Hon. Charles Grey, and of his brother officers to an astonishing degree, as was communicated after his death to the Editor, on the part of the regiment.

There is every reason to believe that neither Sir Edward Paget nor Sir Samford Whittingham were ever made fully acquainted with *the details* of the negotiation which was carried on, almost in spite of Sir Samford, between Sir Rufane Donkin and Sir William Napier, in which the former went so far as to betray the intention of Sir Samford Whittingham not to return the fire of his adversary! Indeed, as Sir Rufane was resolved at all costs to impede the duel, he would naturally, as involving his own breach of confidence, conceal from Sir Samford, those details which under a half transparent veil have been published in the *Life of Sir William Napier*, after the deaths of all concerned. Otherwise the affair could not possibly have ended so peacefully as it did. That Mr. Davis was to withdraw his accusation of unfounded calumny, and that an explanatory note was to appear in future editions about Barrosa, and *that at least partial justice was to be done as regards Talavera*, was it appears all that Sir Samford or Sir Edward Paget were ever told of Sir Rufane Donkin's proceedings; and no direct communications ever took place between Sir William Napier and Sir Samford Whittingham.

It is quite as erroneous therefore, as it is improbable, to suppose that Sir Samford was ever made acquainted with the style and tone of Sir William's conversations with Sir Rufane. Till the publication of the life of the former, the matter appears to have been kept secret between the two officers concerned; and it is to be regretted that it was ever divulged.

But what is certain is that there has been a most lamentable *double breach of faith*. Not only has the explanatory note printed in one edition *since* disappeared for ever; but no attempt it appears was ever made by Sir William Napier to fulfil the other promise made to Sir Rufane Donkin (as recorded in the 'Life of Sir William') to render at least a partial justice to Sir Samford Whittingham in regard to the battle of Talavera. The fact of this breach of promise is not denied by the editor of Sir William Napier's Life, whose defence is that it must have been caused by accidental forgetfulness; and, for the reasons mentioned in the Preface, the Editor of this work would gladly take a charitable view of the question. But all he can do with honour, under existing circumstances, is to leave the matter to the judgment of his readers. Justice and love of fair play are supposed to be precious in the sight of Englishmen, and it is to be hoped that the old Roman saying still holds good in a Christian country, that, 'truth is great and will prevail.'

Before the affair with Napier was settled, Sir Samford applied for an interview with the Duke of Wellington. The following was the reply:—

The Duke of Wellington to Sir Samford Whittingham.

[Apsley House] 'LONDON, 20*th July*, 1835.

'My dear General,—I shall be very happy to see you if you will call here on Wednesday at 12 o'clock.

'Ever yours most faithfully,
'WELLINGTON.'

'General Sir S. Whittingham, K.C.B.,
'No. 38, Conduit Street, Hanover Square.'

What took place on this occasion has never been recorded, at least as far as the Editor is aware. Indeed so little given to boasting was the subject of this Memoir, that his own children would now know very little of his merits, had these not been so liberally done justice to in the writings (lately come to light) of others; and these the great and distinguished amongst men.

Another interview took place the following month, as testified in the following note:—

'COLONIAL OFFICE, 10th August, 1835.

'Lord Glenelg presents his compliments to Sir S. Whittingham, and begs he will favour him with a call here on Wednesday, at 12 o'clock.'

The General was still desirous of employment in the colonies; his pecuniary losses, chiefly from causes over which he had no control, though partly owing to his too great generosity and hospitality, prevented his deriving any permanent advantage from his long service in India.

This interview with Lord Glenelg did not lead to any immediate employment. Mr. Davis was no longer in Parliament, and the great Duke had long since retired from the command of the army. The regiment which the Duke had, in September 1830, assured Mr. Davis should be quickly given to Sir Samford Whittingham, was still withheld, from want of sufficient interest to press the point. Not that his political opinions interfered with his advancement. His friend, Lord William Bentinck, was of the Liberal party, and his Lordship had convinced him— so far as he meddled with politics—that moderate progress and reform was the wisest and safest course in England. But in truth he belonged to no party, and such men are apt to be neglected.

While waiting for employment in London, he carried out his favourite plan of sending his eldest military son to Berlin, his admiration of the Prussians and their system being always very great; and surely recent events have strikingly manifested the prescience of his judgment in this particular case.*

Towards the close of this year Sir Samford must have received the following rather hurried note from the compiler of the 'Wellington Dispatches':—

---

* At this time, excepting an officer attending on the Duke of Cumberland (now Sir Charles Wyke late envoy at Hanover) there was not another British officer in Berlin, so little was the merit of the Prussian system *then* appreciated in Great Britain!

Lieutenant-Colonel Gurwood * to Sir Samford Whittingham.

'PORTSMOUTH, 4th December, 1835.

' My dear General,—I am much obliged to you for the paper enclosed in your letter of the 2nd, the perusal of which was very instructive. I wish I could have had it [in time] to insert [it] in its proper place, in the 4th volume, just published; although not being of the Duke, I should be subjected to criticism. But the memorandum elucidates points not elsewhere defined. Do you wish me to return it? If so I will, when your pleasure on the subject is made known to me. Previous to my visit to Paris in September I waited upon Mr. B. Frere to request he would have the goodness to copy, or have copies [made] of Lord Wellington's letters to him when Chargé d'Affaires at Seville, after Marquis Wellesley's departure. There are thirteen of them, of which I gave him the heads taken from the Duke's Indexes, and they are of December 1809. All the Duke's papers of that month and of the following year were lost in the Tagus; and the only means I have of filling up the vacuum is by applying to those to whom they were written. Mr. Frere had the goodness to tell me that he would search for them. As you are so near a neighbour to him in Savile Row, would you oblige me by presenting my compliments to him, and ascertain[ing] whether he has yet had the opportunity of visiting his papers for those in question? I will also trouble you, as a Spaniard, to tell me how Cazalegas or Casalegos, near the Alberche, is written. In the names of places, I always adhere to Lopez when I am in doubt. Notwithstanding, I find in the hurry and annoyance of correcting the press, the following errors have escaped me, which is the more

---

* Colonel Gurwood was also one of the many officers who had reason to complain of the injustice or inaccuracy of the great military historian. See *United Service Magazine* of February 1868.

stupid in me, as I pledged myself to adhere (in the preface) to the exact spelling of the country:—

> Naval Moral for Navalmoral.
> Fuente Dueñas for Fuentidueña.
> Zarga Mayor for Zarza la Mayor.
> Puente de Arzob for Puente del.
> Brigel for Brujel.
> Casalejos for Cazalegas.
> Albuquerque for Alburquerque.
> Fuente del Mestre for Fuentes del Maestro.

All these I should have put right with more attention to Lopez. Your letter staggered me about Albuquerque; but on referring to three of his own letters to the Duke of Wellington, in 1810, I found it Albu*r*, the correct spelling of the town in which I was quartered in 1808.

'Very sincerely yours,
'J. GURWOOD.'

'Major-General, Sir S. Whittingham, K.C.B.'

On the 24th August, 1835, Sir Samford received an invitation from Lord Auckland, then First Lord of the Admiralty, to dine at the Admiralty the following Wednesday, to meet the Hon. William Osborne,* his Lordship's nephew, and the friend of the General; but temporary indisposition prevented the meeting.

Lord Auckland to Sir Samford Whittingham.
(Private.)
'ADMIRALTY, 27*th August*, 1835.

'My dear Sir,—I was sorry yesterday not to have had the pleasure of your company to dinner, and trust that the cause of your absence will not be of long continuance. If you should be well to-morrow, perhaps you would favour me with a visit between one and two o'clock.

---

* Mr. (now Lord) William Godolphin Osborne was about to re-enter the army as Ensign 26th Cameronians, to become Military Secretary to the Governor-General of India.

Otherwise I would endeavour to find you at home on Sunday.

'I am, most faithfully yours,
'AUCKLAND.'

The Editor was at this time on the Continent, and was ignorant of the cause of these meetings. Probably Lord Auckland was already appointed to the Governor-Generalship of India, or contemplated its acceptance, and was therefore glad to obtain information from so experienced and able an Indian as Sir Samford Whittingham. No copies of the letters of the latter to Lord Auckland are now extant.

From the Same to the Same.
(Private.)

'ADMIRALTY, 5th September, 1835.

'My dear Sir,—I have to thank you for the letter which I have received here this morning, and to express my regret that I did not see you when we interchanged visits on Sunday. But I will give my best attention to the suggestions I have from time to time received here in writing from you, both in regard to persons and to measures; though with the latter I am afraid that considerable hesitation must be felt in any case where they are liable to be attended with great expense.

'Most faithfully yours,
'AUCKLAND.'

It was not till July 1836, that Sir Samford was offered any employment. He then accepted the command of the Forces in the Windward and Leeward Islands, which was now separated from the civil government, and therefore so wretchedly paid, that the mere outfit required would absorb more than the first year's salary. Otherwise the appointment was a flattering one, as it was pointed out that the regiments scattered over the extensive command were many of them in a slack state of discipline, and required an energetic and able commander to remedy the evil. He was moreover to have the local rank of Lieutenant-General, with a military secretary and two aides-de-camp. In thanking Sir Herbert Taylor, who appears to have been instrumental in obtaining the employment, Sir Samford pointed out to him that however gratifying to him the manner of his appointment, it was in a pecuniary point of view very unsatisfactory. Moreover, he took that opportunity of alluding to the long-deferred promised Regiment. But his patience on that matter was still to be further tried, though five years had elapsed since the memorable promise of the great Duke to Mr. Hart Davis.

In 1836 Sir Samford and his son, who had returned from Berlin, passed some days at Sheerness, as the guests of the Hon. Admiral and Mrs. Fleeming, at the Admiral's official residence. There they met for the first time, the Admiral's nephew John, thirteenth Lord Elphinstone, who had just been appointed Governor of Madras, and whom the Admiral's eldest son was one day to succeed for a very brief space as fourteenth lord. Lord Elphinstone was then a tall handsome aristocratic-looking Captain of the Blues, and his selection for so high a post, whilst still so young and inexperienced, created a considerable sensation both in England, and in India.

Before embarking for Barbadoes, a dinner at which Sir Samford and his son were present is worthy of recollection.

It took place on a Friday in the season of 1836, at the Clarendon Hotel,* when Lord William, the ex-Governor-General of India, entertained Lord Auckland, his successor, and about a dozen other gentlemen several of whom had been, or were about to be, Governors.

* The private note of invitation has no date but 'Clarendon Hotel,' and asks Sir S. Whittingham and his son for the following *Friday*.

Lord Elphinstone, and Mr. Mountstuart Elphinstone, and Mr. Cole, brother to Lord Enniskillen, were amongst the gubernatorial guests. Lord George Bentinck, then a handsome young gentleman of sporting celebrity, was also present; but no one then imagined the important position which he would one day hold in the political world. It was a very interesting party, and the kind and unaffected manners of the distinguished host extended its genial influence over all the guests. It is probable that Lord Burghersh (the late Earl of Westmoreland) was present at this dinner, though the Editor does not remember the fact. It is certain that Sir Samford Whittingham met his Talavera friend at Lord William Bentinck's table about this period.

Before leaving England, Sir Samford Whittingham was presented to King William IV. by Lord Glenelg; and he has left in his own handwriting a memorandum of the interview with His Majesty. It does not state the locality, but it was probably at Windsor that it took place. The King was personally unknown to him. In comparison with George IV. it was 'a King that knew not Joseph':—

'On the 5th October, 1836, I was presented to His Majesty by Lord Glenelg, to kiss hands on my appointment to the command of His Majesty's forces in the Leeward and Windward Islands.

'Upon kissing the royal hand, and returning thanks for the honour of the appointment and the rank of Lieutenant-General, the King was pleased to say,

'"Your rank of Lieutenant-General was a necessary consequence of your appointment to the command of the largest body of troops I have in my colonies, except the East Indies. It is, next to the East, the most important command I have to give."

'His Majesty here paused for a short time, and then continued :

'" What events may take place, in the course of a few years, in the West Indies it is impossible to say. But I feel quite sure, that in any and every case, the command of my forces in the Leeward and Windward Islands could not be in better hands than yours."

'The King then asked in what regiment I had commenced my services, I said, "in the 1st Life Guards, and then in the 13th Light Dragoons, in which regiment I was Captain when I sailed with Brigadier Craufurd, as Deputy Assistant Quartermaster-General, for South America. After the failure of the attack on Buenos Ayres I returned to England."

'" I knew you had been in the 13th Light Dragoons," said the King, " though some one said not; and after your return from South America where did you go?"

'" To Spain, Sire, where I was present at the battle of Baylen under General Castaños, and at the battle of Talavera under Sir Arthur Wellesley. From that time I served till the end of the war on the Eastern Coast; having under my command a *corps d'armée* of Spanish troops, composed of ten regiments of infantry, twelve of cavalry, and a considerable train of horse and foot artillery. After the peace, I went to the West Indies as Governor of Dominica."

'" I knew you had been in the West Indies," said His Majesty, "but I did not know in what Island."

'" I remained in the West Indies two years, and then went to the East as Quartermaster-General of the King's troops. On my promotion to the rank of Major-General, I was appointed to the military districts of Cawnpore and Meerut. In the first, I had 24,000 men under my command; in the second, 26,000. After thirteen years' service in India, I returned fifteen months since, to England. Your Majesty has now been graciously pleased to appoint me to the command of your army in the Leeward and Windward Islands, and assuredly no effort on my part shall be wanting to the faithful and effective discharge of the duties of the high post with which your Majesty has been pleased to honour me."

'"I am fully satisfied," said the King, "I could not have made a better choice; and you carry with you my best wishes for your health, happiness, and success."

'"I hope you are satisfied," said Lord Genelg, on our returning from the presence.'——

Of course in so brief an interview Sir Samford had not time to give the King more than an outline of his services, confined to what he could remember on the spur of the moment. He left out indeed the most important of them; his having raised, organized, and led to victory, the Majorca division.

At this period Sir Samford Whittingham lost one of his best and most estimable friends, the late Sir William Knighton, so long the friend and confidant of George IV. The letter which he wrote to Sir Herbert Taylor, announcing the probably approaching end of that amiable and distinguished man is not forthcoming, but the following was the reply:—

Sir Herbert Taylor to Sir Samford Whittingham.

'WINDSOR CASTLE, 9*th* October, 1836.

'My dear Sir Samford,—I feel very grateful to you for your kind attention in writing to me respecting our poor friend Sir William Knighton, and I sincerely lament that your account of his state is so unfavourable, and holds out so little hope of recovery. I shall deeply regret his loss as I love and respect him; and I am greatly indebted to him for many and unceasing acts of kindness and friendship to myself and mine, and of confidence under circumstances which proved his sincerity.

'You have done me a real favour by expressing to this

excellent man my feelings towards him, and my sympathy in his present state of suffering; especially as the close attendance to which I am doomed here and elsewhere deprives me of the facilities of calling personally in Stratford Place to enquire after him. There is, however, no day that I do not receive an account of him. I hope that poor Lady Knighton is able to bear up. I heard that it was not till very recently that she was made aware of poor Sir William's critical state. It is satisfactory to know that he received the sacrament yesterday, which would so much contribute to the ease and comfort of his mind.

'Believe me to be, ever, my dear Sir Samford, most sincerely yours,

'H. TAYLOR.'

'Major-General Sir Samford Whittingham, K.C.B.'

'P.S.—I made the communication which you wished me to make to the King, who received it kindly. His Majesty also entered with kind interest into the situation of our suffering friend.'

Sir Samford Whittingham appears soon afterwards to have transmitted to the Duke of Wellington the news of Sir William Knighton's death, as proved by His Grace's reply :—

The Duke of Wellington to Sir Samford Whittingham.

'WALMER CASTLE, 12th October, 1836.

'My dear General,—I sincerely lament with you the loss of our friend Sir William Knighton.

'I beg you to take an opportunity of presenting my best respects and condolence to his afflicted family.

'I shall have occasion hereafter to communicate with his son upon the late King's affairs. I am not acquainted with him excepting from the report of his poor father; and I entertain a great respect for him.

'Believe me, ever yours most faithfully,
'WELLINGTON.'

'Lieut.-General Sir Samford Whittingham, K.C.B.' *

Sir Samford Whittingham to the Duke of Wellington.

'UNITED SERVICE CLUB, 14*th October*, 1836.

'My Lord Duke,—I took an opportunity this morning of obeying your Grace's orders by presenting your best respects and condolence to the afflicted family of the late Sir William Knighton; and, at the same time, of informing his son, that you would, hereafter, have occasion to communicate with him upon the late King's affairs. He desired me to express to your Grace how much he feels honoured by the flattering mention you are pleased to make of him, and to say that at an early period after the funeral of his poor father, he will be ready to attend your pleasure.

'I have the honour to be, your Grace's most obedient humble servant,

'SAMFORD WHITTINGHAM.'

'His Grace the Duke of Wellington, K.G.,
'&c., &c., &c.'

The following letter alludes to one of the visits which Sir Samford had paid to Sir Edward and Lady Harriet Paget since his return to England, no other records of which now exist. The worry and anxiety which the Napier affair had given to Sir Edward Paget had evidently not cooled his affection for his dear and valued friend, any more than the poverty of his circumstances which made employment, however badly paid, indispensable to him :—

* The Duke in the original wrote 'G.C.B.' by mistake, for Sir Samford did not live long enough to have the K.C.B. converted into G.C.B.

'ROYAL MILITARY COLLEGE, 18*th October*, 1836.

'Many thanks to you, my dear Whittingham, for your letter of the 15th; which somehow or other has only reached me this day. As you *must* go, I will only say that I am glad that "everything is at last settled," and, I ardently hope and pray—in a manner much more suitable to your interests than you gave me any reason to expect when I had the happiness of last seeing you at Sandhurst. When I make use of this word "happiness," I pray you to consider it as exclusively applicable to the sight (perhaps the last) and society of one, whose ardent and unmerited friendship and attachment to me, I never can be sufficiently grateful for. *Au reste* I must acknowledge, that your departure for the West Indies, the inadequacy of the means afforded you to maintain the high position in which you are placed there, the circumstances which led you to accept of this command . . . . have occasioned me a degree of sorrow and distress of mind, which nothing alleviates but the contemplation of the noble and buoyant spirit which enables you so manfully to defy the shafts of adversity. . . . . . . It is most kind of you to think of writing to me from the West Indies. . . . I will ascertain and let you know whether Polchet * has received your cigars. Poor old fellow, he is nearly done. I ought to have written and thanked you a fortnight ago for the beautiful specimen you have sent us, through Grey,† of your military drawing of Hampstead and its neighbourhood. I had no idea till I saw it of your powers in this way. It will be framed and hung up in the office in the good company of some of old Jarry's best performances.

* A professor of the Senior Department, Sandhurst, who had also held a similar situation at High Wycombe, when Sir Samford was there as a pupil.

† Then a subaltern in the 83rd regiment (as was Sir Samford's son), now the well-known Governor, Sir George Grey. He was at this period a student at the senior department of the College.

'God bless you, my dear good friend, and with kindest regards from Lady Harriet, believe me ever
'Most faithfully and affectionately yours,
'Edward Paget.'

Another friend did not conceal his surprise at Sir Samford's acceptance of so wretchedly paid a post, as may be seen by the following letter:—

Lord William Bentinck to Sir Samford Whittingham.

'Welbeck, 22*nd October*, 1836.

'My dear Sir S. Ford,—So you are again about, after so many wanderings and gallant adventurings, to set out upon a new course, which I sincerely trust may obtain for you all the honour and gratification that you can possibly desire. For riches you have shown your contempt, and there are few men who go to the East who possess this noble self-denial. One may regret, though one cannot but admire, this singular quality: and I hope, at any rate, this additional claim, which this new service gives to distinction, may ensure an early appointment to a regiment. I am glad you were well pleased with His Majesty's reception. There cannot be a better hearted man than our gracious Sovereign; and his decided, and above all his equal patronage of the two professions entitle him to the gratitude and respect of every soldier and sailor. . . . . .

'I am sorry to say that Lady William is not so well as she was, and we fear she will be obliged to go to some warmer climate, and we think of Tours. It is not far removed either from Paris or from England; and it must be equally dry with Paris if not warmer; with less temptations to exposure and fatigue. In the early spring we may yet make a march upon Paris. . . . . .

'Yours ever sincerely,
'W. Bentinck.'

One more letter from Lord William, Sir Samford received before sailing for Barbadoes:—

Lord William Bentinck to Sir Samford Whittingham.
(Extract.)

'WELBECK, 6*th November*, 1836.

'My dear Sir S. Ford,—Although in the midst of the hurry of your departure, I must still be allowed to occupy a moment of your time, with my acknowledgments for your most kind and friendly letter. The contents of it have given more pleasure to Lady William than myself, who feels a great deal more for my reputation than I do. I look for no praise and for no public gratitude. The curse of India is that private interest not only predominates over that of the public, but [that] it is exclusively the reigning power. It is a foreign dominion without any control from the voice of the governed. And it is nominally controlled by those in Europe, with whom private interest is as much so as in India, the exclusively reigning power. I have just gone counter to all these sordid and selfish interests, and in this generation, I must have the natural reward, odium, calumny, and ill will. But these principles, like all others of reform founded on reason, moderation and the general good, which I have upheld, must have their triumph in the end. And I am quite satisfied in the meantime with the satisfaction of my own conscience, and the certainty of these results upon the happiness of the Indian Empire. Pardon so much egotism.

. . . . . .

'Ever with great regard,

'W. BENTINCK.'

Sir Samford Whittingham appears to have had some interviews with Lord Palmerston before leaving England, and to have presented him with a copy of his Memoir on Russia and British India. The following is a copy of a letter he subsequently addressed to that popular statesman, then Minister for Foreign Affairs:—

Sir Samford Whittingham to Viscount Palmerston.

'United Service Club, Pall Mall, *7th November*, 1836.

'My Lord,—The accompanying map, which comprises in one sheet the country between Constantinople and the Burmese empire, was published a short time before I left Calcutta. It should have accompanied the Memoir I had the honour of presenting to your Lordship.

'In the sketch of the Russian empire her immense latter acquisitions are brought to notice by being coloured with green.

'Will your Lordship permit me to beg your acceptance of both these maps, of little cost, but of much convenience. I have the honour to be, my Lord,

'Your obedient humble servant,

'Samford Whittingham.'

'The Lord Viscount Palmerston.'

The following was his Lordship's reply:—

Viscount Palmerston to Sir Samford Whittingham.

'Stanhope Street,* *8th November*, 1836.

'My dear Sir,—I beg you to accept my best thanks for the very interesting paper which you left with me the other day, and which I have read with all the attention due to the importance of the subject of which it treats, and to the ability with which it has been drawn up. The local knowledge and the military experience which have been brought to bear upon the matters which you have discussed, render the Memorandum peculiarly valuable. I am also much obliged to you for your per-

---

* Stanhope Street is the address written on the back of the letter, in Sir Samford's hand, but the writing in the note itself is illegible.

mission to keep the two maps which you sent me yesterday.

'My dear Sir, yours faithfully,
'PALMERSTON.'

'Lieut-General Sir S. F. Whittingham, &c., &c., &c.'

Before sailing for Barbadoes contrary winds detained the General and his Staff for many days at an hotel in Portsmouth, where, by his invitation, his son's friend Thomas St. Aubyn of the 83rd † joined the party. The Lieutenant-Governor Sir Thomas MacMahon, and (especially) the Port-Admiral Sir Philip Durham, lightened the tediousness of delay by their hospitalities. At the table of the former the travellers met the second son of *the* Duke, the late Lord Charles Wellesley then quartered with his regiment in the garrison. Captain Considine of the 69th Regiment (formerly of the 52nd Regiment) the Military Secretary to Sir Samford, who was one of the best officers in the army, though amongst the least fortunate in promotion, joined his Chief at Portsmouth, as did Lieutenant Henry B———s, who then commenced his long and fortunate career on the Staff as aide-de-camp.

After embarking in the '*Tulloch Castle*,' towards the close of November, baffling winds occasioned a return of the party to Portsmouth, and it was not till the 22nd December that the wind became fair enough to allow of quitting the harbour.

* Brother of Lady Knollys.

CHAPTER XXII.

1837—1839.

SIR SAMFORD'S SECOND SERVICE IN THE WEST INDIES—SEEDS OF DISSENSION SOWN IN VAIN AT BARBADOES—A PROFITLESS COMMAND—CARES FOR THE HEALTH AND COMFORT OF SOLDIERS — MUTINY OF THE BLACK TROOPS IN TRINIDAD—A ROMAN VIEW OF MILITARY DISCIPLINE—A FRATERNAL DIFFERENCE—'THE BEST INSPECTING GENERAL WE HAVE '—SIR CHARLES PAGET'S FLATTERING LETTER TO SIR SAMFORD—POPULARITY AT THE EXPENSE OF DISCIPLINE DESPISED—APPOINTED COLONEL OF THE 71ST HIGHLAND LIGHT INFANTRY—CONGRATULATIONS OF SIR JOHN MACDONALD THE ADJUTANT-GENERAL — SIR CHARLES PAGET'S 'HEART AND SOUL REMARK' TO HIS BROTHER—AN INVALUABLE INSPECTING GENERAL—SIR DE LACY EVANS—THE HOUGOMONT HERO—DR. ARCHIBALD HAIR'S CONGRATULATIONS—LORD GLENELG'S LETTER—DOCTOR COLERIDGE, BISHOP OF BARBADOES—SIR SAMFORD'S JOY AT THE EMANCIPATION OF THE NEGROES—INSPECTION VISIT TO DOMINICA—SIR SAMFORD'S CAPACITY FOR LABOUR—A FIERY INTERVIEW BETWEEN WELLINGTON AND PICTON—YELLOW FEVER IN ITS LAST STAGE—SATISFACTION OF HOME AUTHORITIES—DEATH OF ADMIRAL SIR CHARLES PAGET—HIS RELATIVES ADVISE SIR SAMFORD TO RESIGN—MR. B. FRERE'S LETTER TO SIR SAMFORD — APPOINTED COMMANDER-IN-CHIEF AT MADRAS — PARTING COMPLIMENTS FROM THE GOVERNOR AND ASSEMBLY—DEPARTURE.

IT was in an exceptionally important command that Sir Samford Whittingham served for the second time in the West Indies; and although on this occasion his post was nominally only a military one, he was really also much employed by Government in matters of a civil nature. Moreover, according to the best authority, the then large garrison of the Windward and Leeward Islands was generally in rather slack order, and required a firm and able hand to restore due discipline and military efficiency. In some of the stations the military Commander was also *ex officio* the civil ruler, and if found unfit in the latter capacity (in the eyes of the Governor-General at Barbadoes, or of the Secretary of State for the Colonies, at home), the only remedy was to remove him from his military command, which gave rise to unpleasant complications in one instance, accompanied by a most harassing and voluminous correspondence.

Again, the Governor-General at Barbadoes was a general officer, acting solely in his civil capacity, and as such superior in authority to his senior military officer, the Commander of the Forces. In such a situation (to which a truly wise and prudent Administration should never expose any person), a high sense of duty, great temper, and a certain modest abnegation of self, became indispensably necessary, on the part of the military commander, to the successful management of business. The only rational course would have been, to have had one instead of two generals, and to have united the civil and military administration in his hands; or, if that was undesirable, to have appointed a civilian Governor, to act with a military commander. But the exigencies of patronage too often set at defiance all the dictates of reason and experience; and in this particular case, the exceptional character of the Commander of the troops saved the British Government from reaping that discord which it had inadvertently done its best to sow. Lieutenant-General Sir Samford Whittingham and Major-General Sir Evan Murray Macgregor were excellent friends both publicly and privately during the whole period in which they acted together; nor did the former ever make the slightest difficulty in marching past and saluting his junior officer on the Royal birthday with all the respect due to the representative of his Sovereign.

In preparing the West Indian negroes for emancipation, the Colonial Secretary of State and the Secretary-at-War (as he was then styled) gave plenty of occupation to the military as well as to the civil commander. In 1837 the prospect was that in 1838 domestic apprenticeship was 'to cease altogether, and in the year 1840 the field labourers were to participate in the same advantages, and the whole population to become free.'* But eventually the Island Assembly decreed the total emancipation on the 1st August, 1838.

Meantime, Sir Samford's private affairs were in a bad way; and remembering the great Duke's speech to Mr. Davis in 1830, few readers will wonder if some despondency had at last possessed the mind of one of the most sanguine of mortals:—

To his Brother-in-law.

'BARBADOES, 12*th April*, 1837.

'As to the Regiment, I really have lost all hope. And were I not surrounded by those I so much love, and who look to me for aid, assistance, and support, I should give up the service altogether; for a Commander of the Forces on 2000*l*. per annum cuts, I am sorry to say, a deplorable figure. In a former letter to Hart I have entered into minute details on financial matters, and have pointed out the hardship of imposing poverty, in addition to a bad climate, on the few remaining years of an old soldier's life. And, having said my say, I shall not again refer to the subject; but, on the contrary, repeat what I have so often said, that we are as happy a quartet as ever yet met together; and whilst we all do our duty to the very best of our power, we shall continue, under God's blessing, to sit at ease, and hope for better times. For myself there is no merit in all this. I am never so happy as when living amongst soldiers, and doing everything in my power to mitigate the sufferings and evils to which they are of necessity exposed. They now get, five days in the week, fresh provisions;

---

* Letter to Mr. Davis, dated 'Barbadoes, 23rd February, 1837.'

and I am doing everything in my power to exempt the European soldier from those distant night duties which have proved so very detrimental to his health. If the suggestions contained in the letters I have sent to Hart * be attended to, I have no doubt of making the troops of this command a model of good discipline, whilst the mortality will be, *under God's blessing*, reduced to one-half!'———

On the 21st May, he recapitulates to Mr. Davis the advantages which he hopes to gain for soldiers and their families in the West Indies. 'The men, women, and children will have fresh provisions instead of salt; distant night-duties will be done by black troops instead of white; the white troops will be removed from the most unhealthy islands. The garrison of Barbadoes will be the reserve of this army, and a real school of instruction. All this and more I hope to see realized before I again embark for old England. Do not think that I am building castles in the air. To the best of my power and ability, I do my duty in that station of life unto which it has pleased God to call me; and my ambition is "to live and die in the saddle," in conformity to my duty to my country and to my children.'†

In another letter he tells the same correspondent that, even with the greatest economy, he could not hope in five years to save enough in this command to repay the cost of his outfit! Assuredly he was not one of the Sovereign's hard bargains.

His Military Secretary, Captain Considine, an excellent and highly esteemed officer, was now obliged from illness to return on sick leave to England, from whence he kept up a copious and interesting correspondence with his Chief in Barbadoes.

* He had sent to his nephew a copy of the suggestions he had sent to the official authorities.
† This wish was granted, but sooner than the asker intended.

This year was marked by a mutiny of the black troops in Trinidad, very easily put down by a company of the 89th Regiment, but necessitating a court-martial, which condemned three men to be shot and a few others to be transported.

In a letter dated 'Unionville, 30th July,' he reverts to the standing grievance in these words: 'The mystery of the Regiment I cannot solve! I suppose they think I can live upon sweet words.'

His high sense of duty when the Military Secretaryship vacated was exhibited in an almost old Roman manner. His son and aide-de-camp had for change of air and scene volunteered to be a member of the General Court-Martial at Trinidad, appointed to try the mutineers, and was therefore absent when Captain Considine left on sick leave. An aide-de-camp's duties are whatever the General chooses to employ him upon. Having had from long absence actually to make the acquaintance of his son, on return to Europe, almost as a stranger, a mutual shyness at first subsisted. Finding that he was not consulted on business, and considered as devoted to pleasure, the son resigned himself to his fate, and doubtless somewhat too willingly, youth being fond of pleasure. The General, therefore, in the absence of him he deemed an idler, appointed his other aide-de-camp, a most excellent and exemplary officer, to the vacant Secretaryship, as he was most fully justified in doing. The only rebuke, which the Editor believes Sir Samford ever gave to his beloved brother-in-law, was for his interference in this matter. Mr. Davis and his clever eldest son regarded these matters as nearly everyone does; that if an advantage is available, a son should have the preference, if not unfitted for the situation. And as they had brought up their young relative, they thought that they might express their opinions in his favour. And this Mr. Davis evidently did, although the letter is lost.

The following was Sir Samford's reply :—

To his Brother-in-law.

'BARBADOES, 21st *October*, 1837.

' I grieve that you should have entered into a question purely military, and the discussion upon which must be *exclusively* left to the judgment of every general officer commanding, for upon him the whole responsibility of everything connected with his command must rest. No private considerations, however strong or closely connected, must even for a moment be put in competition with his views of what his duty exacts. This has been my creed through life, and as a public servant I have never deviated from it.' [He then describes how he was obliged at once to name some one present, and named his senior aide-de-camp, who most generously desired it should be only 'till further orders,' and continues]: 'It was Considine's opinion that ―— would not accept, because he would subject himself to the extreme drudgery of an office the most difficult and most laborious in the army, and particularly as he had never from his first arrival at Barbadoes taken the smallest interest in any military concern whatever. However, I am happy to say he appears to have now made up his mind to dedicate himself entirely to the execution of his manifold duties.' [He then notifies his intention of appointing his son Acting Military Secretary from the 1st of the next month, and adds] : 'If ―— chooses to give up his whole time and exclusive attention to his military duties, he will ever find me most anxious to promote his welfare; but as a general officer in command, I must act according to my views of the good of the service.'——

On the 1st December, 1837, he writes, ' ―— is working hard, and constant in his attendance at the office,' and so the General and father was satisfied. Owing to the number of islands and dependencies, and also because so many of the commanding officers were also Governors, the Military Secretaryship required not only a good man of business, but one of sound judgment, and the Chief was therefore justified in requiring other qualities than relationship to himself as a recommendation for the appointment.

Before this time Sir Samford must have received a letter from Captain Considine, dated '26, Duke Street, St. James's, 22nd October, 1837,' containing amongst other things the account of a long conversation which he had just had with Sir John Macdonald, the Adjutant-General, ' who pronounced the highest *eulogiums on you*, for ability, tact, prudence; and wound up by declaring emphatically, " *Whittingham is the best inspecting General we have. His Reports, all are excellent.* We are much pleased with him, and pray *tell him so from me.*"

' He then got into good humour, praised your letters, so good, so well put together, called you " a clever fellow," and said a number of kind things, " it was *a shame* you had not a Regiment, one you must have very soon." Warmly praised your judgment in settling *so well* " *that fool*,"—as he termed him—Sir ⸺ ⸺'s business, and expressed the highest satisfaction, when I told him on what friendly terms you and Sir Evan Macgregor were. This, he said, would delight Lord Hill, please the Colonial Office, and that you were just the prudent man to get on with these Governors.'

In the same voluminous letter occurs this passage : ' You will be pleased to learn, for Sir John slipped it out, that Cutlar Fergusson is actively employed, arranging for the sanction of Parliament, a plan to pay Judge Advocates well, and employ military men of talent exclusively, having one at every large station. Sir John little knew it was *your plan.* For it appears, from his statement to me, that it is exactly what you recommended.'

Another passage is worthy of extraction: 'You have seen M.-General *George* Napier's appointment to the Cape. I met him yesterday with his son, who was in my company, 52nd [Regiment], and accompanies his father as A. D. C. George Napier is the *quiet* one of the family,—very different from the author of the "Peninsula." He asked me about you, *and spoke handsomely of your character.** He is a fine, generous, nice fellow, minus the right arm, but spare and active. He tells me that they gave him £600 to find his passage, but added he, "they charge me £560 for my commission fees as Governor." However, his income, £5000 a-year, will fully compensate him.'

On the 25th October, Captain Considine mentions his interview with Lord Fitzroy Somerset: 'His Lordship then got on the Trinidad mutiny, and expressed himself gratified at your promptitude in the whole affair.'

Towards the close of 1837, being applied to from Halifax (during the rebellion in Canada), Sir Samford Whittingham took upon himself the responsibility of sending there the 65th Regiment, as a reinforcement. This will be best and most briefly explained by the following demi-official letter to him from the brother of his dearest friend:—

Admiral the Hon. Sir Charles Paget to Sir Samford Whittingham.

'ADMIRALTY HOUSE, BERMUDA, 24*th January*, 1838.

'Dear Sir,—I beg leave to seize the first opportunity to express to your Excellency my humble thanks for

---

* It is pleasant to the Editor to find that even thirty years ago one Napier at least did justice to Sir Samford.

the admirable decision and promptitude which has been manifested by your Excellency in embarking so immediately the 65th Regiment on board the "*Cornwallis*" for Halifax, where they were most heartily welcomed by Sir Colin Campbell, who was enabled by the arrival of that efficient corps, to detach his only remaining regiment, the 34th, to Lower Canada.

'Your Excellency will be further pleased to know that you have thus anticipated the intentions of Her Majesty's Government; since I find orders have been sent from England to forward the 65th from the West Indies to the station where it has already arrived.

'By the last accounts I have received from Sir Colin Campbell, there is every reason to hope that rebellion has received such prompt and signal defeat as to make it reasonable to believe that no further effort will be made to disturb the peace and subordination of those provinces. I have the honour to remain,

'Your Excellency's most faithful servant,
'CHARLES PAGET.'

'His Excellency Lieut.-General
  'Sir S. Whittingham, K.C.B.,
    '&c., &c., &c.'

Exceedingly popular with all good officers, Sir Samford Whittingham was nevertheless a terror to the inefficient and undeserving, in spite of the habitual extreme gentleness of his manner of proceeding. He had sometimes to displace officers from their governments or commands, and sometimes to report them for unfitness for their duty. He was averse to that system where there is one law for the officer, and another for the non-commissioned officer and soldier. He was not afraid (as many Generals are) to do his duty, and the authorities in our easy-going system sometimes considered him too severe to effete and inefficient commanders. He scorned to gain popularity at the expense of discipline and efficiency. Neither, however, did he go to the other extremity, which has been witnessed, that of courting the men by publicly telling them that their insubordination was the fault of their officers. It was this conscientious performance of his duty and distribution of equal justice, that justified the praise given to him by the Adjutant-General of the army, speaking of course the sentiments also of Lord Hill. All the voluminous documents concerning his command in the West Indies would, if investigated, bear out this judgment. Indeed his merits were never denied. It may be truly said of him, that few men ever got more praise, or less rewards.

The Regiment came at last, late though it was. He was appointed Colonel of that regiment, at the head of one of the battalions of which (having two battalions in the Peninsular war) his early friend the gallant Henry Cadogan had fallen at Vittoria; thus losing, in the service of his country, the earldom that awaited him.

Captain Considine to Sir Samford Whittingham.

(Extract.)

'CARGREEN, CORNWALL, 1st *April*, 1838.

' Nothing which has occurred for many years has afforded me more pleasure, than seeing in the ' Gazette' of the 30th March, your appointment to the colonelcy of the 71st [Highland] Light Infantry. I do most sincerely felicitate you on the occasion, as Lord Hill could hardly have selected a finer regiment to place you at the head of. The longed for event has been a tardy boon; but you have every reason to be satisfied with the 71st! Charles Grey,[*] its Lieutenant-Colonel, is an excellent promising young chief of battalion, and he already knows your predilection for light troops from my correspondence with him, and will, I am persuaded, be glad

---

[*] A younger son of Earl Grey, the Premier of the Reform Bill, now Major-General, and well-known member of the Royal Household: also the Editor of " *The Early Days of the Prince Consort.*"

to see your name on the top of the list of the 71st. They embark on the 12th.'

From Sir John Macdonald, Adjutant-General.

'Horse-Guards, 2nd April, 1838.

'My dear Whittingham,—Pray accept my heartiest congratulations upon your appointment to the Colonelcy of the 71st, one of the finest regiments in the army; an appointment which cannot fail to be gratifying to you in the extreme, and which has given me the sincerest pleasure. I am happy to be able to assure you, that all your measures, in your high and responsible situation, have hitherto given Lord Hill the utmost satisfaction, and I can say, as head of this department, that all your intercourse with it is most creditable to you, and highly beneficial to the interests of the public service.

'Your regiment is in splendid order, and all but on the beach for Canada. Your Lieutenant-Colonel (Grey)* is a clever capable young fellow, that has been bred in the best schools (the 60th and 43rd) and thoroughly understands his business. Always my dear Whittingham,
'Most faithfully yours,
'John Macdonald.'

The Hon. Sir Edward Paget to Sir Samford Whittingham.

'Royal Hospital, Chelsea,† 31st March, 1838.

'My dear Whittingham,—I now, thank God, can write and thank you for your letter of the 19th January, with a light heart. Yesterday's Gazette announced your appointment to the Colonelcy of the 71st Regiment; and I verily believe I do not deceive myself in thinking that the event will not be more joyous to you than it is to me. You have too long waited for it: but it

---

* General Grey is now *Colonel* of the same regiment himself.

† Sir Edward had left the Military College, and been appointed Governor of the Royal Hospital, Chelsea.

has come at last, and may you long live to enjoy the honour, and its emoluments. It is no trifling gratification to me moreover to learn, that your services in the West Indies are duly appreciated at the Horse-Guards. I promise you that your zeal and ready acquiescence in the appeal made to you by my brother Charles for aid to Canada, are estimated by him as they deserved to be, and drew from him the heart and soul remark, " Would that I could always find a Whittingham in my hour of need." We talked you well over before he left this country, and I shall rejoice to hear that you have met; for I am greatly mistaken if you do not find him a fellow quite to your taste.

'Most affectionately yours,
'EDWARD PAGET.'

Captain Considine to Sir Samford Whittingham.
(Extract.)

'ARMY AND NAVY CLUB, ST. JAMES'S SQUARE,
'11*th April*, 1838.

[After describing some conversations with the influential Dr. Hair]—'I next saw Sir John Macdonald. He was very kind indeed. He always has a very long chat with me; and in the present case said: "My friend Sir Samford gives me great satisfaction. He is an invaluable *Inspecting General*. We have none like him anywhere employed. Here are some of our distinguished men, such as Sir J. Colborne, Sir Lionel Smith, and the late poor Ponsonby! from whom we never could get more extended information in the way of answers to our queries in the Confidential Reports, than *yes! no!* to the end of the chapter."

'I have seen Sir De Lacy Evans, and dined with him.* He asked a good deal about you, and told the story Sir Loftus Otway had before mentioned to me,

---

* Captain Considine had been Military Secretary to Sir De Lacy, in Spain.

relative to your having had the power to have made [King] Ferdinand, on his return after the war, swear to the Constitution, and I explained that it was a mistake .... Many other points I dwelt on, which appeared to set his mind right about you, and he in conclusion expressed himself complimentarily about you.

'I met at the Horse-Guards Sir James Macdonnel (the Hougomont hero), who is on the eve of starting for Canada in the "*Edinburgh*" (74), to command the Brigade of Guards. Sir James asked me many questions about you and your inspections of the troops. He made me describe your person, &c. He is himself a rigid inspector and drill man.

'Whilst writing Hair has appeared at my side. He reiterates his promise of writing to you by the packet: but the little man is so occupied with the Duke of Richmond and Lord Hill, that I know not how to depend on his promise.'——

'The little man,' the friend of Lord Hill, and of the late popular Duke and Duchess of Richmond, did keep his promise of writing to Sir Samford Whittingham better than Captain Considine expected:—

Doctor Archibald Hair to Sir Samford Whittingham.
(Extract.)
'HYDE PARK BARRACKS, LONDON, 16*th April*, 1838.

'Dear Sir Samford,—I know not how to tell you how much pleasure I feel in being able, *at last*, to offer you my most sincere congratulations on your appointment to a Regiment. I am more pleased and delighted than I can tell you, although I am well aware no General in the service merits it more than you do. The *Regiment* itself must, I am sure, be very satisfactory to you. There are few better in the service; and it is, I understand from various quarters, in first-rate order, and is commanded by an old friend of Considine's and mine, Charlie Grey, than whom there is not a better officer in the service.

'Believe me, my dear Sir Samford, none of your friends rejoice more than I do at your appointment to the 71st Highland Light Infantry.

'Canada and the Coronation are the chief topics of conversation at present. There must be a brevet, I should think, but as yet little or nothing is known on the subject. With a thousand best wishes for your welfare in every respect, believe me to be, with the greatest respect and esteem, dear Sir Samford,

'Yours most faithfully and sincerely,
'ARCHIBALD HAIR.'

The Minister for War and the Colonies also was pleased to express his satisfaction on this occasion, to Sir Samford's nephew,—in a manner implying that his own recommendation of the appointment had not been wanting :—

Lord Glenelg to Mr. Harford.

'LONDON, 30th March, 1838.

'My dear Harford,—I am delighted to tell you that Whittingham is to have the 71st Regiment.

'Yours ever truly,
'GLENELG.'

'J. S. Harford, Esq.'*

To resume the fraternal correspondence :—

'*Barbadoes*, 9*th May*, 1838.—It would be impossible to express half my grateful feelings to Her Majesty for her gracious favour in appointing me to the 71st Regiment; a regiment second to none in the whole army, and for which there were so many pretenders. The strongest feeling in my mind is the deepest humility, proceed-

* Author of the 'Recollections of Wilberforce.'

ing from the magnitude of the mercies I am daily experiencing, and the complete conviction of my own unworthiness.

'It is most grateful to me to learn that the publication of that paper on India has done me no harm with the Directors.* It was not my fault; but that in public affairs is a poor excuse. India is the land of ambition; but Madras is the spot my heart is set upon. For there I have two sons, who would derive great advantage from my presence; at the same time that the large force under my command would enable me to render the State good service.'

'*Unconville*, 22*nd May.*—I never recollect being so absorbed in business as in the last few weeks. Nor is it to be wondered at when we recollect that this is the year '38, and that the complete emancipation on the first of August next, though adopted here and in many other colonies, is still rejected in others; where, in consequence, a bad feeling may arise, and produce mischief. But the blessed work of emancipation will assuredly find favour in the sight of our Lord; and success will attend those efforts which are *constantly* and *firmly* directed to the extension of Christianity.

'We dine with the Bishop to-morrow; and I shall have a long talk with Mrs. Coleridge and his Lordship on the subject of schools. I have received Sir William Knighton's Life, but have not a moment to spare as yet.'

'*Barbadoes*, 26*th June.*—I should not like to quit this command before the spring of '42, when I trust all Lord Glenelg's just and honourable plans will be consolidated, and placed on such a footing, as to give his Lordship no further trouble. The emancipation of the blacks on

---

* The Editor cannot explain this affair. The publication, whatever it was, took place evidently without the authority of its author, as might readily be believed.

the 1st of August next will be carried into effect, I have no doubt, throughout this command; and Jamaica has already set the brilliant example! How would Mr. Wilberforce rejoice, how would he bless the name of that Colonial Minister, under whose able guidance the great, the blessed work of freedom to the poor negro has been effected, could he witness the realization of the hopes he had from the commencement of his career so fondly cherished. I cannot tell you how my soul rejoices to see the noble work so nearly completed. You, who know me better than I know myself, will enter into all my feelings of joy, at having been permitted to be an humble instrument in the completion of the great and good work!'

On the 21st of June he writes to Lady William Bentinck that he had at last succeeded in procuring for her a small collection of humming birds, and expected a larger supply from Jamaica.

It has been shown that when he considered his son as idle and fond of pleasure, he had delayed appointing him to act as Military Secretary in the absence of Captain Considine. Perhaps that trial was useful; or, possibly, in spite of his old Roman theories, his paternal feelings got the better of the General. At all events he at this time writes of the new acting secretary, '—— is become one of the best and steadiest men of business I am acquainted with. He never neglects, delays, or misunderstands any business I put into his hands. But his health has suffered from excess of occupation in this trying climate, and he will return to England for six or eight months, as soon as Considine and B——s arrive. I shall go to Antigua, St. Kitts, Nevis, &c., previous to their arrival; then return to Barbadoes, take them up, and proceed to Berbice.'

Of the official visits of Sir Samford Whittingham to the

various islands in his command, it will here only be observed that about the end of February 1838 he had paid his first inspection visit to Dominica, where he was well received, and found that the memory of his former popularity as Governor there was, after the lapse of sixteen years, still green and fresh on the island.

On the 26th October, 1838, he announces to Mr. Davis that his acting Military Secretary is going on sick leave, his Military Secretary and other Aide-de-Camp being about to return from their leaves; the Commander of the Forces himself alone obtaining no change or relaxation, though also needing it greatly.

In this letter he observes of the Military Secretaryship:—

'This command is so extended and the duties so complicated; cases are so continually occurring which require a clear judgment, the quantity of business is so very great, the correspondence so enormous, that I don't think a better school could be found in the whole British army; and —— has now conducted this important department for twelve months!'

At this time the civil as well as military correspondence was very great; the Colonial Office, and that of the Secretary-at-War, having called upon the General for a variety of reports relating to the negroes, and to their future emancipation and conduct, such as are not usually addressed to a military commander. The collection of this information from many islands was an arduous task. Moreover, Sir Samford was not the man to do a thing in a perfunctory manner, just enough to escape censure; but whatever he undertook was thoroughly done, making work enough for himself and his Staff. He however invariably took the lion's share, even of the details, his capacity for mental labour having ever been perfectly astonishing.

That portion of his general Staff, which he appointed himself, in the lower grades of the Adjutant-General's and Quartermaster-General's department, were invariably able and zealous officers, whatever might be the case with those appointed from home. Captain Martin—of a family of almost hereditary admirals, Captain Trollope, now Major-General, and Captain King, now Colonel, were most useful, excellent, and laborious assistants, as was Lieutenant, now Major-General, O'Halloran.

The head of the Adjutant-General's department was an amiable and willing man, and that of the Quartermaster-General's department, if not great at pen and ink, was a Peninsular hero, and a very popular Amphitryon, from whom the General acquired a first-rate receipt for turtle soup, and whose dinners rivalled those of his Chief. He had been the principal aide-de-camp of Sir Thomas Picton in the war, and the manager of his household. He had a fund of amusing anecdotes, which he was fond of relating at the social board. There was one of a fiery and hasty interview between Wellington and Picton, as they stood on a high hillock apart from their Staff, who could hear their loud voices without distinguishing the words; though they were evidently angry. And the narrator greatly amused his listeners by imitating the gradually increasing loudness of the speakers, up to the parting climax and hurried separation.

He also told how on one occasion he had gone on ahead, and had ordered a dinner to be prepared for his General and Staff at the house of a Spaniard. When they had all sat down a few minutes, Sir Thomas became quite indignant to find that he was taken little notice of; and that all the attentions of the master of the house and of his servants were bestowed on the aide-de-camp; whom it turned out, from his handsome and portly appearance and cocked hat, had been mistaken for the General.

In the early part of October 1838, the General's

English valet named Prior, died of yellow fever. After a few hours' illness, the acting Military Secretary was called up at two in the morning to see him nearly expiring in the convulsions of the black vomit, and he died in the course of the day. The Secretary then took fever, though not of the same fatal kind; but his life was saved by taking the prescription of a coloured woman—a kind of herb tea—which acted, when the medicines of the regular practitioners had wholly failed.

Sir Samford Whittingham to his Niece, Miss Davis.
(Extract.)

'BARBADOES, 15th *October*, 1838.

'What a week of suffering and of sorrow this has been. In the midst of poor Prior's fatal illness, —— was seized with fever, and for two days he remained in a very precarious state. He is, however, thanks be to the God of mercy, at present out of danger, and I trust will soon be convalescent. But it is the opinion of all the medical advisers that European air is quite requisite. He will therefore sail from hence for Falmouth, on Nov. 11th, at latest.

'No sooner had —— fallen ill than Captain King,* my right-hand man in the Adjutant-General's department, was also seized with a most serious attack of fever.

'In the midst of all these grievous afflictions I am truly thankful to God that my own health is quite restored, and that I feel equal to all the duties which must now devolve on me.'

'18*th October*. —— is now considered out of danger, and King is doing very well; and the uncle is still permitted to flourish like an old oak, and to resist the trials under which so many have fallen. ——'s infinite applica-

---

* Now Colonel King, son of General The Hon. Sir Henry King, and nephew to the Earl of Kingston and to Viscount Lorton. An excellent officer; one of the many whose fortune has been below their merits.

tion and incessant labours have in great measure brought on his illness—a clearer or a sounder judgment upon every difficult question submitted to him (and in this extended command they are innumerable) I never saw. As a real man of business —— is invaluable.'

From the Same to the Same.
(Extract.)
'BARBADOES, *4th November*, 1838.

' Yesterday evening, at six o'clock, —— embarked for England. King came back to me at eight o'clock, having seen him on board, and reported all well. For the first time since the commencement of my military career I find myself an insulated and lonely being! But a due humility leads me to the conviction that I have infinite cause for gratitude to the Almighty, and that to repine at any part of a lot so favoured as mine is a crime.

' I feel that our communion in this world can be but of short duration; for my life must be dedicated to the performance of those duties which it is not permitted to neglect. But I am comforted by the blessed hope that we shall meet hereafter.'——

The return of Captain Considine, his able and excellent Military Secretary, and of his beloved aide-de-camp, B——, from their sick leaves, soon afterwards, cheered the exile; and the arrival of the famous 52nd Regiment at Barbadoes, to join his command, afforded him much pleasure. At the same time he was cheered by a letter dated 'Simla, 17th September,' from his friend Captain (now Lord William) Godolphin Osborne, giving him, as secretary to his uncle, Lord Auckland, the account of Sir John Keane's capture of Ghuznee.

In 1837 Sir Samford had given a gold medal prize to every regiment in his command for the best shot, on condition that the officers would provide silver ones for the best company shots. This was long before Government had instituted any rewards for good shooting.

On the 17th January, 1839, he writes to Mr. Davis: 'All the great people at home express their satisfaction at my mode and manner of carrying on the business of this command. Some years back so much praise from such various and high quarters would have made me love my stirrups, and have puffed me up with vanity. In the present day, thanks be to God, my good fortune only impresses me with a more lively sense of my own unworthiness, and a more humble feeling of gratitude to the Almighty for all the blessings he has conferred on me! The fever has at length left us, and the garrison is now perfectly healthy: but the ravages of the earthquake in many of the islands, and particularly in Guadalupe have been terrible.

'Everything here proceeds smoothly and quietly. My black soldiers are behaving exceedingly well. They mount guard with the white troops, and the oldest non-commissioned officer commands, be his face white or black. My own guard alone is *exclusively* black.* This flatters them, and pleases me; for I have always held that to make men trustworthy, you must begin by trusting them.'

In a letter to Sir Edward Paget, dated 28th February, 1839, Sir Samford thus alludes to the death by fever at Bermuda of Admiral Sir Charles Paget. 'Ere you rereceive this letter you will have heard of the sad loss we have sustained in the death of your excellent brother. In a public as well as a private point of view, deeply and justly is the loss deplored. For the British navy possessed not a brighter ornament, nor could our country boast a more perfect model of the real English gentleman.'

'*Barbadoes*, 2*nd July*, 1839.—Many thanks for your

* To appreciate this confidence, the reader must remember the previous mutiny of the black troops at Trinidad, and the executions which had followed.

conversation with Lord Hill. I am not surprised at his Lordship finding it difficult to supply my place in this command. The duties of it are laborious and difficult from its extent. But Lord Hill has been so uniformly friendly to me, that there is no *personal sacrifice* I would not make to meet his wishes; and nothing but the duty I owe to my children could induce me to oppose them. In the meanwhile my trust is in God; fully satisfied that his wisdom and goodness and mercy will ordain all for the best.'

From the reduction of the troops in the West Indies, and other causes, the military command of which Barbadoes is the head-quarters, has of late years much lessened in importance, and is indeed the command only of a Major-General. But at the period referred to it was considered in a very different light, though always greatly disliked, and not without good reason. There is little doubt that this second service in the West Indies shortened a life, which, from original excellence of constitution, had promised to be long. His letter last quoted to his brother-in-law concludes with these words: 'There is one ambition, however, which still clings to my heart, and gains more and more over me. I would wish to spend six months *at least* in the much loved circle, on my transit from the West to East. It will probably be our last meeting on this side the grave; and I should fervently hope it may be as prolonged as I know it will be warm and affectionate. God love you, my dearest, best, and oldest friend. Ever your attached brother, Samford Whittingham.'

His relatives in England, most anxious about his health, pressed him to resign his present profitless and unhealthy command. They feared, moreover, that whilst he remained there nothing better would be offered him; as the authorities at home were desirous of keeping him in a post where he was so useful, and which most officers of his standing and merit would refuse to accept.

'*Barbadoes, 3rd August.*—I enclose duplicate copy of a letter I have written to Lord Fitzroy on the subject of my return to England, in conformity with your opinion, and that of Hart and ——.'

It must be here observed that the fears of his friends in England had arisen from the nature of Lord Hill's first reply through Lord Fitzroy Somerset to Sir Samford's application for employment in the East Indies, namely:— 'I am directed to state that a memorandum will be made of your wishes, although his Lordship would regret extremely that any circumstance should arise to withdraw you from your present command, the duties of which you discharge to his perfect satisfaction.'

The following letter which he received about this time from his diplomatic connexion in London, was not calculated to lessen his repugnance to remaining longer in the country denounced nearly twenty years previously as a '*pays sans souvenirs et sans espérances:*'—

Mr. Bartle Frere to Sir Samford Whittingham.

'SAVILE ROW, 1*st July*, 1839.

'My dear Whittingham,—I have to thank you for your letter of the 19th April, and its very interesting enclosures, since the receipt of which Vaughan [Davis] has been kind enough to send me a copy of your Memoir of May 1836, which you had requested him to do.

'On reading this paper over again at this time, one cannot but be struck with the prophetic spirit with which it was written. I only wish that you were entrusted with the execution of the measures which you recommend for averting the danger that you so distinctly foresaw and predicted. The Shah's providential failure in the last campaign before Herat has given us a breathing time, upon which we had no right to calculate. Had he succeeded, Russia would probably not have scrupled to throw off the mask, which under present circumstances she does not appear to be prepared to do; and our troops seem advancing without opposition to occupy the important points of the line of operations. But after all, it is to me an appalling consideration, how, with the very limited means which we have at our disposal, we are to be prepared to meet all the exigencies of such a gigantic scale of proceedings.

'—— and I have at length paid our visit to Alava,* who received him very cordially. I think he is looking much better for his visit to Paris, of which, no doubt, he will have given you a full history. I was sorry to hear the melancholy account he gave of Turenne.† I had looked to him as a person who would prove his most useful acquaintance. . . . .

'You will have seen by the "Gazette," that Richard [Frere] has got his Lieutenancy in the 13th. His friends heard of him lately from an officer of his regiment who is returned to England, and who spoke very favourably of him.

'I see there is a Mediterranean mail come in, so I shall leave this open till I take it to Downing Street, for the sake of learning whether it brings me any letter from *Don Patricio*.

'Ever, my dear Whittingham,
'Yours most affectionately,
'B. FRERE.'

The gallant and truly excellent young Richard Frere was destined to an early death, as one of the victims to the hardships of the retreat from Cabool. Don Patricio, that is Colonel Campbell, was now Consul at Cairo: and

* General Don Miguel Alava, then Spanish Ambassador in London.
† According to the testimony of his son (the Marquis de Turenne), the health of Count Turenne, the old (and wine-catering) friend of Sir Samford, had so broken down by this time as to cause him to live in strict retirement.

on the 14th January, 1839, he addressed a long letter to his old Chief, detailing the overland route to India, which Sir Samford—always anticipating an Indian command—at first was inclined to proceed by, though eventually he went by sea. The first sentence, therefore, of the gallant Consul's letter alone is given; and, alas, his affectionate good wishes were not destined to be realized:—

'Another year has commenced for us; and it appears almost a dream to think that thirty years have revolved since our first campaigns in Spain; and on the remembrance of which and of yourself, and of my most happy days, I always dwell with so much pleasure. May every happiness attend you, and may you see many new years.'

At length, in September, 1839, Sir Samford Whittingham was unanimously appointed by the Court of Directors to be Commander-in-Chief of the Madras army; but he was directed to remain in Barbadoes till the arrival of his successor. Now at length he had obtained a high and lucrative command in the British service. His own salary was to be £8,600 a year, with an outfit of £2,000. The Staff-pay of his Military Secretary was more than £1,000 a-year, and if exchanged to a regiment in India, he might draw Indian regimental pay in addition; so that father and son would together draw about £10,000 a-year. Two aides-de-camp were also allowed. Everything looked bright and hopeful. Health and strength only were required for the veteran to finish his career in comfort at least, if not with augmented fame and honours. The only question was, had these rewards come too late? Had that second exile to the West Indies shattered a constitution that promised a longevity equal to that which has been obtained by so many veteran soldiers?

He had still to tarry, awaiting his successor for nearly three months in that detestable climate. Meantime all his spare minutes were devoted to correspondence regard-

ing his future command, and to writing memorandums on Indian politics; civil and military subjects, which probably few men living had more deeply studied. To mention only one of many subjects he was anxious to discuss with Mr. James Cosmo Melvill, of the India House:
'*Firstly.* The last Burmese War cost upwards of ten millions sterling, principally caused by imperfect arrangements as to means of transport, and to the consequent duration of the war.

'*Secondly.* A struggle thus protracted with an enemy so inferior to us is always injurious to that opinion of our irresistible superiority which forms the basis of our power in India.

'*Thirdly.* Under existing circumstances, it is of vital importance that a war with Ava should be finished in one campaign.'

He then enumerates the faults of the former campaign in detail, such as beginning the campaign in the rainy season; not brigading the Native and English troops in proper proportions together; not securing by armed steamers the command of the Irawaddy; and neglecting to protect the ordnance and commissariat stores.

Want of space forbids any further extracts on this subject. Suffice it to say that his whole energies were now turned towards effectually serving his country in its greatest and most important foreign possession.

Extract from the Speech of the Governor-General of the Windward Islands, Sir Evan Murray Macgregor, Baronet, at the meeting of the Legislature in Barbadoes, on Monday, the 25th October, 1839.

'In former instances you have participated in my acknowledgments of the obligations due by the Colony for the solicitude which the Lieutenant-General has ever evinced in its prosperity. I cordially embrace the last public opportunity of recording my high appreciation of his Excellency's firm, judicious, and most friendly cooperation pending an eventful crisis in these Islands. And I feel assured that you will cheerfully unite with me in congratulating Sir Samford Whittingham on the mark of Royal favour graciously manifested towards his Excellency, in the Lieutenant-General's approaching transfer to an important command in the Asiatic dominions of the Crown.'

The House of Assembly presented the General an address, signed by their Speaker, Mr. R. Bowcher Clarke, in which they state that they 'cannot suffer your Excellency to leave the shores of Barbadoes without giving expression to the deep sense they entertain of your services to this Colony, during a period unparalleled in its history for difficulty and importance, and their gratitude for the lively interest which your Excellency has, on all occasions, evinced in the welfare and prosperity of the Island. And while they cannot but regret your Excellency's approaching departure, they beg leave to tender their cordial congratulations on the fresh proofs you have received of the favour and approbation of your Sovereign, and their best wishes for your health and happiness.'

Sir Samford made a suitable and grateful reply, which it is unnecessary to produce.

To his Brother-in-law.

'BARBADOES, 16th December, 1839.

'I love to hope that General Maister must speedily arrive. I shall not want forty-eight hours after making over the command to him. How I do long to come again amongst you! Could I have returned in the steamer which will bring out the General, what a blessing! But I fear that cannot be, as the "*Firefly*" is destined to this station.'——

He did not, however, sail from Barbadoes till after

Christmas had passed, and the new year had fairly began, and it was not till the 7th February, 1840, that he re-landed in Old England for the last time of his life. During the last year of his stay in Barbadoes, to his own satisfaction and especially to that of his returned Military Secretary, Captain Considine, the gallant 52nd, one of the crack regiments of the army, served under his immediate command at St. Anne's Barracks, and there fully maintained, (in spite of much suffering from yellow fever),* its excellent and long-established reputation.

He left the Island with Captain Considine and Lieutenant Bates, amidst universal regret and respect, having greatly ameliorated the discipline and the comforts both of the white and black troops, and having obtained the warm thanks and sympathies of the local authorities, and the ungrudging approval of the home authorities at the Horse-Guards, Colonial Office, and War Office, as expressed by Lord Hill, Lord Glenelg, and Lord Howick, now Earl Grey.

* Losing several officers and many men.

CHAPTER XXIII.

1840—1841.

RETURNS TO ENGLAND FOR THE LAST TIME—LAST RECORDED MEETING OF TWO OLD FRIENDS—MOORE AND DICKENS—DUKE OF WELLINGTON'S KIND NOTE—LETTER TO SIR JOHN HOBHOUSE ON CORPORAL PUNISHMENT—WRITES HIS 'RECOLLECTIONS' AT SEA—ARRIVES AT MADRAS DURING LORD ELPHINSTONE'S ABSENCE—LORD ELPHINSTONE'S NATURAL BUT NEEDLESS FEARS—REINFORCEMENT TO CHINA—LETTER FROM LORD BURGHERSH—LETTER TO THE HON. W. G. OSBORNE—SIR CHARLES FELIX SMITH'S EULOGISTIC LETTER—A TRUE PROPHET ON INDIAN AFFAIRS—SIR SAMFORD RECOMMENDS RAPIDITY OF MILITARY MOVEMENTS—A BE-JEWELLED RAJAH—AN UNWORTHY ENGLISHMAN—EVIL EFFECTS OF THE WEST INDIES—SIR HARRY SMITH'S SPONTANEOUS LETTER TO SIR SAMFORD—EVIL RESULTS OF PATERNAL OBSTINACY—LETTER FROM THE BISHOP OF MADRAS—SIR SAMFORD'S LOYALTY TO THE GOVERNMENT—CORRESPONDENCE ABOUT THE 'WELLINGTON DISPATCHES'—SIR SAMFORD'S LETTER TO COLONEL GURWOOD—SIR SAMFORD'S LAST LETTERS—HIS SUDDEN DEATH—LORD FITZROY SOMERSET'S LETTER TO THE EDITOR—THE FUNERAL.

SIR SAMFORD WHITTINGHAM relanded in England on the 7th February, 1840, and immediately reported his arrival from Devonport to the authorities at the Horse-Guards. On the following day he, from the same place, forwarded a copy of his 'Memoir on the means of attack by Russia on British India,' to Sir John Cam Hobhouse then President of the Board of Control; acquainting him that it had formerly merited the approval of Lord William Bentinck, and had been subsequently presented to Lord Palmerston and to Mr. Melvill in 1836.*

* Vide *Appendix* F for a list of such of the manuscript memoirs and other papers and essays on various subjects as have reached the Editor's hands.

At the close of this letter he states: 'I arrived here from Barbadoes in H.M.'s Frigate "*Inconstant*" yesterday, and the probably short time of my stay in England will, I trust, plead my excuse for this early intrusion on your time and attention. On my arrival in London, I shall be most happy to afford any further information you may judge fit. My address will be "Fenton House, Hampstead Heath."'

He had not landed long, when there commenced that rush of applications for appointments to which all high Indian officials were especially subject, before the necessity of passing any examination for Staff employments had put limits to the general desire to obtain them.

How Sir Samford enjoyed his few months in England in the society of his beloved relatives and friends may be readily imagined. It was at the end of February or the beginning of March that the Editor accompanied him to a dinner at the house of his best friend—the excellent Sir Edward Paget, at this time Governor of Chelsea Hospital. Their manners to each other were those of affectionate brothers. Most of the evening the two friends occupied Sir Edward's social double arm-chair shaped like the letter S, where *vis-à-vis* they could carry on their conversation privately, undisturbed by the rest of the company.

There were romantic circumstances attending that dinner calculated to stamp it on the unwritten tablets of the memory, from which it is taken. The lordly heir of a great and illustrious inheritance, separated from his wife, owing to his own vagaries, was invited to Chelsea there to meet his fair young daughter, whom he could only see on such occasions. She was a charming person, and married a few years later, for love, a younger son and her own excellent and handsome first cousin. A few days after this dinner, the Editor heard one gentleman mention to another the death of a certain Duke, by which the member of the House of Commons at the dinner party was transferred to the House of Lords. This fact, aided by the 'Peerage,' has enabled the writer to fix within a few days, the last time at which he saw together the two old friends firmly bound together by the ties of mutual esteem and affection.

Of another interesting dinner, the date has been taken from the Register of the lady who was its fair and accomplished hostess. On Tuesday, the 25th of March, 1840, in Hanover Terrace, Regent's Park, Sir Samford Whittingham, with his newly appointed Military Secretary, and his first aide-de-camp (brother of the hostess), had the pleasure of meeting at the hospitable table of Mr. Thomas Longman, whose parents were also present on the occasion, both Moore and Dickens. The former made himself very agreeable. He had a son in India, unfortunately in the Bombay instead of the Madras Presidency; but he hoped that Sir Samford might in some way or other be of service to him. Dickens, at that time a handsome picturesque-looking young man with flowing hair, was very silent on that occasion as compared with the poet, but no doubt, he *thought a great deal.* The most lively talker at that dinner was Mr. Hayward. In those days it was a great pleasure to hear Moore sing his own songs, as he probably did on that occasion also.

Sir Samford found time one day to go to Greenwich to dine with his old friend, Admiral the Hon. Elphinstone Fleeming, whose son long afterwards for a brief period, enjoyed the ancient family title.

The Duke of Wellington held no office of any kind at this time, and Sir Samford Whittingham had consequently no claim to see him. The Duke was considered, even when Commander-in-Chief, very inaccessible to old Peninsular officers unconnected with the aristocracy, and, indeed, inaccessible generally.* Sir Samford Whitting-

---

* Some years later a noble and distinguished General, who insisted on seeing his Grace at the Horse-Guards one day, in spite of advice from the

ham, owing to almost perpetual exile, had become nearly a stranger to his Grace personally, but as in his last brief stay in England, so now he sought the honour of a personal interview with him whom he ever deemed the most illustrious of Englishmen:—

Sir Samford Whittingham to the Duke of Wellington.

'UNITED SERVICE CLUB, 7*th March*, 1840.

'My Lord Duke,—My departure for Madras to assume the command of the troops of that presidency, being fixed for the 15th of April, I beg leave to submit how highly I should appreciate the honour of being permitted to wait upon your Grace previous to my again quitting England. I leave town for Chatham on Monday next, but shall return on Thursday the 12th instant.

'I have the honour to be, &c.,

'SAMFORD WHITTINGHAM,
'Lieutenant-General.'

'His Grace The Duke of Wellington, K.G.,
&c., &c.'

The Duke of Wellington to Sir Samford Whittingham.

[Apsley House] 'LONDON, 8*th March*, 1840.

'My dear Sir,—I shall be at all times very happy to receive you. Friday is a Parliamentary day, on which I am generally engaged all day. But if you will come here on Saturday the 14th, at twelve at noon, I shall be very happy to receive you.

'Ever yours most faithfully,

'WELLINGTON.'*

'Lieut.-Gen. Sir S. Whittingham, K.C.B.'

Secretary to abstain, had the surprise of hearing through a door not closed, these energetic words: 'What does the d—— old fool want?'

* No record remains of what passed at either of the interviews with the Duke of Wellington in 1835 or 1840. Their occurrence became known to the Editor only by finding his Grace's notes, when Sir Samford's papers reached his hands last year.

The visit to Chatham was to Colonel, afterwards General Sir Charles Pasley, of the Royal Engineers, to which he was accompanied by his son. The visit lasted two or three days, and was passed in investigations and experiments of a scientific military nature, as well as in friendly intercourse.

The Commander-in-Chief, Lord Hill, gave Sir Samford a dinner, at which, amongst other guests, he met the Earl of Cardigan, and all the heads of the Staff of the army. At the usual dinner given by the Chairman and Court of Directors in Leadenhall Street, Sir John Cam Hobhouse, in his wonted grand style, proposed, as President of the Board of Control, the health of Sir Samford Whittingham, to which he responded in his usual easy and unembarrassed manner. His Staff were invited with him; but he alone, of all the guests present, had to appear in uniform. Lord Seymour, now Duke of Somerset, was present, and, the Editor thinks, spoke also on this occasion.

On the 24th February, 1840, Sir Samford had written a long letter to the President of the Board of Control (he wrote to him many letters, for which there is not space even to allude), after 'having perused with great attention the whole of the Indian correspondence relative to the expediency or otherwise of annulling the General Order of Lord William Bentinck, abolishing corporal punishment in the native army of India.'

He declares to Sir John that he had always advocated its abolition, as far as was consistent with discipline, and had greatly diminished its infliction in his late command, with very beneficial results to the service. But he thought it necessary in the field; and at the same time he considered it ill-advised that the Articles of War, or the Act of Parliament, should recognize such distinction. He also thought it invidious and dangerous that in the same command the black troops should be exempt from, and the white troops be subjected to, corporal punishment.

Practically, he was disposed in time of peace to do away with all corporal punishment, except in cases of gross insubordination, accompanied by violence to a superior, such as are in Continental armies visited with death. 'Still,' he adds, 'it will be obvious that it would be highly disadvantageous and injurious to appear to affix by Act of Parliament, or by general regulations, a special penalty on going into active service: a result likely to make taking the field most unpopular with the soldier, and to impress his mind with the feeling that active service was the road to disgrace instead of honour.'

On the 16th April, 1840, Sir Samford Whittingham and his Staff embarked for Madras. Knowing the difficulty of finding in India a horse strong enough to carry a man of his weight and stature, he had requested General Brotherton to purchase for him a first-rate English charger, which was effected at a considerable price, viz. 147*l*. Most unfortunately this very superior acquisition perished on board ship on the 5th May, from inflammation in the bowels. His first aide-de-camp wrote home: 'He is certainly a great loss to Sir Samford, as he fears he will not be able to replace him at Madras.' It is not too much to say that this mishap was in all probability the main cause of his premature decease some seven months later, in the midst of promises of prosperity and success, such as had never before shone so brightly on the whole of his career! The ways of Providence are awfully inscrutable; but those convinced that there is a Providence must feel that all will come right at last under its wise and beneficent rule.

To Sir John Cam Hobhouse.

'AT SEA, 22nd *May*, 1840.
'Lat. 5° 10' North, Long. 20° 17' West.

'Dear Sir,—As you have kindly permitted me to submit to your consideration two Memoirs on the attack and defence of British India, I now beg to call your attention to the enclosed memorandum on the same subject. It is probably the last time I shall trouble you with my comments on this truly interesting topic; as my time and attention on arriving at Madras will, I imagine, be directed to another quarter.

'I have, &c.
'SAMFORD WHITTINGHAM.'

To Sir Willoughby Gordon, Quartermaster-General.

'AT SEA, 16th *June*, 1840.
'Lat. 35° 4' South, Long. 7° 20' West.

'My dear General,—As the busy scene which India at present offers will probably absorb my whole time and attention on my arrival at Madras, I avail myself of the leisure of a sea voyage to offer to you the expression of my sincere gratitude for all your unwearied kindness to me since the commencement of my military career, and at the same time to request your acceptance of two Memoirs, and a Memorandum written by me, on the subject of India as connected with England and Russia.

'Ever, my dear General, gratefully and truly yours,
'SAMFORD WHITTINGHAM.'

The old Quartermaster-General had long ceased to be that channel and dispenser of favours which, as Military Secretary to the Duke of York, he had been in the earlier part of the Peninsular War: the more graceful was the warm and disinterested tribute of gratitude.

It was in the course of this voyage that the General

wrote out the small manuscript that exists of his Peninsular 'Recollections.'

On the 1st August the Commander-in-Chief and his Staff landed at Madras, propelled over the breakers in the way so novel and exciting to strangers, and was received with the usual salutes and honours. Two kind letters awaited him from the absent Governor, then on the Nilgherry Hills. The first was dated 12th July, inviting him either to join his Lordship at once on the hills, or to take possession of Government House at Madras, till he had time to hire his own house, for which there was a fixed annual allowance.

It also stated that the temporary Chief, Major-General Gough,* was at Bangalore with the General Staff of the Army. The two civil members of the Council, Messrs. Lushington and Sullivan, were with the Governor on the hills, a visit to which during summer is so beneficial to mental and bodily health and activity that it is difficult to understand the violent objections constantly made to it by the great officials sitting at home at ease in England. Lord Elphinstone in the same letter mentioned, amongst other matter of business, a plan for converting beautiful and salubrious Outacamund into a military station. Also he had left at Madras an excellent aide-de-camp, Lieutenant Thornhill, to attend and assist Sir Samford, as one experienced in the ways of the country. The letter concludes as follows: 'I do not think of descending into the plains before the middle of October at soonest. I need hardly say that carriages, horses, and everything I have at Madras, are entirely at your disposal. Servants and everything are ready at Government House, and I have only to entreat you to make use of them and to excuse my absence.'

Lord Elphinstone's second letter, dated Outacamund, 20th July, 1840, exhibited a fear, implied rather than

---

* Now Lord Gough.

expressed, that the new Commander-in-Chief might be offended at the absence of his Lordship and Council on his arrival. In spite of his health, he would have come down, 'if I had not some hopes of seeing you here; or, indeed, if I thought that my presence at Madras could be of any use to you, either private or public. Your commissions provide for your assumption of office in both capacities—as Commander-in-Chief and Member of Council—on your landing; and Colonel Steel, the Secretary of Government at Madras, will immediately wait upon you with all the necessary papers, and will explain to you the manner in which business has been done since I left Madras, and the mode in which it is proposed to carry it on, should you prefer to remain there during the remainder of the hot season. I know it is hardly necessary to enter with you into these details; for I am not apprehensive of any misunderstanding between us upon these or any other points. But I am anxious to explain everything to you beforehand, as I fear that there may be some who are interested in giving a contrary interpretation to my conduct, and who, I perceive, have already began in the newspapers to speculate upon the effect which my " want of courtesy," as they term it, may produce upon your mind. Such obvious trash I am really almost ashamed to notice. For not only on personal grounds, but from a conviction that our mutual comfort and happiness—and, I will add, success in our public duties—mainly depends upon the existence of harmony, and of a perfect understanding with each other; you may rest assured that I am most anxious to welcome you, not only with courtesy, but with the most perfect cordiality, and with the strongest desire to renew and cultivate your friendship, and to secure your confidence and support. . . . . If I have dwelt too much on this subject, you must attribute it to my anxiety, both on your account and my own, to *déjouer* a game which has too often been played here, and at the other presidencies.'

The reader, who knows the character of Sir Samford Whittingham better than Lord Elphinstone then did, will easily believe how groundless were his Lordship's apprehensions. Yet these were rationally grounded on precedents, in cases where conscientious performance of duty, and loyal and generous support of authority, were not first principles of action. In a letter dated, 'Government House, 2nd August, 1840,' Sir Samford set his Lordship perfectly at ease, in acknowledging his letters of the 12th and 20th July. The fashionable young Captain of the Blues, whose first appointment was a job, had now ruled some years in Madras, and was daily becoming fitter for his office. He was a man of much tact and common sense, and made a fair average Governor; and later in life, when he again returned to India as Governor of Bombay, he contributed with zeal and energy to the suppression of the mutiny of 1857 by speedily despatching reinforcements from that presidency to the scene of action.

For want of space, Sir Samford's reply to Lord Elphinstone is omitted, except a few sentences, fair samples of the whole letter.

'I should have been much grieved had you come down from the hills to meet me.' (He then states his intention of shortly joining his Lordship on the hills, and expresses the greatest satisfaction at the prospect of the meeting, and adds:)—' A very few days before leaving England I had the very great pleasure of dining with the Admiral [Elphinstone Fleeming] at Greenwich, in company with your uncle Mountstuart Elphinstone, and all the ladies of the family. I shall follow your directions as to the journey to the Nilgherries. I will not enter into further details till we meet; but I am quite certain that our co-operation in every respect will leave neither of us anything to desire.'

He adds great praises of Lieutenant Thornhill, the Governor's aide-de-camp, who truly was a model of a personal Staff Officer, beloved and respected by every one.

As Commanders-in-Chief visited only a few persons of position, and these were mostly on the hills in August, Sir Samford had not much to do in this way; but the Military Secretary and the two aides-de-camp were duly taken on a visiting tour of Madras society. The hot dry wind then blew, and though the insides of the houses were cooled with *tatties*, the air outside resembled that of an oven.

On the 9th August Sir Samford wrote home a long joint letter to his brother-in-law and two nephews, stating that after a very prosperous voyage he had landed on the 1st August. The letter, chiefly full of private affection and chit-chat, describes the departure of the expedition for China from Calcutta, that had previously taken place. He adds: 'I shall send them a reinforcement of a Madras battalion in a few days; but I must change the commanding officer; the present is too old and infirm.'

The effects of those three years passed in his second service in the West Indies had began to tell on Sir Samford's constitution before leaving England, and he was unwell for some days soon after arriving in Madras. The loss of the English horse also was irreparable. He bought others, but it was impossible to find one that could carry safely, except at a walk, a man of his weight and size; and as it was not a good climate for walking, he was thus debarred from that exercise which had become necessary to his existence.

Early in August he received a letter from a distinguished statesman and amiable man, Lord J —— ——, as follows:—

'DOWNING STREET, 26th *March*, 1840.

'My dear Sir Samford,—I have been asked to recommend to your notice Major H——, who will be under your authority at Madras. I understand that he has served in India many years. His father-in-law, Mr. L——, the artist, has asked me to introduce him to your favourable notice. I should therefore be very glad if you should be able to do anything to serve him.'

'Yours, &c.,
'J. —— ——.'

To this letter, Sir Samford made on the 12th August a brief reply assuring his Lordship that he would do everything in his power to meet his Lordship's wishes.

About the same time he must have received the following application:—

Lord Burghersh* to Sir Samford Whittingham.

'LONDON, 24th *April*, 1840.

'My dear Whittingham,—I am very sorry I missed you while you were in England: but I wish you joy of your appointment to Madras; and indeed of the high and distinguished services you have so constantly rendered since our first meeting at the battle of Talavera. I enclose you a letter from the widow of my former tutor. . . . . . . She requests me to recommend to you her son-in-law, ——, a Lieutenant in the Madras Native Infantry; and if you can do anything for him I should be very much obliged to you. I give you no news from

---

* The late Earl of Westmoreland, soldier, diplomatist, and eminent musician.

hence—there is none of any importance. Prince Albert, as you see, has got the 11th Dragoons.

'With every wish, &c.,

'BURGHERSH.'

To which on the 15th August Sir Samford replied that he would do his best to meet the wishes of Lord Burghersh, and adds; 'When I met you at dear Lord William Bentinck's, previous to my departure for the West Indies, I was much gratified to see how little impression time had made upon you. For truly you appeared to me as well and as young as when we sat together on the hill of Talavera. May you long continue thus to prosper, and as one of the High Councillors of the Crown, lend your powerful support to the stability of the British monarchy.'

The following was addressed to the nephew and Military Secretary of the Governor-General:—

Sir Samford Whittingham to the Hon. William Godolphin Osborne.

'MADRAS, 20*th August*, 1840.

'My dear Osborne,—I have delayed writing to you for some days, in the hope of the arrival of an overland mail. But as that hope has not been realized, and as I leave this place for the Hills on the 22nd instant, I write these lines to request you will present my respectful compliments to Lord Auckland and to the ladies of his family.

'I had the pleasure of seeing Lady Godolphin a short time before my departure, and also your uncle, Lord Sidney, at Hampstead; and I have to thank her Ladyship for a copy of your very excellent description of "Runjeet Singh, his Court and Camp."

'Nothing can exceed the enthusiastic admiration in

England of Lord Auckland's celebrated campaign in Affghanistan.'*

'Yours very sincerely,
'SAMFORD WHITTINGHAM.'

Amongst the General Officers, whose congratulations and applications, he received and replied to, were Sir Frederick Adam, and Sir George Walker; both greatly distinguished in the Peninsular War; and the latter himself Commander-in-Chief at Madras, at an earlier period.

Sir Charles Felix Smith, R.E., to Sir Samford Whittingham.†

(Extract.)

'GIBRALTAR, 14th *April*, 1840.

'My dear General,—When I heard of your appointment to India, I became desirous of offering congatulations on a destiny which I knew would be so entirely in accordance with your wishes. But I hesitated from not being certain whether your command in the West was to terminate at your own pleasure, or on the arrival in Barbadoes of your successor; who, for the sake of the poor old West Indians, I hope may be guided by the sound and able example you have left him. Unprofitable as was your command in a pecuniary point of view, it must have been rich in the opinions it gained for you—if indeed your former distinguished career could derive lustre from actions short of absolute triumphs in the field.

'Hitherto you have been a true prophet: but, query, will not the road opened by Sir John Keane tend to increase alarm, and render more important than ever the views you had taken with regard to the Indian

---

* No one then anticipated the evils which misfortune and mismanagement subsequently occasioned.

† This letter probably reached Sir Samford in August, and has this peculiarity, that the congratulations were not accompanied with any requests!

empire? It is well for them that one so enlightened as yourself should have been at hand to aid them in the crisis which is rapidly approaching. Don Fernando will doubtless accompany you. My *memorias* to him: and you will, my dear General, accept the renewed, the reiterated expressions of respect, from your faithful friend and humble servant,

'C. F. SMITH.'

Sir Charles, then commanding Royal Engineers, had been the second in command in Barbadoes, under Sir Samford, and had also known him well in the Peninsula. Sir Charles's conspicuous valour made him the hero of many a Peninsular anecdote, familiar to veterans. He had a very strong head, as well as a very stout heart, and his warm voluntary testimony to the merits of his late commander, is not unworthy of record in this military Memoir.

Mr. W. O. Osborne, on his way with dispatches to the Governor-General from China, addressed a letter to Sir Samford, dated 'Macao Roads, 1st August, 1840,' giving an account of his career in China, since leaving Lord Auckland's Staff to join the 26th Cameronians. The letter is written with characteristic ability, and its criticisms on the first incompetent commander sent to China were but too well founded.

The following letter was addressed to Mr. (afterwards Sir) James Cosmo Melvill, Secretary to the Court of Directors of the East India Company.

From want of space and also of present interest, the local details regarding the politics of Madras are omitted:—

Sir Samford Whittingham to Mr. Melvill.
(Extract.)
'MADRAS, 11*th August*, 1840.

'My dear Mr. Melvill,—I landed here on the 1st instant, and am getting on entirely to my satisfaction.

Nothing can be more delightful than the commencement of the intercourse between Lord Elphinstone and myself. I never saw a man more popular, and apparently most deservedly. He is in the Hills at present for his health; but no delay of business takes place, as the Secretary of Government is here, and he is as indefatigable as able.

'A battalion, 37th Native Infantry, is here under orders for China. I shall inspect them in a few days and probably have to change the commanding officer. When the troops have sailed I shall endeavour to join Lord Elphinstone on the Hills. You will receive, by this mail, a memorandum on the importance of our present position in Affghanistan and the Lower Scinde, written by me at sea. The case there assumed as more than probable, has already occurred, and Bombay has become the grand base of our future operations. . . . . For God's sake, my dear Mr. Melvill, let us keep always in mind, that we hold this country by *the magical charm of our supposed invincibility*, and by *the rapid progress of our* movements. A reinforcement, such as I propose of all arms, arriving suddenly at the scene of action—full of health and strength and European energy—would create an effect equal to that of ten times that number, arriving in the usual slow and ordinary manner. Our sentiments on Chinese affairs so entirely coincide, that we really have no case for discussion. Asiatic power can only be supported by splendid victories. If England ever *attempt to play a little game* in the East, she is lost. . . . Pray tell Colonel Pasley not to forget to send me out *a detailed account of the powder bags*. If he is too busy, Captain Rutherford will do it. I am much interested in the result.

'Yours very truly,
'SAMFORD WHITTINGHAM.'

Before leaving Madras to join Lord Elphinstone on the Hills, Sir Samford with his Staff paid an official visit to the Regent Azeem Jah Bahadur, the young Nawab of Arcot being a minor. Colonel Walpole, the then Resident, regulated all the proceedings connected with the interview in the usual manner.

On the way to the Hills, passing through Tanjore, a visit was due to its Rajah, but the Commander-in-Chief being unwell, his Military Secretary was allowed to represent him, and accompanied by the Resident of Tanjore, the visit was duly paid. The party, including the Resident and Military Secretary, consisted of six officers. At the interview the Rajah sat at the head of the table on his little throne, and the visitors were seated three on either side—the Resident on the right and the Secretary on the left of his Highness. The only peculiarity about the fat and comfortable-looking Rajah was, that he was covered with jewels. In that respect he was quite a sight. The Resident declared that, taken together, the pearls, diamonds, rubies, emeralds, &c., which his Highness then wore, were worth 50,000*l.*; and no doubt his mouth watered when he said so. For, sad to relate, this representative of the Governor of Madras, afterwards fled as an outlaw for systematic robbery of his Highness, which he effected by making the Rajah believe that the high-minded Lord Elphinstone had *an itching palm*; and that by a golden key, the Rajah might open his way to the gratification of all his wishes! It was a sad tale, fraught with shame and dishonour to a family and to connections that did not merit such disgrace and exposure, at the hands of one of its most high-placed members. But nothing was suspected at this time, and the Resident was held in great respect and honour.

Lord Elphinstone received Sir Samford and his Staff in the most friendly manner, and they renewed their former acquaintance with mutual satisfaction.

Sir Samford Whittingham to Vaughan Davis, Esq.
(Extract.)

'OUTACAMUND, 7th September, 1840.

'Dearest Vaughan,—I have come up to this place to transact business with Lord Elphinstone, whose health had suffered very seriously from a severe fall on horseback, when the horse fell over on him. I have found him all I could wish—sensible, well-informed, and possessing talents which his extreme modesty alone prevents from commanding the high respect and consideration they deserve. Be assured that the longer Lord Elphinstone is employed, the more he will be appreciated by the India House, and by Her Majesty's Government. I have only brought up —— with me, and Bates and Dundas have remained at Madras to get the house, &c. in order for my return, which will be about the end of this month. In the meantime, even this little sojourn on these most healthy hills has done me much good. On a well-arranged system, no delay takes place here in business, and the quantum one can get through is tenfold. On public grounds, and for the good of the service, I should strongly recommend our passing the hot months of the summer on these hills; when (the Council sitting and the heads of a few of the military departments being with me), everything else would remain at Madras, and business would be done better and more speedily. I wish you would have a little private conversation with Mr. Melvill on this really important subject.

'C—— is now employed at Madras, and his prospects are very good, and he is giving me the greatest satisfaction in *every point of view.* God be praised for all things. I am truly glad to hear such good accounts of dear B——. Give him my best love. Hatley Frere is going to be married to our Bishop's daughter. She stands very high in the opinion of the best people here.

'*The vile West Indies have sadly shaken the old oak, more indeed than I could have imagined*;* but as long as I can sit in the saddle, I will never forget that a soldier's existence belongs to his country, and that it is his duty to die in the trench when necessary. I have not been able to replace the horse I lost on the voyage, and I sadly feel the want of that best of all exercises.

'Adieu, my beloved Vaughan,
    'Your devotedly attached uncle,
            'SAMFORD WHITTINGHAM.'

This letter greatly alarmed his affectionate relatives in England; knowing how buoyant and sanguine were his spirits, and how little disposed he was to dwell on, or to magnify his ailments. It prepared them in some measure for the approaching catastrophe.

Colonel H. Smith † to Sir S. Whittingham.
(Extract.)
'CALCUTTA, 17*th September*, 1840.

'My dear Sir Samford Whittingham,—There is a sort of freemasonry amongst old soldiers, who mutually shared the dangers of their eventful lives, which so unites them that I cannot refrain from addressing your Excellency, although I do not call to my recollection that I have ever had any personal intercourse with you since a period of time so long ago as when you were A.D.C. to poor ill-used General Whitelocke, and I a more humble performer, adjutant to *los Cazadores*, the 95th Regiment. I say ill-used General Whitelocke, for as a boy I thought so; and, since a more mature knowledge of our profession has en-

---

* These words are placed in italics by the Editor, for in the opinion of all the relatives and friends of Sir Samford Whittingham, that second service in the West Indies, greatly shortened a life that seemed made by Nature to endure far beyond the limits set by the Psalmist.

† The Adjutant-General of the Queen's troops in India, afterwards the well-known Sir Harry Smith, made a Baronet of *Aliwal*. He had married a Spanish lady during the Peninsular War.

abled me better to judge, I say so still for many reasons. I can call you to my recollection in those days as clearly as if the many wonderful scenes of our lives had never occurred, or Time, that imperceptible destroyer of us all, had never progressed. The object of my letter is one which I hope your Excellency will regard as it is humbly intended, to offer to your acceptance any service which it may be in my power at any time to render you. This done, I leave the power of so doing to future circumstances, and pray you to calculate upon *Obras y no palabras*.

'Your Excellency's command having been *indented on*—that elegant expression—for the 55th and 62nd Regiments, has an enlivening appearance; but whether they may enjoy a mountainous climate or not, is a question to be solved. The tea trade, in commercial language is looking up, and everything has been done by Admiral Elliot which was expected. I think old Sir *Varment Willoughby** has his hands full, and Shah Shooja. *Vivas el Rey* are very likely to end in *Vivas el Emperador*; that barony of Ghuznee is far from being settled.

'I hope your Excellency will not consider me intrusive in thus addressing you; but accept as my apology the high regard I cannot fail to entertain for every soldier of conspicuous and bright career, and in which [number] you stand grouped. May you continue to enjoy your high command in good health, the great requisite of this or any country. Did you see that noble-hearted *old Radical* Admiral Fleeming? Many is the anecdote I have heard of you from him. Believe me, General,

'Very faithfully and sincerely yours,
'H. G. SMITH.'

The Editor also possessed a later letter or rather note

---

* A playful *nom de guerre*, for General Sir Willoughby Cotton.

from Colonel Smith to Sir Samford, which is unfortunately lost or mislaid. It contained one important passage; the pleased expectation of the Staff at Calcutta, that the Commander at Madras would shortly succeed to the supreme Commander-in-Chief-ship. By science and by experience assuredly no one, then available, was fitter for the post, but the race is not always to the swift nor the battle to the strong. At length Sir Samford had obtained in the British army rank equal to that which twenty-six years previously he had obtained in the Spanish army. Was he at last to have that opportunity on a great scale, which Sir Willoughby Cotton had written was all that he wanted, and which in speech and in writing Wellington had practically confirmed? That final crowning of his labours was denied him by an unscrutable but allwise Providence. That, indeed, was decided when the prejudices of his father had retarded for ten or twelve years the entrance of his son into the service, which brought him to the Peninsula bereft of that rank, without which it is rarely possible to make a great name, whilst many men younger than himself were already English Generals. The long and severe tropical services, with the brain ever at work, and finally the injurious second stay in the West Indies, completed the evil, and deprived of his well-merited rewards a servant of the Crown whose great talents and unwearied zeal and abilities are proved by testimonies which, in number and in weight, could hardly be surpassed.

On most cordial terms with the Governors, both in public and in private matters, Sir Samford was equally on the best of terms with all the other authorities. Space will not allow of many proofs; but here is one:—

Dr. Spencer, Bishop of Madras, to Sir Samford Whittingham.

'KOTAGHERRY, 10th *October*, 1840.

'Dear Sir Samford,—Accept my best thanks for the copy of your Excellency's most *Christian* and sensible letter.* If such principles are steadily acted upon, our blessed religion cannot be kept back from this benighted land, and I am indeed thankful that they are held by one occupying so very distinguished and important a station in India.

'I most sincerely hope that your Excellency continues in good health, and that you do not feel the Madras climate disagreeable. My duties call me to the Western coast, and it will be long before I can hope to visit the Presidency. May I be permitted to add then one inducement to wish myself there would be the opportunity it would afford me of improving an acquaintance, which, however, I hope to be allowed to cultivate next year under a more genial sky. I have the honour to be, dear Sir Samford,

'Your Excellency's most faithful servant,

'G. T. MADRAS.'

The extreme courtesy he displayed to the amiable young Governor did not prevent the Commander-in-Chief from asserting his rights, and especially when the good of the service required their assertion. In all his correspondence with his Lordship, constant and copious, only in one letter is there the slightest cloud, namely in one dated 'Madras, 19th October.' He there writes to the Governor, that while it is his duty to carry his wishes into effect as regards the movement of troops, he is anxious

---

* This probably refers to a letter written to Mr. James Cosmo Melvill advocating the general secular education of the Natives, as the best means of gradually destroying their superstitions, without risk of creating jealousy or animosity.

the details should be left to him. He goes on: 'There is not a company of artillery in the command which can be said to be fit for service; for there is not one with its complement of officers. Your private letter to me, my dear Lord, was just as satisfactory as though it had come in the most official form. And I was only anxious to call your attention to the state of the *personnel* of our artillery, in support of the minute I have submitted to the Council on that subject.'

'I quite agree with you that everything must be left to the decision of the Bombay Government; and I rejoice that your Lordship has done everything in your power to aid and assist that Government.'

On the 8th November, he informs Lord Elphinstone: 'I know of nothing in which officers in command are more often neglectful than in furnishing *correct returns* of the *real efficiency* of the different arms. We shall at last arrive doubtless at the truth; but unless attention be paid to the requisite changes of system, recommended in my minute on the artillery of this Presidency, we shall never be efficient in that most important of all arms.

'Unless the Punjab were conquered and in our possession, that line of our operations from our North-west frontier to Affghanistan must always be more or less insecure. Nevertheless the assembling of a large force on that frontier to protect our advance to the Sikh country is a wise and prudent measure. But under existing circumstances too much attention cannot be paid to Herat as the real pivot of all our operations in Scinde; as securing to us the command of the Indies, and of the Bolan Pass; and consequently of our communicating from Bombay to Candahar and Cabool.'

The letter is not extant to which the following is a reply:—

Sir Samford Whittingham to the Hon. J. Sullivan,
(Member of Council).

(Extract.)

'MADRAS, 24*th November*, 1840.

'I cannot tell you how much I regret the not seeing you again before your departure for England; but I trust we shall pass many days together on your return. My opinion of your delightful hills can never vary; but there is a point of view to which we have none of us hitherto given due weight. I allude to the colonization of that interesting part of the country; which would be the certain consequence of locating a regiment in the vicinity of Outacamund. You, better than any man, are acquainted with the importance of those hills in the military and civil view. I recommend them to your protection at home. The cultivation of coffee alone would be of infinite value.

'If you are still inclined to let me have your house on the Hills, I shall be happy to rent it on your own terms, from the 1st April* next to the 1st October.

'With regard to my Memoirs on Indian affairs, I will state to you frankly, that as I predicted too truly many of the evils which have occurred, and as the Government have taken most active measures to remedy these evils, I should not wish to appear to criticize any acts of my superiors, when the time for rendering my opinions useful has gone by,

'Ever &c., &c.,
'SAMFORD WHITTINGHAM.'

Noble sentiments the reader will allow; and worthy of the man who was soon to die, as he had lived, in the arduous and zealous service of his country; with nothing to transmit to his family, but a name that he alone had raised from insignificance, and under the greatest dis-

---

* Ominous date; which he lived not to see. *L'homme propose, mais Dieu dispose.*

advantages, to a height which had gained the esteem of the most illustrious and most aristocratic of Englishmen; as recorded on many memorable occasions.

Sir Hugh Gough was now sent to China; and was destined soon to be Sir Samford's nominal successor at Madras, and thence to pass on to the chief command in Calcutta, on his road to many victories and two peerages, pensions, and prize money, with fairy-tale-like rapidity.

The following letter can hardly fail to interest the reader:—

Major Stokes, Resident of Mysore, to Sir Samford Whittingham.

'ELWAK, 16*th November*, 1840.

'Your Excellency,—I had the honour to receive in due course of post, your letter of the 5th October, with its enclosed copy of a letter from Colonel Gurwood to your address on the subject of the 'Wellington Dispatches.' I also had the honour to receive a letter from Lord Elphinstone on the same subject.

'I am much obliged to your Excellency for having given me an opportunity of aiding, in however slight a degree, in rendering more perfect a work of such great national interest as that referred to.

'As required by Colonel Gurwood, I have carefully compared the letters and other papers in the records of my office, bearing the signature, "Arthur Wellesley" (the present Duke of Wellington), with the printed copies of them published in the first volumes of His Grace's 'Dispatches.' With this day's post, you will receive a packet containing the particulars of the inaccuracies in the letters, which this comparison has led to the discovery of, together with correct copies of *eighteen* letters, bearing his Grace's signature, which are not to be found in the printed volumes referred to.

'As indicative of the industry of his Grace—and as every particular connected with his career must be interesting to every lover of his country—I have added a column to the statement which I forward to your Excellency, which will show that, with very few exceptions, the whole of his letters on the records of this department are in his own handwriting.

'To one who loves the Duke, as I know your Excellency does, it will be a gratification to hear that though it is thirty-five years since he was last in the town of Mysore, the name of "Wellesley" is still generally and publicly known in it.

'I have, &c., &c.,
'T. D.* Stokes.'

In his reply dated 25th November, apologizing for delay in consequence of his suffering from ophthalmia Sir Samford thanks the Resident, and promises to forward all the papers and also his letter to Colonel Gurwood by the first opportunity.

Sir Samford Whittingham to Colonel Gurwood.

'Madras, 4th December, 1840.

'My dear Colonel Gurwood,—I have now the pleasure to enclose the papers received from Major Stokes, the Resident at Mysore, in answer to your queries on the subject of the "Dispatches."

'Major Phillips of the 15th Hussars, who proceeds to England in the merchant ship "*Reliance*," to sail from hence in a few days, has undertaken to deliver them to you.

'Should you have any further investigations to make on this most interesting subject, I shall be too happy to be employed; for I consider myself in common with every

---

* The second initial of Christian names can only be guessed at in the signature.

British subject,* as owing to you a debt of gratitude we never can repay.

'Believe me, &c.,
'SAMFORD WHITTINGHAM.'

One of his last extant letters is of the 23rd December, and addressed to the late Lord (then Sir Hussey) Vivian, in praise of his relative Major Vivian, 'a promising young officer,' whom he intends to provide for as soon as possible.

Of his private letters, the following are extracted from those of latest date, supposed to be now in existence. A merciful providence was gilding his last days with happiness and contentment, and preparing a bright and cheerful sunset for the close of a somewhat harassing and agitated, though honourable career.

Without entering deeply into religious matters, which, though precious to friends, might be out of place in this work, it must here be stated, that the state of mind of Sir Samford Whittingham had been for some years such, as to render the idea of sudden death terrible neither to himself, nor to his friends; and his last letters fully establish his possession of that peace of mind, which practical Christianity nearly always instils into its votaries.

On the 28th November he writes to Miss Davis, his youngest niece: 'Our overland communications being stopped, I avail myself of the expected arrival of the "*Reliance*" from Calcutta for England, to prepare a letter for dear home. C——is still with me, and is the delight and comfort of my life. —— is an able and enlightened Military Secretary. My house is a home of peace and tranquillity; and I am more thankful to Almighty God than I have words to express, for all his many mercies to me and mine. The weather here is now very pleasant, but I have not yet regained my former strength and vigour.

---

* More than most men he had cause for gratitude; for these Dispatches by doing him justice have helped to neutralize *in*justice.

On the 30th he writes in the same contented and cheerful strain. 'I cannot tell you how very happy we all are, and what a charming little family circle we form. They all study my happiness and comfort. This house is by far the best I have ever lived in, and we are all well lodged. How truly thankful do I feel to the Almighty for all the blessings I enjoy! My health is fast amending, and all the young ones are quite blooming.'

Two more proofs will suffice to demonstrate the happy and religious state of mind, in which his sudden summons found him, to the great consolation of his surviving relatives.

On the 4th December, 1840, he writes to his younger nephew: 'Our overland correspondence having been brought to a close, we are bound to avail ourselves of every private channel which may present itself. I have latterly been a great sufferer from an attack of ophthalmia; but it is now, thank God, well over, and has merely left a little weakness in the eyes, which makes me abstain from writing more than I like. Our domestic luck is quite heart cheering. C―― is living with me; and is the charm and comfort of my life. I hope to obtain for him very shortly a really good situation.* ―― is as steady as an old man of business, and a really able Military Secretary. B―― is my right hand; and I shall be indebted to him for whatever may be my future independence.† In short, such a family of love and happiness I have only witnessed at home.'

Owing to some stoppage in the overland route at this period, and the state of his eyes, Sir Samford did not write much during the last few weeks of his life. His latest (extant) letter was written to his first, oldest and

* In the Civil Service.
† This aide-de-camp successively served on the Staff of Sir Samford Whittingham, Lord Elphinstone, Sir Robert Dick, Lord Gough, and then with Lord Elphinstone a second time, equally valued and esteemed by all.

best friend, his brother-in-law, an extract from which closes Sir Samford's correspondence:—

'MADRAS, 24*th December*, 1840.

'My dearest Brother,—The long-expected overland mail has arrived at last, and brought letters up to October 12th from you, and the darling C——, my dear Hart, B——, and D——. Only conceive what a treat after so long a privation, and such a state of uncertainty as to the future! The only drawback is the exceedingly short space allowed us to answer the numerous arrivals. I only received the letters last night, and the express goes off to-morrow evening; and to-morrow is *Christmas Day*. There was a time when that consideration would have had little weight with either you or me; but I thank God that time is over. . . . . . It is indeed a blessing to find C—— all I could wish, just the dear amiable creature he used to be. He is without exception the pleasantest domestic companion I have known. In the house he is the delight and comfort of us all. Alas! for how short a time he has been with us. He was obliged to join his station at Cuddalore, where he has already arrived. Pray tell my much-loved V—— to send me "Blunt's Lectures." They are intended as a present to C—— from me. ——'s judgment, ability, and steadiness, fill me with admiration and pleasure. He is an excellent Military Secretary. . . . . There is not in existence a human being whose heart more overflows with humble gratitude to God than mine. . . . B—— is a treasure in every sense of the word.' [After many long and endearing messages to all his relatives the writer continues]: 'I cannot tell you, my dearest brother, with what delight I look forward to the time of my returning to England, and to the renewal of that intimacy which has for so many years been a source of comfort and happiness to us both! May our friendship and love go on increasing to the last day of our lives; and may God's mercy grant that we may yet pass a few happy years together.

'Your affectionate and devotedly attached brother,
'SAMFORD WHITTINGHAM.'

On the 19th January 1841, one of the dragoons of the Commander-in-Chief's escort was dispatched for the Chief's son, then taking his afternoon ride on the Madras beach, who gallopped home in time to witness the last breath, and no more. This sudden call was a mercy to the departed, whose last moments were thus spared the grief of knowing that he was leaving his family before making adequate provision for them. And nothing could exceed the kindness of Lord Elphinstone to the sons of the deceased General, and to his personal Staff.

Mr. Melvill, in the name of the Chairman of the Court of Directors, and the Adjutant-General of the Horse-Guards, also forwarded their kind and valued condolences. That of Lord Fitzroy Somerset, the Military Secretary to Lord Hill, with the account of the funeral, will now close this Memoir :—

To Lieutenant F. Whittingham, 67th Regiment.

'HORSE-GUARDS, 31st *March*, 1841.

'My dear Sir,—The last mail from India brought me your letter of the 22nd January, conveying to me the melancholy intelligence of the sudden death of your father, Sir Samford Whittingham; and I avail myself of the earliest opportunity to condole with you upon an event, which has not only deprived you of a kind and affectionate father, upon whose assistance and exertions you naturally relied for advancement in your profession, but has likewise deprived the service of a distinguished General Officer, who was devoted to his duty, and by the zeal and ability he had ever displayed, when the occasion was afforded him, had obtained the esteem and confidence of the Government and the Commander-in-Chief.

'Lord Hill most sincerely laments his loss, and desires me to assure you that he feels very much for you, and will be happy when circumstances may enable him to select you for advancement. In the meantime, his Lordship has granted you leave of absence to enable you to remain in India: and as no officer has yet been selected as successor to your much-regretted father, and in the absence of Sir Hugh Gough, Sir Robert Dick is supposed to be acting Commander-in-Chief, I have received Lord Hill's directions, to express to him his Lordship's hopes, that he would, if he should be able, place you in some employment.

'I remain, dear Sir,
'Your very faithful servant,
'FITZROY SOMERSET.'

SOME PARTICULARS OF THE DEMISE AND FUNERAL OF THE LATE LIEUTENANT-GENERAL SIR SAMFORD WHITTINGHAM. &c.*

'IT is with extreme regret we have to announce the death of Sir Samford Whittingham, K.C.B. and K.C.H., Commander-in-Chief of this Presidency. The melancholy event took place about half-past seven o'clock on Tuesday evening last (19th January, 1841).

'His Excellency had attended Council in the course of the day; and, on his return home about four o'clock, partook of some slight refreshment, and lay down for a short time, desiring his servant to call him precisely at five, at which hour he had ordered his carriage, for the purpose of taking his evening's drive. After coming down stairs, he went into the compound to give some directions regarding the pitching of a tent, and almost immediately

* Taken from *The Athenæum*, Madras Newspaper, of Thursday, January 21, 1841.

returned complaining of indisposition. Dr. Cole was sent for, and arrived about a quarter to six, and proceeded at once to take from his Excellency a considerable quantity of blood; but apoplexy quickly succeeded, and, notwithstanding that most prompt means were adopted, both by Drs. Cole and Lane, to prevent fatal consequences, he expired shortly after the attack.

'We believe but one feeling exists with regard to the departed, and that of the most favourable character. During the short time that he had been amongst us, he had secured to himself the respect and esteem of all who came in contact with him. The army had just begun to reap the fruits of his unremitting concern for its welfare; and, from his known reputation as a soldier, the highest expectations were formed as to the measures he would in future adopt, to perfect its mechanism, and uphold its efficiency. This sudden stroke at once disappoints the hopes entertained, and deprives the soldier of a warm and zealous friend, and Her Majesty's and the Honourable Company's Army of an officer of consummate military talent and ability.

'It is an event calculated to produce a serious, and we hope also a salutary impression, throughout all ranks of society, and especially in the army. To his family it is a severe visitation. The suddenness of his death reads an affecting lesson to the living. It should not, therefore, be permitted to pass by, without fixing in the mind the necessity of preparing for so solemn an event. The records of every day are fraught with instructions to this effect; but, when a great man falls—a mighty man, a man of war—it points a moral, the neglect of which argues an insensibility distressingly painful to every individual who feels interested in the happiness of the human family.

'The undermentioned Official Orders were issued in the course of the following day: we merely insert them for the information of our up-country readers, and to show the deep interest excited by this unexpected and truly affecting event.

> '*Garrison Morning Orders.*
>
> ' Fort St. George, 20*th January*, 1841.

' It is with extreme regret the Right Honourable the Governor announces to the garrison the death of Lieutenant-General Sir S. F. Whittingham, K.C.B. and K.C.H., Commander-in-Chief of all the Forces on this Establishment, which melancholy event occurred about half-past seven o'clock last night. In testimony of respect for the memory of the deceased, his Lordship directs that the colours of the Fort be immediately hoisted half-staff high, and to continue so until after the interment has taken place; and minute guns (15), corresponding with the rank of the deceased, be fired from the saluting battery, on the arrival of the procession at the Government Bridge.

' A serjeant, corporal, and twelve privates, from the light company of H. M.'s 57th Regiment to be sent immediately to the residence of the late Commander-in-Chief, as a guard of honour over his remains.

' F. L. Doveton,
' Town Major.

' *Garrison After Order.*

' A funeral party, for the interment of the late Lieutenant-General Sir Samford Whittingham, K.C.B. and K.C.H., to be formed at half-past five this evening, on the road leading from his Excellency's garden towards the Fort, by the Mount Road, near the Dispensary. The party to consist of the whole of the effective troops in garrison, with the Right Honourable the Governor's bodyguard, and a proportion of artillery from St. Thomas's Mount.

'Detailed instructions respecting its order of formation will be issued from the Adjutant-General's office.

'A salute of 15 guns to be fired from the saluting battery immediately after the infantry has ceased firing.

'The Right Honourable the Governor directs that all officers belonging to the garrison, not on duty with the troops, will attend; and that every officer will wear a piece of black crape on his left arm, and have their ornaments, on hat or cap, also the sword-knot, covered with the same material.

When the troops halt, to form a street, no carriages or other conveyance will be permitted to enter it, with the exception of those belonging to the Right Honourable the Governor, the members of Council, the judges of the Supreme Court, and the chief mourners.

'Twelve privates of the light company to be selected as under-bearers.

'F. L. DOVETON,
'Town Major.

'With deep regret the Right Honourable the Governor in Council announces the demise of his Excellency Lieutenant-General Sir Samford Whittingham, K.C.B. and K.C.H., and requests the attendance of all officers, civil and military, of Her Majesty's and the Honourable Company's service, and of all other gentlemen at the presidency, at his Excellency's funeral this evening. The procession will move from his residence to Fort St. George at five o'clock, p.m.

'FORT ST. GEORGE, 20th January, 1841.

'By order of the Right Honourable the Governor in Council.

'H. CHAMIER,
'Chief Secretary.

'*General Orders by the Right Hon. the Governor in Council.*

'Fort St. George, 20*th January*, 1841.

'With great grief the Right Hon. the Governor in Council announces to the army the demise of his Excellency Lieutenant-General Sir Samford Whittingham, Knight Commander of the Most Honourable Military Order of the Bath and of the Royal Hanoverian Guelphic Order, Commander-in-Chief at this Presidency, which event took place at Madras, on the 19th instant.

'On this melancholy occasion, the flag of the Fort will be hoisted half-mast high; and 15 minute guns, corresponding with the rank of the late Commander-in-Chief, will be fired at each of the principal military stations under this government.

'The Governor in Council further directs, that the Officers of Her Majesty's and the Hon. Company's Army will wear mourning for a fortnight from this present date.

'By Order of the Right Hon. The Governor in Council.

'H. Chamier,
'Chief Secretary.

'*Programme.*

'The arrangements made by the authorities for conducting the procession were in conformity with the following programme:—

'The troops ordered for the funeral of his Excellency Lieutenant-General Sir Samford Whittingham, K.C.B. and K.C.H., Commander-in-Chief, &c., &c., assembled yesterday afternoon (the 20th), at a quarter to five o'clock, on the Mount Road,—under the command of Lieut.-Colonel E. E. Jones, K.H., of H. M.'s 57th regiment. The troops in the garrison formed in column of quarter distance, left in front, facing to the Fort; the rear of the column halted opposite to the Athenæum Library.

'The artillery marched down left in front, and formed in rear of H.M.'s 57th regiment.

'The procession moved in the following order:—

    Garrison Band.
    39th Reg. N. I.
    H. M.'s 57th Regiment.
    Golundauze Battalion of Artillery.
    2nd Battalion of Artillery.
    The Right Honourable the Governor's Body Guard.
    Band of H.M.'s 57th Regiment.
    His Excellency the Commander-in-Chief's Charger, led
    by Non-commissioned Officers of Cavalry.

Flanked by his Excellency the Commander in Chief's Escort, in file.	𝕮𝖍𝖊 𝕭𝖔𝖉𝖞.	Flanked by his Excellency the Commander in Chief's Escort, in file.

    His Excellency the Commander in Chief's Carriage.
    The Right Honourable the Governor's Carriage.
    The Honourable the Chief Justice's Carriage.
    The Honourable the Councillors' Carriages.
    The Honourable the Puisne Judge's Carriage.
    Other Carriages in succession.

'No carriages but those of the chief mourners, the Right Hon. the Governor, the Members of the Council, and Judges of the Supreme Court, were allowed to pass beyond the Wallajah Bridge, where the procession halted.

'The infantry and foot-artillery moved forward into the Fort, passing by the Town Major's house and main guard, toward St. Mary's church, where the column halted, and the troops formed street.

'The body-guard passed over the bridge, and formed up in line to the right and left on the road leading to the Saluting Battery and General Hospital, fronting the river, resting upon their swords reversed, and the trumpets sounding a Dead March as the hearse passed.

'The procession then moved forward, the troops resting upon their arms reversed, bands of music playing the Dead March in " Saul."

'The garrison band fell back to the front of the hearse, and preceded it in its progress to the church.'

'*The Funeral.*

'The procession followed the corpse in the following order :—

> The Right Honourable the Governor and Staff.
> The Councillors and Judges.
> Commander in Chief's Personal Staff.
> Secretaries to Government.
> Members of Boards.
> Officers and Gentlemen two and two, the juniors leading.

'When the procession reached the church, the artillery and infantry formed in line, broke into columns of sub-divisions, left in front, and the left resting upon St. Mary's church, the right thrown back, and prolonged towards St. George's gate. The body was then taken from the hearse, accompanied by pall-bearers, in the persons of his Excellency the Governor,[*] Col. Monteith, Col. Doveton, Sir R. Comyn, and the Hon. Mr. Bird. The corpse was then met at the gate by the Rev. Mr. Mahon, A.M. and the Rev. Mr. Knox, B.A. The funeral service was chiefly performed by Mr. Mahon, assisted by Mr. Knox, who read the Psalms and Lessons usual for such occasions. After which the corpse was lowered into the grave by 24 grenadiers of H.M.'s 57th regiment, when three volleys were fired by word of command and by signal, which was made by the garrison flag being hoisted to the mast-head.

'During the procession 15 minute guns were fired from the Saluting Battery, which commenced when the hearse reached the Government Bridge ; and a further salute of 15 guns after the body was deposited in the grave, next to Lord Pigott, late Governor of Madras, on the north side of the pulpit, facing the communion table, which was made known by the hoisting of the garrison flag.

'The parade was then dismissed, and the troops

---

[*] Lord Elphinstone, then Governor of Madras ; and, many years later Governor of Bombay.

marched to their respective quarters, right in front, no drums beating until outside of the Fort.

'The inner coffin was of wood, covered with lead, and this was again enclosed in a wooden case. We understand the Governor gave instructions for an arch to be thrown over the grave, which work commences this day.

'The sight was one of the most affecting and solemnly imposing that has been witnessed in Madras for many a day. Nearly the whole of the civil and military service at the Presidency were in attendance, and a great multitude of people from among all classes of the population.

'The flag-staffs at the Fort and the Custom House had the union jack flying half mast high, as was also the case with all the ships in the roads. The general feeling harmonized in every respect with the mournful occasion.'*

---

* A tablet was subsequently put up by his sons to the memory of Sir Samford Whittingham, in the Garrison Church at Madras.

APPENDICES.

APPENDIX A.

Copy of Original Report of Major-General Whittingham to Lieutenant-General La Peña, Commander-in-Chief, of his Share in the Battle of Barossa, fought on March 5, 1811.

'Exmo. Señor,—Como á las dos de la tarde del dia 5 del corriente recibí órden de V. E. para quedarme con tres escuadrones y dos compañias de Caballeria, y mil trecientos cincuenta hombres de la Infanteria que mandaba el Brigadier Don Antonio Begines de los Rios en el campo del Cerro del Puerco, en consecuencia iba á tomar posicion, uniendome á la Infanteria, cuando me avisó el Coronel Don Luis Michelena que se veian tropas que parecian enemigas por su marcha acia nosotros. Acceleré la reunion, y reconocí al enemigo que marchaba en dos fuertes columnas, llevando un batallon de tropas ligeras á su vanguardia; la una marchaba directamente á mi posicion, y la otra se prolongaba por su izquierda para envolverme. Mandé formar la Infanteria en cuadros, y la Caballeria al flanco izquierdo en escalones para sostener el punto. Á este tiempo recibí la órden de V. E. para replegarme sobre el grueso del exercito, y descubrí ademas de las dos columnas enemigas ya dichas, otra mas fuerte que venia aceleradamente sobre mi izquierda para interponerse al Pinar que mediaba entre mi campo y el del exercito, unico paso que me quedaba para cumplir, replegandome, la última resolucion de V. E. Las fuerzas enemigas eran quadruplas cuando menos á las que yo tenia.

'Determiné, en virtud de dicha órden, que la Infanteria emprendiese su retirada cubierta por la Caballeria. El batallon Ingles, á las órdenes del Coronel Bran, rompió la marcha, y en seguida las tropas Españolas. Llevé conmigo el destacamento de Carabineros Reales, y una compañia de Husares Ingleses para cubrir el flanco derecho de la linea de marcha retrograda, y interponiendome entre esta y el enemigo, continuando la retirada hasta tomar posesion del bosque, donde inmediatamente coloqué al Brigadier Don Juan de la Cruz, encargandole cubriese el flanco derecho de la posicion que el enemigo ya intentaba envolver. En cumplimiento á mis instrucciones, el Mayor Bush, con los Husares Ingleses, los Tenientes Coroneles Don Francisco Ramonet y Don Francisco Serrano con un escuadron de Granaderos, y él de la misma clase Don Santiago Wall con dos compañias del de su mando, se sostuvieron con algunas guerillas de Infanteria, hasta que se retiró la Infanteria, todo el bagage del exercito, y las dos piezas de artilleria, que hasta el momento de ser atacadas vivamente, hicieron firmes un muy acertado y vigoroso fuego sobre los enemigos.

'La Caballeria cubrió perfectamente la retirada, y en buen órden, no obstante las continuadas escaramuzas que hizo la enemiga en todo su avance, reunida desde que se avistó, y mas fuerte en una tercera parte contra la nuestra, repartida entónces en varios puntos.

'En este momento divisé el cuerpo del General Graham, que salia del bosque, dirigiendose sobre su antigua posicion de las alturas ya ocupadas por el enemigo. Dificil seria dar una justa idea del impetu con que fué arrojado de todas ellas por las bayonetas Inglesas el enemigo comun que venia cargandonos con tanto orgullo y confianza, como si tuviera ya la victoria conseguida. Su fuerza era doble de la Inglesa, pero la victoria, aunque costosa, fué completa, y decidida por el acero de las bayonetas. Se hubiera recogido el fruto de esta señalada jornada, aun mas allá del objeto principal, si los enemigos en su precipitada retirada—pues abandonaron allí sus heridos de todas clases y caracter, tres piezas, y dos carros de municiones—hubieran sido cargados de flanco, ó amenazados por la retaguardia.

'Un escuadron de Husares Ingleses que estaba á mi mando atacó al de Guardia del Mariscal Victor, lo destrozo, y dispersó completamente. Dicho escuadron de Husares Ingleses, juntamente con el ya indicado de Granaderos Españoles al mando del Baron de Carondelet, y las dos compañias de Don Santiago Wall, cubrian el ala derecha, y sostenidos por las tropas de los Brigadieres Don Antonio Begines y Don Juan de la Cruz, evitaron por su bizarra conducta, y maniobras, que el enemigo nos envolviese por la playa como lo intentó por dos veces. Aquellas dos compañias se portaron con bizarria, retirandose y avanzando oportunamente sobre el enemigo, como igualmente el destacamento de Carabineros Reales. Toda la Caballeria en fin cumplió brillantemente con su deber.

'El exercito enemigo, despues de verse rechazado de las alturas, emprendió su retirada en órden, cubierto por su Caballeria. Este fué el instante en que me prometí reunir y obrar ofensivamente con los cuatrocientos caballos que tenia á mi disposicion, para lo que avisé á Ramonet, y Serrano, que en union con Wall observasen y cooperasen á los movimientos de los Husares Ingleses y Carabineros Reales que yo llevaba conmigo, cuando se dejó ver sobre la derecha de toda la linea una columna de Infanteria como de quinientos hombres, precedida de una partida de Caballeria, y moviendose como para ganar nuestra espalda. Fué indispensable maniobrar en su observacion mientras la reconocia un sargento y seis hombres del escuadron de Granaderos, y se me escapó la ocasion de cargar al enemigo, que se retiraba de priesa, con toda mi Caballeria disponible. Á la cabeza de los Husares Ingleses seguí sobre el, y resolví atacar un trozo de Caballeria situado al lado de una laguna, que cubria su flanco izquierdo; mas en mi marcha descubrí que toda la Infanteria enemiga se habia colocado á su derecha, y sostenido por su Artilleria, apoyandose en el Pinar, situacion que no permitia un movimiento aislado ó parcial contra dicho trozo protegido tan inmediatamente. En esta situacion se colocaron en posicion por el General Graham dos piezas de artilleria, que tirando con acierto, obligaron al enemigo á continuar su retirada entre la laguna y el Pinar con direccion á Chiclana.

'No puedo menos de suplicar á V. E. haga presente á S. A. S. el particular merito á toda prueba que han contrahido todos los gefes, oficiales, y tropa que en esta accion se hallaron á mis órdenes, sin resolverme á individualizar ante V. E. á ninguno, pues todos á porfía llenaron cumplido, y honrosamente, con su deber, al paso que les llegaba la ocasion feliz de mostrar á la nacion que son sus defensores.

'Dios guarde á V. E. muchos años.
'Campo del Cerro de los Martires, 7 de Marzo de 1811.
    'Exmo. Señor Don Santiago Whittingham.

'Exmo. Señor Don Manuel de la Peña,
 General en Gefe.'

APPENDIX B.

Return of Corps of different Arms of the Spanish Army under the Orders of Lieutenant-General Whittingham, when only Lieutenant-Colonel in the British Army.

Saragossa, Head-quarters, April 1, 1814.

Regiments of Infantry	Regiments of Cavalry	Horse Artillery
5th Battn. of Grenadiers 1st Regt. of Cordova 1st do. Guadalaxara 1st do. Grenada 2nd do. Majorca 2nd do. Burgos 2nd do. Murcia 1st do. Nueva Creacion Cazadores of Majorca Company of Sappers	The Prince's Regt. of Horse Santiago do. Calatrava do. Queen's Dragoons Almanza do. Madrid do. Soria do. Olivenza Chasseurs Ubrique do. La Mancha do. Ferdinand VII.'s Hussars	Squadrons 5th and 6th, each squadron consisting of 3 troops, each troop 4 pieces of 8, and 2 howitzers of $5\frac{1}{2}$ inch.

Total:—9 regiments of infantry; 11 regiments of cavalry; 18 pieces of artillery.

Military College at Majorca, founded by General Whittingham, and under his direction.

General Cavalry Depôt, established by General Whittingham, and under his orders.

APPENDIX C.

Sir Samford Whittingham's Letter to Viscount Combermere concerning Lieutenant (now Lieutenant-Colonel) Caine.

'CAWNPORE, *November* 26, 1827.

'My Lord,—In compliance with your Lordship's wishes, I have the honour to state officially the gallant conduct of Lieutenant Caine (late of the 14th Foot), 3rd, or Buffs, at the assault of Bhurtpore on the 18th January, 1826.

'Lieutenant Caine accompanied the right column of attack (in his capacity of Major of Brigade of the 1st Brigade), under the command of Major Everard, 14th, and continued at its head, during the day. Whilst leading a small party of ten or twelve men in advance of the column, he found his progress arrested by a deep cut in the rampart of Gopalgurh, which he leaped across, but his men being unable to follow in a similar manner, were obliged to descend and reascend the rampart before they could join the Lieutenant, who found himself singly opposed to three of the enemy, two of whom he killed with his double-barrelled pistol, and destroyed the third man by closing with and throwing him over the rampart into the ditch, as the Lieutenant found his sword could not make any impression through the armour of the Jaut, which was worn over a cotton jacket.

'Lieutenant Caine was the first officer up at the taking of the Kumbheer Gate, which was carried by him, with about thirty men of the 14th. On Major Everard's column halting at the bastion beyond the Kumbheer Gate, the Major found his numbers, which were originally 300, dwindled down to not more than 100 or 120 bayonets, without one round of ammunition or any support whatsoever, having in his rear a rampart of nearly two miles in extent, on which the enemy were reassembling from the town. The Major, finding his party in this helpless situation, asked who would volunteer to head a few men back, and to bring him a reinforcement and ammunition. Lieutenant Caine instantly stepped forward and volunteered his services, which were accepted, and with one serjeant, one corporal, and twelve men, he cut his way through the enemy, drove them from their guns, which they had re-manned, and was the first person who reported to the Commander-in-Chief, Lord Combermere, the success and situation of Major Everard's column; and having received the required reinforcement and ammunition, he returned. The Lieutenant was slightly wounded by a grape-shot in the foot whilst leading his small party of volunteers in charging the enemy's guns at the Goverdhun Gate.

On the morning of the 19th January, Captain Meade, Aide-de-Camp to General Reynell, waited upon Lieutenant Caine, and told him that the General had sent him, and had been pleased to approve of the Lieutenant's conduct during the assault, in consequence of a report made by Major Everard, and that therefore the Major-General had introduced his name in the following manner, in his despatch dated 19th January, 1826:—

'" Major Everard reports that Brigade-Major Caine, of the

14th Regiment, accompanied him throughout, and distinguished himself particularly." 'I have, &c.

'SAMFORD WHITTINGHAM,
'Major-General.
'His Excellency the Lord Viscount Combermere, G.C.B., &c.
'Commander-in-Chief in India.'

APPENDIX D.
Sir Samford Whittingham's Commissions.
In the British Service.

Born	29th January, 1772
Ensign	20th January, 1803
Lieutenant	10th March, 1803
Captain	14th February, 1805
Major	12th March, 1810
Lieutenant-Colonel (back dated to)	30th May, 1811
Colonel	4th June, 1814
Major-General	27th May, 1825
Lieutenant-General	28th June, 1838
Colonel of 71st Highland Light Infantry	28th March, 1838

In the Spanish Service.

Colonel	20th July, 1808
Brigadier-General	2nd March, 1809
Mariscal de Campo	12th August, 1809
Lieutenant-General	16th June, 1814

APPENDIX E.
Commanders-in-Chief of India, under whom Sir Samford Whittingham served from 1822 to 1835.

	Date of Appointment.
The Marquis of Hastings*	12th March, 1813
The Hon. Sir Edward Paget	3rd January, 1822
Viscount Combermere	14th March, 1825
The Earl of Dalhousie	28th February, 1829
Sir Edward Barnes	7th June, 1831
Lord William Bentinck †	17th May, 1833

* Lord Hastings was Governor-General and Commander-in-Chief during the whole of his stay in India.

† Lord William Bentinck was Commander-in-Chief during a part of the latter half of his rule as Governor-General. Lord Amherst succeeded Lord Hastings as Governor-General, and was himself succeeded by Lord William Bentinck. Thus Sir Samford Whittingham served under three Governor-Generals and six Commanders-in-Chief. Lord William left India in February, 1835.

APPENDIX F.

List of such Memoirs and Memoranda written by Sir Samford Whittingham for Sir Edward Paget or Lord William Bentinck, as are now in the Possession of the Editor.

Dates		Full Foolscap Pages	Half Margin
1823			
June 10	Observations on the Consequences of a Russian Invasion of India	15½	
July 5	Memoirs on the Burmese Empire, commencing in 1752	10	
Sept. 30	Memoir on the Bengal Army	14½	
1824			
March 31	Some Observations on the Possibility of an Invasion of India by Russia; and on the Nature and Extent of their Means of Execution	20	
April 25	Memorandum of the State of the Bengal Army, as handed over to Sir Edward Paget by the Marquis of Hastings	17	
June 28	Propositions on the Survey Department	9	
July 19	Memorandum on the Campaign in Burmah		7
Nov. 25	Indian Army	30	
Nov. 25*	Probability of a Russian Invasion	11	
—	Proposed Distribution of Bengal Army	13	
not dated	Expedition of the Burmese against Mannipore and Cachar in 1774		17
not dated	India, as it should be governed	14	
1833			
Feb. 22	On the Indian Army (*sent to Lord W. B. from Dinapore*)		16½
Dec. 16 Dec. 30 Dec. 31	} Papers on similar Subjects; altogether nearly		20
1834			
Feb. 28	Distribution of Southern Army of India	3	
March 5	Russian and British Administration of Eastern Colonies compared		10
April 7	Proposed Organization and Distribution of Madras Army		10½
April 16	On the proposed Equalization of Bengal and Madras Armies		6
1836			
May 15	An Inquiry into the Means of Attack on British India, and of the Defence to be opposed to it	24	

* The dates refer to the completion of the papers. Two appear to have been completed on the same day. Two papers are without date, and one paper has only the year marked on it. These were probably rough copies.

INDEX.*

ADAM Colonel; and next General Sir Frederick. Mentioned in General Orders after *Castalla*, by Sir John Murray; p. 190. Governor of Madras; p. 386.

ALAVA, General Don Miguel. His valour at *Medellin*; p. 63. Ambassador in England; p. 449.

ALBURQUERQUE, Duke of. His character; p. 53. Himself and Staff saved by the vigilance of Col. S. W.; p. 56. His gallantry at *Medellin*; p. 63. His letters in praise of Col. S. W. to the Duke of York and Viscount Castlereagh; p. 68. Saves Cadiz by a rapid march; p. 110. Resigns his command; p. 112. Ambassador in England; p. 114. His death; *note* at p. 114.

ARABIN, Captain. (Afterwards Colonel.) Praised in General Orders after *Castalla*; p. 190.

AUCKLAND, Lord. His notes to Sir S. W.; pages 413 and 414.

BARNES, General Sir Edward. Fifth Commander-in-Chief over Sir S.W.; p. 380. Signs his own official death-warrant; p. 382. Is superseded by Lord William Bentinck; p. 391.

BENTINCK, General Lord William. Employs Col. S. W. at *Aranjuez*; pages 50 and 401. Relieves Sir John Murray in the east of Spain; p. 201. Consults, in India, Sir S. W. regarding his personal Staff; p. 355. Adopts the Duke of Wellington's opinion of Sir S. W.; p. 372. Styles Sir S. his Friend and Counsellor; p. 393.

CADOGAN, Colonel, the Hon. Henry. Meets Capt. S. W. at Buenos Ayres; p. 24. Two letters to him by S. W.; pages 43 and 98. His heroic death; p. 201.

CAINE, Captain. (Now Lieut.-Colonel.) His great valour at *Bhurtpore*; p. 329. Made A.D.C. to Sir S. W.; p. 345. Second to Sir S. in a duel with an Ensign; p. 388.

CALCUTTA, Dr. Middleton, Bishop of. Sir S. W. introduced to him by Wilberforce; p. 290. His death; p. 305.

CAMPBELL, Colonel Patrick. His letter to Sir S. W. concerning the English Officers in Spain; p. 252.

CASTAÑOS, General. (Afterwards Duke of Baylen.) His generous conduct to General Dupont; p. 35. Sends Col. S. W. on special mission; p. 36. His kindness to S. W. after *Tudela*; p. 47. Gives away the bride at the marriage of Gen. S. W.; p. 109. Capt.-Gen. of Andalusia; p. 109. Appointed to the Regency; p. 133. Commands Army of Catalonia in 1815; p. 254.

CASTLEREAGH, Viscount. (afterwards Marquis of Londonderry). Offers Sir S. W. commissionership of Austrian army; p. 257. His opinion of Mr. R. H. Davis; p. 284. His death; p. 304.

COLLINGWOOD, Lord. Visit of Col. S. W. to him about treaty of Baylen; p. 37.

COMBERMERE, General, (afterwards Field-Marshal) Viscount. His coldness to Sir S. W.; p. 326. His visit to him; p. 345. His friendliness to him; pages 346 and 353. His confidence in him; p. 357.

CONSIDINE, Captain William. His letters to Sir S. W. on the praises of the Adjutant-General; pages 432 and 437. His remarks on Sir George Napier; p. 433.

COTTON, Colonel. (Afterwards General Sir Willoughby.) His affectionate letters to Sir S. W.; pages 350 and 353. His admiration of Sir Edward Paget; p. 352.

CRAUFURD, General Robert. His high opinion of Capt. S. W.; p. 27.

CUESTA, General. His folly loses the

---

* In this Index S. W. stands for Samford Whittingham.

battle of *Medellin*; p. 62. S. W. was his earliest British critic; p. 73. His conduct before *Talavera*; p. 86. His interview with Sir A. Wellesley; p. 86. Resigns command; p. 95. Capt.-Gen. of Balearic Islands; p. 137. His hostility to everything English, and his insolence; p. 148. His death; p. 150.

DALHOUSIE, Earl of. Fourth Com.-in-Chief over Sir S. W.; p. 364.

DALRYMPLE, General Sir Hew. Permits Capt. S. W. to join Gen. Castaños, as a volunteer; p. 30.

DAVIS, Mr. Richard Hart, M.P. for Bristol. Writes to Sir S. W. of the Duke of Wellington's repeated praise of him; p. 371.

DONKIN, General Sir Rufane. His conduct in the affair between Sir S. W. and Colonel Napier; pages 407 and 409.

ELIOT, Hon. William Writes to Mr. Murdoch to appoint Lieut. Whittingham to meet Mr. Pitt, the Premier; p. 6.

ELPHINSTONE, Lord. Governor of Madras; (and afterwards Governor of Bombay). His fears that Sir S. W. might on arrival take offence at his absence; p. 461. Chief pall-bearer at the funeral of Sir S. W.; p. 490.

FIFE, James Earl of. His coolness at *Talavera*, when Lord Macduff; p. 90. His letter to S. W., conveying *Marshal Suchet's* opinion of the latter, and of the Majorca Division; p. 239. His Lordship's letter to Editor; vide *Preface*.

FRERE, Mr. Bartle. Acts as Minister on departure of Marquis Wellesley; p. 104. Marries by proxy the sister-in-law of Gen. S. W.; p. 271.

FRERE, Right Hon. John Hookham. Minister in Spain, S. W.'s letters to him; pages 58, 60, 65, 69, 70, 73, and 80.

GEORGE IV. H. M.'s eulogistic letter, introducing Sir S. W. to the Hon. Sir E. Paget; p. 292. H. M.'s high opinion of Mr. R. H. Davis; p. 284.

GLENELG, Lord. Secretary of State for Colonies. Presents Sir S. W. to King William IV., at a private audience; p. 416. Expresses to Mr. Harford his *delight* at Sir S. W.'s being appointed Colonel of 71st Regt.; p. 439. Credit due to his Lordship for the emancipation of negroes in the West Indies; p. 441. His approval of Sir S. W.'s conduct in that command; p. 453.

GORDON, Colonel. (Afterwards General Sir Willoughby.) His praise of S. W.; pages 27 and 41.

GRAHAM, General. (Afterwards Sir Thomas, and eventually Lord Lynedoch.) His laudatory letter to Gen. S. W.; page 118. His mention of him in his *Barrosa* dispatch; p. 124.

GURWOOD, Lieut.-Colonel. His correspondence with Sir S. W. regarding the *Wellington Dispatches*; pages 412, 478 and 479.

HASTINGS, Marquis of. His kind reception of Sir S. W.; p. 297. His confidential conversations with Sir S.; pages 298 to 301.

HILL, Lord. Gen. Comg.-in-Chief. His opinion of Sir S. W.; pages 379 and 484.

HUGEL, Baron. His terse description of the West Indies in a letter to Sir S. W.; p. 284.

INFANTADO, Duke of. His want of decision causes the defeat of General Venegas and his own supersession; p. 56.

KENT, H.R.H. the Duke of. His two letters to Mr. H. Davis in praise of Gen. S. W.; pages 83 and 132.

KNIGHTON, Sir William. His first acquaintance with Gen. S. W.; p. 95. His testimony to the abilities of Sir S. W.; p. 331.

LA PEÑA, Lieut.-General. By joining him, Capt. S. W. took part in battle of *Baylen*, and thus became *the first Englishman who fought in Spain during the Peninsular War*; p. 36. Is rejoined by S. W.; p. 44. His generous resignation in favour of the Duke of Infantado; p. 53. Commander-in-Chief of Allied Army at Barrosa; p. 122. His conduct that day a matter of controversy still; pp. 122–123. One of the Generals employed in regulating the order of San Fernando; p. 264.

LINIERS, General. General Whitelocke's capitulation with him; p. 21. His dinner to the British chiefs, and modest behaviour; p. 22.

LIVERPOOL

LIVERPOOL, Earl of. His letter to Mr. Davis on Sir S. W.'s defence of the Bengal Government; p. 331.

MACDONALD, General Sir John, Adjutant General. His praise of Sir S. W.; p. 432 and 437. His congratulatory letter on the Colonelcy of 71st Regt.; p. 436.

MADRAS, Dr. Spencer, Bishop of. His letter of thanks to Sir S. W.; p. 475.

MAJORCA, Llaneres, the Bishop of. His great liberality to the Military College, founded by Gen. S. W.; p. 154.

MONTENEGRO, Count. Congratulates Sir S. W. on having greatly contributed to the suppression of the Spanish *Slave-Trade*; p. 275.

MONTIJO, Count of. His base conduct occasions Sir S. W. to make a very effective speech to a furious Spanish mob; p. 48.

MURDOCH, Mr. Thomas. Introduces Lieut. S. W. to Mr. Pitt, the *Premier*; p. 6.

MURRAY, Lieut.-General Sir John. Mentions Gen. S. W. three times in General Orders, pages 183 and 190; again names him in his dispatch after *Castalla*; p. 195. His trial and virtual acquittal; p. 250.

O'REILLY, Colonel. Barbarously murdered by French soldiers; p. 213.

PAGET, Admiral the Hon. Sir Charles. Thanks Sir S. W. for sending the 65th Regt. to Canada during the rebellion; p. 433. His 'heart and soul' remark regarding Sir S. W.; p. 437. His death; p. 446.

PAGET, General, the Hon. Sir Edward. His rapid promotion; p. 8. Comr.-in-Chief in India; p. 302. Employs Sir S. W. in drawing up 'a General State of India'; p. 307. Resolves to keep Sir S. always with him; p. 309. Writes to Earl Bathurst that Sir S. W. *created* the means by which *Bhurtpore* was taken; p. 340. Declines to be *second* in any duel; p. 405. His dinner to Sir S. W. and son at Chelsea Hospital; p. 455. What Gen. Sir Charles Napier thought of Sir Edward Paget; see *Preface*.

PALMERSTON, Viscount. His letter of thanks to Sir S. W. for a Memoir on Russia and India, and a plan; p. 424.

VENEGAS

PELLEW, Admiral Sir Edward. (Afterwards Viscount Exmouth.) His correspondence with General S. W.: pp. 141, 154, and 161.

PITT, Right Hon. William. Employs Lieut. S. W. on a secret mission; p. 7.

ROCHE, Colonel. (Afterwards Sir Keating Roche.) His letter to Mr. R. H. Davis on the gallantry and wound of Sir S. W. at *Talavera*; p. 91.

RUTI, Captain. The gallantry and energy of this Spanish Officer; pages 180 and 215.

SMITH, Colonel, Sir Charles Felix. His eulogistic letter to Sir S. W.; p. 467.

SMITH, Colonel. (Afterwards General Sir Harry Smith of *Aliwal*.) His spontaneous letter to Sir S. W.; p. 472.

SOMERSET, Lord Fitzroy. (Afterwards Lord Raglan.) His letter to the Editor, on the death of Sir S. W.; p. 483.

SPAIN, Ferdinand King of. His first meeting with Gen. S. W.; p. 231. The Royal gift; p. 233. Account of the King's return to Spain, from the *Recollections*; p. 243. Gen. S W. gives H. M. a paper on the *Slave Trade*; p. 261. H.M. invites him to ask for favours which are declined; p. 266. His last visit from Sir S. W.; p. 277.

TATISCHEFF, M. de. Russian Ambassador to Spain. His great influence with king Ferdinand; pages 246 and 273.

TAYLOR, Sir Herbert. His eulogistic letter to Sir S. W.; p. 336. Deems Sir E. Paget to have ensured the success in *Burmah*, and at *Bhurtpore*; p. 356.

TORRENS, Colonel. (Afterwards General Sir Henry.) Successively Military Secretary, and Adjutant-General at the Horse-Guards. His praises of S. W.; pages 142 and 223. His very striking letter to Sir E. Paget introducing Sir S.; p. 293.

VAUGHAN, Right Hon. Charles. H.M.'s Minister in Spain. His grateful mention to Lord Castlereagh of Sir S. W.'s diplomatic services; p. 268.

VENEGAS, General. General S. W. sent to him on mission by Lord Welling-

WALKER

ton; pp. 107 and 109. Lord W.'s confidence in Venegas; p. 110.

WALKER, Colonel (afterwards General) David. He and the officers of 58th Regt. most happy to serve under General S. W.; p. 175.

WELLESLEY, Right Hon. Henry. (Afterwards Sir Henry. Eventually the first Lord Cowley.) His arrival in Spain; p. 111. His letter praising Gen. S. W.'s formation of a Spanish cavalry corps; p. 119. Requests him not to resign his Spanish command; p. 164. Congratulates him on the success, in the field, of the Majorca Division; p. 187. His first letter to Lord Castlereagh on the *military* services of Gen. S. W.; p. 237. His letter to the Duke of York, regarding his great *diplomatic* obligations to Sir S. W.; p. 271. His second letter to Lord Castlereagh on the services of Sir S. W. and their being unrewarded by the Spanish Government; p. 279.

WELLESLEY, Marquis. His letter to Mr. R. H. Davis, regarding certain papers written by S. W.; p. 82. Attaches S. W. to the Embassy; p. 95. His letter of thanks and praise at his departure from Spain; p. 105. His kind letter to Gen. S. W. from England, when Secretary of State for Foreign affairs; p. 120.

WELLINGTON (the Hon. Sir Arthur Wellesley, successively Lord and), Duke of. His honourable mention in his dispatch of Brig^r.-Gen. S. W.'s being wounded at *Talavera* whilst bringing two Spanish battalions into action; p. 92. Some of his proofs of confidence in Gen. S. W.; pages 106 and 107. Grants the Inspectorship which he had at first refused, as irregular; p. 177. Extract of his dispatch to Earl Bathurst forwarding Sir John Murray's report of two of Gen. S. W.'s affairs of advanced guards, and specially reporting him-

YORK

self that Gen. S. W. had driven *Suchet's* advanced guard through the pass of *Albayda*; p. 184. Declines in the matter of Inspectors of Spanish troops (writing to Lord William Bentinck) to do for 'anybody else' what he had done for Gen. S. W.; p. 205. 'Feels the utmost concern' at the resignation of Gen. S. W., and persuades its withdrawal; p. 216. Indirectly confirms the estimate formed by Gen. S. W. of King Ferdinand; *note* at p. 233. His comprehensive official letter to the Duke of York on the Peninsular services of S. W.; p. 234. States and repeats (sixteen years later) to Mr. R. H. Davis that '*We had not such another officer in the army*' as Sir S. W.; p. 371. His Grace's note to Sir S. W. on the death of Sir William Knighton; p. 419. Writes to Sir S. W. that he 'shall be at all times very happy to receive him;' p. 457.

WHITELOCKE, Lieut.-General. Appoints Captain S. W. to be one of his aides-de-camp; p. 12. Employs him on very hazardous service; p. 16. His trial, condemnation, and sentence; p. 25.

WILBERFORCE, Mr. William, M.P. His dictated letter introducing Sir S. W. to the Bishop of Calcutta; p. 290. His autograph letter to Sir S.; p. 291.

WILLIAM IV. His Majesty's audience to Sir S. W. before starting for the West Indies, and his gracious remarks; p. 416.

YORK, H.R.H. the Duke of. Recommends Sir S. W. to Sir Henry Wellesley; p. 258. His letter to Mr. Davis in praise of Sir S. W.; p. 271. His letter to Sir E. Paget recommending Sir S. W. as 'highly deserving of his confidence;' p. 292. Expresses, through Sir Herbert Taylor, the interest with which he had read Sir S. W.'s journal of the siege of *Bhurtpore*; p. 337.

THE END.

LONDON: PRINTED BY
SPOTTISWOODE AND CO., NEW-STREET SQUARE
AND PARLIAMENT STREET

EXTRACTS FROM REVIEWS

(Which appeared up to the completion of the printing of the New Edition).

PALL MALL GAZETTE.

'Sir Samford Whittingham was one of those men whose lives ought to be written . . . . and though he died Commander-in-Chief of the Madras army, we may safely hazard the assertion that few soldiers who have done so much have received so little public recognition of their courage, loyalty, and military capacity as that which fell to his lot. His career is specially interesting, as being that of one who was born to be a soldier, and who, in many respects, came up to the popular ideal of a soldier, *sans peur et sans reproche.* . . . The story of the battle [of Talavera], so far as it came under Whittingham's own eyes, is as lively an account of the horrors, and moreover of the ludicrous aspects, of a murderous conflict as we have ever come across.'

EXAMINER.

'The estimate of his character, which his son leaves the reader to draw for himself, is that of a brave, clear-headed, just, and stern warrior, apt at organising raw levies, and capable of any work that might be entrusted to him. His generosity, amiability, and unselfishness are patent everywhere to the most careless reader. Many of the sentiments expressed in his correspondence, and not a few of the ideas worked out in his memoranda, show his sagacity, wisdom, and foresight.'

MORNING POST.

'He [*Sir Samford*] was constantly occupied in the negotiations between the English and Spanish Governments, as well as in the various military operations during the campaigns, and describes with much ability the scenes that he witnessed. His opinions on passing events are written with soldier-like frankness, and display remarkable powers of discrimination and foresight. . . . The biographer has displayed much impartiality, although coupled with a natural pride in his father's distinguished services. . . . The memoirs . . . . are altogether very interesting, and afford a valuable study for young soldiers.'

UNITED SERVICE MAGAZINE.

'An officer whose services are not so well known as they ought to be, and though recorded by Wellington, and published in the *London Gazette*, are not to be found in "Napier." . . . . Though only an English Captain till 1810 . . . . he was, in fact, a General Officer in command of large bodies of [*Spanish*] troops that did good service; among them the Majorca division . . . . of which Marshal Suchet, after the war, spoke as being "in as high a military state as any of his own troops." . . . . The reader will find many acute remarks on men and things in India . . . . which, had they received the attention that they merited, would have caused the transfer of the Government to the Crown, and might probably have averted the Indian Mutiny. . . . The care that he took of the health of his troops shows that he was as earnest and enlightened as any sanatory reformer of the present day. Taken altogether, this memoir is one that deserves an attentive perusal, which it will well repay.'

JOHN BULL.

'This goodly volume records the gallant deeds of one of England's bravest soldiers, of whose history it is to be feared his countrymen generally are ignorant. Yet his military career .... was one of no ordinary character; and the testimony borne to his worth by the great Duke must be not only satisfactory to his family, but should commend the work to the general public, for Sir S. F. Whittingham was not merely a soldier, though devoted to his profession, but performed important civil functions.'

PRESS.

'These memoirs, published by his son, are worthy of this permanent record. They illustrate the history of two important epochs, by throwing light on the state of the Peninsula during the first quarter, and by explaining the position of affairs in India during the early portion of the second quarter, of this century.'

STAR.

'The name of Sir Samford Whittingham is one little known, yet he was a brave soldier, a good administrator, and an able general. The memoir seems to be well and conscientiously done. It is extremely interesting.'

OBSERVER.

'It is never too late to correct statements of historical events. . . . The memoirs will, no doubt, be read with great satisfaction.'

DAILY NEWS.

'He had the .... disadvantage of being an Englishman. If he had only had the good fortune to hail from north of the Tweed, or west of the Irish Channel, we should have had no end of solos on the trumpet of Fame to his honour. As it is, we are glad to receive this record of his services.'

ATHENÆUM.

'He was held in high esteem by appreciating adversaries (*the reviewer here quotes Marshal Suchet's testimony*), and may be said to have fought his way to distinction. He was a gentleman as well as a soldier, and had a quick eye to see what was before him. . . . King Ferdinand have a valuable general in our hero. . . . If our readers would refresh their memories touching the *fiasco* at Buenos Ayres .... and if they have curiosity about incidents of military life in various parts of the world, they will find their account by looking into these memoirs of a gallant old English soldier.'

UNITED SERVICE GAZETTE.

'The subject of this biography is, in fact, made to tell his own story, and a very pleasant and instructive story it is for all military readers.'

BRISTOL TIMES.

'The subject of the memoir .... may be readily accepted as one of old Bristol's sons, of whom she may be justly proud.'

STANDARD.

'He [*the Editor*] tells us all the facts concerning a career that ought to interest every soldier of England's army. . . . The imputations against his father the author effectually rebuts .... the vindication of Sir Samford's conduct and motives is complete .... whose reputation will be not inconsiderably enhanced by these memoirs of a life well spent in the service of England.'

THE NAVAL & MILITARY PRESS
Specialist Books For The Serious Student Of Conflict

Military book enthusiasts now have a place on the internet dedicated to themselves. Our site is the most extensive devoted to military history on the web. You can browse and shop through our vast range of titles by time period or by theme, or use our advanced search facilities to find areas of specific interest.

The Naval & Military Press Ltd was founded in 1991 and quickly established itself as a mecca for the military enthusiast. Over 35,000 customers worldwide enjoy receiving our booklist which contains many hundreds of first-class books. With the advances in technology we are now pleased to show all of you with access to the internet our full catalogue. Updated regularly, you can count on the same level of service that our existing customers enjoy.

Our own publications feature strongly on both our list and our website. The innovative approach we have to military bookselling and our commitment to publishing have made us Britain's leading independent military bookseller.

Many titles featured on this website are not unavailable through any other source in the world.

www.naval-military-press.com

General Sir Ian Hamilton's
Staff Officer's Scrap-Book during the Russo–Japanese War 1904–1905
9781474538077

As Hamilton was the military attaché of the British Indian Army serving with the Japanese army in Manchuria during the Russo-Japanese War, he was well placed to publish in 1907 this impressive eye witness account to a military confrontation between a well-known European army and a less-familiar Asian army. Good maps (many in colour), a full index and 600+ pages make this facsimile two-volume set a fine reference for the modern scholar, of a war that is still the classic example of a conflict waged for purely imperialistic motives, a rivalry for the control of Korea and Manchuria and indeed for the mastery of the Far East and China.

The Golden Chersonese and the way thither
9781905748198

A delightful description of her travels in Malaya and China in the 1880s by that intrepid lady Isabella L. Bird, first female member of the Royal Geographical Society and doyenne of all women travel writers.

NOTES FROM A JOURNAL OF RESEARCH INTO THE NATURAL HISTORY OF THE COUNTRIES VISITED DURING THE VOYAGE OF H.M.S. SAMARANG under the command of Captain Sir Edward Belcher, C.B., F.R.A.S.
9781905748013

Like Darwin on the Beagle, surgeon Arthur Adams was a naturalist with this 1843-45 Naval expedition to Japan and the Indian and China Seas. Contains fascinating descriptions of the region's flora and fauna.

LOW`S HISTORY of the INDIAN NAVY
9781474536530

This is an extremely rare work, in its original edition, and covers the life span of the Indian Navy, 1600 to 1863. Operations from the Persian Gulf to the Burma and First China Wars, from Aden to New Zealand and the Maori Wars, and the Indian Mutiny. Survey work from the Red Sea to the China Seas.

NARRATIVE OF THE EARL OF ELGIN'S MISSION TO CHINA AND JAPAN IN THE YEARS 1857, '58, '59
9781905748051

Superbly illustrated two-volume account of Lord Elgin's expeditions to the Far East in 1857-59 which resulted in the occupation of Canton, the burning of Peking's Imperial Summer Palace; and the opening of Japan to European trade.

"CHINA JIM" Being Incidents and Adventures in the Life of an Indian Mutiny Veteran
9781845748463

An account of the author's experiences in the Indian Mutiny and the Second China War. The author acquired his nickname as a result of the immense amount of loot he acquired from the Summer Palace at Peking!

CHINESE WAR, AN ACCOUNT OF ALL THE OPERATIONS OF THE BRITISH FORCES 1842
9781843428176
Detailed account of the first Chinese 'Opium war' with Britain. With 53 fascinating illustrations.

VOYAGE OF HIS MAJESTY'S SHIP ALCESTE, to China, Corea, and the Island of Lewchew, with an account of her shipwreck
9781905748068
Rather aptly summed up by the title, this book was written by the ship's surgeon on the 'Alceste' which was charged with delivering the British Embassy of Lord Amherst to China in 1816. Passing through Rio de Janeiro, the Cape of Good Hope and Batavia en-route, they arrived in the China Sea in the summer and their first meetings with the Chinese together with some of the politics of the time are described here.

OFFICIAL ACCOUNT OF THE MILITARY OPERATIONS IN CHINA 1900-1901
9781783311156
This official account of the military operations in China at the time of the Boxer Rebellion and the siege of the Foreign Legations in Peking was originally compiled by Major Norrie, a member of the Intelligence Staff of the British Contingent, China Field Force. It was considerably revised, edited and expanded by the Intelligence Department at the War Office. It begins with the rise of the Boxer Secret Society and the outbreak of hostilities against foreigners in the northern provinces, extends to cover the operations for the relief of Foreign Legations in Peking and concludes with the peace negotiations and withdrawal of the greater part of the allied forces from China, original editions are excessively rare.

THE CRUISE OF THE PEARL WITH AN ACCOUNT OF THE OPERATIONS OF THE NAVAL BRIGADE IN INDIA
9781843428206
Drawn from the unusual diary of a naval Chaplain detailing the exploits of a scratch Naval Brigade, consisting of warship crews fighting on shore, in quelling the Indian Mutiny in 1857-58. Charming, despite the grim nature of much of the material.

THE LAST CRUISE OF THE "MAJESTIC"
George Goodchild from the log book of Petty Officer J.G. Cowie
9781474539166

Interesting personal account of the service of battleship "Majestic" in the Dardanelles arranged by Goodchild from the logbook of Petty Officer J.G. Cowie. "Majestic" was a Majestic-class pre-dreadnought battleship. In early 1915, she was dispatched to the Mediterranean for service in the Dardanelles Campaign. She participated in bombardments of Turkish forts and supported the Allied landings at Gallipoli. On 27 May 1915, she was torpedoed by the German submarine U-21 at Cape Helles, sinking with the loss of 49 men.

THE COMMISSION OF HMS TERRIBLE 1898-1902
9781843425533

Naval Brigades in South African War & China 1900. Various nominal rolls.

THE NAVAL BRIGADE IN SOUTH AFRICA DURING THE YEARS 1877-78-79
9781843429203

An account of the actions of the Naval Brigade from 'HMS Active' in South Africa's Kaffir and Zulu wars in 1877-79. Written by the Brigade's principal medical officer.

THE HISTORY OF THE BALTIC CAMPAIGN OF 1854, FROM DOCUMENTS AND OTHER MATERIALS FURNISHED BY VICE-ADMIRAL SIR C. NAPIER
9781845742126

A full history of the Crimean War's 'forgotten' sideshow in the Baltic, based on the papers of the British Commander, Admiral Napier, which exonerates him from charges of incompetence.

www.ingramcontent.com/pod-product-compliance
Lightning Source LLC
Chambersburg PA
CBHW051352230426
43669CB00011B/1612